BARRON'S

PASS KEY
TO THE

LAW SCHOOL ADMISSION TEST
Second Edition

Jerry Bobrow, Ph.D.
Executive Director
Bobrow Test Preparation Services
Programs at major universities, colleges, and law schools throughout California
Lecturer, consultant, author of over 20 nationally known test preparation books
Dr. Bobrow personally instructs over 2,000 LSAT test takers each year

Contributing Authors and Consultants

William A. Covino, Ph.D.
Professor, Department of English
University of Illinois, Chicago

Daniel C. Spencer, M.S.
Management Services Officer
University of California at Los Angeles
(UCLA)

David A. Kay, M.S.
Computer Analyst, Professor
Moorpark College, California

Merritt L. Weisinger, J.D.
Attorney at Law, Lecturer
Weisinger and Associates

Barron's Educational Series, Inc.

All inquiries should be addressed to:
Barron's Educational Series, Inc.
250 Wireless Boulevard
Hauppauge, New York 11788

Library of Congress Catalog Card No. 96-12081

International Standard Book No. 0-8120-9643-6

Library of Congress Cataloging-in-Publication Data
Bobrow, Jerry.
   Pass key to the LSAT : law school admission test / Jerry Bobrow.
 —2nd ed.
     p.   cm.
   ISBN 0-8120-9643-6
   1. Law schools—United States—Entrance examinations.   2. Law School
Admission Test.
   KF285.Z9B63   1996
   340'.076—dc20   96-12081
                                                                          CIP

PRINTED IN THE UNITED STATES OF AMERICA
987654321

CONTENTS

Chapter 3   Logical Reasoning   111

Chapter 4   Writing Sample 165

PART THREE PRACTICE
Mastering Problem Types and Time Pressures 181

Chapter 5   Model Test One 182

Chapter 6   Model Test Two 240

Chapter 7   Model Test Three 304

PART FOUR FINAL TOUCHES
Reviewing the Important Techniques   365

Chapter 8   A Summary of Strategies   366

PREFACE

The LSAT is a difficult exam and we want to give you every possible advantage!

In this book, *Barron's Pass Key to the LSAT*, the compact version of Barron's best-selling *How to Prepare for the LSAT*, we have gathered the expertise and materials developed in over 20 years of successful LSAT, GMAT, GRE, NTE, CBEST, MSAT, ELM, and SAT preparation courses that are currently offered at over 25 universities, colleges, and law schools.

So how are we going to give you every possible advantage?

By thoroughly analyzing each of the sections of the LSAT and reviewing the thinking processes and the skills necessary for top performance, this text aims at complete preparation. It is up to date with the most recent forms of the latest test. The staff of writers and consultants includes specialists in problem solving, reading, writing, logic, law, and test psychology. All these authors and consultants have been teaching prelaw students in LSAT preparation programs for many years.

An introductory section will acquaint you with the format of the LSAT. Then, a series of insightful chapters on the most recent sections of the test will carefully analyze each question type, pinpoint specific test-taking strategies, and give additional practice. Three full-length practice tests will allow you to get the feel of the real thing while you begin applying new skills and techniques. Your answer sheet will resemble the machine-graded LSAT answer sheet, and an analysis chart will enable you to assess your strengths and weaknesses. The answers to each practice test are fully explained.

Will this be effective?

Complete analysis, thorough instruction, extensive practice, up-to-date examples, and the most successful overall systems of objective test taking are described in detail in this book to give you invaluable insight into the LSAT. The test-taking strategies and approaches we've included have been proven effective for over 2,000,000 graduate and undergraduate students and teachers whom we've assisted in preparing for these important exams. If you're short of time, *Barron's Pass Key to the LSAT* is what you need.

All right, let's get down to business and start with a brief overview of How to Prepare.

PREPARING FOR THE LSAT: A FOUR-STEP APPROACH

Preparing to take the LSAT is no easy task; it takes a well thought-out, focused study plan. This plan should follow these four basic steps:

1. Awareness
2. Understanding the Thinking Processes
3. Applying Strategies and Techniques
4. Practice, Practice, Practice

AWARENESS

Before taking the LSAT, you should know everything possible about the test from the length of each section to the specific types of questions. Be an expert on the structure and construction of the exam.

The LSAT consists of five 35-minute multiple-choice sections. Four sections count toward your LSAT score; one experimental section is a repeat of the other sections and does not count toward your score. An unscored essay is also included. The types of questions are: Reading Comprehension (one section), Analytical Reasoning (one section), and Logical Reasoning (two sections).

Reading Comprehension—one section that includes four fairly sophisticated passages, each ranging from about 400 to 600 words with 5 to 8 questions per passage for a total of about 26 to 28 questions. The passages can be from the fields of science, philosophy, economy, history, law, and so on, but the questions must be answered from the actual passages given, not from your general or specific knowledge of a subject.

Analytical Reasoning—one section that includes four sets of conditions, statements, or rules. You are required to see the relationships among the items being described and discussed. Constructing a simple display or diagram using the information given is an important part of attacking this question type. Each set is followed by 4 to 7 questions for a total of 22 to 24 questions. This section appears to be the most difficult for most test takers, but it also appears to be the most preparable.

Logical Reasoning—two sections that include short passages, statements, arguments, or discussions, each followed by 1 or 2 questions asking about the reasoning involved. Each section contains between 24 and 26 questions. This question type requires good reading and reasoning skills and accounts for 50 percent of your LSAT score. You will have two sections of Logical Reasoning, about 50 of the 100 questions that count toward your score. A course in formal logic is not necessary but could be helpful, as would any course that requires critical reading and reasoning.

These sections total from 96 to 104 questions and are scaled to a scoring range of 120–180 with an average score about 150 or 151. Approximately 60 percent correct is necessary to obtain an average score. There is no penalty for guessing on the LSAT, so never leave a question without at least taking a guess.

Unscored Essay—the multiple-choice sections of the LSAT are followed by a 30-minute unscored essay. This essay is written on a special sheet of paper with about 25 lines and is written in ink (a pen is provided). Scratch paper is given so that you can organize your essay before writing. A copy of your essay is sent to each law school to which you apply. The law schools may use the essay in a number of ways—as a tie-breaker between two applicants, as a measure for admittance, and so on. Test takers who have not seen a sample topic are often worried about the essay topic. You should review a few sample topics and try writing a few essays. The topics typically involve a selection that needs to be made between two people, items, techniques, places, and so on. There is no right or wrong answer. Simply make your selection and support it by using the criteria and information given.

UNDERSTANDING THE THINKING PROCESSES

The LSAT, unlike many other standardized exams, is not content oriented, but is reasoning oriented. Therefore, it is vital to understand the thinking processes involved in obtaining the correct/credited response. You should not memorize information, but focus your preparation on understanding the reasoning involved. Carefully analyzing each question type, the credited response, and the common mistakes will help you understand the thinking processes. You should understand that the correct answer to each question is facing you on the page and that the incorrect answers are called "distracters." An incorrect answer that looks good or is close is often called an "attractive distracter." Learn to avoid the attractive distracters by analyzing the choices and understanding the thinking processes.

APPLYING STRATEGIES AND TECHNIQUES

There are many strategies and techniques that you can and should learn before taking your LSAT. The general strategies include how and when to skip problems, eliminate answers, and circle important words. The specific strategies should include how to draw diagrams or simple displays for Analytical Reasoning, how to actively read Reading Comprehension passages and how to preread questions and focus on Logical Reasoning questions. You should also be very familiar with the many types of questions you could be asked in each section. You should take the test only after reviewing and practicing many specific strategies for the question types.

PRACTICE, PRACTICE, PRACTICE

As with other standardized exams, becoming a proficient LSAT test taker takes lots of practice. This practice helps you get acclimated to working under time pressure as well as dealing with the fatigue factor. When you practice, try to replicate testing conditions. Don't use scratch paper, do your work in the test booklet, and transfer your answers to an answer sheet. Don't practice on a large tabletop, as in most cases you will be taking your test in a classroom with fairly small desktops. When you practice, you should give yourself only 30 minutes to complete a section, even though the time allotted is actually 35 minutes. Shorting yourself on time will force you to work faster and should increase your speed. Another reason for extended practice is to identify the types of mistakes you make when you're tired, that is, dealing with the fatigue factor. Practice taking three 35-minute sections (giving yourself 30 minutes for each section) back to back to back with only about a five second break between each one. Then, take a short break of about ten minutes and try another two sections. When you complete your practice tests, carefully analyze each section and watch for any consistent types of errors. On your next practice session, focus on eliminating those errors.

The LSAT is an important, difficult exam, but you can prepare for it, and you owe it to yourself to be prepared. Read and review this book carefully. You'll be glad you did.

Good Luck!!!
Jerry Bobrow, Ph.D.

Jerry Bobrow, Ph.D., author of *Barron's How to Prepare for the LSAT* and many other national best-selling preparation books, has been teaching and directing preparation programs for most of the California State universities for the past 23 years. He personally lectures and teaches over 2,000 LSAT test takers each year.

ACKNOWLEDGMENTS

I gratefully acknowledge the following sources for granting permission to use materials from their publications:

Pages 32, 37, 185, 252, 307, 330: Dean Seymour Greitzer, Law Reviews from Glendale University College of Law.

Pages 17, 22, 30: George E. Riggs, publisher; news articles and editorials from *The Herald News,* Fontana, California.

Page 34: Arthur Doerr and J. L. Guernsey, *Principles of Geography,* © 1975 by Barron's Educational Series, Inc., Hauppauge, N.Y.

Pages 140, 144: Dr. Albert Upton, *Design for Thinking,* Stanford University Press, Stanford, California

Page 187: Herbert Marder, *Feminism & Art: A Study of Virginia Woolf.* Chicago: University of Chicago Press, 1968.

Page 189: C. Vann Woodward, *The Future of the Past.* New York: Oxford University Press, 1989.

Page 191: Joseph E. LeDoux, "Emotion, Memory and the Brain," *Scientific American,* June 1994. All rights reserved.

Page 254: Roy Sieber and Arnold Rubin, *Sculpture of Black Africa: The Paul Tishman Collection.* Los Angeles: Los Angeles County Museum of Art, 1968. By permission of the copyright holder.

Page 256: John Kenneth Galbraith, *American Capitalism.* Sentry edition. Boston: Houghton Mifflin, 1962.

Page 259: Steve Jones, *The Language of Genes: Unraveling Mysteries of Human Genetics.* New York: Doubleday (Anchor Books), 1994.

Page 275: Law Reviews from the University of California at Los Angeles (UCLA) Law School—Comment, "United States Tax Treaty Policy Toward Developing Countries: The China Example," 35 UCLA L. Rev. 69 (1987).

Page 277: Spiro Kostof, *A History of Architecture.* New York: Oxford University Press, 1985.

Page 279: Robert A. Nisbet, *The Present Age: Progress and Anarchy in Modern America.* New York: Harper & Row, 1988. Reprinted by permission of HarperCollins.

Page 282: P. James E. Peebles, David N. Schramm, Edwin L. Turner and Richard G. Kron, "The Evolution of the Universe," *Scientific American,* October 1994.

xiv Acknowledgments

Page 309: Fred Kaplan, *Dickens: A Biography.* New York: William Morrow & Company, 1988.

Page 311: Robert H. Wiebe, *The Segmented Society: An Historical Preface to the Meaning of America.* New York: Oxford University Press, 1975.

Page 332: Donald Heiney and Lenthiel H. Downs, *Continental European Literature,* Vol. 1, © 1974 by Barron's Educational Series, Inc., Hauppauge, N.Y.

Page 333: Paul Veyne, ed., & Arthur Goldhammer, translator, *A History of Private Life: Volume I—From Pagan Rome to Byzantium.* Philippe Aries and Georges Duby, series general editors. Cambridge, Massachusetts: The Belknap Press of Harvard University Press, 1987. Copyright 1987 by the President and Fellows of Harvard College.

Page 336: C. Leland Rodgers, *Essentials of Biology,* © 1974 by Barron's Educational Series, Inc., Hauppauge, N.Y.

(Note: Some of the Law Reviews have been edited, including changes in names, places, and dates)

My thanks to James Zinger, President, Hypmovation, for the use of excerpts from his writings; to Jean Eggenschwiler, writer and editor, for her contributions; to Stacey Baum, Joy Mondragon, and Kristen Fest-Tennison, for their assistance in assembling the manuscript; to Lynn Turner, Dana Lind, Brenda Clodfelter, and Jennifer Johnson for typing the manuscript; and to Linda Turner for manuscript editing and final preparation.

And finally thanks to my wife, Susan Bobrow, for critical analysis and moral support; and to my three children, Jennifer Lynn, 18, Adam Michael, 15, and Jonathan Matthew, 11, for comic relief.

PART ONE

INTRODUCTION

Getting Acquainted
with the Test

INTRODUCTION
TO THE LSAT

ANSWERS TO SOME COMMONLY ASKED QUESTIONS

What does the LSAT measure?
The LSAT is designed to measure a range of mental abilities related to the study of law; therefore, it is used by most law schools to evaluate their applicants.

Will any special knowledge of the law raise my score on the LSAT?
The LSAT is designed so that candidates from a particular academic background are given no advantage. The questions measure reading comprehension, logical reasoning, and analytical reasoning, drawing from a variety of verbal and analytical material.

Does a high score on the LSAT predict success in law school or in the practice of law?
Success on the LSAT demonstrates your ability to read with understanding and to reason clearly under pressure; surely these strengths are important to both the study and the practice of law, as is the ability to write well, measured by the LSAT Writing Sample. To say that success on the LSAT *predicts* success in law school may overstate the case, however, because success in law school also involves skills that are not measured by the LSAT.

When is the LSAT administered?
The regular administration of the test occurs nationwide four times each year, around the beginning of the fall, winter, spring, and summer seasons. Except for the summer month, the test is usually administered on a Saturday morning from 8:30 A.M. to about 1:00 P.M. For the past few years, the *summer exam* has been given on a Monday afternoon. Dates are announced annually by the Law School Admission Council in Newtown, Pennsylvania.

What if I cannot take the test on a Saturday?
Some special arrangements are possible: Check the LSAS General Information Booklet in your registration packet. Those who must take the exam at a time when the regular administration occurs on Saturday, but who cannot participate on Saturday for religious reasons, may arrange for a special Monday administration.

How early should I register?

Regular registration closes about one month before the exam date. Late registration is available up to three weeks prior to the exam date. There is an additional fee for late registration.

Is walk-in registration available?

For security reasons, walk-in registration is no longer permitted. Students may register by telephone by the telephone deadline. The Law School Admission Services (LSAS) will not permit walk-ins the day of the test. Be sure to read very carefully the General Information Booklet section on "registering to take the LSAT."

What is the LSDAS?

The LSDAS (Law School Data Assembly Service) compiles a report about each subscribing applicant. The report contains LSAT results, a summary of the applicant's academic work, and copies of college transcripts. A report is sent to each law school that the applicant designates. Thus, if you register for the LSDAS, you will not need to mail a separate transcript to each of your prospective law schools. REMINDER: You can register for the Candidate Referral Service only at the same time you register for the LSDAS.

How is the LSAT used?

Your LSAT score is one common denominator by which a law school compares you to other applicants. Other factors also determine your acceptance to law school: a law school may consider your personal qualities, grade-point average, extracurricular achievements, and letters of recommendation. Requirements for admission vary widely from school to school, so you are wise to contact the law school of your choice for specific information.

How do I obtain registration forms?

The registration form covering both the LSAT and the LSDAS is available in the LSAT/LSDAS REGISTRATION PACKET. Copies of the packet are available at the admissions offices of most law schools and the testing offices at most undergraduate universities and colleges. You may also obtain the packet by writing to LAW SCHOOL ADMISSION SERVICES, Box 2000, Newtown, PA 18940.

What is the structure of the LSAT?

The LSAT contains five 35-minute multiple-choice sections followed by a 30-minute Writing Sample. The Writing Sample does not count as part of your LSAT score. The common question types that do count toward your score are Logical Reasoning (two sections), Analytical Reasoning (one section), and Reading Comprehension (one section). In addition to these four sections, one experimental or pretest section will appear. This experimental or pretest section, which will probably be a repeat of one of the common question types, will not count in your score.

How is the LSAT scored?

The score for the objective portion of the test ranges from 120 to 180, and there is no penalty for wrong answers. The Writing Sample is unscored, but copies are sent to the law schools of your choice for evaluation.

What about question structure and value?

All LSAT questions, apart from the Writing Sample, are multiple-choice with five choices. All questions within a section are of equal value, regardless of difficulty.

Should I guess?

There is no penalty for guessing on the LSAT. Therefore, before you move on to the next question, at least take a guess. You should fill in guess answers for those you have left blank or did not get to, before time is called for that section. If you can eliminate one or more choices as incorrect, your chances for a correct guess increase.

How often can I take the LSAT?

You may take the LSAT more than once if you wish. But keep in mind that any report sent to you or to law schools will contain scores for any exams taken over the past few years, along with an average score for those exams. The law school receiving your scores will decide which score is the best estimate of your ability; many law schools rely on the average score as a reliable figure.

Is it at all possible to cancel my LSAT score?

You may cancel your score only within five days after taking the test.

How early should I arrive at the test center, and what should I bring?

Arrive at the test center 15 to 30 minutes before the time designated on your admission ticket. Bring three or four sharpened No. 2 pencils, an eraser, and a watch, as well as your LSAT Admission Ticket and proper identification as described in the LSAT Registration/Information Booklet.

Can I prepare for the LSAT?

Yes. Reading skills and test-taking strategies should be the focus of your preparation for the test as a whole. Success on the more specialized analytical sections of the test depends on your thorough familiarity with the types of problems you are likely to encounter and the reasoning process involved. For maximum preparation, work through this book and practice the strategies and techniques outlined in each section.

BASIC FORMAT OF THE LSAT AND SCORING

THE *ORDER* OF THE FOLLOWING MULTIPLE-CHOICE SECTIONS *WILL* VARY. The Experimental Section is not necessarily the last section.

Section	Number of Questions	Minutes
I. Logical Reasoning	24–26	35
II. Analytical Reasoning	22–24 (4 sets)	35
III. Reading Comprehension	26–28 (4 passages)	35
IV. Logical Reasoning	24–26	35
V. Experimental Section	varies	35
Writing Sample	1 essay	30
TOTALS	118–132 questions (only 96–104 count toward your score)	205 minutes or 3 hours 25 minutes

The LSAT is scored on a 120 to 180 scale.

The following simple chart will give you a very general approximation of the LSAT scoring system. It shows the approximate percentage of right answers necessary on the LSAT to be in a certain score range.

Approximate % of Right Answers	Approximate Score Range
Between 75% and 100%	160–180
Between 50% and 75%	145–159
Between 25% and 50%	130–144
Between 0% and 25%	120–129

Note that this chart is meant to give you an *approximate* score range.

A CLOSER LOOK AT THE TIMING—WHAT IT REALLY MEANS

Although the LSAT comprises five 35-minute multiple-choice sections and a 30-minute unscored essay, it is important to understand the timing breakdown and what it means. The test is actually broken down as follows:

105 min.
- Section I 35 mins.
- Section II 35 mins.
- Section III 35 mins.

Short break—usually 5–10 minutes

70 min.
- Section IV 35 mins.
- Section V 35 mins.

Very, very short break—usually 1 or 2 minutes

30 min.
- Writing Sample (Essay)—30 mins.

Notice that you are given three multiple-choice sections with no breaks in between. When they say "stop" at the end of 35 minutes they will immediately say something like, "Turn to the next section, make sure that you are in the right section, ready, begin." So, in essence, you are working three sections back to back to back. This means that when you practice you should be sure to practice testing for 1 hour and 45 minutes without a break.

After the short break, when you may get up, get a drink, and go to the restroom, you are back for two more back-to-back multiple-choice sections.

For the final 30-minute writing sample you will be given a pen and scratch paper to do your prewriting or outlining.

Keep in mind that there will be some time taken before the exam and after the exam for clerical-type paperwork—distributing and picking up paperwork, filling out test forms, and so on.

IMPORTANT REMINDERS

- At least half of your test will contain Logical Reasoning questions; prepare accordingly. Make sure that you are good at Logical Reasoning!
- The experimental or pretest section will usually repeat other sections and can appear in different places on the exam. At the time of the exam, you will not know which section is experimental. Take the test as if all of the sections count.
- Scoring will be from 120–180. This is the score, and the percentile rank that goes with it is what the law schools look at and are referring to in their discussions.
- All questions in a section are of equal value, so do not get stuck on any one question. The scores are determined by totaling all of your right answers on the test and then scaling.
- There is NO PENALTY for guessing, so at least take a guess before you move to the next question.
- The 30-minute Writing Sample will not be scored, but copies will be forwarded to the law schools to which you apply. Scratch paper and a pen will be provided for the Writing Sample only.
- Keep in mind that regardless of the format of your exam, two sections of Logical Reasoning, one section of Analytical Reasoning, and one section of Reading Comprehension always count toward your score.

SOME WORDS TO THE WISE

ASK A FEW QUESTIONS

Before you actually start your study plan there are four basic questions that you should ask the law schools to which you are applying:

1. Considering my GPA and other qualifications, what score do you think I need to get into your law school?
2. When do you need to get my score reports? Or, When should I take the test to meet your deadlines?
3. What do you do if I take the LSAT more than once? Remember that when the law school receives your score report it will see a score for each time you've taken the test *and* an average of the scores. It is up to the law schools and their governing

bodies as to what score(s) they will consider. Try to do your best on the first try and take the LSAT only once, if possible.

4. What do you do with my Writing Sample? Is it used as a tiebreaker? Do you score it yourself? Is it just another piece of the process?

Knowing the answers to most of these questions before you start your study will help you understand what is expected and will help you get mentally ready for the task ahead.

AN EFFECTIVE STUDY PROGRAM

A THREE-WEEK LSAT STUDY PLAN

Many students don't even bother to read the LSAT bulletin, let alone do any thorough preparation for the test. You, however, should begin your LSAT preparation by reading the LSAT bulletin (book) carefully; information about how to obtain one is on page 3. The bulletin is filled with information about registration and score reporting. Also provided with the registration packet is an "official" practice test. You should also send for copies of old exams (good practice).

With the preliminaries out of the way, begin working through this book. Because it is geared to an intensive three-week study plan, your study time must be well focused and well planned. This study time should be free from distractions. If you plan your study time wisely, you will find the techniques, strategies, practice, and analyses in this book invaluable to your LSAT preparation.

Most people can keep up with the following study sequence by devoting about 7 to 10 hours a week. It is most important that you review and practice *daily,* for about an hour or two each day. Don't "save up" your practice for one long session each week. Shorter, regular practice sessions will allow you to assimilate skills and strategies more effectively and efficiently.

Always spend some extra time reviewing "why" you made your mistakes. Watch for repeated or consistent errors. These errors are often the easiest to correct. As you review, focus on the thinking process involved in reaching the credited response, and note specifically where you made the error.

If you have reviewed an explanation, and still do not understand where you made an error, mark the problem in your book and go on. Return to review this problem later, after you have had an opportunity to review other problems that use similar thinking processes. Don't get stuck on reviewing one problem.

Week 1

- Read the section "Answers to Some Commonly Asked Questions" (p. 2).
- Read carefully "Before You Begin" (p. 9), paying special attention to the "One-Check, Two-Check System" and the "Elimination Strategy." Applying these techniques confidently should make quite a difference in your test taking.
- Read carefully the chapters on Reading Comprehension, Logical Reasoning, Analytical Reasoning, and the Writing Sample.

- Spend some extra time reviewing the chapter on Logical Reasoning. Remember: Logical Reasoning will comprise two of the four scored sections of your exam.
- Review the chapter on Reading Comprehension. Do the Reading Comprehension problems in the chapter, the ones in the LSAT sample test, and those in Model Test One (p. 185). Correct and analyze your performance.

  Note: Do not time yourself on these practice tests. Your task at present is to familiarize yourself with strategies and techniques, a task that is best done slowly, working back and forth between the introductory chapter and the practice problems. You may get an uncomfortable number of problems wrong at this stage, but, instead of being discouraged, you should attempt to understand clearly the reasons for your errors. Such understanding will become a plus in the future.

- Review the chapter on the Writing Sample, and write an essay about one of the given topics. Ask a friend with good writing skills to read your essay and offer constructive criticism.
- Review the chapter on Logical Reasoning. Do the Logical Reasoning problems in the chapter, those in the LSAT practice test, and the ones in Model Test One (pp. 200 and 214). Correct and analyze your performance.

Week 2

- Review the chapter on Analytical Reasoning. Do the Analytical Reasoning problems in the chapter, those in the LSAT practice test, and those in Model Test One (pp. 195 and 209). Correct and analyze your performance.

  Note: At this point you have introduced yourself to the whole test, and have tried some effective strategies. Now you should begin timing each of your practice tests.

- Do the Reading Comprehension problems in Model Test Two (pp. 252 and 275), and the Logical Reasoning problems in Model Test Two (pp. 243 and 267). Correct and analyze your performance.
- Do the Analytical Reasoning problems in Model Test Two (p. 262). Correct and analyze your performance.
- Write another essay about one of the topics given in the Writing Sample chapter, and have a friend read and respond to your effort.

Week 3

- Early in the week, do all of Model Test Three; practice and review three sections each day. For each section, time yourself, then correct and analyze your performance. Again, have a friend read and respond to your efforts on the Writing Sample.

  Note: This long practice testing will familiarize you with some of the difficulties you will encounter on the actual test—maintaining focus and concentration, dealing with fatigue, pacing, etc. It will also help you build your endurance. Remember, as you analyze your mistakes, to watch for repeated errors. Sometimes these are the easiest to eliminate.

- Review carefully all of the Logical Reasoning problems in the sample test in the LSAT bulletin, Chapter 3, and any others you have completed in the model tests in this book.

- A few days before your exam, review some of the problems you have already completed—focus on the thinking processes. You may wish to reread chapters that gave you the most difficulty.
- Finally, carefully read the review of test-taking strategies at the end of the book (p. 366). It will recap the highlights of the book, and supply a variety of tips for putting yourself into an effective state of mind before the LSAT.

BEFORE YOU BEGIN

THE MAIN FOCUS

Understanding the Thinking Processes

One of the key factors in your success on the LSAT is your mastery of the LSAT "thinking processes." There is no question that this will take lots of time working practice problems, but it will also take a carefully focused analysis of that practice.

As you read each introductory chapter, keep in mind the thinking process involved as it is explained. You are not trying to learn or memorize any actual problem; rather, you are trying to learn the process behind solving each problem type so that you will be able to apply that process to new problems.

Notice that each section is designed to analyze this thinking process and to help you understand what the test maker had in mind when constructing the question. Learn to understand the reasoning behind the construction of each question.

If you focus on this reasoning as you prepare, the techniques carefully explained in each chapter will be easier to apply and will become even more effective. Remember that it is the mastery of this thinking process within the time constraints that will yield success on the LSAT.

SOME GENERAL STRATEGIES

The One-Check, Two-Check System

Many people score lower than they should on the LSAT simply because they do not get to many of the easier problems. They puzzle over difficult questions and use up the time that could be spent answering easy ones. In fact, the easy questions are worth exactly the same as the difficult ones, so it makes sense not to do the hard problems until you have answered all the easy ones.

To maximize your correct answers by focusing on the easier problems, use the following system:

1. Attempt the first question. If it is answerable quickly and easily, work the problem, circle the answer in the question booklet, and then mark that answer on the answer sheet. The mark on the answer sheet should be a complete mark, not merely a dot, because you may not be given time at the end of the test to darken marks.

2. If a question seems impossible, place two checks (√ √) on or next to the question number in the question booklet and mark the answer you guess on the answer sheet. Again, the mark on the answer sheet should be a complete mark, not merely a dot.

3. If you're in the midst of a question that seems to be taking too much time, or if you immediately spot that a question is answerable but time-consuming (that is, it will require more than two minutes to answer), place one check (√) next to the question number, mark an answer you guess on the answer sheet, and continue with the next question.

NOTE THAT NO QUESTIONS ARE LEFT BLANK. AN ANSWER CHOICE IS *ALWAYS* FILLED IN BEFORE LEAVING THAT QUESTION.

4. When all the problems in a section have been attempted in this manner, there may still be time left. If so, return to the single-check (√) questions, working as many as possible, changing each guessed answer to a worked-out answer, if necessary.

5. If time remains after all the single-check (√) questions are completed, you can choose between

   a. attempting those "impossible" double-check (√√) questions (sometimes a question later on in the test may trigger one's memory to allow once-impossible questions to be solved);

   or

   b. spending time checking and reworking the easier questions to eliminate any careless errors.

6. Remember: use *all* the allotted time as effectively as possible.

You should use this system as you work through the practice tests in this book; such practice will allow you to make "one-check, two-check" judgments quickly when you actually take the LSAT. As our extensive research has shown, use of this system results in less wasted time on the LSAT.

The Elimination Strategy

Faced with five answer choices, you will work more efficiently and effectively if you *eliminate unreasonable or irrelevant answers immediately.* In most cases, two or three choices in every set will stand out as obviously incorrect. Many test takers don't perceive this because they painstakingly analyze every choice, even the obviously ridiculous ones.

Consider the following Logical Reasoning problem:

> **According to the theory of aerodynamics, the bumblebee is unable to fly. This is because the size, weight, and shape of its body in relationship to the total wingspan make flying impossible. The bumblebee, being ignorant of this "scientific truth," flies anyway.**

The author's statement would be strengthened by pointing out that

(A) the theory of aerodynamics may be readily tested
(B) the bumblebee does not actually fly but glides instead
(C) bumblebees cannot fly in strong winds
(D) bumblebees are ignorant of other things but can't do all of them
(E) nothing is impossible

A student who does not immediately eliminate the unreasonable choices here, and instead tries to analyze every choice, will find herself becoming confused and anxious as she tries to decide how even silly choices might be correct. Her thinking goes something like this: "I wonder if bumblebees do glide; I've never looked that closely—maybe the test has me on this one . . . come to think of it, I've never seen a bumblebee in a strong wind; (C) is tricky, but it just might be right . . . I can't understand (D); it seems irrelevant but that just might be a trick . . ."

On and on she goes, becoming more and more uncertain.

Using the elimination strategy, a confident test taker proceeds as follows:

(A)? Possible choice.
(B)? Ridiculous. Both false and irrelevant. Cross it out.
(C)? Another ridiculous, irrelevant one. Cross it out.
(D)? Incomprehensible! Eliminate it.
(E)? Too *general* to be the best choice.

This test taker, aware that most answer choices can be easily eliminated, does so without complicating the process by considering unreasonable possibilities.

To summarize the elimination strategy:

- Look for unreasonable or incorrect answer choices first. Expect to find at least two or three of these with every problem.
- When a choice seems wrong, cross it out in your test booklet *immediately,* so that you will not be tempted to reconsider it.

Eliminating choices in this fashion will lead you to correct answers more quickly, and will increase your overall confidence.

Marking in the Test Booklet

Many test takers don't take full advantage of opportunities to mark key words and draw diagrams in the test booklet. Remember that, in the Reading Comprehension and Logical Reasoning sections, *marking key words and phrases will significantly increase your comprehension and lead you to a correct answer.* Marking also helps to keep you focused and alert. In the Analytical Reasoning section, *drawing diagrams is absolutely essential.*

Further, more specific hints about marking are given in the introductory chapters that follow. The important general point to stress here is that active, successful test taking entails marking and drawing, and that passive, weak test takers make little use of this technique.

The "Multiple-Multiple-Choice" Item (Not appeared recently)

Although the "Multiple-Multiple-Choice" Item has not appeared in the last few years, we have included a few samples with some excellent strategies in the event that any do reappear on a future exam.

EXAMPLE

According to the theory of aerodynamics, the bumblebee should be unable to fly. But it flies anyway.

Which of the following can be logically inferred from the above statement?

I.   The bumblebee's behavior contradicts scientific theory.
II. The bumblebee is not really able to fly.
III. Some theories don't hold true in all cases.

(A) I only   (B) II only   (C) I and II only   (D) I and III only
(E) I, II, and III

Analysis

When faced with a problem of this structure, first try to quickly answer each of the roman numerals as true or false and label them accordingly. They would therefore be labeled as follows:

T I.   The bumblebee's behavior contradicts scientific theory.
F II. The bumblebee is not really able to fly.
T III. Some theories don't hold true in all cases.
   (A) I only   (B) II only   (C) I and II only   (D) I and III only   (E) I, II, and III

Therefore, since I and III are true, the answer is (D).

Quite frequently, however, determining each of the roman numerals as true or false is not a quick or easy proposition. In such a case it may be effective (and possibly less time consuming) to skip the difficult roman numerals, solve the easy ones, and then eliminate the final choices, as follows:

? I.   The bumblebee's behavior contradicts scientific theory.
F II. The bumblebee is not really able to fly.
T III. Some theories don't hold true in all cases.
   (A) I only   (B) II only   (C) I and II only   (D) I and III only   (E) I, II, and III

Notice that, since II is false, any choice containing a false II may be eliminated. Thus, (B), (C), and (E) should be crossed out. Continuing, since III is true, any remaining choice must contain a true III for it to be correct. Thus, choice (A) may be eliminated as it does not contain a true III. This leaves only choice (D) as the correct answer.

In some cases you will be able to eliminate all but the correct answer, as above. In other cases you may find several possible choices remaining, and thus have a more educated guess.

Becoming familiar with this technique will often save you time and allow you to take better educated guesses in those cases when you have partial information, when parts of the problem appear too difficult, or when the question itself does not appear to give enough direction.

PITFALLS—WHAT TO WATCH OUT FOR

The Common Mistake—The Misread

The most common mistake for many test takers is the MISREAD. The MISREAD occurs when you read the question incorrectly. For example, "Which of the following *must* be true?" is often read as "Which of the following *could* be true?" and "All of the following must be true EXCEPT" often loses the word "except."

If you MISREAD the question, you will be looking for the wrong answer.

To help eliminate the MISREAD, always underline or circle what you are looking for in the question. This will also help you focus on the main point of the question.

By the way, the MISREAD also occurs while reading answer choices. You may wish to underline or circle key words in the answers to help you avoid the MISREAD.

Distracters and "Attractive" Distracters

When the test makers put together the LSAT they spend a great deal of time and effort not only making sure that "credited response" is the best answer given, but also that the wrong answer choices (distracters) are good possibilities.

Distracters, as the word indicates, are meant to distract you away from the right answer. Some distracters are easily eliminated as they are just "wrong"—they are irrelevant, contradict something, or bring in items that are not addressed. Some distracters are too general, too specific or narrow, or use a word or words that miss the mark or point of the question. Some distracters are very close to the best or right answer. We refer to the wrong answers that are close as "attractive distracters." The choice looked good but was wrong. When you have narrowed your choices down to two, let's say (A) or (B), keep in mind that one is probably an "attractive distracter."

As you prepare for the LSAT it is important that you focus on the difference (in some cases a very fine difference) between the correct answer and the attractive distracter(s). When you analyze your practice tests, focus on what constitutes a right answer and on spotting the differences.

ANALYZING YOUR LSAT SCORE: A BROAD RANGE SCORE APPROXIMATOR

The chart that follows is designed to give you a general approximation of the number of questions you need to get right to fall into a general score range and percentile rank on your LSAT. It should help you see if you are in the "ballpark" of the score you need. This range approximator is *not* designed to give you an exact score or to predict your LSAT score. The actual LSAT will have questions that are similar to the ones encountered in this book, but some questions may be either easier or more difficult. The variance in difficulty levels and testing conditions can affect your score range.

OBTAINING YOUR APPROXIMATE SCORE RANGE

Although the LSAT uses a very precise formula to convert raw scores to scaled scores, for the purpose of this broad range approximation simply total the number of questions you answered correctly. Next, divide the total number of correct answers by the total number of questions on the sample test. This will give you the percent correct. Now look at the following chart to see the approximate percent you need to get right to get into your score range. Remember, on the actual test one of the sections is experimental and, therefore, doesn't count toward your score.

Approximate Scaled Score Range	Approx. % of Correct Answers Necessary	Approx. Score Percentile for 94–95 Test Takers (Est. % below)
171–180	95 and up	99–99.9%
161–170	80–94%	88–98%
151–160	65–79%	53–85%
141–150	45–64%	17–48%
131–140	30–44%	3–15%
121–130	20–29%	0–2%

On the actual LSAT, the percent of correct answers to get certain scores will vary slightly from test to test, depending on the number of problems and the level of difficulty of that particular exam.

An average score is approximately 151.

If you are not in the range that you wish to achieve, check the approximate percent of correct answers that you need to achieve that range. Carefully analyze the types of errors you are making and continue practicing and analyzing. Remember, in trying to approximate a score range, you must take the complete sample test under strict time and test conditions.

PART TWO

ANALYSIS

Understanding the Sections
and the Key Strategies

1

READING COMPREHENSION

INTRODUCTION TO QUESTION TYPE

The entire LSAT is, generally speaking, a test of reading comprehension. However, the Reading Comprehension section itself is a test of general reading skills rather than the more particular analytical skills stressed in the Analytical Reasoning section.

Each Reading Comprehension section consists of four passages that range in length from 400 to 600 words. Each passage is followed by six to eight questions relating to the passage. These 26 to 28 questions are to be answered in 35 minutes.

The four passages are drawn from the humanities, the natural sciences, the social sciences, and law. No specialized knowledge is necessary to answer any of the questions. All of the questions can be answered by referring to the passage.

Some of the common types of Reading Comprehension questions that follow a passage include questions about:

- the main point of the passage or the passage's primary purpose;
- the meaning or function of specific words or phrases in the context of the passage;
- information that is explicitly stated in the passage;
- inferences and implications related to the passage;
- the author's tone or attitude;
- the function of a paragraph within the passage as a whole;
- the organization of the passage.

ACTIVE READING

The Reading Comprehension section presents long passages demanding your steady concentration. Because such passages are complex, you must approach them actively, focusing on a specific plan of attack.

Suppose that midway through the first paragraph of a passage you encounter a sentence like this:

> Ordinarily, of course, we are invited only to criticize the current neglect of government programs; politicians cling to their own fringe benefits while the strife in our inner cities is only nominally contained with a plethora of half-baked local projects whose actual effect is the gradual erosion of trust in the beneficence of the republic.

Different students may respond in different ways:

"What? Let me read that again" (and again and again).
"I used to know what beneficence meant; uh. . . ."
"Boy, am I tired."
"I should have eaten a better breakfast; my head aches."
"I wonder what I'll do tonight. . . ."
"This writer is screwy; I was a senator's aide and I know he's wrong."
"How can I read this!? It's written so poorly; that word *plethora* is a terrible choice."

These typical responses—getting stuck, getting distracted, getting angry—all work against your purpose: understanding the information given in the passage to answer the questions that follow. The techniques described below should help you avoid some common reading test pitfalls.

Essentially, active reading consists of marking as you read. But the marking you do must be strategic and efficient. To present some effective active reading techniques, we will consider seven typical LSAT questions and a sample reading passage that is shorter and less complex than those in the exam.

EXAMPLE

With the possible exception of equal rights, perhaps the most controversial issue across the United States today is the death penalty. Many argue that it is an effective deterrent to murder, while others maintain there is no conclusive evidence
(5) that the death penalty reduces the number of murders, and go on to contend that it is cruel and inhuman punishment, that it is the mark of a brutal society, and finally, that it is of questionable effectiveness as a deterrent to crime anyway.

But, the death penalty is a necessary evil. Throughout
(10) recorded history there have always been those extreme individuals who were capable of terribly violent crimes such as murder. But some are more extreme, more diabolical than others. It is one thing to take the life of another in a momentary fit of blind rage, but quite another to coldly plot and carry out
(15) the murder of one or more people in the style of an executioner. Thus, murder, like all other crimes, is a matter of relative degree. While it could be argued with some conviction that the criminal in the first instance should be merely isolated from society, such should not be the fate of the latter type
(20) murderer. To quote Moshe Dayan, "Unfortunately, we must kill them." The value of the death penalty as a deterrent to crime may be open to debate, but there remains one irrefutable fact: Gary Gilmore will never commit another murder. Charles Manson and his followers, were they to escape, or—God forbid—
(25) be paroled, very well might.

The overwhelming majority of citizens believe that the death penalty protects them. Their belief is reinforced by evi-

dence that shows that the death penalty deters murder. For example, the Attorney General points out that from 1954 to 1963,
(30) when the death penalty was consistently imposed in California, the murder rate remained between three and four murders for each 100,000 population. Since 1964 the death penalty has been imposed only once (in 1967), and the murder rate has skyrocketed to 10.4 murders for each 100,000 population. The
(35) sharp climb in the state's murder rate, which commenced when executions stopped, is no coincidence. It is convincing evidence that the death penalty does deter many murderers. If the governor were to veto a bill reestablishing the death penalty, an initiative would surely follow. However, an initia-
(40) tive cannot restore the death penalty for six months. In the interim, innocent people will be murdered—some whose lives may have been saved if the death penalty were in effect.

1. The primary purpose of the passage is to

   (A) criticize the governor
   (B) argue for the value of the death penalty
   (C) initiate a veto
   (D) speak for the majority
   (E) impose a six-month moratorium on the death penalty

2. The passage attempts to establish a relationship between

   (A) Gary Gilmore and Charles Manson
   (B) the importance of both equal rights and the death penalty
   (C) the murder rate and the imposition of the death penalty
   (D) executions and murders
   (E) the effects of parole and the effects of isolation

3. It can be inferred that the author assumes which one of the following about a governor's veto of the death penalty legislation?

   (A) It might be upheld.
   (B) It will certainly be overridden.
   (C) It represents consultation with a majority of citizens.
   (D) The veto is important, but not crucial.
   (E) It is based on the principle of equal protection for accused murderers.

4. The author's response to those who urge the death penalty for all degrees of murder would most likely be

   (A) strongly supportive
   (B) noncommittal
   (C) negative
   (D) supportive
   (E) uncomprehending

5. In the passage the author is primarily concerned with

    (A) supporting a position
    (B) describing an occurrence
    (C) citing authorities
    (D) analyzing a problem objectively
    (E) settling a dispute

6. In lines 39–40 "initiative" refers to

    (A) a demonstration against the governor's action
    (B) a rise in the murder rate
    (C) a more vocal response by the majority of citizens
    (D) the introduction of legislation to reinstate the death penalty
    (E) overriding the governor's veto

7. The passage provides answers to all of the following questions EXCEPT

    (A) Are all murders equally diabolical?
    (B) Does the public believe the death penalty deters murder?
    (C) What happened to Gary Gilmore?
    (D) Will Charles Manson be paroled?
    (E) Should the governor support the death penalty?

FOUR-STEP APPROACH

STEP ONE: SKIM THE QUESTIONS

Before reading the passage, spend a short time familiarizing yourself with the questions. You should preread or "skim" the questions for two reasons: (1) to learn what *types* of questions are being asked; and (2) to learn what specific *information* to look for when you do read the passage. In order to skim efficiently and effectively, you should read over only the portion of each question that *precedes* the multiple choices, and you should mark *key words* as you do so.

A *key word* or phrase is any segment that suggests what you should look for when you read the passage. Marking these key words will help you remember them as you read (luckily, the questions will be printed directly below and alongside the passage, so that as you read the passage you will be able to glance at the questions and remind yourself about what you've marked). In order to further explain and clarify these tips on skimming, let's examine the questions that follow the preceding passage.

The key words for each of them are circled.

1. The primary purpose of the passage is to. . . .

This is a "main idea" or "primary purpose" question; most LSAT reading passages are followed by at least one of these. You are asked what the passage is trying to *do* or *express,* as a whole. Here is a list of possible purposes that may be embodied in a reading passage:

to inform	to criticize	to show
to persuade	to argue for or against	to question
to analyze	to illustrate	to explain
to change	to represent	to prove
to restore	to parody	to describe

This list is by no means exhaustive; the possible purposes are almost endless, and you might try thinking of some yourself.

The main idea or primary purpose of a passage is usually stated or implied in the *thesis sentence* of one or more of the paragraphs. A thesis sentence tells what the paragraph as a whole is about; it states a main idea or primary purpose. For example, the second sentence of paragraph 3 in the passage is the thesis sentence; it sums up the evidence of that paragraph into a single statement.

A primary purpose or main idea question should direct your attention to the thesis sentences in the passage, that is, the *general statements* that sum up the specific details.

2. The passage attempts to establish a relationship between. . . .

This question requires that you locate *explicit* (established) *information* in the passage, information that defines a relationship. The question allows you to anticipate the mention of at least one relationship in the passage, and warns you through its wording that the relationship is not "hidden," but is instead one that the author deliberately attempts to establish.

3. It can be inferred that the author assumes which of the following about the veto of a governor's death penalty legislation?

This question requires that you locate *implicit,* rather than explicit, information; you are asked to draw an *inference* (a conclusion based on reasoning), not just to locate obvious material. It is more difficult than question 2. When you read about the governor's veto in the passage, you should take mental note of any unstated assumptions that seem to lie behind the author's commentary.

4. The author's response to those who urge the death penalty for all degrees of murder would most likely be. . . .

This question type, usually more difficult than the types previously discussed, requires you to *apply* the information in the passage itself. As you read the passage, you should pay special attention to the author's attitude toward types, or degrees, of murder; applying this attitude to the situation described in the question should lead to the answer.

5. In the passage the author is ⟨primarily concerned⟩ with. . . .

This is another variety of the "primary purpose" or "main idea" question.

6. In lines 39–40, "initiative" refers to. . . .

The question requires you to focus on specific language in the passage and define it in context. Such a question is relatively easy insofar as it specifies just where to look for an answer; its difficulty varies according to the difficulty of the word or phrase you are asked to consider.

7. The passage provides answers to all of the following questions EXCEPT. . . .

Although many questions that you skim will lead you to useful information in the passage, some like this one, do not. It is still important, however, to circle key words in the question to avoid the <u>misread</u>.

In general, spend only a few seconds skimming the questions. Read each question, mark key words, and move on.

DO NOT:

- dwell on a question and analyze it extensively.
- be concerned with whether you are marking the "right" words (trust your intuition).
- read the multiple choices (this wastes time).

STEP TWO (OPTIONAL): SKIM THE PASSAGE

Some students find skimming the passage helpful. Skimming the passage consists of quickly reading the first sentence of each paragraph, and marking key words and phrases. This will give you an idea of what the paragraph as a whole is about. The first sentence is often a general statement or thesis sentence that gives the gist of the paragraph.

Consider the passage given above. Reading the first sentence of each paragraph, we mark the key words and phrases, and may draw the following conclusions:

Paragraph 1: "With the possible exception of equal rights, perhaps the most controversial issue across the United States today is the death penalty." This sentence suggests that the passage will be about the death penalty, and the word "controversial" suggests that the author is about to take a stand on the controversy.

". . . that it is cruel and inhuman punishment, that it is the mark of a brutal society, and finally that it is of questionable effectiveness as a deterrent to crime anyway." This sentence presents opposition arguments, and because those arguments are presented as the views of others, not the views of the author, we begin to suspect that he does not align himself with the opposition.

Paragraph 2: "But, the death penalty is a necessary evil." This confirms our suspicion; the author is beginning an argument *in favor* of the death penalty.

"For example, it is one thing to take the life of another in a momentary fit of blind rage but quite another to coldly plot and carry out the murder of one or more people in the style of an executioner." Here the author is distinguishing between *degrees* of murder, and you may at this point recall question 4; this information seems relevant to that question.

"The value of the death penalty as a deterrent to crime may be open to debate, but there remains one irrefutable fact: Gary Gilmore will never commit another murder." The most significant feature of this sentence is that the author's tone is so absolute, indicating his strong belief in his own position.

Paragraph 3: "The overwhelming majority of citizens believe that the death penalty protects them." This sentence points toward statistical evidence in favor of the author's view.

"If the governor were to veto a bill reestablishing the death penalty, an initiative will surely follow." Coincidentally with the author's faith in the will of the majority, here he suggests that the death penalty will be upheld one way or another, by overriding a veto or through initiative.

Do not expect your own skimming of the passage to necessarily yield a series of conclusions such as those expressed above. Most of the knowledge you gather as you skim will "happen" without a deliberate effort on your part to translate your intuitions into sentences. Just read and mark the sentences, without slowing yourself down by analyzing each sentence. The preceding analysis suggests some possible conclusions that may occur to a reader, but drawing such full conclusions from sentence clues will take both practice and a relaxed attitude; don't push yourself to make sense out of everything and don't reread sentences (skimming the passage should take only a few seconds). Some sentences you read may be too difficult to make sense of immediately; just leave these alone and move along. Remember that getting stuck wastes time and raises anxiety.

STEP THREE: READ AND MARK THE PASSAGE

Now you are ready to read the entire passage. To read quickly, carefully, and efficiently, you must be *marking* important words and phrases while you read. At least such marking will keep you alert and focused. At most it will locate the answers to many questions.

Skimming the questions will have helped you decide what to mark. If a question refers to a specific line, sentence, or quotation from the passage, you will want to mark this reference and pay special attention to it. Whenever a key word from a question corresponds with a spot in the passage, mark the spot. In the scheme for marking a passage, these spots are called, simply, ANSWER SPOTS. There are two other kinds of "spots" that you should mark as you read: REPEAT SPOTS and INTUITION SPOTS. Repeat spots are sections of the passage in which the same type of information is repeated.

Consider the following excerpt from a passage:

> **Proposed cutbacks in the Human Resources Agency are scheduled for hearing 9 A.M. on the 17th. Included in possible program reductions are cutbacks in the veterans' affairs pro-**

gram, including closure of the local office; in potential support for the county's Commission on the Status of Women; and in payments provided by the county for foster home care, which are not being adjusted for cost-of-living increases this year.

Programs in the Environmental Improvement Agency will be examined by the board beginning 9 A.M. Friday, August 18. The milk and dairy inspection program has been recommended by County Administrative Officer Fred Higgins for transfer to state administration. In addition, budget recommendations do not include funds for numerous community general plans which have been discussed previously by the board of supervisors. Such areas as Joshua Tree, Crestline, Lytle Creek, and Yucaipa are not included in the Planning Department's program for the upcoming year.

A special session to discuss proposed budget cuts in the county's General Services Agency will be conducted at 9 A.M. Saturday, August 19. A number of county branch libraries have been proposed for closure next year, including the Adelanto, Bloomington, Crestline, Joshua Tree, Mentone, Morongo, Muscoy, and Running Springs locations. A rollback in hours of operation will also be considered. Branches now open 60 hours a week will be cut to 52 hours. Other 50-hour-a-week branches will be reduced to 32 hours a week. Testimony will be heard on cutbacks in various agricultural service programs, including the county trapper program in the Yucaipa region and support for 4-H activities.

Generally, this excerpt stresses information about times, dates, and locations; we are conscious of repeated numbers and repeated place names. Marking the spots in which such information is found will help you to sort out the information, and also to answer more efficiently a question that addresses such information, a question such as "Which of the following cities are (is) *not* included in the Planning Department's program and *are* (is) liable to lose a branch library?" Having marked the REPEAT SPOTS that contain location names, you may be better able to focus on the appropriate information quickly.

INTUITION SPOTS are any spots that strike you as significant, for whatever reason. As we read, we tend to pay special attention to certain information; marking those spots that your intuition perceives as important will help increase your comprehension and will therefore contribute to correct answers.

You may notice that ANSWER SPOTS, REPEAT SPOTS, and INTUITION SPOTS are not necessarily different spots. An answer spot may also be a spot that contains repeat information AND appeals to your intuition.

Don't overmark. Some students, fearing that they will miss an important point, underline everything. Such misplaced thoroughness makes it impossible to find any specific word or phrase. Just mark the main idea of each paragraph and several important words or phrases. And vary your marks. You may want to underline main ideas, use cir-

cles or brackets or stars to indicate other important spots, and jot some notes to yourself in the margin. Here is how you might mark the death penalty passage:

With the possible exception of equal rights, perhaps the
most controversial issue across the United States today is the
death penalty. Many argue that it is an effective deterrent to
murder, while others maintain there is no conclusive evidence
(5) that the death penalty reduces the number of murders, and go
on to contend that it is cruel and inhuman punishment, that it
is the mark of a brutal society, and finally that it is of questionable effectiveness as a deterrent to crime anyway.

But, the death penalty is a necessary evil. Throughout
(10) recorded history there have always been those extreme individuals who were capable of terribly violent crimes such as murder.
But some are more extreme, more diabolical than others. It is
one thing to take the life of another in a momentary fit of blind
rage, but quite another to coldly plot and carry out the murder of
(15) one or more people in the style of an executioner. Thus, murder,
like all other crimes, is a matter of relative degree. While it could
be argued with some conviction that the criminal in the first instance should be merely isolated from society, such should not
be the fate of the latter type murderer. To quote Moshe Dayan,
(20) "Unfortunately, we must kill them." The value of the death
penalty as a deterrent to crime may be open to debate, but there
remains one irrefutable fact: Gary Gilmore will never commit
another murder. Charles Manson and his followers, were they to
escape, or—God forbid—be paroled, very well might.

(25) The overwhelming majority of citizens believe that the
death penalty protects them. Their belief is reinforced by evidence that shows that the death penalty deters murder. For example, the Attorney General points out that from 1954 to 1963,
when the death penalty was consistently imposed in Califor-
(30) nia, the murder rate remained between three and four murders
for each 100,000 population. Since 1964 the death penalty has
been imposed only once (in 1967), and the murder rate has
skyrocketed to 10.4 murders for each 100,000 population. The
sharp climb in the state's murder rate, which commenced
(35) when executions stopped, is no coincidence. It is convincing
evidence that the death penalty does deter many murderers. If
the governor were to veto a bill reestablishing the death
penalty, an initiative would surely follow. However, an initiative cannot restore the death penalty for six months. In the in-
(40) terim, innocent people will be murdered—some whose lives
may have been saved if the death penalty were in effect.

Margin notes: contrast / opposition points; degrees of murder; penalty; irrefutable fact ←; STATS; veto effects

Your marking method should be active, playful, and personal. While you are marking, don't worry about whether you are doing it correctly. You may notice that, in the discussion of skimming the passage, some sentences are marked differently than they are here, in order to stress that there is no single, "correct" method.

Remember not to react subjectively to the passage, or add to it. Your own background may have you disagreeing with the passage, or you may be tempted to supply information from your own experience in order to answer a question. You must use only the information you are given, and you must accept it as true.

Avoid wasting time with very difficult or technical sentences. Concentrating on the sentences and ideas you do understand will often supply you with enough material to answer the questions. Rereading difficult sentences takes time, and usually does not bring greater clarity.

STEP FOUR: ANSWER THE QUESTIONS

As you attempt to answer each question, follow these steps:

1. assess the level of difficulty, and skip the question if necessary;
2. eliminate unreasonable and incorrect answer choices;
3. make certain that information in the passage supports your answer.

We will follow this procedure, using the questions on the "death penalty" passage as examples.

Question 1

The primary purpose of the passage is to

(A) criticize the governor
(B) argue for the value of the death penalty
(C) initiate a veto
(D) speak for the majority
(E) impose a six-month moratorium on the death penalty

Analysis

The correct answer is B. Remember that this sort of question asks for the *primary* purpose, not a subsidiary purpose. Often the incorrect answer choices will express minor or subsidiary purposes; this is true of (A) and (D). Another type of incorrect answer choice *contradicts* the information in the passage. So it is with (C) and (E). Both contradict the author's expressed support of the death penalty. Having marked thesis sentences in the passage, you should be aware of the author's repeated arguments for the value of the death penalty, and choose (B).

Question 2

The passage attempts to establish a relationship between

(A) Gary Gilmore and Charles Manson
(B) the importance of both equal rights and the death penalty
(C) the murder rate and the imposition of the death penalty
(D) executions and murders
(E) the effects of parole and the effects of isolation

Analysis

The correct answer is C. "Equal rights" is mentioned only in passing, and a relationship between parole and isolation is scarcely even implied; therefore (B) and (E) should be eliminated. (A) is not a good answer because, strictly speaking, Gary Gilmore and Charles Manson are not compared; their *sentences* are. (D) is a true answer, but not the best one because it is more vague and general than the best choice, (C); paragraph 3 makes this specific comparison.

Question 3

It can be inferred that the author assumes which of the following about a governor's veto of the death penalty legislation?

(A) It might be upheld.
(B) It will certainly be overridden.
(C) It represents consultation with a majority of citizens.
(D) The veto is important, but not crucial.
(E) It is based on the principle of equal protection for accused murderers.

Analysis

The correct answer is A. We are looking for information that is (1) assumed but not explicit, and (2) relevant to the governor's veto. Having marked the appropriate section of the passage, you are able to return immediately to the final two paragraphs, which discuss the veto. (B), (C), and (D) contradict passage information. (C) contradicts the author's earlier explanations that most citizens approve of the death penalty, and (D) contradicts the author's final statement. (B) contradicts the author's assumption that the veto might be upheld. (E) is irrelevant to the veto issue. (A) is correct because the assumption that the veto might be upheld would certainly underlie an argument against it.

Question 4

The author's response to those who urge the death penalty for all degrees of murder would most likely be

(A) strongly supportive
(B) noncommittal
(C) negative
(D) supportive
(E) uncomprehending

Analysis

The correct answer is C. Having marked the section that refers to different degrees of murder, you are once again able to focus on the appropriate section. In paragraph 2 the author argues that unpremeditated murder may not warrant the death penalty. This argument suggests his negative attitude toward someone who urges the death penalty for all murderers.

Question 5

In the passage the author is primarily concerned with

(A) supporting a position
(B) describing an occurrence
(C) citing authorities
(D) analyzing a problem objectively
(E) settling a dispute

Analysis

The correct answer is A. With your general knowledge of the passage, you should immediately eliminate (B) and (D), because the author is *argumentative* throughout, never merely descriptive or objective. Citing authorities (C) is a *subsidiary* rather than a primary concern; the author does so in paragraph 3. (E) is incorrect because it is the author himself who is *creating* a dispute over the death penalty. A review of the thesis sentences alone shows that the author is consistently supporting a position; (A) is certainly the best answer.

Question 6

In lines 39–40 "initiative" refers to

(A) a demonstration against the governor's action
(B) a rise in the murder rate
(C) a more vocal response by the majority of citizens
(D) the introduction of legislation to reinstate the death penalty
(E) overriding the governor's veto

Analysis

The correct answer is D. Skimming this question has allowed you to pay special attention to "initiative" as you read the passage. The sentence suggests that the initiative is a response to a governor's veto of the death penalty; and it is a *certain* response, as indicated by "surely." It is also an action that can eventually restore the death penalty; this fact especially signals (D) as the answer. (B) states information mentioned apart from the initiative; the murder rate will rise "in the interim." Demonstrations (A) or vocal responses (C) are not suggested as possibilities anywhere. (E) is eliminated because the last sentence of the passage urges an override, thus distinguishing this action from an initiative.

Question 7

The passage provides answers to all of the following questions EXCEPT

(A) Are all murders equally diabolical?
(B) Does the public believe the death penalty deters murder?
(C) What happened to Gary Gilmore?
(D) Will Charles Manson be paroled?
(E) Should the governor support the death penalty?

Analysis

The correct answer is D. The passage answers all of these questions except the question of Manson's parole, which remains a possibility.

Active Reading, A Summary Chart

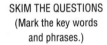

SKIM THE QUESTIONS
(Mark the key words
and phrases.)

SKIM THE PASSAGE
—OPTIONAL—
(Quickly read and mark the first
sentence of each paragraph.)

READ AND MARK THE PASSAGE
• Answer Spots
• Repeat Spots
• Intuition Spots

ANSWER THE QUESTIONS
• Skip if necessary.
• Eliminate weak choices.
• Don't "read into" the passage.

AN ALTERNATIVE GENERAL APPROACH

Some students, regardless of how much they review, analyze, and practice, cannot seem to finish the Reading Comprehension section. They simply cannot work fast enough and continue to maintain a high level of comprehension. If you find that you consistently have a problem getting to or into the fourth passage, you may wish to try this alternative approach: Focus your time on three of the four passages. That is, try to do well on the three passages and the questions that follow, and simply guess at the questions for the remaining passage. You can skip a passage and still receive a good score. The idea is to significantly raise your percentage of correct answers on the passages and questions you are completing. Remember, this is an alternative approach that you may wish to try if you are having a real problem getting to all four passages and maintaining a good level of comprehension.

BASIC TRAINING: EXTRA, EFFECTIVE PRACTICE

The following procedure, *practiced daily,* should strengthen precisely the kinds of skills that you will need for the Reading Comprehension section of the LSAT:

1. Locate the editorial page in your daily newspaper. There you will probably find three or four editorials on different subjects.
2. Read several editorials at your normal reading speed, marking them, if possible.
3. Set the editorials aside, and try to write a summary sentence describing each editorial. Make your summary as precise as possible. Do not write, "This editorial was about the economy." Instead, try to write something like this: "This editorial argued against the value of supply-side economics by referring to rising unemployment and interest rates."

   You may not be able to write so precise a summary right away, but after a few days of practicing this technique, you will find yourself better able to spot and remember main ideas and specific details, and to anticipate and understand the author's point of view.

   It is most important that you *write down* your summary statements. This takes more time and effort than silently "telling" yourself what the editorial means, but the time and effort pay off.
4. Every few days, create some of your own multiple-choice questions about an editorial. What would you ask if you were a test maker? Putting yourself in the test maker's shoes can be very instructive. You will realize, for instance, how weak or incorrect answer choices are constructed, and that realization will help you to eliminate such choices when you take the LSAT.

EXTRA PRACTICE: READING COMPREHENSION

Directions: Read the passages and answer the questions following each passage by blackening the appropriate space on the answer sheet. You may refer back to the passages when answering the questions. Answer all questions on the basis of what is stated or implied.

Use the answer sheet found on page 45.

Passage 1 (Written in 1982)

A recent Harris Survey revealed that a majority of Americans say the price of gasoline would have to go to $1.50 a gallon before they would cut back on
(5) the use of their automobiles for pleasure driving. The survey, conducted among 1,517 adults nationwide, also found that gasoline prices would have to go to $1.85 per
(10) gallon before adults would cease to use their own cars to go to work and would turn to public transportation and car pooling.

In fact, the price of gasoline is
(15) presently going *down* rather than up. Major oil companies have announced plans to reduce wholesale prices by as much as eight cents a gallon. As a result, those drivers who insisted that
(20) only rising gasoline costs would cut their consumption will now probably begin to drive more rather than less. Already, according to the Highway Patrol, highways are becoming more
(25) crowded with cars carrying only one passenger, and with gas-guzzling recreational vehicles.

These results are interesting when one considers that we are presently at
(30) the height of the smog season. As most of us know by now, the majority of our smog problem is caused by exhaust emissions from cars. Yet how many of us have actually made an

(35) effort to drive less? In fact, how many of us have even made an effort to drive more slowly to help conserve gasoline? Unfortunately, the answer to both questions is: not very many. Even
(40) though we all are aware—or certainly should be by now—that there is a desperate need both to conserve fuel and to clean up our air, far too few of us are willing to make even a small
(45) sacrifice to help.

Recently, we read that a small group of botanists is busily attempting to develop a strain of pine tree that can resist the smog. It seems that as the
(50) smog has gotten worse each year it has taken an increasingly greater toll on the pines in mountain areas. Now the situation is becoming critical, either we develop a hardier tree or they will all
(55) die. It's sad to think that in a country which professes so much love for nature, and where so much natural beauty abounds, we have to develop a breed of "supertrees" which can cope
(60) with the polluted air we create.

The solution to our smog problem lies not in eliminating the steel industry's coke oven emissions, or any other industrial emissions, but in
(65) convincing the millions of people who traverse our freeways daily to try at least to drive less. Obviously, it's necessary to drive in order to get to and from work, but if each of us could
(70) at least reduce the pleasure driving a

little, drive the speed limit, and have
our automobile engines tuned
regularly, the improvement would be
immediately noticeable. If we make
(75) these small sacrifices we won't have to
worry about eventually paying $1.85
per gallon for gasoline. The reduced
consumption will keep prices low
because there will be enough for
(80) everyone without having to increase
prices to "force" us to use less.

1. The primary purpose of this passage is
   to

   (A) convince smog producers to
       reduce emissions
   (B) convince drivers to reduce smog
   (C) convince drivers to drive less
   (D) describe an instance of the
       supply/demand phenomenon
   (E) argue against higher gasoline
       prices

2. The author puts the blame for air
   pollution on

   (A) individuals
   (B) institutions
   (C) corporations
   (D) botanists
   (E) pollsters

3. With which one of the following
   statements about the effects of smog
   would the author be most likely to
   agree?

   (A) A greater number of vans and
       campers at our national parks
       threatens the parks' beauty.
   (B) Smog encourages the survival of
       hardy vegetation.
   (C) The price of gasoline may rise in
       the future.

   (D) People who drive alone have no
       respect for nature.
   (E) Smog will gradually become
       something we can live with.

4. Who of the following would be most
   likely to object to the author's
   argument?

   (A) an industrialist
   (B) an auto mechanic
   (C) a botanist
   (D) a Highway Patrol officer
   (E) a manufacturer of recreational
       vehicles

5. The author implies which one of the
   following in his argument?

   (A) Industrial emissions are
       uncontrollable.
   (B) Reduced driving will occur even if
       drivers do not follow his advice.
   (C) Reduced driving will not
       inconvenience drivers.
   (D) The diminishing supply of fuel is
       not a problem.
   (E) Gasoline prices should not go
       down.

6. The author's tone in this passage is

   (A) cynical
   (B) analytical
   (C) satirical
   (D) urgent
   (E) objective

7. To accept the author's argument, we
   must assume which one of the
   following about the Harris Survey?

   (A) The people conducting the survey
       were opposed to pleasure driving.
   (B) The people conducting the survey
       were not drivers.
   (C) The survey was conducted recently.

(D) The 1,517 adults actually represent a majority of Americans.

(E) The people conducting the survey were not employed by the steel industry.

Passage 2

A recent study surveyed 3,576 trials in two reporting samples. Over 500 judges cooperated in the study. The survey was conducted using judges as (5) reporters for jury trials. Two major questions were explored in the survey, "First, what is the magnitude and direction of the disagreement between judge and jury? And, second, what are (10) the sources and explanations of such disagreement?"

The study found that judges and juries agree (would decide the same case the same way) in 75.4 percent of (15) the cases. If cases in which the jury hung are eliminated, the overall agreement rate rises to 78 percent. Thus at the outset, whatever the defects of the jury system, it can be (20) seen that the jury at least arrives at the same result as the judge in over three-fourths of the cases.

The direction of disagreement is clearly toward a more lenient jury than (25) judge. The trend was not isolated to any particular type of offense but was spread throughout crime categories. Additionally, the pattern found was that in convictions, juries tended to be more (30) lenient as far as counts, degrees, and sentencing.

For civil cases the percentage of agreement and disagreement was about the same except that there did (35) not appear to be any strong sentiment in favor of plaintiff over defendant (or vice versa) by the jury.

In cases decided differently because the judge had facts the jury did not, (40) generally, these facts related to suppressed evidence, personal knowledge of the defendant's prior record, etc. The factors that made the difference between judge and jury in (45) these cases, then, were all facts that we as a society purposefully keep from juries because the information is irrelevant or because it is highly prejudicial. From the study it can be (50) assumed that the judge, hearing the information, did not disregard it but, quite the contrary, used it in reaching his (harsher) judgment.

The overwhelming number of cases (55) in which judge and jury agree argue for the jury's understanding of the evidence because it is not to be expected that a jury deciding cases it does not understand and a judge (60) deciding cases he does understand (we presume) would not agree in their results so often. Also, judges themselves generally did not identify "jury misunderstood the facts" as the (65) reason for disagreement.

The level of sympathy that the jury had with the defendant did make some difference. Although generally the jury was neutral, in about 36 percent of the (70) cases the jury had some reaction (positive or negative) because of the personal characteristics, occupation, family, or court appearance. These factors affected juries differently (75) depending on the age, race, or sex of the defendant. Through various statistical evaluations the study is able to state that "the sympathetic defendant causes disagreement in . . . (80) 4 percent of all cases." Similar figures apply for the unsympathetic defendant.

8. This passage was probably written in response to an argument for

   (A) the appointment rather than the election of judges
   (B) the election rather than the appointment of judges
   (C) the wider use of the trial by jury
   (D) the reduced use of the trial by jury
   (E) the increased use of statistics in the courts

9. According to the passage, judge and jury are likely to reach the same verdict in

   (A) criminal cases rather than in civil cases
   (B) civil cases rather than in criminal cases
   (C) cases where the judge has facts denied to the jury
   (D) cases in which the jury hung
   (E) roughly three-quarters of the cases

10. The results of this study suggest that, when there is disagreement between a judge and a jury, the judgments of the judge are

   (A) harsher than those of juries
   (B) less harsh than those of juries
   (C) very nearly the same as those of juries
   (D) less likely to be influenced by irrelevant or prejudicial information
   (E) less harsh than those of juries in criminal cases only

11. From the results of the study we can infer that withholding from a jury information that is irrelevant or prejudicial to a defendant

   (A) has no significant effect on the results of a trial
   (B) works to the disadvantage of most defendants

   (C) works to the advantage of most defendants
   (D) works to increase the objectivity of the judge
   (E) works to decrease the objectivity of the jury

12. The author's argument for the jury's understanding of the evidence presented in trial is based upon

   (A) his assumption that the judge understands the evidence
   (B) his assumption that evidence too complex for the jury to understand would not be admitted
   (C) the fact that evidence is rarely complex
   (D) the fact that juries are able to reach verdicts
   (E) the fact that no judges have accused juries of misunderstanding

13. With which one of the following statements would the author be most likely to disagree?

   (A) Juries are likely to be influenced by the personal characteristics, occupation, family, or court appearance of defendants.
   (B) Juries are influenced by the age, race, or sex of the defendant.
   (C) The judge's misunderstanding the evidence is not a likely cause of judge-jury disagreements.
   (D) The jury's misunderstanding the evidence is not a likely cause of judge-jury disagreements.
   (E) The jury's sympathy with a defendant is a major cause of judge-jury disagreements.

14. By including the information in the final paragraph about the effect of sympathy with the defendant upon the jury, the author of the passage

  (A) unfairly denigrates the opposing argument

  (B) undermines the case he has presented

  (C) suggests that his arguments are objective

  (D) conceals a weakness in his case

  (E) underscores the lack of objectivity in judges

15. The author includes statistical information in the passage chiefly in order to

  (A) demonstrate his familiarity with social science research methods

  (B) support his case for the use of juries

  (C) make what is really a hypothesis appear to be factual

  (D) give an appearance of objectivity to a subjective view

  (E) support a case against the use of juries

Passage 3

Although different plants have varying environmental requirements because of physiological differences, there are certain plant species that are
(5) found associated with relatively extensive geographical areas. The distribution of plants depends upon a number of factors among which are (1) length of daylight and darkness, (2)
(10) temperature means and extremes, (3) length of growing season, and (4) precipitation amounts, types, and distribution.

Daylight and darkness are the keys
(15) by which a plant regulates its cycle. It is not always obvious how the triggering factor works, but experiments have shown day length to be a key. A case in point is that many
(20) greenhouse plants bloom only in the spring without being influenced by outside conditions other than light. Normally, the plants keyed to daylight and darkness phenomena are
(25) restricted to particular latitudes.

In one way or another, every plant is affected by temperature. Some species are killed by frost; others require frost and cold conditions to fruit. Orange
(30) blossoms are killed by frost, but cherry blossoms will develop only if the buds have been adequately chilled for an appropriate time. Often the accumulation of degrees or the
(35) direction of temperatures above or below a specific figure critically affects plants. Plant distributions are often compared with isotherms to suggest the temperature limits and ranges for
(40) different species. The world's great vegetation zones are closely aligned with temperature belts.

Different plant species adjust to seasonal changes in different ways.
(45) Some make the adjustment by retarding growth and arresting vital functions during winter. This may result in the leaf fall of middle latitude deciduous trees. Other plants
(50) disappear entirely at the end of the growing season and only reappear through their seeds. These are the *annuals,* and they form a striking contrast to the *perennials,* which live
(55) from one season to another.

Precipitation supplies the necessary soil water for plants, which take it in at the roots. All plants have some limiting moisture stress level beyond which
(60) they must become inactive or die. Drought resistant plants have a variety

of defenses against moisture deficiencies, but *hygrophytes,* which also are adapted to humid environments, have hardly any defense
(65) against a water shortage.

16. According to the passage, the temperature belts aligned with the world's great vegetation zones may be characterized by

    (A) extreme frost
    (B) either frost or warmth
    (C) extreme cold, but not frost
    (D) the accumulation of degrees
    (E) directed temperatures

17. From this passage we must conclude that a long drought striking a humid environment must inevitably

    (A) render most plants inactive
    (B) result in legislation aimed at building new canals
    (C) reduce or extinguish the hygrophytes
    (D) affect the plant's responses to daylight and darkness
    (E) produce a corresponding change in drainage conditions

18. The passage implies that plants affected by length of day are normally located in

    (A) random locations
    (B) regions where nights are longer
    (C) regions where days are longer
    (D) certain regions east or west of the prime meridian
    (E) certain regions north or south of the equator

19. The behavior of annuals may be compared to

    (A) senility
    (B) eternal life

    (C) reincarnation
    (D) exfoliation
    (E) hibernation

20. According to the passage, the phrase "distribution of plants" (paragraph 1) refers to

    (A) factors too numerous to be listed in this brief passage
    (B) the marketing of plants in areas conducive to further germination and reproduction
    (C) the varieties of size, shape, and color among plants
    (D) the locations in which plants grow and thrive
    (E) certain species only

21. As the author discusses each of the factors affecting the distribution of plants, the overall implication that he does not stress is that

    (A) each of the factors produces notable effects
    (B) no one of these factors operates independently of the others
    (C) soil conditions have one of the most pronounced effects upon plant life
    (D) environmental factors either promote or retard growth
    (E) isotherms affect every factor surveyed

Passage 4

No sooner had the British forces in June 1944 carried out their part in the Allied invasion of Germany than they were faced with the fact that among the
(5) prisoners of war captured there were Russians in German uniforms. By the time the war in Europe ended, between two and three million Soviet citizens had passed through Allied hands. This

(10) extraordinary situation, certainly never before known in the history of war, was the consequence of the policy of both the Soviet and the German regimes. On the Soviet side, the very existence of

(15) prisoners of war was not recognized: the Soviet government refused to adhere to the Geneva Convention, and washed its hands of the millions who fell into German power.

(20)   The Germans, in turn, treated their Soviet prisoners with such callous brutality that only a relatively small number of them survived. For a Soviet prisoner in German hands to enlist in

(25) the German armed forces was about the only way open to him of saving his life. There were also Soviet citizens whose hatred of the Communist regime was so strong that they were

(30) prepared to fight alongside the Germans in order to overthrow Stalin: nominally headed by General Andrey Vlasov, they saw little combat until the end of the war, largely because of

(35) Hitler's suspicion of Vlasov's claims to maintain his political independence of the National Socialist regime even as a prisoner of war. There were also some other combat units composed of

(40) Russians, some of them noted for their savagery. Then there were hordes of civilians in German hands—some compulsorily swept into the German labor mobilization drive, many more

(45) borne along the wave of the German retreat from Russia and thereafter drafted for labor duties. These civilians included many women and children.

    The problem facing the British
(50) government from the outset was what policy to adopt toward this mass of humanity that did not fall into any of the accepted categories thrown up by war. Quite apart from the logistic

(55) problems, there existed a well-established tradition in Britain which refused to repatriate against their will people who found themselves in British hands and the nature of whose

(60) reception by their own government was, to say the least, dubious. The first inclination of the Cabinet—to send all captured Russians back to the Soviet Union—was challenged by the minister

(65) of economic warfare, Lord Selborne, who was moved by the fact that the Russians in British hands had only volunteered to serve in German uniforms as an alternative to certain

(70) death; and that it would therefore be inhuman to send them back to be shot or to suffer long periods of forced labor. Winston Churchill was also swayed by this argument.

22. The primary purpose of this passage is to

    (A) explain one of the problems facing British forces near the end of World War II
    (B) reveal the savagery of both the German and the Russian forces
    (C) stress America's noninvolvement
    (D) detail a "war within a war"
    (E) give evidence for Churchill's position

23. "Repatriate" in paragraph 3 means to

    (A) send back to the country of birth
    (B) send back to the country of allegiance
    (C) send back to the victorious country
    (D) reinstill patriotism
    (E) reinstill British patriotism

24. The author's position is

    (A) pro-Russian
    (B) anti-Russian
    (C) anti-British

(D) pro-German
(E) neutral

25. The problem in World War II concerning the disposition of Soviet prisoners of war was very similar to

(A) the plight of Armenian refugees
(B) Hitler's own loss of identity after 1944
(C) the plight of British prisoners of war
(D) no previous situation
(E) several instances in the history of war

26. Lord Selborne's opinion disregards which of the following facts?

(A) The Soviet Union posed a nuclear threat to the United States.
(B) Traditionally, repatriation was not imposed by Great Britain.
(C) Certain Soviet citizens wanted to overthrow Stalin.
(D) General Andrey Vlasov was politically independent.
(E) Soviet prisoners were treated brutally.

27. The German labor mobilization drive consisted partly of

(A) women and children
(B) retreating German soldiers
(C) followers of General Andrey Vlasov
(D) savage combat units
(E) those born during the retreat

28. The Soviet policy toward their prisoners of war was one of

(A) nonrecognition
(B) nonaggression
(C) nonproliferation
(D) noncontempt
(E) nonadherence

Passage 5

The right to an unbiased jury is an inseparable part of the right to trial by jury as guaranteed by the Seventh Amendment of the United States
(5) Constitution. This right guarantees that twelve impartial jurors will hear and "truly try" the cause before them.

In September 1982, the California Supreme Court upheld a lower court's
(10) $9.2 million verdict against Ford Motor Company despite the fact that three jurors had been working crossword puzzles and one juror had been reading a novel during the presentation of
(15) testimony. Four of the twelve jurors hearing the case were admittedly participating in the activities charged and were clearly guilty of misconduct, yet the California Supreme Court found
(20) no resultant prejudice against Ford's position.

In the United States, citizens are called upon by the government to serve as jurors. Only under
(25) extraordinary circumstances may a citizen be excused from such service. Juries are therefore not necessarily composed of willing volunteers, but instead, are sometimes made up of
(30) individuals who are serving against their will, and justice is adversely affected when citizens are "forced" to serve on juries. In "Reflections of a Juror," the author, who served as a
(35) juror himself, recognized two distinct perspectives shared among jurors. Some jurors have a very positive attitude about their being asked to serve on a jury. Their perspective is
(40) that of rendering a public service by fulfilling their jury duties. On the other hand, some jurors view their obligation as just that, a burdensome obligation, and nothing more. Their attitude is one

(45) of getting through with the ordeal as soon as possible, a let's-get-out-of-here-by-this-afternoon approach.

A study conducted with mock juries, concerned specifically with the issue of (50) juror prejudgment, revealed that 25 percent of the jurors polled reached their decision early in the trial. The jurors in the study who admitted to having made up their minds before (55) having heard all the evidence also stated that they generally held to their first-impression assessments. By prejudging the outcome of the case the jurors had, in effect, breached their (60) sworn duty.

From a reading of the California Supreme Court's opinion, it appears that the Court itself has committed the one form of conduct universally (65) prohibited, that of prejudgment. Ford's battle was lost before it had even begun to present its case. In the first place, Ford is a multibillion-dollar international corporation with (70) "pockets" deeper than most. Secondly, Ford had experienced a great deal of negative publicity resulting from recent jury verdicts awarding large sums of money to victims of Pinto automobile (75) accidents wherein it was determined that Ford had defectively designed the Pinto's gasoline tank so that it was prone to explode upon rear end impacts. Finally, the plaintiff was a (80) nineteen-year-old college freshman whose pursuit of a medical career was abruptly ended when he suffered extensive brain damage after the brakes on his 1966 Lincoln failed, (85) causing him to crash into a fountain after careening down a steeply curving hillside street. Ford presented a considerable amount of evidence in an attempt to prove that the cause of the (90) accident was driver error and faulty

maintenance and not defective design. The Supreme Court responded to Ford's arguments by stating that the jury was responsible for judging the (95) credibility of witnesses and it would be wholly improper for the Court to usurp that function by reweighing the evidence. How ironic that the Court should so gallantly refuse to upset the (100) decision of the jury, a jury wherein four members admittedly were engaging in extraneous activities when they were supposed to be "judging the credibility of witnesses." It would appear from the (105) misconduct of the jury and the conclusionary statements of the California Supreme Court that Ford's liability was indeed a predetermined, prejudged fact.

(110)   If the decision has any impact upon our present system of justice, it will regretfully be a negative one. The California Supreme Court has, in effect, approved a standard of jury conduct so (115) unconscionable as to, in the words of dissenting Justice Richardson, "countenance such a complete erosion of a constitutional command," namely, the right to a fair and impartial jury (120) trial.

29. Which one of the following best states the central idea of the passage?

(A) By not questioning the decision in the Ford case, the California Supreme Court, like the jury, was guilty of prejudgment.

(B) There are serious defects in the system of trial by jury.

(C) The jury in the Ford case was guilty of prejudging the case.

(D) The Supreme Court's handling of the Ford case may lead to an erosion of the constitutional right to a fair and impartial jury trial.

(E) Studies suggest that a large number of the men and women serving on juries fail to "truly try" the cases they hear.

30. All of the following data from the passage could be used to argue against the jury system EXCEPT

(A) in the Ford case, three jurors were working crossword puzzles and one was reading a novel during the presentation of testimony

(B) juries are likely to include individuals who are serving against their will

(C) in a study of mock jurors, 25 percent reached a decision early in the trial

(D) pretrial publicity about Ford Pintos resulting in large jury verdicts to victims influenced the Supreme Court's decision

(E) some jurors view their service as an ordeal to be ended as quickly as possible

31. The author's belief that Ford was denied a fair trial in the lower court is best supported by the fact that

(A) the jury was unduly sympathetic to the nineteen-year-old accident victim who suffered extensive brain damage

(B) the jury was influenced by unfavorable publicity about the defective gas tanks on the Ford Pinto

(C) three of the jurors were admittedly working crossword puzzles during the testimony

(D) the California Supreme Court refused to reverse the decision of the jury

(E) the California Supreme Court refused to judge the credibility of the witnesses

32. An argument in favor of the Supreme Court decision in the Ford case might include all of the following EXCEPT

(A) if the case were retried, the jury would probably include jurors who were serving against their will

(B) it is probable that the jurors working puzzles and reading were also paying attention to the testimony

(C) if the case were retried, some members of the jury are likely to come to a decision early in the trial

(D) if the case were retried, those jurors who made up their minds early would be unlikely to alter their verdicts later in the trial

(E) the jury at the original trial is in a better position to judge the credibility of the witnesses than the Supreme Court

33. The author suggests that the California Supreme Court reached its decision in the Ford case for all of the following reasons EXCEPT

(A) a prejudice against Ford because of its wealth

(B) a prejudice against Ford because of recent negative publicity

(C) an agreement with the lower court's evaluation of the credibility of the witnesses

(D) a bias in favor of the young accident victim

(E) a refusal to find fault with deplorable jury conduct

34. In the next to last paragraph of the passage, the author uses irony when he writes

    (A) "Ford's battle was lost before it had even begun to present its case."
    (B) "Ford is a multibillion-dollar international corporation with 'pockets' deeper than most."
    (C) The plaintiff's "pursuit of a medical career was abruptly ended when he suffered extensive brain damage . . ."
    (D) ". . . the Court should so gallantly refuse to upset the decision of the jury. . . ."
    (E) ". . . Ford's liability was indeed a predetermined, prejudged fact."

35. From information given in lines 110–120, it is clear that the Supreme Court decision

    (A) was unanimous
    (B) was not unanimous
    (C) will have a significant impact on the justice system
    (D) reverses that of the lower court
    (E) will be appealed

ANSWERS AND EXPLANATIONS

Passage 1

1. **C** This purpose is stated most explicitly in paragraph 5, although there are several other points in the passage where the author urges drivers to drive less. (A) is weak because it is too general and inclusive; (B) is vague about the means of reducing smog; (D) and (E) are very minor points.

2. **A** This is stated explicitly in paragraph 5, where the author blames individual drivers rather than industry.

3. **A** The second paragraph implies that recreational vehicles create more smog, and the fourth paragraph describes smog's effects on nature; therefore, we may conclude that gas-guzzling vacation vehicles help to damage the natural beauty of vacation spots. The author *might* also agree with (D), but the evidence in the passage itself points more substantially to (A).

4. **E** The author criticizes the increased use of recreational vehicles (see explanation for question 3).

5. **B** The final sentence in the passage implies that we will be "forced" to conserve if we do not do so voluntarily. (A) is neither stated nor implied; the author does imply that industrial emissions *should not be controlled,* but this is not the same as suggesting that they are *uncontrollable.*

6. **D** The author is almost pleading that drivers make immediate changes in their habits; the urgency of his purpose coincides with the urgency of his tone.

7. **D** The author begins the passage by claiming that the Harris Survey represents a "majority of Americans"; we must share that assumption in order to accept the importance of his argument. All other choices are irrelevant.

Passage 2

8. **D** The passage is part of a longer essay written to refute the arguments of Judge Jerome Frank, who holds that a judge alone is likely to be more reliable than a jury.

9. **E** The second paragraph says that judges and juries agree in 75.4 percent of the cases, according to the study.

10. **A** The third paragraph discusses the greater harshness of judges in all categories of crime—in counts, degrees, and sentencing.

11. **C** Because the effect of this information upon judges is to make their judgments harsher, we can infer it would have the same effect on juries and the withholding of this information is, predictably, to the defendant's advantage.

12. **A** The author assumes the judge understands the evidence and because the juries agree with the judge so often, he argues the juries must also have understood the evidence to come to the same conclusion as the judge.

13. **E** The passage supports each of the first four statements, but the jury's sympathy with a defendant according to the last paragraph leads to judge-jury differences in only 4 percent of all the cases studied and so could not be called a "major" cause of disagreement.

14. **C** By admitting frankly that juries are not always fully objective the author

demonstrates a willingness to discuss facts that may not advance his case. All of the four other options are false.

15. **B** The statistics are used to support the author's case for the use of juries. Because the statistics are the result of other writers' research, and are based upon a large sample, they give more than an "appearance" of objectivity.

Passage 3

16. **B** Paragraph 3 states, "Some species are killed by frost; others require frost and cold conditions to fruit."

17. **C** Paragraph 5 tells that hygrophytes have little defense against a water shortage.

18. **E** The final sentence in paragraph 2 aligns plants affected by light and darkness with "particular latitudes," that is, particular regions north or south of the equator.

19. **C** Reincarnation (C) might be associated with *annuals,* which disappear and reappear again through new seeds ("new life").

20. **D** The factors that account for distribution are all related to geographic location, and all affect the plant's growth and sustenance; this becomes more obvious through the remainder of the passage. (A) must be eliminated because, although the author may have left other factors unmentioned, she does not acknowledge their existence within the passage.

21. **B** Each of the factors is accorded a separate paragraph, and although we must reasonably suppose that such factors must coexist, the author does not express interrelationships among factors. (E) is not stressed in the passage, but neither

is it implied. Each of the other choices is an expressed fact.

Passage 4

22. **A** The passage discusses the past and present facts contributing to the British problem with captured Russians.

23. **A** The final paragraph discusses at length the question of whether to send Russians back to Russia despite their lack of allegiance to Russia. This is the repatriation question and is consistent with the dictionary definition of *repatriate*—to send back to the country of birth.

24. **E** The author does not himself argue for or against a particular position or nationality. He simply presents facts and the arguments of others. His comments in paragraph 2 might be called anti-German, but this attitude is not one of the choices.

25. **D** Paragraph 1 states, "This extraordinary situation [was] . . . never before known in the history of war."

26. **C** Selborne argued that Russians served the Germans only "as an alternative to certain death" (paragraph 3). But paragraph 2 states that some Russians fought with the Germans "in order to overthrow Stalin."

27. **A** Paragraph 2 says that "the German labor mobilization drive . . . included many women and children."

28. **A** Paragraph 1 states, "On the Soviet side, the very existence of prisoners of war was not recognized."

Passage 5

29. **A** The author wishes to criticize both the jury, which was inattentive, and the Supreme Court, which allowed the jury's decision to stand. Some of the other options are stated or im-

plied ideas of the passage but not its central idea.

30. **D** (D) is relevant to the Supreme Court decision but not to the jury system. (A), (B), (C), and (E) all expose deficiencies in the jury system.

31. **C** The inattentiveness of four jurors is explicit support for a charge that Ford's case was not fairly heard. We don't know for certain if (A) or (B) is true. (D) and (E) are true but do not support the author's belief in the unfairness of the trial.

32. **B** The limitations of all juries discussed in the passage would apply as well to the jury retrying the case as to the jury who reached a decision already. The Supreme Court's argument that the original jury was in a better position to judge the credibility of the witnesses is surely correct; the Supreme Court did not see the witnesses who testified. Though (B) is remotely possible, it is not a point one would wish to use in support of the Supreme Court decision.

33. **C** Though the Supreme Court agreed with the lower court jury, it specifically asserted the impropriety of its attempting to reweigh the evidence and the credibility of the witnesses.

34. **D** A case could be made that (B), an understatement, is ironic but a clearer instance is the sarcasm of "gallantly"; the author does not believe the Supreme Court acted gallantly.

35. **B** Because Justice Richardson dissented, the decision cannot have been unanimous.

ANSWER SHEET
EXTRA PRACTICE: READING COMPREHENSION

1. Ⓐ Ⓑ Ⓒ Ⓓ Ⓔ
2. Ⓐ Ⓑ Ⓒ Ⓓ Ⓔ
3. Ⓐ Ⓑ Ⓒ Ⓓ Ⓔ
4. Ⓐ Ⓑ Ⓒ Ⓓ Ⓔ
5. Ⓐ Ⓑ Ⓒ Ⓓ Ⓔ
6. Ⓐ Ⓑ Ⓒ Ⓓ Ⓔ
7. Ⓐ Ⓑ Ⓒ Ⓓ Ⓔ
8. Ⓐ Ⓑ Ⓒ Ⓓ Ⓔ
9. Ⓐ Ⓑ Ⓒ Ⓓ Ⓔ
10. Ⓐ Ⓑ Ⓒ Ⓓ Ⓔ
11. Ⓐ Ⓑ Ⓒ Ⓓ Ⓔ
12. Ⓐ Ⓑ Ⓒ Ⓓ Ⓔ

13. Ⓐ Ⓑ Ⓒ Ⓓ Ⓔ
14. Ⓐ Ⓑ Ⓒ Ⓓ Ⓔ
15. Ⓐ Ⓑ Ⓒ Ⓓ Ⓔ
16. Ⓐ Ⓑ Ⓒ Ⓓ Ⓔ
17. Ⓐ Ⓑ Ⓒ Ⓓ Ⓔ
18. Ⓐ Ⓑ Ⓒ Ⓓ Ⓔ
19. Ⓐ Ⓑ Ⓒ Ⓓ Ⓔ
20. Ⓐ Ⓑ Ⓒ Ⓓ Ⓔ
21. Ⓐ Ⓑ Ⓒ Ⓓ Ⓔ
22. Ⓐ Ⓑ Ⓒ Ⓓ Ⓔ
23. Ⓐ Ⓑ Ⓒ Ⓓ Ⓔ
24. Ⓐ Ⓑ Ⓒ Ⓓ Ⓔ

25. Ⓐ Ⓑ Ⓒ Ⓓ Ⓔ
26. Ⓐ Ⓑ Ⓒ Ⓓ Ⓔ
27. Ⓐ Ⓑ Ⓒ Ⓓ Ⓔ
28. Ⓐ Ⓑ Ⓒ Ⓓ Ⓔ
29. Ⓐ Ⓑ Ⓒ Ⓓ Ⓔ
30. Ⓐ Ⓑ Ⓒ Ⓓ Ⓔ
31. Ⓐ Ⓑ Ⓒ Ⓓ Ⓔ
32. Ⓐ Ⓑ Ⓒ Ⓓ Ⓔ
33. Ⓐ Ⓑ Ⓒ Ⓓ Ⓔ
34. Ⓐ Ⓑ Ⓒ Ⓓ Ⓔ
35. Ⓐ Ⓑ Ⓒ Ⓓ Ⓔ

✂ To remove, cut along dotted rule.

2

ANALYTICAL REASONING

INTRODUCTION TO QUESTION TYPE

The Analytical Reasoning section is designed to measure your ability to analyze, understand, and draw conclusions from a group of conditions and relationships. This section is 35 minutes long and contains from 22 to 24 questions (usually four sets of conditions, statements, or rules). Each set is followed by four to seven questions.

The Analytical Reasoning type of question first appeared officially on the LSAT in June 1982, but a similar form of Analytical Reasoning has been used on the Graduate Record Exam since 1977.

Analytical Reasoning situations can take many forms, but you should be aware of some general things before reviewing the problem types.

WHEN YOU START A SET, FOCUS ON:

Reading the Conditions

1. Read each statement carefully and actively, marking important words.
2. As you read, learn to flow with the information given, looking for relationships between items.
3. Remember that making simple charts, diagrams, or simply displaying information is essential on most sets, so read the conditions as though they are describing a display or diagram.
4. If you wish to read through all of the conditions of a set before starting a diagram, begin your diagram on the second reading.
5. If no diagram seems apparent or conducive to the information given, look at a few questions. Sometimes the questions can give you some good hints on how to display the information.

Marking the Conditions

1. Because you will probably be drawing some sort of diagram or display, place a check mark next to each statement or condition as you read it or use it in the diagram. This will help you avoid skipping a statement or condition as you work back and forth in setting up your diagram.
2. Put a star or an asterisk next to big, general, and important statements. Sometimes these statements will affect a group, category, or placement. (Examples are, "No two people of the same sex are sitting in adjacent seats," and "All of the members of a department cannot take the same day off." Two other examples might include:

"At least two graduate students must be on the team," and "People with pets with them must stay in hotel room 1 or 8.")

3. Put a star or an asterisk by statements that are difficult to understand. Try to rephrase these statements to yourself for better understanding.

WHEN YOU START DRAWING YOUR DISPLAY, FOCUS ON:

Finding Key Items

1. Look for a simple way to display the information. Don't complicate the issue.
2. Look for the setup, frame, or framework. Sometimes this is given in the first statement, but in other cases you may need to read a number of conditions before constructing the type of drawing that will be most effective.
3. If you discover the frame or framework, fill in as much of the diagram as possible, but do not spend a great deal of time trying to complete it. This may not be possible or necessary to answer the questions.
4. Be aware that you may have to redraw all or part of your diagram several times (typically, a few times for each set) as different conditional information is given for specific questions.
5. If a framework is not given, see if the information can be grouped by similarities or differences.
6. As you read each statement, look for concrete information that you can enter into your chart or that you can simply display. (For example, "Tom sits in seat 4," or "Cheryl is Elma's mother.")

Drawing and Placing Information

1. Locate off to the side any information that you cannot place directly into your chart. (Whatever you can't put in, goes out; for example, "Jill will not sit next to Helen," or "A biology book must be next to a science book.")
2. Some very important statements may not fit into your chart. Remember to put a star or an asterisk by these big, general, and important statements.
3. If some statements are not immediately placeable in your chart (and they are not the big, general statements), you may have to return to them for later placing, after you have placed other statements. Remember to mark such statements with an arrow or some other symbol so you don't forget to return to them.
4. As you place information, use question marks (?) to mark information that is variable or could be placed in a number of different places in the diagram.
5. Underline and abbreviate or write out column headings and labels. Don't use single letters as they may be confused with the actual items (If you use "m" for males, it could be confused with an "m" for Manuel, one of the males).
6. If, as is true in many cases, no standard type of chart will apply to the problem, be aware that you can merely pull out information in a simple display or through simple notes. Remember to flow with the information given, looking for relationships between items.

Reasoning from the Conditions

1. No formal logic is required.
2. Apply evidence in both directions. For instance, if a statement tells you that a condition must be true, consider whether this means that certain other conditions must not be true. (For example: "All blue cars are fast" tells you that a slow car is *not* blue.)
3. Notice what information is used, and what is left to use. (For example, "Bob, Carl, Don, Ed, and Fred are riding the school bus home. Don, Ed, and Fred are sitting in seats one, two, and three, respectively." You should realize that Bob and Carl are left to be placed.)
4. Watch for actions and the subsequent reactions in initial conditions or from information given in the questions. (For example, "Dale, Ralph, and Art cannot be on the same team. Dale is on Team A." Your action is that Dale is on Team A, your immediate reaction is that Ralph and Art cannot be on Team A.)
5. Watch the number of items, places, and people (males to females, adults to children, etc.) you are working with. Sometimes these numbers are the basis for correct answers, and they can even tip off how to construct a diagram.
6. If the diagram you construct shows positions or specific dates or other limits, watch for items that will force you off the end or out of the limits. (For example, "There are five houses in a row on the north side of the street numbered 1, 2, 3, 4, 5 consecutively. There is one yellow house that is between two blue houses." Therefore, the yellow house cannot be in place 1 or 5, because there would be no room for a blue house. It would be forced off the end or out of bounds.)

WHEN YOU START ANSWERING THE QUESTIONS, FOCUS ON:

Reading the Questions

1. Read the questions actively, marking the important words. You should first always circle what you are looking for (Which of the following must be true? All of the following are possible except . . .).
2. Notice and underline any *actions* given to you in a question (If <u>Bob is selected</u> for the team, who else must be selected?). Watch for any subsequent *reactions* (If Bob is selected, Tom can't be selected).
3. Keep in mind that any information given to you in a specific question (Usually starting with the words "If . . . ," "Assume . . . ," "Suppose . . . ," "Given the fact that . . . ," and so on.) can be used only for that question and not for any other questions.
4. Don't take any information from one question to another question. That is, if you get an answer on one question, don't use that information (answer) in any other questions.

Working with the Answer Choices

1. Using the elimination strategy mentioned in the introduction can be invaluable here. Watch for rule breakers, that is, statements that contradict initial conditions. If the

conditions state "X cannot sit next to Y" then any answer choice with X sitting next to Y can be eliminated (unless of course, the initial condition was changed in the question for that particular question).

2. Watch for certain types of wrong answers known as *distracters*. Since *"could be"* and *"must be"* are often confused, a *"could be true"* answer choice is a great distracter (*attractive distracter*) for a question that asks what *must be true*.

Understand the distinction between *must be* and *could be:*

Must Be	Could Be
No exceptions All the time Always	May be, but doesn't necessarily have to be

3. If a question looks like it's going to be difficult or time-consuming, you may wish to **scan the answer choices.** When you scan, **look for winners, losers, workers, and question marks**:

Winners—right answers that jump at you or are easy to spot (circle the answer in your question booklet, mark it on your answer sheet, and move on)

Losers—answers that you can eliminate instantly or very easily (cross out the answer choice and move on)

Workers—answer choices that can be fairly easily worked out to determine if they are right or wrong (go on and work this one)

Question Marks—answer choices that you either can't work or don't know what to do with (put a question mark ? and move on)

AND A FINAL REMINDER: KEEP THE DRAWING SIMPLE; DON'T COMPLICATE YOUR THINKING.

The following sections provide some detailed examples of typical problem types and charts. These samples are intended to give you insight into the methods of charting that are possible. REMEMBER: Different students may prefer different types of charts. Use what is effective and efficient for you!

THE APPROACH

ANALYZING TYPES OF CHARTS

The Connection Chart

One of the many types of charts is the connection chart. In constructing this chart, you should follow these steps:

1. Group or align items into general categories (remember you group items by similarities and differences).

2. Draw connections according to relationships between specific items. Your markings should indicate whether items always go together (x—y), never go together (x⤬y), are conditional (if x goes then y goes; x → y), and so on.

After you've drawn your chart, remember to take information forward and backward (what can and can't happen) and to watch for actions and subsequent reactions.

EXAMPLE

Sales manager Phil Forrester is trying to put together a sales team to cover the Los Angeles area. His team will consist of four members—two experienced and two new salesmen.

Sam, Fred, Harry, and Kim are the experienced salesmen.
John, Tim, and Dom are new.
Sam and Fred do not work together.
Tim and Sam refuse to work together.
Harry and Dom cannot work together.

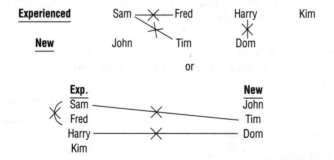

Analysis—The setup

When drawing a connection chart, always prefer fewer connections to many connections. In this case, drawing connections between the workers who can work together will result in a complicated system of intersecting lines. Connecting those who *do not* or *cannot* work together results in a simple, clear chart:

Experienced   Sam —✕— Fred   Harry   Kim
                                      ✕
New   John   Tim   Dom

or

Exp.   **New**
✕ Sam ————————✕———— John
  Fred   ———— Tim
  Harry ————✕———————————— Dom
  Kim

Each chart encourages you to use information in both directions, recognizing that, because connected workers *cannot* work together, unconnected workers *can* work together.

Notice that the conditions gave initial information about those who cannot work together, helping you to formulate the most efficient method of connecting the diagram. If the conditions had stated that some salesmen always work together and some never work together, you would have used a different type of marking to denote each type of connection. Also notice that the labels or headings should be written out or abbreviated *and* underlined.

Question 1

If Sam is made part of the team, the following must be the other members:

(A) John, Tim, Dom
(B) John, Dom, Kim
(C) Tim, Harry, Kim
(D) Dom, John, Fred
(E) John, Dom, Harry

Analysis

The correct answer is B. The team must consist of two experienced and two new salesmen. Sam is experienced, so the rest of the team must include one experienced and two new salesmen. (C) should be eliminated both because it contains two experienced salesmen and because Sam does not work with Tim; also eliminate (A) because it includes Tim. Eliminate (D) because Sam does not work with Fred, and eliminate (E) because Dom does not work with Harry.

Question 2

If Sam is not chosen as part of the sales team and Tim is, then which one of the following must be true?

(A) Dom and Harry are on the team.
(B) Kim and John are on the team.
(C) Harry and Fred are on the team.
(D) John or Dom is not on the team.
(E) Fred or Kim is not on the team.

Analysis

The correct answer is D. With Tim on the team, there is room for one other new salesman. Therefore, *either* John *or* Dom is on the team, but not both.

Question 3

Which one of the following must be true?

(A) Fred and Sam always work together.
(B) Kim and Dom never work together.
(C) Kim and Fred always work together.
(D) If John works, then Kim doesn't work.
(E) If Sam works, then Dom works.

Analysis

The correct answer is E. The key word in this question is *must,* which excludes possible but not necessary combinations. (A) is false, as the chart reveals. (B) is false because they *could* work together if Harry does not work. (C) is false because Kim and Fred do not have to work together. You could have the team of Kim, Sam, John, and Dom.

This also eliminates (D). (E) must be true since Sam and Tim never work together; Sam must always work with Dom and John.

Question 4

If Dom is chosen as part of the sales team but John is not, then the other three members must be D, T, F, K

- (A) Fred, Tim, and Harry
- ✓(B) Fred, Tim, and Kim
- (C) Harry, John, and Tim
- (D) Tim, Dom, and Kim
- (E) Sam, Fred, and Harry

Analysis

The correct answer is B. If Dom is chosen as part of the team and John is not, then Tim must be the other inexperienced member. So, if Dom and Tim both are chosen, then Sam and Harry are not chosen. The team now consists of Dom, Tim, Fred, and Kim.

Question 5

Which one of the following must be true?

- ✓(A) If Harry works, then John works.
- (B) If Kim works, then John works.
- (C) If John works, then Dom works.
- (D) If Dom works, then John works.
- (E) If John works, then Kim works.

Analysis

The correct answer is A. Since Harry will not work with Dom, then John must be one of the other inexperienced members in the group when Harry works. The other combinations (Kim and John, John and Dom) do not always work together.

The Position Chart

Another type of diagram is the position chart. The position chart is very common on the LSAT and appears in a variety of forms. In constructing this type of chart, you should follow these steps:

1. Look for a frame or framework (often given in the first condition or in a statement preceding the conditions).
2. Look for concrete information (that is, specific information to fill in the positions or information that shows restrictions or connections). Have techniques and symbols for showing restrictions (B cannot be next to A—BA) and connections (C is adjacent to D—CD) before you take the test.
3. List the items, people, or letters that will be used to fill in the positions, and mark the relationships and/or restrictions between them.

4. Watch for and mark large, general, important statements (statements that cover a group or category). Remember to place a small check mark next to each statement as you read it, and an asterisk next to general statements.

5. Fill in as many of the positions as possible, but don't be concerned if you can't fill in any immediately; the questions themselves may give you information to fill in the positions. (For example, if X sits in position 4, then which of the following sits in position 6?)

6. Watch for situations that push you out of bounds (for example, if Bill sits between Alice and Jan, then Bill cannot sit on either end—that would push Alice or Jan out of bounds).

7. If you can't fill in any positions from the initial conditions, read some of the questions to get a feel for how much you should know and have filled in.

Keep in mind, whatever won't go in the chart immediately, goes out to the side for possible placement later (whatever won't go in, goes out).

EXAMPLE

John, Paul, George, and Herman sit around a square table with eight chairs, which are equally distributed.

Bob, Carol, Ted, and Alice join them at the table.

The two women (Carol and Alice) cannot sit next to each other.

John and Herman are seated on either side of George and are next to him.

Ted is seated next to Herman.

Carol is seated next to John, but not directly across from George.

John is directly across from Alice.

Handwritten annotations:

Men   Women
B   C ✓
T ✓   A ✓
J ✓
P
G ✓
H ✓

A ✱ C
J — G — H
H — T
C — J
C ✱ G
J ≡ A

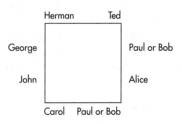

Analysis—The setup

Note that the statement preceding the six conditions immediately suggests that you draw a square table with two spaces on each side. The first piece of concrete information is condition 3, which tells you to seat John, George, and Herman in that order. Next, seat Ted next to Herman (#4), seat Carol next to John (#5), and seat Alice across from John (#6). Note that Carol and Alice are not sitting next to each other (#2), and that Paul and Bob are in *variable* positions on either side of Alice. The resulting chart is as follows:

	Herman	Ted
George		Paul or Bob
John		Alice
	Carol	Paul or Bob

Question 1

Which men could switch positions without contradicting the seating arrangement?

(A) George and Herman
(B) John and George
(C) Paul and Ted
(D) Bob and Paul
(E) Bob and George

Analysis

The correct answer is D. As the chart points out, only Bob and Paul are in variable positions and, thus, interchangeable.

Question 2

Which of the following must be FALSE?

T (A) George is not next to Ted.
T (B) Alice is not next to Carol.
F (C) Herman is next to Carol.
(D) George is across from Paul.
(E) Bob is not next to Paul.

Analysis

The correct answer is C. Working from the answer choices and inspecting the chart, you see that (C) *must* be false in any case, and that (D) *may* be false, depending upon where Paul is seated.

Question 3

Which of the following could be true?

(A) Herman sits next to Carol.
(B) Herman sits next to John.
(C) Ted sits next to Paul.
(D) John sits next to Paul.
(E) George sits next to Alice.

Analysis

The correct answer is C. From the diagram you can see that Paul could be in the seat next to Ted. None of the other choices are possible.

Question 4

Which of the following must be true?

(A) Ted sits next to Paul.
(B) Alice sits next to Paul.
(C) George sits next to Carol.
(D) Ted sits next to Bob.
(E) Bob sits next to John.

Analysis

The correct answer is B. Since the two seats next to Alice are tak[en]
then Alice must sit next to Paul.

Question 5

If Arnold were now to take Ted's seat, then Arnold

(A) must now be next to Bob
(B) must be next to Alice
(C) must be across from Bob
(D) is either next to or across from Paul
(E) is either next to or across from George

Analysis

The correct answer is D. If Arnold takes Ted's seat, then either
Paul, or else Paul is seated across from him.

EXAMPLE

A graphic artist is designing a modern type style for the alphabet. This type style is based on artistic design and relative sizes of the letters. At this point, the relative sizes among the letters that the artist has designed are as follows:

A is taller than B but shorter than C.
B is shorter than D but taller than E.
F is shorter than A but taller than B.
G is taller than D but shorter than F.
H is shorter than B.

Analysis—The setup

From the information given, a simple chart may be constructed using the following steps:

The first statement reads, "A is taller than B but shorter than C." Using a position chart where the top is the tallest and the bottom is the shortest, you have:

C

A

B

The first part of the second statement reads, "B is shorter than D. . . ." Notice that D can be *anywhere* taller than B, so a "range" for D has to be drawn:

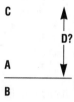

Adding the second part of the second statement gives "B is shorter than D but taller than E." Since B is taller than E, E will be placed under B:

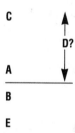

The third statement reads, "F is shorter than A but taller than B." Therefore F must fit between A and B:

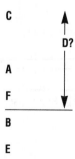

According to the fourth statement, "G is taller than D but shorter than F." Therefore G is above D, but since it's below F, both G and D must fit between F and B:

C

A

F

G

D

B

E

The fifth statement reads, "H is shorter than B," so H must have a possible range anywhere under B:

C

A

F

. G

D

B _____

E   ↑
        H?

        ↓

Note that H is in a variable position.

Question 1

Which one of the following could be FALSE, but is not necessarily false?

(A) E is shorter than D.
(B) C is taller than E.
(C) D is taller than F.
(D) H is taller than E.
(E) E is shorter than A.

Analysis

The correct answer is D. H may be taller than E, or it may be shorter than E. This is the only part of the chart that isn't definitely resolved.

Question 2

Which of the following could be true?

(A) D is taller than most of the others.
(B) A is the tallest.
(C) H is the shortest.
(D) D is not shorter than G.
(E) H is taller than F.

Analysis

The correct answer is C. H may be the shortest, because it could possibly be shorter than E.

Question 3

Which one of the following must be true?

(A) F is taller than D.
(B) H is the shortest of all.
(C) H is taller than D.
(D) E is the shortest of all.
(E) E is taller than H.

Analysis

The correct answer is A. Inspection of the chart reveals that F is taller than D. It also reveals that H cannot be taller than D and that H or E *could* be the shortest of all, since H is in a relatively variable position.

Question 4

If Q is added to the group and Q is taller than B but shorter than G, then Q must be

(A) taller than F
(B) shorter than D
(C) between D and F
(D) taller than only three of the others
(E) shorter than at least three of the others

Analysis

The correct answer is E. If Q is added to the group, it may be either taller or shorter than D. Therefore, only (E) is true.

Question 5

If Q and Z are both added to the group, and both are taller than H, then

(A) H is the shortest of all
(B) E is the shortest of all
(C) C is the tallest of all
(D) either Q or Z is the tallest of all
(E) either H or E is the shortest of all

Analysis

The correct answer is E. If Q and Z are added, and both are taller than H, we know little more except that H or E must still be the smallest. Q or Z could possibly be the tallest, but not necessarily so. Only (E) *must* be true.

EXAMPLE

> In a parking lot, seven company automobiles are lined up in a row in seven adjacent parking spots.
>
>> There are two vans, which are both adjacent to the same sports car.
>> There is one station wagon.
>> There are two limousines, which are never parked adjacent to each other.
>> One of the sports cars is always on one end.

Analysis—The setup

From this information, you could have made the following display:

V S V (van–sports car–van)
1 SW
1 L
2 S

Question 1

If the station wagon is on one end, one of the sports cars must be in the

(A) 2nd spot
(B) 3rd spot
(C) 4th spot
(D) 5th spot
(E) 7th spot

Analysis

The correct answer is C. In this question, two charts are possible:

S	___	___			___	___	SW

and

SW	___	___	___	___		S

Now notice that for *both* of the vans to be adjacent to the same sports car, there must be another sports car, and they must always be in the order V S V. Thus, the only way to place V S V in either of the above diagrams so that two limousines are never adjacent is to place V, S, and V in spots 3, 4, and 5, as follows:

S	___	V	S	V	___	SW

or

SW	___	V	S	V	___	S

Thus, the limousines will not be adjacent if one of the sports cars is in the 4th spot.

Question 2

If one of the vans is on one end, then the station wagon must be

(A) only in the 4th spot
(B) either in the 2nd or the 6th spot
(C) only in the 3rd spot
(D) either in the 3rd or the 5th spot
(E) only in the 6th spot

Analysis

The correct answer is D. Again there are two possible diagrams for this question:

V	S	V	___	___	___	S

and

S	___	___	___	V	S	V

Now notice that, in order that the limousines not be adjacent, the station wagon must be in either the 5th spot or the 3rd spot.

Question 3

If a limousine is in the 7th spot, then the station wagon could be in

(A) the 2nd spot
(B) the 3rd spot
(C) the 6th spot
(D) either the 2nd or 6th spot
(E) either the 2nd, 3rd, or 6th spot

Analysis

The correct answer is E. If a limousine is in the 7th spot, then a sports car, to be on an end, must be in the 1st spot:

S						L
—	—	—	—	—	—	—

Notice that the station wagon could now be in the 6th spot:

		V	S	V	L	
S	L	V	S	V	SW	L

or else in either the 2nd or the 3rd spot:

	L	SW				
S	SW	L	V	S	V	L

So the station wagon could be in either the 2nd, the 3rd, or the 6th spot.

Question 4

If one of the sports cars is in the 2nd spot, then the station wagon

(A) could be in the 5th spot
(B) could be in the 6th spot
(C) must be in the 5th spot
(D) must be in the 6th spot
(E) must be in the 3rd spot

Analysis

The correct answer is C. If one of the sports cars is in the 2nd spot, the other sports car must be in the 7th spot:

V	S	V				S

Thus, in order for the limousines not to be adjacent, the station wagon must be in the 5th spot.

Question 5

If both sports cars are adjacent to a van, the station wagon must be in

(A) the 2nd spot
(B) the 4th spot
(C) the 6th spot
(D) either the 2nd or 4th spot
(E) either the 2nd or 6th spot

Analysis

The correct answer is E. Two diagrams are necessary for this problem. If both sports cars are adjacent to a van, your diagrams will be:

S	V	S	V			

and

			V	S	V	S

Thus, in order for the limousines not to be adjacent, the station wagon must be in either the 2nd spot or the 6th spot.

Question 6

If an eighth car (a limousine) is added, and another parking spot is also added, then in order not to violate any of the original statements EXCEPT the number of limousines

(A) a limousine must be parked in the 2nd spot
(B) the station wagon must be parked in the 2nd spot
(C) the station wagon must be parked in the 6th spot
(D) a limousine must be parked on one end
(E) a limousine cannot be parked on either end

Analysis

The correct answer is D. If another limousine is added along with an eighth parking spot, all the original statements can be obeyed ONLY if a limousine is parked on one end. For example:

S	L	V	S	V	L	SW	L

Position Chart with the Diagram Provided

On occasion, the position chart or diagram will be provided. That is, instead of, or along with, a description of the set up, an actual diagram is given. Use the following steps if a chart or diagram is given:

1. Either redraw the chart or diagram or mark the diagram dark enough so you can understand your notes but also so you can erase without losing information.
2. Follow the same procedures you would use in filling in or completing the position chart.

Nine guests—A, B, C, D, E, F, G, H, I—attend a formal dinner party. Ten chairs are arranged around the rectangular dining room table as follows:

Seat 1 is directly across from seat 9.
Seat 2 is directly across from seat 8.
Seat 3 is directly across from seat 7.
Seat 4 is directly across from seat 6.

Seats 5 and 10 are at the ends of the table and are directly
across from each other.

A, B, C, and D are females.

E, F, G, H, and I are males.

A and E are a married couple.

B and F are a married couple.

C and G are engaged to each other.

Each married couple always sits next to his or her spouse
on one side of the table.

Members of the same sex never sit in adjacent seats.

Guests in end seats 5 and 10 are considered adjacent to
seats on each side of them.

If G is in seat 10, then C is not in seat 5.

I is never in seat 6.

A is always in seat 1.

Analysis—The setup

From the initial conditions, the diagram and markings would look like this:

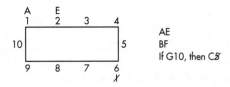

Question 1

Which one of the following could sit in seat 10?

(A) A
(B) C
(C) D
(D) F
(E) H

Analysis

The correct answer is E. Since guest A sits in seat 1, a male must sit in seat 10 if it
is not empty. This eliminates (A), (B), and (C) since guests A, C, and D are females (A is
in seat 1 anyway). Since guests B and F are a married couple, they must sit next to each
other on a side. This eliminates (D). Guest H is a male and could sit in seat 10.

Question 2

Which one of the following is a complete and accurate list of guests who could sit in seat 3?

(A) A, B, C, D, E, F, G
(B) B, C, D, E, F
(C) B, C, D, E
(D) B, C, D
(E) B, C

Analysis

The correct answer is D. Since guest E is in seat 2, only a female could sit in seat 3. Since guest A is in seat 1, the remaining females are guests B, C, and D.

Question 3

If seat 9 is empty and G sits in seat 10, which one of the following could sit in seat 5?

(A) B
(B) D
(C) C
(D) H
(E) I

Analysis

The correct answer is B. From the information given in the question and the initial conditions, the diagram should look like this:

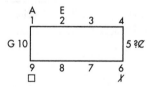

It can now be determined that seat 3 is a female, seat 4 is a male, and seat 5 is a female. You may have added to your diagram so it would now look like this:

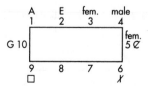

Seat 5 cannot be guest B, since guest B cannot be on the end. Guest H and I are males so (D) and (E) are eliminated. Since guest G is in seat 10, then guest C cannot be in seat 5 (from initial conditions), so only guest D is left.

Question 4

If C sits in seat 5, and F sits in seat 4, which one of the following could be the arrangement of seats from 1 to 10 respectively?

	1,	2,	3,	4,	5,	6,	7,	8,	9,	10
(A)	A,	B,	E,	F,	C,	G,	—,	I,	D,	H
(B)	A,	E,	B,	G,	C,	F,	D,	H,	—,	I
(C)	A,	E,	B,	F,	C,	I,	D,	—,	G,	H
(D)	A,	E,	B,	F,	C,	H,	D,	I,	—,	G
(E)	A,	E,	B,	F,	C,	G,	D,	H,	—,	I

Analysis

The correct answer is E. From the information given, the diagram should look like this:

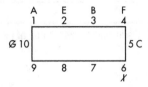

You could eliminate (A) because guest B cannot be in seat 2. Since guest F is in seat 4, guest B is in seat 3. This eliminates (B). (C) can be eliminated since male guests G and H cannot be seated next to each other. Since guest C is in seat 5, guest G cannot be in seat 10, so (D) is eliminated. (E) is a possible arrangement.

Question 5

If D sits in seat 5, and the engaged couple sits together in seats 7 and 8, which one of the following seats must be empty?

(A) 3
(B) 4
(C) 6
(D) 9
(E) 10

Analysis

The correct answer is D. From the information given, your chart should now look like this:

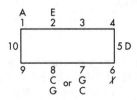

You should also be able to fill in seats 3 and 4 and determine that seats 6 and 10, if not empty, must be males. Your diagram should now have this information:

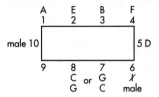

Since only male guests H and I are not seated, guest H must be in seat 6 and guest I in seat 10. This leaves seat 9 empty. In any other arrangement, two males are next to each other.

Question 6

Which one of the following is a complete and accurate list of guests who could sit in seat 5?

(A) C
(B) D
(C) C, D
(D) B, C, D
(E) C, D, G

Analysis

The correct answer is C. First eliminate (D) since guest B must be on a side. If guest G is in seat 5, then the diagram would look like this:

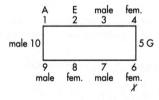

This requires two males to be next to each other, so seat 5 must be a female, either guest C or D.

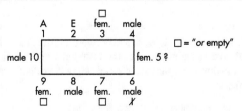

Question 7

If a female sits directly across from A, which one of the following must be true?

(A) Seat 3 is empty.
(B) Seat 4 is empty.
(C) Seat 6 is a female.
(D) Seat 7 is a female.
(E) Seat 8 is a male.

Analysis

The correct answer is E. If a female sits across from guest A, your diagram would now have the following information:

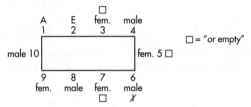

Since seats 3, 5, or 7 could be empty, only (E), a male is in seat 8, must be true.

The Map

Another type of display is the map. This is really a takeoff of the position diagram with some more possibilities. When completing a map display, keep the following in mind:

1. Maps can include actual distances (miles, yards, etc.) from one place to another, or simply relative alignments.
2. While constructing a map, you will be placing houses, cities, objects, or people in general areas, limited areas, or zones—north, south, east, west, northeast, southwest, and so on.
3. Placements often will be relative to a central location or other placements.
4. Sometimes the houses, cities, objects, or people will be placed directly north (due north), directly southeast, and so on.
5. Watch for limited areas or zones, as opposed to exact locations. This takes careful reading, reasoning, and placement.
6. Place question marks next to items that are movable (that is, not stuck in one spot).

EXAMPLE

Six cabins—A, B, C, D, E, and F—were constructed on a small flat area in the mountains. The focal point of the area was a statue that was constructed years before the cabins were constructed.

Cabin A is directly north of the statue.
Cabin C is directly west of the statue.

Cabin D is south of Cabin C.
Cabin E is west of Cabin A.
The statue is directly southeast of Cabin B and directly
   northwest of Cabin F.

Analysis—The setup

From the information given, a simple chart may be constructed as follows (possible ranges are denoted with arrows):

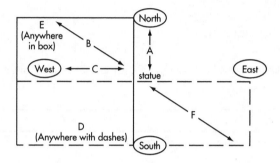

Or an even simpler map (if you can remember the zones) is possible:

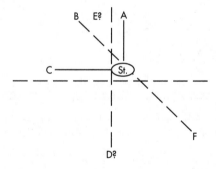

Question 1

Which one of the following must be true?

(A) Cabin B is east of Cabin C.
(B) Cabin B is west of Cabin C.
(C) Cabin F is west of Cabin E.
(D) Cabin D is south of Cabin B.
(E) Cabin D is east of Cabin A.

Analysis

The correct answer is D. Statements (A), (B), and (E) *could* be true, but do not necessarily have to be true. (C) is false. Only (D) must be true.

Question 2

Which one of the following must be FALSE?

(A) Cabin A is north of Cabin E.
(B) Cabin C is east of Cabin E.
(C) Cabin B is south of Cabin F.
(D) Cabin D is north of Cabin F.
(E) Cabin D is east of Cabin E.

Analysis

The correct answer is C. Choices (A), (B), (D), and (E) *could* be true, but (C) *must* be false.

Question 3

How many cabins must be west of Cabin A?

(A) 0
(B) 1
(C) 2
(D) 3
(E) 4

Analysis

The correct answer is D. Cabins E, B, and C must be west of A. Cabin D does not have to be west of Cabin A.

Question 4

What is the maximum number of cabins you could encounter traveling directly east from Cabin C?

(A) 0
(B) 1
(C) 2
(D) 3
(E) 4

Analysis

The correct answer is B. Traveling directly east from Cabin C, you could encounter Cabin E.

Question 5

If another cabin, Cabin G, is constructed directly north of Cabin F, then all of the following must be true EXCEPT

(A) Cabin A is west of Cabin G
(B) Cabin G is east of Cabin C
(C) Cabin D is south of Cabin G
(D) Cabin G is east of Cabin A
(E) Cabin B is west of Cabin G

Analysis

The correct answer is C. Adding Cabin G to the chart results in:

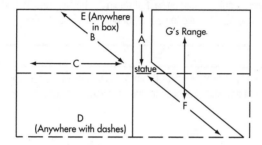

Statements (A), (B), (D), and (E) must be true. Statement (C) could be true, but does not necessarily have to be true.

Question 6

If Cabins H and J are constructed so that H is directly east of J, and H is directly north of A, then which one of the following must be true?

(A) Cabin H is north of Cabin B.
(B) Cabin C is west of Cabin J.
(C) Cabin H is south of Cabin D.
(D) Cabin E is south of Cabin H.
(E) Cabin F is east of Cabin J.

Analysis

The correct answer is E. Adding Cabins H and J to the chart results in:

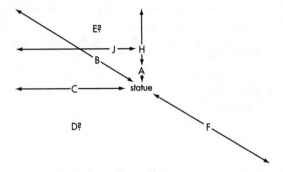

From the chart, Cabin F must be east of Cabin J. Choices (A), (B), and (D) could be true, but do not necessarily have to be true. Choice (C) must be false.

Question 7

If Cabin M is constructed west of Cabin A, which one of the following is a possible order of cabins a traveler could encounter while traveling directly northwest from F?

(A) BEDM
(B) DMBE
(C) MDEBC
(D) DMCBE
(E) MDABE

Analysis

The correct answer is B. Adding Cabin M to the chart results in:

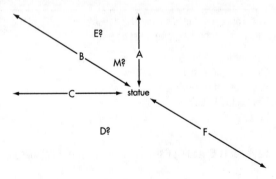

From the chart, you could possibly encounter DMBE while traveling northwest from F.

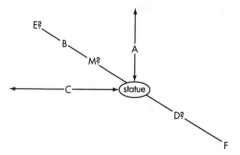

The Numerical Display or Numerical Position Diagram

This type of display or diagram deals with numerical relationships—lengths, heights, scores, and so on. When working with numerical information, keep the following in mind:

1. You may first need to simply list the relationships before making a display. This may help you see the complete picture.
2. When converting the information into a positional display, be sure to mark or signify what the directions mean (top-most, bottom-least, tallest, shortest, etc.).
3. Place question marks next to variables that can be moved or are not locked into a certain position.

EXAMPLE

Alice, Bobby, Carole, Dwight, and Elva were playing a game with marbles. When the game ended, Alice wrote down the following information:

Carole has more marbles than Alice and Bobby together.
Alice's total is the same as the total of Dwight and Elva together.
Alice has more marbles than Bobby.
Bobby has more marbles than Elva.
Everyone has at least one marble.

Analysis—The setup

From the information given, you can set up the following relationships:

$$C > A + B$$
$$A = D + E$$
$$A > B$$
$$B > E$$

Then you can construct the following diagram (Note: This chart is more easily realized by starting with the last condition and working up.):

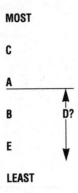

MOST

C

A

B   D?

E

LEAST

Question 1

Who ended the game with the most marbles?

(A) Alice
(B) Bobby
(C) Carole
(D) Dwight
(E) Elva

Analysis

The correct answer is C. Using the relationships you can see that Carole has more marbles than Alice and Bobby together. Because Alice has more marbles than Dwight, Elva, or Bobby each have alone, Carole must have most of all.

Question 2

If Dwight has more marbles than Bobby, who ended the game with the least marbles?

(A) Alice
(B) Bobby
(C) Carole
(D) Dwight
(E) Elva

Analysis

The correct answer is E. If Dwight has more marbles than Bobby, then Elva must have the least number of marbles. The arrangement would be as follows:

MOST

C

A
___

D
___

B

E

LEAST

___

Question 3

Which one of the following is a possible order of children going from most marbles to least?

(A) Alice, Bobby, Carole, Dwight, Elva
(B) Carole, Alice, Bobby, Elva, Dwight
(C) Carole, Bobby, Alice, Dwight, Elva
(D) Dwight, Carole, Alice, Bobby, Elva
(E) Carole, Alice, Elva, Bobby, Dwight

Analysis

The correct answer is B. From the original chart, we can see that Carole must have most of all, followed by Alice. Because Bobby has more marbles than Elva, only answer (B) can be a possible correct order.

___

Question 4

Which of the following must be true?

(A) Elva has more marbles than Dwight.
(B) Dwight has fewer marbles than Bobby.
(C) Alice has more marbles than Elva.
(D) Dwight and Bobby have the same number of marbles.
(E) Elva and Dwight have the same number of marbles.

Analysis

The correct answer is C. Only (C) *must* be true. In (A) and (E) Elva *could* have more marbles than Dwight, but not necessarily. She could have less *or the same*. Notice the possible range of placement for Dwight on the original chart. Again, in (B) and (D) Dwight's placement is uncertain: Dwight could have fewer, *the same,* or more marbles than Bobby.

Question 5

If Elva has 3 marbles and everyone has a different number of marbles, which of the following could NOT be the number of marbles that Alice could have?

(A) 5
(B) 6
(C) 7
(D) 8
(E) 9

Analysis

The correct answer is B. Using the relationships you can see that if Elva has 3 marbles, then Dwight can have any number *but* 3. Because Alice's total equals Dwight's and Elva's total together, Alice cannot have 3 + 3, or 6.

EXAMPLE ▬▬▬▬▬▬▬▬▬▬▬▬▬▬▬▬▬▬▬▬▬▬▬▬▬▬▬▬

Five students, A, E, I, O, and U, were comparing the scores each received on a test and a quiz. The following was discovered:

A's quiz score was 80.
A's test score equals U's quiz score.
U's test score equals A's quiz score.
A's quiz score is 15 less than U's quiz score.
O's test score is 20 more than his quiz score and is 20 more than I's test score.
O's test score is 40 more than E's quiz score.
I's quiz score is 10 less than E's quiz score.

▬▬▬▬▬▬▬▬▬▬▬▬▬▬▬▬▬▬▬▬▬▬▬▬▬▬▬▬▬▬▬▬▬▬

Analysis—The setup

You could have set up the following relationships from the information given

$$
\begin{aligned}
Aq &= 80 \\
At &= Uq \\
Ut &= Aq \\
Aq &= Uq - 15 \\
Ot &= Oq + 20 \\
Ot &= It + 20 \\
Ot &= Eq + 40 \\
Iq &= Eq - 10
\end{aligned}
$$

and you could have discovered that Ut = 80 (since Aq = Ut), Uq = 95 (since Aq = Uq – 15), At = 95 (since At = Uq), and Oq = It (since Ot = Oq + 20 and Ot = It + 20).

You might have used the following diagram to help visualize the solutions to these problems:

```
Quiz                        A           U
----------------------------80----------95-------------------------------
Test                        U           A
Quiz            I <- - - - 10 - - - ->E<- - - - 20 - - - ->O
-------------------------------------------------------------------------
Test                                            I<- - - - 20 - - - ->O
```

Question 1

If E's quiz score is 60, what is O's quiz score?

(A) 80
(B) 70
(C) 60
(D) 50
(E) 40

Analysis

The correct answer is A. From the preceding information we can see that O's quiz score is 20 greater than E's quiz score. Thus, 80 is the correct answer.

Question 2

Which one of the following must be true?

(A) I's quiz score equals O's test score.
(B) E's quiz score equals U's quiz score.
(C) A's quiz score equals U's test score.
(D) E's quiz score equals O's quiz score.
(E) I's quiz score equals I's test score.

Analysis

The correct answer is C. From the diagram, A's quiz score equals U's test score. We do not have a relationship between E's quiz scores and A's or U's scores.

Question 3

What is U's test score?

(A) 55
(B) 65
(C) 80
(D) 95
(E) 100

Analysis

The correct answer is C. Because U's test score equals A's quiz score, and that is 80, the answer must be C.

Question 4

If I's test score is 45, what is O's test score?

(A) 25
(B) 35
(C) 45
(D) 55
(E) 65

Analysis

The correct answer is E. Because O's test score is 20 greater than I's test score, and I's test score is 45, O's test score must be 65.

Question 5

If E's quiz score is 50, which one of the following must be true?

(A) I's test score is 70.
(B) O's test score is 100.
(C) I's quiz score is 30.
(D) O's quiz score is 60.
(E) O's test score is 70.

Analysis

The correct answer is A. From the diagram, I's test score is 70. Using the relationships gives Ot = 50 + 40 = 90, Ot = It + 20; therefore It = 70.

Question 6

If O's quiz score is the same as U's quiz score, which one of the following must be true?

(A) I's test score is 90.
(B) O's test score is 110.
(C) I's quiz score is 70.
(D) E's quiz score is 75.
(E) O's quiz score is 80.

Analysis

The correct answer is D. This problem relates the two groups of scores together. Because A's quiz score is 80, U's quiz score is 95. Therefore, O's quiz score is 95. Thus, I's test score is 95. E's quiz score is 20 less than O's quiz score, thus it is 75, making (D) true.

The Information Chart

The information chart is helpful for spotting information and making deductions quickly. When putting together an information chart, you should follow these steps:

1. Carefully decide on the type of framework, categories, or labels. You may need to read all of the statements or conditions before deciding how to arrange the information.
2. If you have selected a good way of showing the information—proper labels, categories, and so on—the information should fit in fairly easily and be easy to understand and interpret.
3. Be sure to note variable positions or possibilities in your information chart (for example, Bob can work on Mondays or Tuesdays).

EXAMPLE

In order to open a new furniture store the following week, Mr. Worble hired a painter, a carpet layer, an electrician, and a carpenter. In scheduling the workmen, he had to consider the following conditions:

The painter is available only on Tuesday morning, Wednesday afternoon, and all day Friday.

The carpet layer is available only on Monday, Wednesday, and Friday mornings.

The electrician is available only on Tuesday morning and Friday afternoon.

The carpenter is available only on Monday morning, Tuesday all day, and Wednesday afternoon.

Unless otherwise stated, each workman must work alone in the store.

Unless otherwise stated, each workman is able to complete his own job in half a day.

Analysis—The setup

An information chart is suggested whenever you are trying to determine the points at which two sets of facts coincide. In this case, we chart the daily schedule of each worker, simply following the explicit information given.

	M	T	W	T	F
Painter		Morning	Afternoon		All day
Carpet layer	Morning		Morning		Morning
Electrician		Morning			Afternoon
Carpenter	Morning	All day	Afternoon		

Although we have written out "morning," "afternoon," and "all day," you may wish to abbreviate such terms.

Question 1

If the carpenter and the electrician must work on the same day to coordinate their efforts, but cannot work at the same time, who of the following will NOT be able to start work until Wednesday, at the earliest?

(A) painter
(B) carpet layer
(C) electrician
(D) carpenter
(E) carpet layer and electrician

Analysis

The correct answer is A. The carpet layer may work on Monday, and the carpenter and the electrician *must* work Tuesday (the only day they are available together). In this case, the painter (A) may not begin until Wednesday.

Question 2

If the painter needs the whole day on Friday to complete his job, the

(A) carpenter must work on Thursday
(B) electrician and carpet layer must work on the same day
(C) total job cannot be completed in one week
(D) electrician must work on Tuesday
(E) carpet layer and carpenter must work on the same day

Analysis

The correct answer is D. The electrician *must* work Tuesday, because his only other working day, Friday, interferes with the painter's work.

Question 3

Mr. Worble is expecting a supply of furniture on Thursday morning. Which one of the following must be true?

(A) The carpenter will be the only one finished before the merchandise arrives.
(B) Before the merchandise arrives, the painter will be finished, but the electrician will have to work Wednesday night.
(C) The carpet layer, the carpenter, and the electrician will be the only ones finished before the merchandise arrives.
(D) The carpet layer will have to work on the Tuesday before the merchandise arrives.
(E) All of the workers could have their jobs completed before the merchandise arrives.

Analysis

The correct answer is E. One possible plan is this: The carpet layer works Monday morning, the electrician works Tuesday morning, the carpenter works Tuesday afternoon, and the painter works Wednesday afternoon.

Question 4

If the store must be closed Monday and Tuesday and no worker may enter on those days, then, for all the work to be completed by the end of the week,

(A) the carpet layer must work Friday morning
(B) the painter must work Friday morning
(C) the painter must work Wednesday afternoon
(D) the painter must work Friday afternoon
(E) the carpet layer must work Friday afternoon

Analysis

The correct answer is B. If the store must be closed on Monday and Tuesday, then the carpenter must work Wednesday afternoon, and the electrician must work Friday afternoon, as these workers have no other available days to work. Since the painter cannot work Wednesday afternoon (the carpenter is already working then), he must work Friday morning. This leaves the carpet layer Wednesday morning to complete his work.

Question 5

If the store must be painted before any of the other work may begin, then, for all the work to be completed, all the following are true EXCEPT

(A) the carpenter may work Tuesday or Wednesday afternoon
(B) the electrician must work Friday afternoon
(C) the carpet layer must work Wednesday or Friday morning
(D) the electrician and the carpet layer may work the same day
(E) the painter and the electrician may work the same day

Analysis

The correct answer is E. If the store must be painted first, then the painter could do his work Tuesday morning. All of the choices then are true, except (E). The painter and electrician may not work the same day, because if it's Tuesday, then they both would work in the morning, which is not allowed. The only other day they could both work is Friday, but that wouldn't allow all the work to be completed if the painter first works Friday morning.

The Elimination Grid

This type of chart will assist you in eliminating many possibilities, thus narrowing your answer choices and simplifying the reasoning process. To set up an elimination grid you should:

1. Decide on the column and row headings.
2. Mark X's in squares or situations that are not possible.
3. Place check marks or fill in squares or situations that are possible.
4. Fill in any items that you can deduce or "eliminate" with the grid (for example, if Ann receives an A, she cannot receive a B, C, or D).

EXAMPLE

Two boys (Tom and Sal) and two girls (Lisa and Molly) each receive a different one of four different passing grades (A,B,C,D) on an exam.

(1) Both boys receive lower grades than Lisa.
(2) Sal did not get a B.
(3) Tom got a B.
(4) Molly did not get an A.

Analysis—The setup

Although a chart is not necessary to answer question 1, you could have constructed the following using the information given in the statements:

First, since both boys received lower grades than Lisa, we know that Lisa could not have gotten the C or D, and that neither of the boys could have gotten the A. Thus, your chart will look like this:

	A	B	C	D
Tom	X			
Sal	X			
Lisa			X	X
Molly				

From statements 2 and 3, we can fill in that Tom received the B (and thus the others didn't):

	A	B	C	D
Tom	X	✓	X	X
Sal	X	X		
Lisa		X	X	X
Molly		X		

Statement 4 allows us to indicate on our chart that Molly didn't get an A. Thus, we can see from our chart that Lisa *must* have gotten the A:

	A	B	C	D
Tom	X	✓	X	X
Sal	X	X		
Lisa		X	X	X
Molly	X	X		

Notice that we could have deduced that even without statement 4, as there was no other grade Lisa could possibly receive.

Now we know that Lisa received the A, and Tom received the B. But we cannot deduce Sal's or Molly's grade. Be aware that, on many problems like this, you will have to proceed to the questions with an incomplete chart.

Question 1

Which statement(s) may be deduced from only one of the other statements?

(A) statement 1
(B) statement 2
(C) statement 3
(D) statement 4
(E) statements 1 and 3

Analysis
The correct answer is B. Statement 2 may be deduced from statement 3. If Tom got the B, it must be true that Sal did not get the B.

Question 2

If Molly received the lowest grade, then Sal must have received

(A) the A
(B) the B
(C) the C
(D) the D
(E) either the A or the B

Analysis
The correct answer is C. Using the chart, if Molly received the lowest grade (D), then Sal must have gotten the C. Note that by elimination on the grid, the only possibilities for Sal and Molly were Cs and Ds.

Question 3

Which one of the following is a complete and accurate list of the grades that Sal could have received?

(A) A
(B) A, C
(C) B, D
(D) C, D
(E) B, C, D

Analysis

The correct answer is D. From our chart we can easily see that Sal could have received either the C or the D.

Question 4

Which one of the following is a complete and accurate list of the grades that Molly could NOT have received?

(A) A
(B) B
(C) B, C
(D) C, D
(E) A, B

Analysis

The correct answer is E. From our chart we can easily see that Molly could not have received either the A or the B. We could also have determined this from statements 3 and 4.

Question 5

If Sal received the D, then Molly received

(A) the A
(B) the B
(C) the C
(D) the D
(E) either the A or the D

Analysis

The correct answer is C. From our chart we can easily see that, if Sal received the D, then Molly must have received the C.

Question 6

If the grades that Sal and Lisa received were reversed, then which one of the original statements would no longer be true?

(A) statement 1
(B) statement 2
(C) statement 3
(D) statement 4
(E) statements 2 and 3

Analysis

The correct answer is A. If Sal and Lisa reversed their grades, then

Sal would get the A.
Tom would get the B.
Lisa received either the C or the D.
Molly received either the C or the D.

Therefore, only statement 1 ("Both boys receive lower grades than Lisa") would no longer be true.

Pulling Out Information

In some instances, no chart or diagram appears to fit the situation. If this is the case, then:

1. Simply pull out or note whatever information seems important to you.
2. Mark any relationships between the items you have pulled out.
3. Go on to the questions.

EXAMPLE

Tongo is a sport similar to racquetball, except in each game three players oppose each other. Sandy, Arnie, and Betsy are the only entrants in a tongo tournament. Sandy is a left-handed tongo player, while Arnie and Betsy are right-handed tongo players. The players must compete in the tournament according to the following rules:

The winner of each game receives 5 points; the second place finisher gets 3 points; and the third place finisher gets 1 point.

There are no tie games.

The one player with the most game points at the end of the tournament is the grand winner.

If, at the end of the tournament, two or more players have the same total number of points, there will be a play-off.

Analysis—The setup

You probably found that this set of conditions was not conducive to constructing any standard chart. As soon as this was evident, you should have simply pulled out information as follows:

L—Sandy	1st—5 pts.
R—Arnie	2nd—3 pts.
R—Betsy	3rd—1 pt.

Question 1

Which one of the following must be true?

(A) Betsy plays only right-handed opponents
(B) Arnie never plays a right-handed opponent.
(C) Arnie plays just right-handed opponents.
(D) Sandy never plays right-handed opponents.
(E) Sandy always plays right-handed opponents.

Analysis

The correct answer is E. Since Sandy is the only left-handed player, then she must play only right-handed opponents.

Question 2

If, after three games, both right-handed players have each scored 9 points, which one of the following could be true?

(A) One of the right-handed players finished first twice.
(B) At least one of the right-handed players finished second three times.
(C) Both right-handed players each finished first, second, and third.
(D) The left-handed player finished first twice.
(E) The left-handed player was ahead after three games.

Analysis

The correct answer is C. Only (C) may be true. (A) is blatantly false, since two first-place wins would result in 10 points. (B) is incorrect because, if one player finished second in all three games, then there is no way a second player could score exactly 9 points in three games. (D) and (E) are incorrect since there must be 27 points scored during the three games with each player scoring 9 points.

Question 3

Which one of the following must be true?

(A) A player with no first-place game points cannot win the tournament.
(B) A player with only second-place game points can win the tournament.
(C) A player with no first-place game points can win the tournament.
(D) A player with no third-place game points must win the tournament.
(E) A player with no second-place game points cannot come in second.

Analysis

The correct answer is A. Only (A) is true. With no first-place game points, the most a player could score per game is 3 points. The best that that player could hope for would be that the other two players would split first place and third place on all the games. But even then, the other two players would average 3 points per game. At best a playoff would be necessary, and the player without a first-place finish would thus lose the tournament. (D) and (E) are false by example.

Question 4

If, after three games, Arnie has 11 points, Betsy has 9 points, and Sandy has 7 points, which one of the following must be false?

(A) After four games, there is a three-way tie.
(B) After four games, Betsy is alone in first place.
(C) After four games, Betsy is alone in third place.
(D) After four games, Sandy is alone in first place.
(E) After four games, Sandy is alone in third place.

Analysis
The correct answer is D. The only statement that could not be true is (D). Since the most Sandy could score after four games would be 12 points, Betsy and/or Arnie will at least tie her for first place.

Question 5

If, just before the last game, it is discovered that the left-handed player has finished first in every even-numbered game, then

(A) Sandy must win the tournament
(B) Sandy cannot win the tournament
(C) Arnie may win the tournament
(D) Betsy can't win the tournament
(E) Betsy must win the tournament

Analysis
The correct answer is C. Even though Sandy may have scored 5 points in every even-numbered game, she may not necessarily win the tournament. For instance, if, say, Arnie scores 5 points in every odd-numbered game, and if the tournament consists of an odd number of games, then Arnie will win the tournament. Sandy *can* win the tournament, but not necessarily *must* win the tournament. Betsy, also, could possibly win the tournament, if she scores first-place wins in every odd-numbered game.

Venn Diagrams/Grouping Arrows

Another type of charting (also mentioned later in Chapter 4, Logical Reasoning) is the Venn Diagrams/Grouping Arrows. This type of diagram can be useful when information is given that shows relationships between sets or groups of sets. Keep in mind that:

1. Venn diagrams should be used only in very simple situations involving small numbers of items.

2. Grouping arrows seem to be more effective and simpler to work with, especially in complex situations.

Some very basic Venn diagrams and grouping arrows look like this:

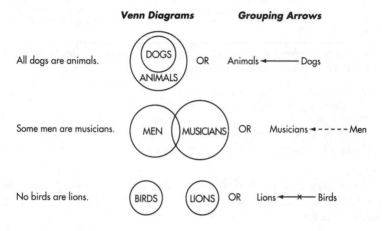

Venn Diagrams   *Grouping Arrows*

All dogs are animals.   DOGS / ANIMALS   OR   Animals ◄——— Dogs

Some men are musicians.   MEN / MUSICIANS   OR   Musicians ◄ - - - - - Men

No birds are lions.   BIRDS   LIONS   OR   Lions ◄——✕——— Birds

In diagramming more than two groups, you may find it helpful to draw the most general or largest category before drawing any of the others.

EXAMPLE

A pharmacist has labeled certain pills—A, B, C, D, and E—by the categories they fall into. Some of the categories overlap as follows:

   (1) All As are Bs.
   (2) All Bs are Cs.
   (3) Some, but not all, Ds are As.
   (4) All Ds are Bs.
   (5) No Es are Cs.

Analysis—The setup

From statement 1 we may draw a Venn diagram or grouping arrows as follows:

(A) B   OR   B ◄——— A

From statement 2 our diagrams or grouping arrows grow to look like this:

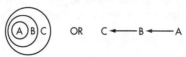

(A)B)C   OR   C ◄——— B ◄——— A

Now statements 3 and 4 add another circle in the Venn diagram (note that we need the fourth statement in order to "contain" the D circle within the B circle) or another element to the grouping arrows as follows:

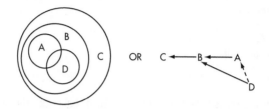

And, finally, from statement 5 we get:

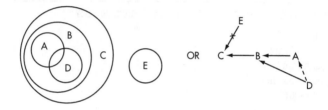

Now it will be relatively simple to answer the questions simply by referring to our final Venn Diagram or grouping arrows.

Question 1

Which one of the following must be true?

(A) All Cs are As.
(B) Some Es are Bs.
(C) All As are Ds.
(D) No Bs are Es.
(E) Some Es are As.

Analysis
The correct answer is D. From the grouping arrows or Venn Diagram, you can see that Bs and Es do not connect, so no Bs are Es must be true. Notice that (A) is false, all As are Cs, but not all Cs are As. Choice (B) is false because the Es are separate from the Bs. Choice (C) could be true, but doesn't have to be true. Choice (E) is false since no Bs are Es, no Es are Bs.

Question 2

Which one of the following must be FALSE?

(A) All Ds are As.
(B) No As are Es.
(C) Some As are Ds.
(D) Some Cs are Ds.
(E) No Bs are Es.

Analysis
The correct answer is A. Statement (3) says "Some, but not all, Ds are As."

Question 3

If all Es are Fs, then which one of the following must be true?

(A) All Fs are Es.
(B) Some Fs are Es.
(C) All As are Fs.
(D) Some Bs are Fs.
(E) No Fs are Cs.

Analysis
The correct answer is B. Note that this problem requires us to add another circle to our Venn diagram, as follows:

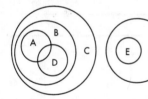

(Note that Fs must contain at least Es, but could possibly also contain other circles.)

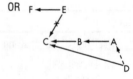

Question 4

If some Gs are As, then which one of the following must be true?

(A) Some Gs are Ds.
(B) All Ds are Gs.
(C) All Bs are Gs.
(D) Some Es are Gs.
(E) Some Gs are Cs.

Analysis
The correct answer is E. This problem, too, requires us to add to our original Venn diagram. If some Gs are As, our Venn diagram must *at least* contain some Gs in the A circle (x notes location of some Gs):

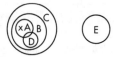

but it *could* also look like this:

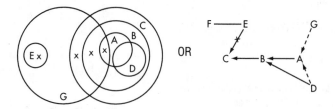

IN CONCLUSION

You have just worked through some of the basic types of charts that you may encounter on the LSAT. Be aware that there are *many other possible charts and modifications of the charts presented.* In the following practice tests, as you work through some of the other possible charts, carefully review the explanations of each to assist you in understanding these other types.

Remember that the exact type of chart you make is not of critical importance. What is important is that you can get the necessary information from your chart, and that it is simple to understand. Do not spend a great deal of time trying to make an elaborate chart; a simple one will usually serve the purpose.

AN ALTERNATIVE GENERAL APPROACH

Some students, regardless of how much they review, analyze, and practice, cannot seem to finish the Analytical Reasoning section. They simply cannot work fast enough or make displays or rough diagrams quickly enough to see relationships and maintain a high level of correct answers. If you find that you consistently have a problem getting to or into the fourth set, you may wish to try this alternative approach: Focus your time on only three of the four sets. That is, try to set up and do well on the three sets and the questions that follow, and simply guess at the questions to the remaining set. You can skip one of the four sets and still receive a good score. The idea is to significantly raise your percentage of correct answers on the questions you *are* attempting. Remember, this is an alternative approach that you may wish to try if you are having a real problem getting to all four sets and maintaining a good level of correct answers. In using this method, you may wish to decide which set of questions you are going to skip after you have read the conditions and realize that the set is going to be problematic and difficult to complete.

EXTRA PRACTICE: ANALYTICAL REASONING

Directions: In this section you will be given a group of questions based on a specific set of conditions. Drawing a simple diagram may be helpful in answering some of the questions. You are to choose the best answer and mark the corresponding space on your answer sheet.

Use the answer sheet found on page 109.

Questions 1–4

There are four books standing next to each other on a shelf. The books are in order from left to right. The colors of the books are red, yellow, blue, and orange, but the placement of these books has not been determined. The following is known about the placement of the books:

The red book is between the yellow and blue books.

The blue book is between the orange and red books.

The orange book is not fourth.

1. If the orange book could be fourth, then which one of the following can be deduced?

   (A) The red book is fourth.
   (B) The blue book is not third.
   (C) The red book is next to the orange book.
   (D) The blue book is next to the yellow book.
   (E) The yellow book is not second.

2. If a white book is added to the shelf, and the fourth book is not necessarily an orange book, then which one of the following is a possible order of the books?

   (A) yellow, red, orange, blue, white
   (B) white, yellow, blue, red, orange
   (C) yellow, red, blue, white, orange
   (D) orange, blue, red, yellow, white
   (E) blue, red, yellow, orange, white

3. Which one of the following pairs are next to each other on the shelf?

   (A) yellow and blue
   (B) blue and orange
   (C) yellow and orange
   (D) red and orange
   (E) No books are next to each other on the shelf.

4. If a green book were placed just to the left of the blue book, what position would it be in (counting from the left)?

   (A) first
   (B) second
   (C) third
   (D) fourth
   (E) fifth

Questions 5–8

Doctors at Ventana Hospital have been researching an outbreak of three rare diseases, which they have labeled J, K, and L. In tracking the diseases and some of the people possibly infected, they have come up with the following information:

Disease J is always communicable; its symptoms are red splotches, which appear the day after infection.

Disease K is only communicable the day after infection; its symptoms

are blue lips or red splotches,
which appear the day of infection.
Disease L only infects concurrently
with Disease J; its symptoms—
swollen ears, which appear the day
after infection—are negated by
Disease K.

Peter had lunch with Paul on Tuesday.
Paul had dinner with Mary on
Wednesday.

Symptoms appear for only one day.

The diseases J, K, and L are the only
diseases involved in the outbreak
and are the only ones being
researched.   *The* Pe & Pa
                  Wed   Pa + M

5. If Peter broke out in red splotches on
Tuesday, which one of the following
must be true?

(A) Peter was infected with Disease K.
(B) Peter was infected with Disease J.
(C) Peter was infected with Disease L.
(D) Peter could have given Disease K to
    Paul on Tuesday.
(E) Peter didn't give Paul Disease K on
    Tuesday.

6. Which one of the following is a
complete and accurate list of possible
pairs of symptoms from the diseases?

(A) blue lips and swollen ears
(B) blue lips and swollen ears; red
    splotches and swollen ears
(C) swollen ears and red splotches
(D) blue lips and red splotches
(E) swollen ears and red splotches;
    blue lips and red splotches

7. If Paul had red splotches on Tuesday,
then he could NOT have given

(A) Peter Disease J
(B) Peter Disease K
(C) Mary Disease J
(D) Mary Disease K
(E) Mary Disease L

8. If on Monday Peter was infected only
with Disease K, then which of the
following is a complete and accurate
list of Mary's possible symptoms on
Wednesday because of Peter's passing
on Disease K?

(A) swollen ears
(B) blue lips
(C) red splotches
(D) swollen ears and blue lips
(E) blue lips and red splotches

Questions 9–17

A head counselor is choosing people to go
on a hiking trip. The head counselor must
choose from among 3 adult counselors (A,
B, C) and 9 campers (boys D, E, F, G, H,
and girls J, K, L, M).

At least two adult counselors must go
on the hike.

Camper D will not go without friends E
and F.

Campers J and L will not hike together.

Camper M will not hike with counselor
C.

There can never be more boy campers
than girl campers.

9. If camper D is chosen for the hike

(A) camper L must be chosen
(B) camper J cannot be chosen
(C) camper L cannot be chosen
(D) camper G cannot be chosen
(E) camper H must be chosen

10. If camper K is NOT chosen for the hike

(A) camper G cannot be chosen
(B) camper H cannot be chosen
(C) camper E cannot be chosen
(D) camper D cannot be chosen
(E) camper L cannot be chosen

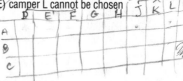

11. If camper D is chosen for the hike, which one of the following CANNOT be true?

    (A) Camper H goes on the hike.
    (B) Camper K goes on the hike.
    (C) Counselor A goes on the hike.
    (D) Counselor B goes on the hike.
    (E) Camper M goes on the hike.

12. An acceptable combination of campers and counselors is

    (A) ABCDEFJKM
    (B) ABDEFJLM
    (C) ABGHJKM
    (D) ACDEFJK
    (E) ACEFGKLM

13. If counselor A is NOT chosen for the hike, then

    (A) camper D must be chosen
    (B) camper D cannot be chosen
    (C) camper J must be chosen
    (D) camper L cannot be chosen
    (E) camper F cannot be chosen

14. If counselor A is NOT chosen for the hike, then which one of the following must be true?

    (A) If camper E is chosen, camper K must be chosen.
    (B) If camper F is chosen, camper K must be chosen.
    (C) Camper J cannot be chosen.
    (D) Camper D cannot be chosen.
    (E) If camper L is chosen, camper F must be chosen.

15. If camper D is chosen for the hike, which one of the following could represent the other hikers?

    (A) ACEFJKM
    (B) ABGHKML
    (C) ABEFJKM

    (D) ABFGJKL
    (E) ACEFGKLM

16. What is the largest number of hikers that can go on the hike?

    (A) 5
    (B) 6
    (C) 7
    (D) 8
    (E) 9

17. Which one of the following must be true?

    (A) Campers K and M never hike together.
    (B) Campers E and G never hike together.
    (C) Campers D and G never hike together.
    (D) Campers J and M never hike together.
    (E) Campers D and M never hike together.

Questions 18–23

At 4:00 P.M. Howard, Iris, Jessie, Kelly, Lance, and Murray start playing video-games A, B, C, D, E, and F, respectively. They will play video games for one hour. At 4:15; 4:30, and 4:45, these players will switch video games using a different set of rules at each of the three designated switch times. The rules that are used are as follows:

Rule 1: The player of video game A switches games with the player of video game B. The player of video game C switches games with the player of video game D. The player of video game E switches games with the player of video game F.

Rule 2: The player of video game A
switches games with the
player of video game C. The
player of video game B
switches games with the
player of video game D. The
player of video game E
switches games with the
player of video game F.

Rule 3: The player of video game A
switches games with the
player of video game F. The
player of video game B
switches games with the
player of video game E.

Rule 4: Howard switches video games
with Lance, and Kelly switches
video games with Murray.

18. If at 4:35, Howard is playing video
game D, which one of the following
must be true at 4:35?

(A) Lance is playing video game F.
(B) Jessie is playing the same game he
started with at 4:00.
(C) Iris is playing video game C.
(D) Kelly is playing the same game she
started with at 4:00.
(E) Murray is playing video game B.

19. If at 4:20, Jessie is still playing the
same game he started with at 4:00,
which one of the following CANNOT be
true at 4:20?

(A) Kelly is playing video game D.
(B) Murray is playing the video game
that Howard was playing at 4:10.
(C) Lance is playing the video game
that Iris was playing at 4:05.
(D) Iris is playing video game F.
(E) Howard is playing video game E.

20. If at some time during the hour, Jessie
is playing video game F, which one of
the following could have been true 15
minutes earlier?

(A) Howard was playing video game C.
(B) Iris was playing video game E.
(C) Kelly was playing video game A.
(D) Lance was playing video game B.
(E) Murray was playing video game D.

21. Which one of the following is a list of
the times that Murray could be playing
video game B?

(A) 4:15–4:30 only
(B) 4:30–4:45 only
(C) 4:45–5:00 only
(D) 4:15–4:30 and 4:45–5:00
(E) 4:30–4:45 and 4:45–5:00

22. Which one of the following is a list of
video games that Howard could be
playing at 4:50?

(A) A and B
(B) A and C
(C) B and D
(D) C and D
(E) D and E

23. If Jessie plays the same video game
from 4:00 to 4:45, which one of the
following must be true at 4:50?

(A) Howard is playing video game A.
(B) Iris is playing video game F.
(C) Kelly is playing video game B.
(D) Lance is playing video game D.
(E) Murray is playing video game C.

Questions 24–27

The Alto family's children—Do, Rey, Mi, Fa, and So—are planning to sing at the annual holiday festival. All singers at the holiday festival are dressed in animal costumes, so it is impossible to distinguish who are the boys and who are the girls. The following is known about the Alto family's children:

> Do is Rey's brother.
> Rey is Mi's sister.
> Mi is Fa's brother.
> So is Rey's sister.

24. Which one of the following must be true?

   (A) Do is a boy.
   (B) Fa is a girl.
   (C) Rey is a boy.
   (D) Mi is a girl.
   (E) So is a boy.

25. Which one of the following could be FALSE?

   (A) Fa is Rey's brother.
   (B) Do is Mi's brother.
   (C) So is Fa's sister.
   (D) Rey is Fa's sister.
   (E) Mi is Rey's brother.

26. Which one of the following could be true?

   (A) Do is So's sister.
   (B) Mi is not Do's brother.
   (C) Rey is Mi's brother.
   (D) Fa is Rey's brother.
   (E) So is Do's brother.

27. If Fa is a girl, from the information given which one of the following must be true?

   (A) There are more brothers than sisters.
   (B) Fa is So's sister.
   (C) Do is older than Fa.
   (D) Mi is younger than So.
   (E) Rey is Fa's brother.

Questions 28–35

Four men, A, B, C, and D, and three women, E, F, and G, are auditioning for a new TV pilot. The director is deciding the order in which they should audition. Since many of the actors have other auditions to attend at different locations, the director must observe the following restrictions:

> A must audition first or last.
> D and E must audition consecutively, but not necessarily in that order.
> Neither F nor G can audition last.
> E cannot audition until B has auditioned.

28. Which one of the following must be true?

   (A) F cannot audition first.
   (B) D cannot audition first.
   (C) B cannot audition first or second.
   (D) A must audition before D auditions.
   (E) G must audition second.

29. If A auditions first, which one of the following CANNOT be true?

   (A) G auditions second.
   (B) F auditions before B auditions.
   (C) D auditions second.
   (D) B auditions fifth.
   (E) G auditions before B auditions.

30. If F and G audition first and second respectively, then which one of the following must be FALSE?

(A) C auditions fourth.
(B) B auditions fourth.
(C) E auditions sixth.
(D) D auditions fifth.
(E) B auditions fifth.

31. Assume that B auditions first, and that F and G audition second and third respectively. Which one of the following must be FALSE?

(A) E auditions sixth.
(B) C auditions fifth.
(C) D auditions fourth.
(D) C auditions sixth.
(E) E auditions fifth.

32. Suppose that D auditions ahead of E. If A auditions first and B auditions fifth, who must audition sixth?

(A) D
(B) E
(C) F
(D) G
(E) C

33. Which one of the following is a possible order of auditions?

(A) A, E, B, D, F, G, C
(B) A, B, D, E, C, F, G
(C) C, B, G, F, E, A, D
(D) B, F, G, D, E, C, A
(E) F, B, E, G, D, A, C

34. If the director decides NOT to audition two men consecutively, and if C auditions first, which one of the following must be true?

(A) F auditions second.
(B) G auditions second.
(C) E auditions fifth.

(D) D auditions fourth.
(E) B auditions third.

35. Assume that all the women must audition consecutively. If F auditions third and G does NOT audition second, then which one of the following must be true?

(A) A auditions first.
(B) B auditions second.
(C) C auditions seventh.
(D) G auditions fifth.
(E) D auditions sixth.

Questions 36–41

Eight weight lifters, Aaron, Bryan, Clifford, David, Ellen, Jason, Logan, and Prescott, have joined a local gym. No two of these lifters lift the same weight. The following statements describe the relative strength of the lifters:

Ellen lifts more than Aaron.
Bryan lifts less than Logan but more than Prescott.
David lifts more than Logan.
Jason lifts less than Aaron but more than Clifford.
Logan lifts more than Jason.

36. Which one of the following statements must be true?

(A) David lifts more than Jason.
(B) Jason lifts more than Prescott.
(C) Ellen lifts more than Bryan.
(D) Clifford lifts more than Ellen.
(E) Bryan lifts more than David.

37. If Prescott lifts more than Aaron, then which one of the following must be true?

(A) Logan lifts more than Aaron.
(B) Aaron lifts more than Bryan.
(C) Ellen lifts more than Bryan.

(D) David lifts more than Ellen.
(E) Clifford lifts more than Logan.

38. If Aaron lifts more than David, what is the maximum number that can lift more than Logan?

(A) 0
(B) 1
(C) 2
(D) 3
(E) 4

39. If 5 people lift less than Logan, then which one of the following must be true?

(A) Bryan lifts more than Aaron.
(B) Prescott lifts more than Aaron.
(C) Clifford lifts more than Prescott.
(D) Jason lifts more than David.
(E) David lifts more than Aaron.

40. If Bryan lifts more than Aaron and Jason lifts more than Prescott, then who can lift more than Ellen?

(A) Prescott, Bryan, Logan.
(B) David, Prescott, Clifford.
(C) Logan, Bryan, Prescott.
(D) David, Logan, Jason.
(E) Logan, David, Bryan.

41. If Prescott lifts more than Jason, then which one of the following must be false?

(A) Bryan lifts more than Aaron.
(B) Prescott lifts more than Ellen.
(C) Ellen lifts more than David.
(D) Aaron lifts more than Logan.
(E) Bryan lifts more than David.

Questions 42–47

There are nine cans of soft drinks lined up on a shelf. The cans are numbered from 1 to 9, from left to right.

The first and fourth are different brands of cola.
The sixth and eighth are different brands of root beer.
The second, fifth, sixth, seventh, and ninth are the only caffeine-free soft drinks.
The second, third, fifth, seventh, and ninth cans contain unflavored beverages.

42. How many of the cans contain unflavored beverages that contain caffeine?

(A) 0
(B) 1
(C) 2
(D) 3
(E) 4

43. In which one of the following places is a beverage that contains caffeine?

(A) second
(B) fourth
(C) fifth
(D) sixth
(E) ninth

44. Which place contains a caffeine-free beverage that is not unflavored?

(A) first
(B) third
(C) fourth
(D) sixth
(E) seventh

45. If the two root beers were replaced with two cans of orange flavored beverage containing caffeine, how many cans would contain either cola or caffeine but not both?

(A) 0
(B) 1
(C) 2

(D) 3
(E) 4

46. If someone randomly chose two cans of caffeine-free beverage, which places could they be?

(A) second and third
(B) fourth and fifth
(C) third and seventh
(D) sixth and ninth
(E) eighth and ninth

47. How many cans of flavored beverage are next to at least one can of caffeine-free beverage?

(A) 0
(B) 1
(C) 2
(D) 3
(E) 4

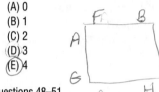

Questions 48–51

Eight people—A, B, C, D, E, F, G, H—are to be seated at a square table, two people on each side.

B must sit directly across from H.
A must sit between and next to F and G.
C cannot sit next to F.

48. Which one of the following must be true?

(A) C sits next to either B or H.
(B) H must sit next to G.
(C) F sits next to D or E.
(D) A sits directly across from B.
(E) F sits directly across from C or D.

49. If B does not sit next to G, then which one of the following is NOT possible?

(A) If C sits next to B, then D could sit directly across from F.
(B) If C sits next to D, then E could sit directly across from G.

(C) C could sit next to G.
(D) If C sits next to H, then B could sit between D and E.
(E) If C sits next to B, then A could sit next to H.

50. If C sits directly across from F, who could NOT sit next to H?

(A) C
(B) D
(C) E
(D) G
(E) A

51. How many different people could be seated directly across from A?

(A) 1
(B) 2
(C) 3
(D) 4
(E) 5

$B + T \rightarrow O$
only $A + Z \rightarrow T$
$A + T \rightarrow Z$
$A + B \rightarrow Z$
$Z + T \rightarrow B$
$Z + B \rightarrow A$

Questions 52–57

A scientist starts experimenting with four chemicals—Alpha, Beta, Theta, and Zeta. These chemicals combine in the following ways:

Alpha combines with Beta, giving Zeta.
Theta combines with Zeta, giving Beta.
Zeta combines with Beta, giving Alpha.
Beta combines with Theta, giving Omega, which is the only odorless chemical.
Theta is formed only when Alpha and Zeta combine.
Alpha combines with Theta, giving Zeta.
The order of the combinations makes no difference in their outcome.

52. An odorless chemical may be formed from a combination of

(A) Theta and Beta
(B) Alpha and Beta

(C) Beta and Zeta
(D) Theta and Zeta
(E) Alpha and Theta

53. Beta may be involved in the combination if the outcome is

(A) Alpha or Theta
(B) Alpha, Omega, or Zeta
(C) Beta
(D) Beta, Theta, or Zeta
(E) Alpha, Beta, or Theta

54. If an odorless chemical combines with Zeta, the outcome is

(A) Alpha
(B) Beta
(C) Theta
(D) Zeta
(E) unknown

55. Which one of the following must be true?

(A) Zeta and Theta combine to give Beta.
(B) Beta and Zeta combine to give Omega.
(C) Alpha and Beta combine to give Theta.
(D) Theta and Alpha combine to give Beta.
(E) Alpha and Zeta combine to give Omega.

56. If the outcome of Alpha and Beta combine with the outcome of Alpha and Zeta, the result is

(A) Alpha
(B) Beta
(C) Omega
(D) Theta
(E) Zeta

57. If Omega combines with Theta, the outcome is Zeta or Theta. Then the outcome of a combination of Omega and Theta is similar to the outcome of

(A) Alpha with any other
(B) Beta with any other
(C) Theta with any other
(D) Zeta with any other
(E) Beta with Zeta

ANSWERS AND EXPLANATIONS

Answers 1–4

By following statements 1–3, you could have made these two possible orders:

Y R B O or O B R Y

but statement 4 eliminates the first order, Y R B O.

1. **E**   From statements 2 and 3, the red and blue books are between other books; thus, they cannot be first or fourth. Therefore, they are second and third. This leaves first and fourth positions for the orange and yellow books.

2. **D**   Orange, blue, red, yellow, white is a possible order. Notice that each of the other orders could have been eliminated because each broke an initial statement:

    (A) Orange and blue are switched.

    (B) Blue and red are switched.

    (C) White must be on an end since the other four must be next to each other.

    (E) Blue cannot be on an end.

3. **B**   This follows the order discovered from the initial conditions, YRBO.

4. **B**   Because the blue book was in the second position, it will move to the third position, and the green book will take the second.

Answers 5–8

The following simple chart may be helpful in answering the questions:

Disease	When Communicable	Symptom
J	Always	Red splotches appear DAY AFTER INF.
K	Day after infection	Blue lips OR red splotches appear DAY OF INF.
L	Only with J	Swollen ears appear DAY AFTER INF. NEGATED BY DISEASE K

Tuesday	Wednesday
Peter and Paul	Paul and Mary

5. **E**   Either (A) or (B) may be true, but neither necessarily *must* be true. (C) could be true if Disease L is concurrent with Disease J, but it doesn't necessarily have to be true. Choice (D) is false since Disease K wouldn't be communicable until the day after, Wednesday. Thus (E) *is* true: Peter did not give Paul Disease K, because Disease K isn't communicable until a day later, on Wednesday.

6. **E**   A complete and accurate list of pairs is swollen ears and red splotches and blue lips and red splotches. Blue lips and swollen ears are not possible together: Disease L's symptoms are negated by Disease K. Swollen ears and red splotches will both appear the day after infection with Diseases J and L. Blue lips and red splotches will appear together if a person is infected with Disease K a day after infection by Disease J.

7. **B** If Paul had red splotches on Tuesday, then he either was infected with Disease J on Monday or was infected with Disease K on Tuesday. Therefore:

Paul could have given Peter Disease J because J is always communicable.

Paul could *not* have given Peter Disease K on Tuesday, because Disease K isn't communicable until the day after (Wednesday).

Paul could have given Mary Disease J because Disease J is always communicable.

Paul could have given Mary Disease K because Disease K is communicable a day after infection (Wednesday).

8. **E** If Peter was infected with Disease K on Monday, then:

Peter could have infected Paul with Disease K on Tuesday (one day later); Paul in turn could have infected Mary on Wednesday. Thus, Mary could have blue lips.

Mary's ears could not have been swollen because simply passing on Disease K would not manifest such a symptom.

Peter could have given Paul Disease K on Tuesday; Paul in turn could have given it to Mary on Wednesday. Red splotches are also a symptom of Disease K, which Mary could have shown on Wednesday.

Answers 9–17

Drawing the simple diagram, below, will help answer the questions.

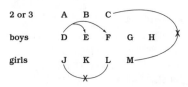

9. **D** If camper D is chosen, then campers E and F are also chosen. Thus three boys have been picked to go on the hike. Note that three girls, at most, can go on the hike. Since boys cannot outnumber girls, no other boys can be chosen.

10. **D** If camper K is not chosen, the maximum number of girls chosen can be two. Therefore, since boys cannot outnumber girls, D cannot be chosen, since selecting D means also selecting two more boys, E and F.

11. **A** If camper D is chosen, then boys E and F are also chosen. Since the maximum number of girls chosen can be three, no other boys may be chosen, since boys may not outnumber girls.

12. **C** Choices (A) and (E) include both C and M, which is not permitted. Choice (B) includes J and L, who will not hike together. In choice (D), boys outnumber girls, which is not permitted. Only choice (C) is an acceptable combination of campers and counselors.

13. **B** If counselor A is not chosen for the hike, then counselors B and C are chosen as there must be at least two counselors on the hike. Since counselor C is chosen, camper M (a girl) cannot be chosen. Therefore, the maximum number of girls on the hike can be two. Since boys cannot

outnumber girls, D cannot be chosen, since selecting D would mean also selecting E and F, a total of three boys.

14. **D**   If counselor A is not chosen, then counselors B and C will be chosen as there must be at least two counselors on the hike. If counselor C is chosen, camper M cannot be chosen, leaving the maximum number of girls possible on the hike at two. Therefore, since boys may not outnumber girls, D cannot be chosen as choosing D would mean also selecting E and F, thus outnumbering the girls.

15. **C**   Choices (A) and (E) included both C and M, which is not permitted. Choices (B) and (D) do not include camper E, who must accompany camper D. Only choice (C) includes acceptable companions for a hike with camper D.

16. **D**   The largest number of hikers that can go on the hike is eight, as follows: three boys, three girls, and counselors A and B. (Example: A, B, D, E, F, J, K, M)

17. **C**   The maximum number of girls possible for the hike is three. Therefore, since choosing camper D means also choosing campers E and F, no other boys (for instance, G) can be chosen, as boys would then outnumber girls.

Answers 18–23

From the information given, you could have made a simple chart showing how each rule works:

Rule 1   A B C D E F

Rule 2   A B C D E F

Rule 3   A B C D E F

Rule 4   H L K M

18. **C**   The only way Howard can be playing video game D after two switches is if rule 1 then rule 2, or rule 2 then rule 1, is applied. The following is a diagram showing who is playing each video game after two switches. The order of rules 1 and 2 does not make any difference.

Choices (A) and (E) are incorrect since Lance and Murray are playing the same video games they were playing at 4:00. Choices (B) and (D) are wrong because Jessie and Kelly are playing different games from those they were playing at 4:00.

	A	B	C	D	E	F
	H	I	J	K	L	M
Rule 1	I	H	K	J	M	L
Rule 2	K	J	I	H	L	M

	A	B	C	D	E	F
	H	I	J	K	L	M
Rule 2	J	K	H	I	M	L
Rule 1	K	J	I	H	L	M

19. **D**   If Jessie does not switch video games at 4:15, then either rule 3 or rule 4 must be applied at 4:15.

Choice (A) is incorrect since using rule 3, Kelly is playing video game D.

Choice (B) is incorrect since using rule 3, Murray is playing video game A.

Choice (C) is incorrect since using rule 3, Lance is playing video game B.

Choice (E) is incorrect since using rule 4, Howard is playing video game E.

	A	B	C	D	E	F
	H	I	J	K	L	M
Rule 3	M	L	J	K	I	H

A	B	C	D	E	F
H	I	J	K	L	M
Rule 4 L	I	J	M	H	K

20. **A** The only way Jessie can play video game F is if rule 2 is applied at 4:15 and rule 3 is applied at 4:30. Thus, 15 minutes earlier would be after rule 2 was applied.

Choice (B) is incorrect since Iris is playing video game D.

Choice (C) is incorrect since Kelly is playing video game B.

Choice (D) is incorrect since Lance is playing video game F.

Choice (E) is incorrect since Murray is playing video game E.

A	B	C	D	E	F
H	I	J	K	L	M
Rule 2 J	K	H	I	M	L
Rule 3 L	M	H	I	K	J

21. **E** The switch for Murray from video game F to video game B cannot be made in one switch. Thus, 4:20 is not possible. This eliminates choices (A) and (D). Since it is possible for Murray to be playing video game B after two switches or three switches, choices (B) and (C) are incorrect and choice (E) is correct.

A	B	C	D	E	F
H	I	J	K	L	M
Rule 1 I	H	K	J	M	L
Rule 3 L	M	K	J	H	I

A	B	C	D	E	F
H	I	J	K	L	M
Rule 2 J	K	H	I	M	L
Rule 3 L	M	H	I	K	J

A	B	C	D	E	F
H	I	J	K	L	M
Rule 3 M	L	J	K	I	H
Rule 1 L	M	K	J	H	I

A	B	C	D	E	F
H	I	J	K	L	M
Rule 3 M	L	J	K	I	H
Rule 4 K	H	J	M	I	L
Rule 2 J	M	K	H	L	I

22. **E** After three of the four rules are applied, it is not possible for Howard to be playing either video game B or video game C. Thus, any choice including video game B or C is incorrect.

After applying rules (in any order)	Howard will be playing the following video game
Rules 1, 2, and 3	D or F
Rules 1, 2, and 4	E
Rules 1, 3, and 4	A
Rules 2, 3, and 4	A or D

23. **B** In order for Jessie to play the same video game from 4:00 to 4:45, rules 3 and 4 must be used and 4:15 and 4:30. The order of rule 3 and 4 does not make a difference since both yield the same result.

A	B	C	D	E	F
H	I	J	K	L	M
Rule 3 M	L	J	K	I	H
Rule 4 K	H	J	M	I	L

A	B	C	D	E	F
H	I	J	K	L	M
Rule 4 L	I	J	M	H	K
Rule 3 K	H	J	M	I	L

A	B	C	D	E	F
K	H	J	M	I	L
Rule 1 H	K	M	J	L	I

A	B	C	D	E	F
K	H	J	M	I	L
Rule 2 J	M	K	H	L	I

If rule 1 or rule 2 is applied to the result of rules 3 and 4, Lance must play video game E and Iris must play video game F. Thus, choice (B) is the only one that must be true. Choice (A), (C), and (E) may be true, and choice (D) is false.

Answers 24–27

Constructing the following chart would be helpful in answering the questions:

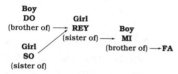

24. **A** Only statement (A) must be true. Because Do is Rey's brother, then Do is a boy. Because Rey is Mi's sister, then Rey is a girl. We do not know if Fa is a boy or a girl.

25. **A** Only statement (A) could be false, because we don't know if Fa is a boy or a girl.

26. **D** We do not know if Fa is a boy or a girl. Thus, (D) could be true. The others are false.

27. **B** We are not given any information about their ages. If Fa is a girl, then we have three sisters and two brothers.

Answers 28–35

From the information given, you could have constructed a diagram similar to this:

```
                            D–E
                   F        B ? E
                   G
A?                 A?
1   2   3   4   5   6   7
```

Notice the information listed off to the side of the diagram.

28. **B** D cannot audition first since D and E have to audition consecutively, and B must audition before E.

29. **C** If A auditions first, then D cannot audition second because B must au-

dition before E, and therefore also before D.

30. **E** If F and G audition first and second respectively, then A must audition last and the diagram for this question would look like this:

```
F   G                   A
1   2   3   4   5   6   7
```

Therefore, A must audition last and B cannot audition fifth (no room for D and E to follow B). C could possibly audition fourth.

31. **B** If B auditions first, and F and G audition second and third respectively, then A must audition last and the diagram for this question would look like this:

```
B   F   G               A
1   2   3   4   5   6   7
```

Therefore, E auditions sixth could be true. C auditions fifth must be false because D and E must be next to each other. If C was fifth, he would split D and E. D auditions fourth could be true.

32. **A** If D auditions ahead of E, and if A auditions first and B fifth, then the diagram for this question would look like this:

```
A               B   D   E
1   2   3   4   5   6   7
```

Since B auditions fifth, then D must be sixth and E seventh.

33. **D** This question is most easily answered by eliminating the orders that are not possible. Choice (A) can be eliminated because E is ahead of B and not next to D. Choice (B) can be eliminated because G cannot audition last. Choices (C) and (A) can be eliminated because A is not first or last.

34. **E** From the new information given, men cannot audition consecutively;

the diagram for this question would now look like this:

```
C       B       D       A
1   2   3   4   5   6   7
```

Therefore, B must audition third.

35. **E** If F auditions third and all the women must audition consecutively, then G must audition next to F, since E must be next to D. The diagram for this question would now look like this:

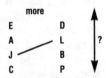

```
        F   G   E   D
1   2   3   4   5   6   7
```

Therefore, D must audition sixth.

Answers 36–41

The following diagram may prove helpful:

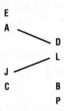

36. **A** Because David lifts more than Logan and Logan lifts more than Jason, David lifts more than Jason. Prescott and Bryan lift less than Logan, but we cannot say anything about their relationship to Jason. It is possible for Prescott to lift more than Ellen.

37. **A** Logan lifts more than Prescott. If Prescott lifts more than Aaron, so must Logan.

38. **D** If Aaron lifts more than David, then Aaron, Ellen, and David each lift more than Logan.

39. **E** If 5 people lift less than Logan, they must be Bryan, Prescott, Clifford, Jason, and Aaron. Thus, David and Ellen lift more than Logan, therefore, David lifts more than Aaron. Answer (C) may be true, but doesn't have to be.

40. **E** Given these additional facts, we can redraw the diagram as follows:

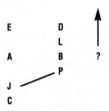

Thus, Logan, David, and Bryan can each lift more than Ellen.

41. **E** From the diagram, all of the following could be true:

Answers 42–47

This diagram shows these relationships:

	CF			CF	CF	CF		CF
1	2	3	4	5	6	7	8	9
Cola				Cola		RB		RB

42. **B**   Can 3 is the only one.
43. **B**   Of the cans listed, only the fourth place (can 4) contains caffeine.
44. **D**   The sixth place (can 6) is the can that meets the requirements.
45. **D**   For this question, you should use the following diagram:

	CF				CF		CF	CF
1	2	3	4	5	6	7	8	9
Cola				Cola		0		0

After the replacement, the cans that meet the conditions are 3, 6, and 8.

46. **D**   The five caffeine-free cans are 2, 5, 6, 7, and 9. Therefore choice (D), the sixth and ninth places, is the only valid one.
47. **E**   All four flavored beverages are next to caffeine-free beverages.

Answers 48–51

From the information given, it would be helpful to construct a diagram to answer the questions.

NOTE: When more than one letter appears at a seat, those letters represent all the possible occupants of that seat.

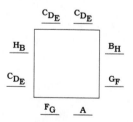

48. **A**   From the diagram, C must sit next to B or H; therefore (A) is true. Taking a second look at the diagram, we can see that H doesn't have to sit next to

G, and F doesn't have to sit next to D or E. Therefore, (B) and (C) are not necessarily true. Also, (D) is false since H sits directly across from B. Statement (E) is false since F could sit across from E.

49. **E**   If B does not sit next to G, then we should adjust the diagram as follows:

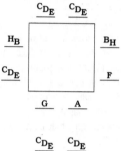

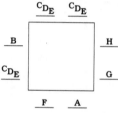

From these diagrams, we see that all statements are possible except (E). Since A sits between G and F, A cannot sit next to H under any circumstances.

50. **E**   If C sits across from F, then H could sit next to any of these four (C, D, E, G) depending on the positions of B and H. A cannot sit next to H since A sits between G and F.

51. **C**   B and H can't, since they must sit opposite each other. F and G can't, since they must sit next to A. That leaves only C, D, and E.

Answers 52–57

From the information given, you could make the following displays:

A + B = Z
T + Z = B
Z + B = A
B + T = O   (O is odorless)
A + Z = T
A + T = Z

OR

	A	B	T	Z
A	?	Z	Z	T
B	Z	?	O	A
T	Z	O	?	B
Z	T	A	B	?

(O is odorless)

52. **A** This answer may be derived directly from the statement: Beta combines with Theta, giving Omega. Omega is the only odorless chemical.

53. **B** From our chart or statements we can see that, if Beta is involved, then the outcome may be Alpha, Omega, or Zeta.

54. **E** We have no information about the results if the odorless chemical, Omega, combines with anything.

55. **A** From the chart or statements we can see that Zeta and Theta combine to give Beta.

56. **B** The outcome of Alpha and Beta is Zeta. The outcome of Alpha and Zeta is Theta. Thus, if the two outcomes (Zeta and Theta) combine, the result will then be Beta.

57. **A** Alpha with any other (with the exception of Omega, which we do not know) produces either Zeta or Theta, which is similar to the outcome of Omega with Theta.

ANSWER SHEET
EXTRA PRACTICE: ANALYTICAL REASONING

1. ⒜ⒷⒸⒹⒺ	20. ⒜ⒷⒸⒹⒺ	39. ⒜ⒷⒸⒹⒺ
2. ⒜ⒷⒸⒹⒺ	21. ⒜ⒷⒸⒹⒺ	40. ⒜ⒷⒸⒹⒺ
3. ⒜ⒷⒸⒹⒺ	22. ⒜ⒷⒸⒹⒺ	41. ⒜ⒷⒸⒹⒺ
4. ⒜ⒷⒸⒹⒺ	23. ⒜ⒷⒸⒹⒺ	42. ⒜ⒷⒸⒹⒺ
5. ⒜ⒷⒸⒹⒺ	24. ⒜ⒷⒸⒹⒺ	43. ⒜ⒷⒸⒹⒺ
6. ⒜ⒷⒸⒹⒺ	25. ⒜ⒷⒸⒹⒺ	44. ⒜ⒷⒸⒹⒺ
7. ⒜ⒷⒸⒹⒺ	26. ⒜ⒷⒸⒹⒺ	45. ⒜ⒷⒸⒹⒺ
8. ⒜ⒷⒸⒹⒺ	27. ⒜ⒷⒸⒹⒺ	46. ⒜ⒷⒸⒹⒺ
9. ⒜ⒷⒸⒹⒺ	28. ⒜ⒷⒸⒹⒺ	47. ⒜ⒷⒸⒹⒺ
10. ⒜ⒷⒸⒹⒺ	29. ⒜ⒷⒸⒹⒺ	48. ⒜ⒷⒸⒹⒺ
11. ⒜ⒷⒸⒹⒺ	30. ⒜ⒷⒸⒹⒺ	49. ⒜ⒷⒸⒹⒺ
12. ⒜ⒷⒸⒹⒺ	31. ⒜ⒷⒸⒹⒺ	50. ⒜ⒷⒸⒹⒺ
13. ⒜ⒷⒸⒹⒺ	32. ⒜ⒷⒸⒹⒺ	51. ⒜ⒷⒸⒹⒺ
14. ⒜ⒷⒸⒹⒺ	33. ⒜ⒷⒸⒹⒺ	52. ⒜ⒷⒸⒹⒺ
15. ⒜ⒷⒸⒹⒺ	34. ⒜ⒷⒸⒹⒺ	53. ⒜ⒷⒸⒹⒺ
16. ⒜ⒷⒸⒹⒺ	35. ⒜ⒷⒸⒹⒺ	54. ⒜ⒷⒸⒹⒺ
17. ⒜ⒷⒸⒹⒺ	36. ⒜ⒷⒸⒹⒺ	55. ⒜ⒷⒸⒹⒺ
18. ⒜ⒷⒸⒹⒺ	37. ⒜ⒷⒸⒹⒺ	56. ⒜ⒷⒸⒹⒺ
19. ⒜ⒷⒸⒹⒺ	38. ⒜ⒷⒸⒹⒺ	57. ⒜ⒷⒸⒹⒺ

To remove, cut along dotted rule.

3

LOGICAL REASONING

INTRODUCTION TO QUESTION TYPE

The LSAT will contain *two* Logical Reasoning sections that will count toward your score. The unscored experimental section could also be Logical Reasoning. Each Logical Reasoning section is 35 minutes in length and contains from 24 to 26 questions. *Since approximately half of your exam consists of Logical Reasoning questions, you should spend additional time reviewing, understanding, and practicing this question type.*

Logical Reasoning questions, which require you to apply your reading and reasoning skills, measure your aptitude for understanding, analyzing, utilizing, and criticizing various short passages and types of arguments. Your ability to reason logically and critically is tested by questions that require you to do the following:

- Recognize a point.
- Follow a chain of reasoning.
- Draw conclusions.
- Infer missing material.
- Apply principles from an argument.
- Identify methods.
- Evaluate arguments.
- Differentiate between fact and opinion.
- Analyze evidence.
- Assess claims critically.

Logical reasoning questions may take many forms. In analyzing these forms, consider their basic component parts:

1. **A *passage*, *argument* or *discussion***
   followed by
2. **A *question* based upon the preceding text**
   followed by
3. **The five *answer choices* (A, B, C, D, and E)**

The following discussion offers some tips for each of these parts.

THE APPROACH

THE BASIC COMPONENTS

1. The Passage, Argument, or Discussion

For the passage, read *actively;* that is, as you read you should mark the important parts with circles, exclamation points, etc., directly on the page of your question booklet. Reading actively helps you stay involved in the passage, it keeps you an active participant in the testing process, and it helps you note and highlight the important points mentioned, should you need to refer to the passage.

As you read you should also note the major issue being discussed, along with the few supporting points, if any.

2. The Question

For the question, it may be helpful to *preread actively;* that is, to read the question first, *before* reading the passage. That way you have an idea of what to look for as you read the passage. This is an effective technique only if the question is short. If the question is as long as (or longer than) the passage, this technique may not be helpful. Use your judgment.

As you read the question, note the key words and *circle* them, in the same manner as you mark the passage. Also note the *reference* of the question. Is it positive or negative? Is it asking what would strengthen the author's argument or what would weaken the author's argument? Is it asking what the author would agree or disagree with? Is it asking what the author believes, or what his critics would believe? Finally, be aware that questions often refer to *unstated* ideas: assumptions (a supposition or a truth taken for granted); implications/inferences (what would logically follow from a previous statement); and conclusions (the necessary consequence or result of the ideas in the passage). Assumptions and implications/inferences are usually not directly mentioned in the passage. Conclusions may or may not be mentioned. You must arrive at all three through logical thinking.

3. The Choices

For the choices, note that you must select the *best* of the five alternatives. Therefore, there may not be a perfect choice. There may also be two good choices. You are to pick the best of the five. Therefore, the elimination strategy (p. 10) is an effective way to approach the answer choices. Eliminate choices that are irrelevant (have nothing to do with the particular topic or issue), off-topic, or not addressed by the passage. Note that often a choice will be incorrect simply because one word in that choice is off-topic. Learn to look for and mark these off-topic key words.

Finally, be very careful as you read the passage, question, and choices, to watch for words that have very special meanings. The following words, for instance, are frequently used:

```
except  some  all  none  only  one
     few  no  could  must  each
```
These types of words will often be the key to finding the best answer. Therefore, make sure to underline or circle them in your reading.

ANALYZING QUESTION CATEGORIES

The following sections give detailed examples of the most common types of Logical Reasoning questions, complete with important techniques and strategies. You should not try to memorize the different categories presented here, but rather use them as an aid in identifying strategies needed and in practicing techniques.

Author's Main Point or Main Idea

A very common Logical Reasoning question type will ask you to identify or understand the main point or main idea of the passage. This is also a common question type in the Reading Comprehension section.

As you read the short passage, focus on what the author is trying to say—the major issue. Each paragraph usually contains only one main idea, often stated in the first sentence.

Let's analyze the following passage:

EXAMPLE

1   As the legal profession becomes more specialized and complex, clerical assistance must become more specialized as well. One legal secretary might be an expert in bankruptcy law, another an expert in criminal justice.

Which one of the following is the main point of the passage?

(A) A legal secretary may understand subjects other than law.

(B) A legal secretary should have special training in a particular branch of law.

(C) A legal secretary must be an expert in several types of law.

(D) Attorneys will hire only secretaries without legal experience so they can be trained on the job.

(E) Attorneys will still need legal secretaries with a very general background.

Analysis

The first sentence of the passage, a general statement about increasing specialization in the legal profession, states the main idea. It is followed by a more specific statement, which gives you additional information.

To help you focus on the main point, you may wish to use the following technique when practicing this question type. As you finish reading each paragraph, try to mentally summarize the paragraph in a few words. For example, after reading the sample above, you might summarize it by saying to yourself, "Legal secretaries should specialize in different types of law."

Next, note whether the paragraph states a particular attitude toward the subject. Typically the author will either <u>approve</u> or <u>disapprove</u> of the main point, or remain <u>neutral</u>. In the Example 1 passage, the author takes no position pro or con, but delivers the additional information in a matter-of-fact way.

The correct answer is (B). In this case, the main point is that legal secretaries must become more specialized, and the correct answer emphasizes "special training." Notice also that the correct answer here refers as well to the second sentence, which contains additional information about particular branches of law.

(A) is irrelevant. Although particular types of law are mentioned, subjects other than law are not. Note that this statement may certainly be true for some legal secretaries, but receives no support from the paragraph. (C) contradicts information in the passage; the passage discusses legal secretaries who specialize in one type of law, not several. (D) and (E) are not addressed in the passage. The passage does not discuss attorneys' hiring requirements or the need for legal secretaries with a very general background.

Remember, when asked for a main point, be sure to differentiate the main point from secondary or minor points.

$+ \quad — \quad$ *Lazy*

EXAMPLE 2

The belief that positive thinking is the key to success can lead to laziness. It encourages some people to engage in slipshod work, in the hope that an optimistic mental attitude will take the place of hard, careful, dedicated work.

Which one of the following is the <u>main idea</u> of this passage?

(A) Laziness is always the result of positive thinking.
(B) Laziness is practiced by successful people.
(C) Laziness is only permissible after one has completed a hard day's work.
(D) Laziness may result from a reliance on positive thinking.
(E) Laziness may result from an assortment of mental attitudes.

Analysis

The correct answer is (D), which restates the opening statement that "positive thinking . . . can lead to laziness." However, the paragraph does not say that laziness is <u>always</u> the result; therefore (A) is incorrect. (B) is unreasonable and is contradicted by the paragraph. (C) is irrelevant; the paragraph does not discuss when laziness is permissible. (E) brings in an assortment of mental attitudes that are not addressed.

EXAMPLE

3   Few people understand poetry, and few prefer to read it. Although English professors speak in glowing terms about the greatness of Pope's *Rape of the Lock* and Tennyson's *Ulysses,* it seems that only other professors share their enthusiasm. To appreciate the greatness of difficult poetry, readers must exercise great patience and concentration, and must tolerate the unusual, compressed language of rhythm and rhyme; with so many urgent issues demanding our attention almost every hour of the day, choosing to figure out a poem seems an unlikely possibility.

In the passage above, the writer makes which one of the following arguments?

(A) English professors pay lip service to great poetry, but, in fact, rarely read it for pleasure.

(B) Even English professors may not really understand difficult poetry.

(C) Few laypeople will spend the time necessary to read difficult poetry.

(D) Simple poetry may continue to be popular, but only English teachers now read difficult poetry.

(E) To read difficult poetry requires patience, concentration, and tolerance.

Analysis

The correct answer is (C). The passage does not suggest that the English professors' enthusiasm is insincere (A) nor that they may fail to understand difficult poems (B). It argues that only English professors have the skills, time, and interest in poetry to deal with its difficulties, that laypeople are now unlikely to do so (C). The passage does not allude to simple poetry. (E) is tempting at first, but the argument of the passage is that understanding or appreciating poetry requires these skills, not simply reading it, so (C) is the best of the five choices.

Author Information or Author's Purpose

Another common Logical Reasoning question refers to a reading passage or paragraph and asks you to understand some things about the author. You may be asked to interpret what the author is trying to accomplish by this statement, or to predict the action and feeling of the author on similar or unrelated subject matter (tell whether the author would agree or disagree with some idea).

To answer this type of question, first look for the values and attitudes of the author. (Ask yourself, "Where is the author coming from?") Second, watch for word connotation: the author's choice of words can be very important. Third, decide the author's purpose and point of view, but don't OVERREAD. Keep within the context of the passage. Sometimes it will be advantageous to skim some of the questions (not the answer choices) before reading the short passage, so that you will know what to expect.

Remember while reading to mark the passage and look for *who, what, when, where, why,* and *how.* (See the section on "Active Reading" that begins on page 16).

EXAMPLE

1   Recent studies show that the general public is unaware of most new legislation and doesn't understand 99% of the remaining legislation. This is mainly because of the public's inattention and lack of interest.

The author of this argument would most likely be

(A) in favor in new legislation
(B) against new legislation
(C) advocating public participation in legislation
(D) advocating the simplifying of the language of new legislation
(E) advocating more interesting legislation

Analysis
The correct answer is (C). The statement does not imply that an increase or decrease in legislation would change the public awareness; therefore (A) and (B) are incorrect. (C) follows in the tenor of the argument because the author's purpose appears to be centered around involvement. He points out that the general public is unaware because of inattention and lack of interest. (D) would be possible, *but* the author is not focusing his criticism on the complex wording of legislation and does not mention it as a reason for unawareness. Remember (1) *whom* the author is talking about—the general public, (2) *what* he mentions—their unawareness of most new legislation, and (3) *why* they are unaware—because of inattention and lack of interest. The author is not advocating more interesting legislation (E).

EXAMPLE

2   Writing Teacher: There are advantages and disadvantages to clear, simple writing. Sentences that are easy to understand are processed more quickly and efficiently by readers; those who can express themselves in simple terms are rarely misunderstood. However, prose that is crystal clear often lacks both complexity and imagination. Whether one chooses a style that is simple and clear or complex and unusual often depends upon the tolerance of one's readers.

The purpose of the writing teacher who makes this statement to a class is probably to

(A) encourage students to write more simply
(B) encourage students to imitate in their own pure style the points the teacher is making about pure style
(C) encourage students to be more imaginative in their writing
(D) remind students of the importance of the audience to a piece of writing
(E) urge students to combine simplicity and complexity, clarity and imagination in all their writing

Analysis

The correct answer is (D). The passage points out the disadvantages and advantages of both simple and complex prose and concludes with the reminder that the readers will determine which is appropriate The passage does not favor one style over another as in (A) and (C), nor does it say that all writing should be both simple and complex (E). It argues for a style suitable to the audience.

Form of Argumentation

In this type of question, you are asked to decide what type of argument, logic, or reasoning the author is using (example, exaggeration, deduction, induction, etc.).

To answer this type of question, carefully follow the author's line of reasoning while focusing on his or her intent or purpose. Notice how the author starts and finishes the argument. Consider what the author has concluded or proved, or what point has been made or argued. Watch "if" and "how" specific points or examples are used in relation to more general statements.

EXAMPLE

1   Once again, refer to the argument used earlier concerning legislation.

Recent studies show that the general public is unaware of most new legislation and doesn't understand 99% of the remaining legislation. This is mainly because of the public's inattention and lack of interest.

To make the point, the author of this statement

(A) gives a general statement followed by supporting facts
(B) argues by pointing out the effects and then the cause
(C) uses specific examples to disprove an argument
(D) infers an outcome and then attempts to support that outcome

(E) assumes the conclusion is true and uses circular reasoning to state the premise

Analysis

The correct answer is (B). The author starts by making specific points about the general public. It is "unaware of most new legislation and doesn't understand 99% of the remaining legislation." This is followed by a statement of the cause: "This is mainly because of the public's inattention and lack of interest."

EXAMPLE
2   In the twelfth century, people used the abacus (a simple device made of beads strung on wire) to perform complex calculations. Today we use electronic calculators, and the abacus has become obsolete. In fifty or one hundred years, the calculator will be as quaint and outmoded as the abacus. Every invention of man, every breakthrough of science will, if we wait long enough, be out of date and used no longer.

Which one of the following is a questionable technique used in the argument in this passage?

(A) It ignores the fact that the abacus is still in use in Asia.
(B) It generalizes from a single instance of obsolescence.
(C) It makes a prediction without specifying exactly when the prediction will come true.
(D) It mistakes a minor premise for a major premise and so deduces erroneously.
(E) It considers only scientific advances, but some inventions are not related to science.

Analysis

The correct answer is (B). The question calls for a questionable technique. The error here is the hasty generalization, based on a single instance of obsolescence. (A), (C), and (E) may be true but they do not point to a technique of argument. (D) is irrelevant and not true of this argument, which is not a syllogism.

Strengthening or Weakening the Author's Statement or Conclusion

This question type is very common on the LSAT. Here you are given a short reading passage or paragraph followed by the question "Which of the following would strengthen the author's statement the most?" or "Which of the following would most weaken the author's statement?" (Both of these questions may be asked. There are many possible varieties of this question type: "least likely to weaken," "strongest criticism of," and so on).

You may find it helpful to preread, or read the question before reading the short paragraph. Focus on the major point of the statement and "how" or "if" it is supported. Be aware of the strength of the statement or argument. Is it a harsh criticism of a certain system? Is it a mildly persuasive paragraph? What point is the author trying to make in supporting this cause?

Remember to always read actively, marking key words or phrases.

EXAMPLE

1   **Psychiatrists and laypeople agree that the best sort of adjustment is founded upon an acceptance of reality, rather than an escape from it.**

Not all

Which one of the following would probably most weaken the author's point?

(A) Psychiatrists and laypeople do not often agree.
(B) Reality is difficult to define.
(C) Escaping reality has worked for many.
(D) Accepting reality is often traumatic.
(E) Psychiatrists' definition of reality and laypeople's definition of reality are different.

Analysis

The correct answer is (C). If escaping reality has worked for many, then it becomes more difficult to defend the acceptance of reality theory. (A) would probably strengthen the point being made. (B) could strengthen or weaken the point. (D) and (E) are irrelevant.

EXAMPLE

2   **The likelihood of America's exhausting her natural resources is growing less. All kinds of waste are being reworked and new uses are constantly being found for almost everything. We are getting more use out of our goods and are making many new by-products out of what was formerly thrown away. It is, therefore, unnecessary to continue to ban logging in national parks, nature reserves, or areas inhabited by endangered species of animals.**

Which one of the following most seriously undermines the conclusion of this argument?

(A) The increasing amount of recycled material made available each year is equal to one-tenth of the increasing amount of natural material consumed annually.
(B) Recent studies have shown that the number of endangered animals throughout the world fluctuates sharply

and is chiefly determined by changes in weather conditions.

(C) The logging industry contributes huge sums of money to the political campaigns in states where it has a financial interest.

(D) The techniques that make recycling possible are constantly improved so that more is reclaimed for lower costs each year.

(E) Political contributions by the recycling industry are now greater than those of the logging or animal protection interests.

Analysis

The correct answer is (A). First, remember to circle the words <u>undermines</u> and <u>conclusion</u> to help you focus on what you're looking for. Now let's look at the choices. (D) would support rather than undermine the conclusion. (B), (C), and (E) neither support nor weaken the argument, though with more information (C) and (E) might be relevant. If the recycled materials are equal to only one-tenth of the natural materials lost each year, the argument is seriously injured.

EXAMPLE
3

Some scientists have proposed that, over two hundred million years ago, one giant land mass—rather than various continents and islands—covered one-third of the earth. Long before there was any human life, and over vast periods of time, islands and continents drifted apart. Australia was the first to separate, while South America and Africa were late in splitting apart. Some islands, of course, were formed by volcanoes and were never part of the great land mass.

All the following would support the author's claim EXCEPT

(A) Many of the plants of the South American rain forests are markedly similar to those of the African rain forest.

(B) Australia has more animals that are not found on any other continent than have several of the much larger continents.

(C) Volcanic islands like Hawaii have ecosystems very different from those of continental lands with the same average temperature.

(D) The plants of similar conditions in South America have less in common with those of Australia than with those of Asia, Africa, or Europe.

(E) The primitive languages of Australia are unlike those of Africa, which resemble those of South America.

Analysis

The correct answer is (E). If Australia was the first continent to separate, it would follow that its flora and fauna would develop in isolation over a longer period of time. Similarly, we may expect the plants and animals of South America and Africa that separated later to be more alike. (A), (B), and (D) support these ideas. That the separately developed islands are different is also in accord with the passage. However, the languages of all the continents would have developed in isolation, since man did not evolve until after the break-up of the land mass and it is surprising that African and South American languages are similar. Human likeness or difference are irrelevant to the claims of the passage.

EXAMPLE
4

In America, a baseball game should be described as a series of solo performances: at any given moment, attention is focused on one player and one play. On the other hand, soccer involves all of the team most of the time: each player interacts with others constantly, so that no single individual seems responsible for success or failure. It is because spectators prefer concentrating on individual personalities that baseball remains a much more popular spectator sport than soccer.

Which one of the following, if true, can best be used to undermine the conclusion of this argument?

(A) Soccer is more popular with spectators in France than baseball.

(B) Among the ten most televised sports in America, by far the most watched is football, and the least watched are tennis and bowling.

(C) Many people watch only the baseball teams of the city in which they live and for whom they root.

(D) Compared to football and basketball, baseball games are much cheaper to attend.

(E) In some sections of the United States, soccer leagues for children under fifteen are more popular than Little League baseball.

Analysis

The correct answer is (B). The weakness of this argument is not its claim that baseball is more popular than soccer with spectators in America. This is true from the passage. The weakness is its claim that the reason for baseball's greater popularity is that it is an individual performance rather than a team sport. (B) cites a team sport that is more watched than baseball and two solo performance sports that are not very popular. (A) makes a good point, but the passage is concerned with spectators "in America." Even if (C) is true, it may be that these people watch the teams to see individual performances.

(D) is true, but not as powerful a criticism as (B). (E) does not necessarily deal with spectators; popularity could refer to the number of participants.

Author Assumptions, Presuppositions, Underlying Principles

This is another very common question type in the Logical Reasoning section. Here you are again given a short reading passage or paragraph followed by questions asking about the author's possible assumptions, presuppositions, or underlying principles.

To answer this question type, you may wish to first read the question actively. Make a careful note of what part of the paragraph the question refers to. Is the question asking about the conclusion of the passage? (Which of the following assumptions must be made for the author to reasonably arrive at the stated conclusion?) Or about the opening statement? Or about the complete paragraph? (The complete paragraph may be only one or two sentences.)

Keep in mind that assumptions and presuppositions are things taken for granted, or supposed as facts. In the same sense, an underlying principle is the basis for the original statement. It is necessary for the conclusion to be logical. There may be a number of assumptions possible, but in most cases you are looking for the major assumption, not a minor one. In some cases the major assumption will be evident; you will know what the author is assuming before you even get to the answer choices. In other cases, the assumptions are more subtle, and the answer choices will be helpful by stating them for you.

EXAMPLE

1   Use the statement in Example 1 on page 119:

Psychiatrists and laypeople agree that the best sort of adjustment is founded upon acceptance of reality, rather than an escape from it.

The author of this statement assumes that

    (A) there is only one sort of adjustment
    (B) escaping reality is possible
    (C) psychiatrists and laypeople disagree on most things
    (D) psychiatrists never escape reality
    (E) laypeople need many sorts of adjustments

Analysis

The correct answer is (B). In stating "rather than an escape from it [reality]," the author is assuming that escaping reality is possible.

EXAMPLE

2   **It has been said that a weed is a flower whose virtue has not yet been discovered. As if to prove this point, a homeowner**

who was tired of constantly maintaining a pretty lawn and shrubbery decided to let weeds run wild in his yard. The result, so far, has been an array of lively shapes and colors. If everyone in the neighborhood would follow this leader, we could save time, effort, money, and water, and soon have one of the most unusual neighborhoods in the city.

Which one of the following is a basic assumption on which this argument depends?

(A) The neighborhood values convenience more than maintaining an attractive environment.
(B) All the other yards will look like the first homeowner's if the weeds are allowed to run wild.
(C) Allowing the weeds to take over will save money spent on maintaining a lawn.
(D) Other neighborhoods in the city will not follow the example of this neighborhood.
(E) The loss of jobs or revenue to gardeners and garden supply businesses is not so important as the time and money that will be saved.

Analysis

The correct answer is (A). Although all five of the propositions here may well be true, it is (A) that is the basic assumption of the argument. No one who highly values an attractive lawn and yard will want to let weeds take over, so for the argument to have any validity, its speaker must assume that an audience willing to allow the gain in convenience outweighs the loss in appearance of the neighborhood.

EXAMPLE 3

Four of the candidates for reelection in this state had been named among those who had more than 100 overdrafts on the House Bank. Two were Democrats, one was a Republican and one an Independent. One other Republican incumbent candidate had bounced over 50 checks. All of the Democrats favored increased federal spending on education and increased government regulation of firearms, while the Republicans opposed these measures. Of the five incumbents, only the Independent candidate was reelected.

Which one of the following is the most likely principle upon which the majority of voters cast their votes in the elections?

(A) The voters opposed any candidate who had more than 49 overdrafts on the House Bank.

(B) The voters opposed any candidates who favored increased federal spending.

(C) The voters opposed reelection of any members of the two major parties who bounced 50 or more checks.

(D) The voters opposed any candidate who favored increased firearms control.

(E) The voters opposed any candidate who opposed firearms legislation.

Analysis

The correct answer is (C). Since the Independent also bounced more than 100 checks, that cannot be the reason for the defeat of the other four candidates. Since we do not know how the Independent candidate stands on spending for education or on firearms regulation, the only factor to explain his victory is his not belonging to one of the two major parties.

EXAMPLE
4

Time and again studies have shown that 85% of the young adults sent to special juvenile prison farms lead productive lives when they are released. On the other hand, 85% of young adults of the same age who are sent to prisons for adults later return to prisons. The bad influence of the older inmates is permanent. We must expand the number of special juvenile prison farms so that all young adults convicted of crimes can be sent to a penal institution that will not maim them for life.

Which one of the following principles most helps to justify this argument?

(A) It is more expensive to house adult prisoners in prisons than to house young adults on prison farms.

(B) Young adults exposed to bad role models will imitate these models.

(C) Some young adults who are sent to prison farms later become criminals who are sent to prisons for adults.

(D) Some of the young adults who are sent to prisons for adults become productive members of society and never return to prison.

(E) Young adults who have been sent to prison farms on two occasions are more likely to return to prison than young adults who have been sent to prison farms only once.

Analysis

The correct answer is (B). This principle is the basis of the argument to prevent young adults from being exposed to adult felons. If the hope of penologists is to reintegrate young adults into society, these young adults must be kept away from bad models they are likely to imitate. (C) and (D) may be true, but they do not justify the argument. (A) is a practical matter, not a principle to justify the case. (E) would not justify the argument, and might, in fact, be used against it.

EXAMPLE

5
Drunken drivers in our state kill or maim people every day. I understand that only one out of 500 drunken drivers on the highway is flagged down by the police. Also, 50% of these arrests are made on four holiday weekends when the policing of highways is greatly increased. With these odds, I can afford to drink heavily and drive, as long as I am careful not to do so on holiday weekends.

Which one of the following is a necessary premise for the speaker's conclusion in the paragraph above?

(A) The odds against being arrested from drunken driving are greater on weekends than on weekdays.
(B) Fear of arrest is a good reason not to drink and drive.
(C) All that drunken drivers need to fear is being arrested.
(D) The chances of being arrested for drunken driving are greatest on four holiday weekends.
(E) The penalties for drunken driving are often incommensurate with the dangers to the public.

Analysis
The correct answer is (C). The speaker of this passage notes that drunk driving can kill and maim, but his concern is solely with the chances of his being arrested. His conclusion is based on the assumption that no other consequence of drunk driving need trouble him. (A), (B), (D), and (E) are not untrue, but they are not the underlying principle in the speaker's conclusion.

Inferences and Implications

In this very common question type you are asked to "read between the lines." Inferences and implications are not expressed in words in the passage, but may be fairly understood from the passage. If you draw or infer something from a passage, it is called an inference. From the author's point of view, if he or she imparts or implies something, it is called an implication. For the purposes of your exam, you should not be concerned with the differences in the terms, but in understanding what unstated information is in the passage. As you read the passage, focus on the main idea, what the author is suggesting but not actually saying, and what information you can be drawing.

As you approach the choices in inference and implication questions, look for the most direct answer that is not explicitly stated. That is the one that most directly ties back into the passage. Remember that your inference is NOT directly stated in the passage, but is implied by the passage.

EXAMPLE

1   Since 1890, the federal government and the individual states have passed a number of laws against corrupt political practices. But today many feel that political corruption is a regular occurrence, and deeply distrust their public leaders.

Each of the following can be reasonably inferred from the passage EXCEPT

(A) Corrupt political practices have been going on for many years.

(B) The laws against corrupt political practices have not been effective.

(C) The federal government and the individual states are against corrupt political practices.

(D) Many public leaders may be distrusted even though they are not corrupt.

(E) Leaders in private industry are also involved in corrupt political practices.

Analysis

The correct answer is (E). Since the passage does not address leaders in private industry, you could not reasonably make an inference regarding their practices. Though (A), (B), (C), and (D) are not stated, all of them are reasonable inferences from the passage.

EXAMPLE

2   The ability to recognize grammar and usage errors in the writing of others is not the same as the ability to see such errors in one's own writing.

The author of this statement implies that

(A) a writer may not be aware of his own errors

(B) grammar and usage errors are difficult to correct

(C) grammar and usage errors are very common

(D) one often has many abilities

(E) recognizing grammar and usage errors and writing correctly use two different abilities

Analysis

The correct answer is (A). The author's statement points out that recognizing errors in others' work involves a different ability than recognizing errors in one's own work.

Since these abilities are different, writers may not possess both abilities and therefore may not be aware of their own errors. (B) is irrelevant because its focus is "difficulty to correct," which is not addressed. (C) and (D) are incorrect because they are too general, addressing items that are not specific to the statement. (E), which is a common mistake, simply restates information in the statement.

EXAMPLE
3

A poll of journalists who were involved in the Senate campaign revealed that 80% believed Senator Smith's campaign was damaged by press reports about his record during his last six years in office. His opponent, the recently narrowly elected Senator Jones, believes he was benefited by press coverage of his campaign. Journalists believe the election was covered without bias, and the Senator was defeated because of his record, not, as he insists, because of unfair press coverage. Ninety percent of the voters who supported Senator Smith believe the press was unfair in this election, while 85% of the voters who supported Senator Jones thought the coverage free of any bias.

Which one of the following can be inferred from this passage?

(A) The press coverage of the Senate election was free from bias.

(B) Senator Smith lost the election because the press reported his record accurately.

(C) The public's view of the objectivity of the press is likely to be influenced by the election results.

(D) The election was close because of different perceptions of the bias of the press.

(E) Journalists are probably the best judges of bias in political campaign reportage.

Analysis

The correct answer is (C). We cannot be sure whether or not the reporting of the press was biased since the election was close and the pros and cons are nearly equal. The press cannot be counted on to be objective, so (A), (B), and (E) are not reasonable inferences. The large percentage of each candidate's supporters, whose views of the press coincide with the success or defeat of their candidates, strongly support the inference of (C). Whether or not (D) is true, we cannot tell.

Deductions

You may be asked to deduce information from a passage. Deductions are arrived at or attained from general premises—drawing information to a specific piece of information—

from general laws to specific cases. In a deduction, if the general premises are true, then the deduction is necessarily true.

To answer this question type you may wish to first actively read the question. Focus on the general premises to see where they lead. As you continue reading, try to follow the logic as it narrows the possibilities of what must be true.

EXAMPLE

1   Years ago, a nationwide poll concluded that there are more televisions than there are bathtubs in American homes. No doubt that fact remains today, especially in light of the growing popularity of home computers. Now, in addition to owning televisions for entertainment, more and more families are purchasing TV monitors for use with a personal computer. We can safely guess that there are still many more people staring at a picture tube than singing in the shower.

Which one of the following statements can be deduced from this passage?

(A) Personal computers probably cost less than installing a shower or a bathtub.

(B) People can wash themselves without a tub or shower, but they cannot watch television unless they own a television set.

(C) TV monitors will work with personal computers in place of regular computer monitors.

(D) As many computers are sold today as television sets a few years ago.

(E) More television monitors are now used with personal computers than are used to watch commercial television broadcasts.

Analysis

The correct answer is (C). Though (A) and (B) may well be true, they are not deductions that we can make from the information in the passage. But (C) can be deduced since, "more and more families are purchasing TV monitors for use with a personal computer." TV monitors must work with these computers. Otherwise, people would not buy them for that purpose. (D) and (E) may or may not be true, but they are not deductions from the passage, simply additional information.

EXAMPLE

2   Antifreeze lowers the melting point of any liquid to which it is added so that the liquid will not freeze in cold weather. It is commonly used to maintain the cooling system in automobile radiators. Of course, the weather may become so cold that

even antifreeze is not effective, but such a severe climatic condition rarely occurs in well-traveled places.

Which one of the following can be deduced from the passage?

(A) Well-traveled places have means of transportation other
than automobiles.
(B) Antifreeze does not lower the melting point of certain liq-
uids in extreme conditions.
(C) Severe climatic conditions rarely occur.
(D) It is not often that many travelers who use antifreeze
have their cooling systems freeze.
(E) Antifreeze raises the melting point of some liquids.

Analysis

The correct answer is (D). Since severe climatic conditions rarely occur in well-
traveled places, it is necessarily true that "It is not often that many travelers who use antifreeze have their cooling systems freeze." (A) mentions other means of transportation,
which is not addressed in the passage. (B) refers to "certain" liquids, which again are not
addressed. You cannot deduce that "severe climatic conditions rarely occur" (C), because the passage alludes to only well-traveled places. (E) discusses raising the melting
point, which is irrelevant to the passage.

EXAMPLE
3

Sociologists have noted that children today are less "childish"
than ever; when they are still very young, perhaps only six or
seven years old, children are already mimicking adult fash-
ions and leading relatively independent lives. Dressed in de-
signer jeans, an elementary school child is likely to spend
much of every day fending for herself, taking charge of her
own life while waiting for her working parents to arrive home.
Children become less dependent on adults for their day-to-day
decisions.

From the passage above, since children are less dependent on
adults for their day-to-day decisions, it must be true that

(A) children need more supervision
(B) children are growing up faster
(C) children should be completely independent
(D) parents should not leave children home alone
(E) parents need to spend more "quality time" with their chil-
dren

Analysis

The correct answer is (B). Since children today are "less childish than ever," and since they are "less dependent on adults for their day-to-day decisions," they must be "growing up" faster. Although (A), (D), and (E) are probably true, they are not necessarily true and therefore cannot be deduced from the passage.

Parallel Reasoning or Similarity of Logic

In this type you will be given a statement or statements and asked to select the statements that most nearly parallel the originals or use similar logic. First, you should decide whether the original statement is valid. (But don't take too much time on this first step because some of the others may tip you off to the correct choice.) If the statement is valid, your choice must be a valid statement. If the statement is invalid, your choice must be an invalid one. Your choice must preserve the same relationship or comparison.

Second, the direction of connections is important—general to specific (deduction), specific to general (induction), quality to thing, thing to quality, and so on.

Third, the tone of the argument should be the same. If the original has a negative slant, has a positive slant, or changes from negative to positive, then so must your choice.

Fourth, the order of each element is important. Remember: Corresponding elements must be in the same order as the original.

It may be helpful to substitute letters for complex terms or phrases, to simplify confusing situations and help you avoid getting lost in the wording. Direction and order are usually more easily followed by letter substitution.

Remember: Don't correct or alter the original; just reproduce the reasoning.

EXAMPLE

1   Alex said, "All lemons I have tasted are sour; therefore all lemons are sour."

Which one of the following most closely parallels the logic of the above statement?

(A) I have eaten pickles four times and I got sick each time; therefore, if I eat another pickle, I will get sick.

(B) My income has increased each year for the past four years; therefore, it will increase again next year.

(C) I sped to work every day last week and I did not get a ticket; therefore, they do not give tickets for speeding around here any more.

(D) All flormids are green. This moncle is red; therefore, it is not a flormid.

(E) Every teacher I had in school was mean; therefore, all teachers are mean.

Analysis

The correct answer is (E). First, the logic of the original is faulty; therefore, the correct choice must also be faulty, eliminating (D). Next, notice the direction of connections: generalization from a *few* experiences → generalization about *all* similar experiences. (A) and (B) each project the result of a few past experiences to only ONE similar experience. (C) starts from a few experiences, but finishes with a result that implies a change in a specific area. You could assume that "they" used to give tickets here.

EXAMPLE

2

Some serious novelists prefer scientific studies to literary studies. All science fiction writers are more interested in science than in literature. Therefore, some serious novelists are science fiction writers.

Which one of the following is most closely parallel to the flawed reasoning in the argument above?

(A) All trees have leaves. Some cactuses have leaves. Therefore, all trees are cactuses.

(B) All orchestras include violins and all chamber groups include violins. Therefore, some chamber groups are orchestras.

(C) Some animals sleep through the winter and some animals sleep through the summer. Therefore, all animals sleep through either the summer or the winter.

(D) All hotels have restaurants. Some shopping malls have restaurants. Therefore, some shopping malls are hotels.

(E) Some sweaters in this store are made of cotton. All shirts in this store are made of cotton. Therefore, all the wearing apparel in this store is made of cotton.

Analysis

The correct answer is (D). The stem asserts that all science fiction writers prefer science to literature and so do some serious novelists. It then concludes that some serious novelists must be science fiction writers. The "some serious novelists" who prefer science do not have to be science fiction writers, though they share a preference with them. The stem would have to say only science fiction writers prefer science to make this conclusion certain. The two terms used in the stem are "all" and "some," so we can exclude (B) and (C), which use "all" and "all" and "some" and "some." (D), though it gives the "some" term first and the "all" term second, is parallel to the passage.

EXAMPLE

3   **Why do you want to stop smoking?**

(with a
slight twist) Which one of the following most closely parallels the reasoning
of this question?

      (A) Why do you want to go to Italy?
      (B) When will you decide on the offer?
      (C) Will you ever play cards again?
      (D) When do you want to learn to play tennis?
      (E) Which desk do you like better?

Analysis
    The correct answer is (C). This response is the only one that implies that the *action*
has already taken place, as in the original question. To stop smoking, one must have
been smoking *before.* To stop playing cards, one must have been playing cards *before.*
(A) appears to be the closest, but this is only true regarding sentence structure, not reasoning. (B) and (D) are asking about future plans without implying anything about past
actions. (D) does imply past lack of action. (E) merely asks for a comparison.

Argument Exchange

    In this question type, two or more speakers are exchanging arguments or merely dis-
cussing a situation. You will then be asked to choose the statement that most strengthens or weakens either argument. Or you may be asked to find the inconsistency or flaw
in an argument, or to identify the form of argument. In some instances you will be asked
to interpret what one speaker might have thought the other meant by his response.
    To answer these questions, you should first evaluate the strength and completeness
of the statements. Are they general or specific? Do they use absolutes? Are they consistent?
    Second, evaluate the relationship between responses. What kind of response did the
first statement elicit from the second speaker?
    Third, evaluate the intentions of the author in making his remarks. What was his pur-
pose?

EXAMPLE

1   *Tom:* It is impossible to hit off the Yankee pitcher Turley.
      Jim: You're just saying that because he struck you out three
           times yesterday.

    Which one of the following would strengthen Tom's argument
most?

      (A) Tom is a good hitter.
      (B) Turley pitched a no-hitter yesterday.
      (C) Tom has not struck out three times in a game all season.

    (D) Tom has not struck out all season.

    (E) Turley has not given up a hit to Jim or Tom all season.

Analysis

The correct answer is (B). Tom's is a general statement about Turley's relationship to all hitters. All choices except (B) mention only Tom or Jim, not hitters in general.

EXAMPLE

2   *Sid:*   **The recent popularity of hot-air ballooning and bungee-jumping are instances of the latest quest for new types of adventure in the modern world.**

    Phil: **That's ridiculous! Certainly these brightly colored floating globes of air are not modern inventions; rather, they recall the spectacle of county fairs and carnivals from the turn of the century.**

    Sid: **Well, bungee-jumping wasn't around at the turn of the century.**

Phil's best counter to Sid's last statement would be

    (A) But bungee-jumping is used in fairs and carnivals.

    (B) No, bungee-jumping is merely a newer version of a Polynesian ritual hundreds of years old.

    (C) You do know that bungee-jumping is more dangerous than hot-air ballooning.

    (D) Yes, but hot-air ballooning is more popular than bungee-jumping.

    (E) No, but lots of other inventions are adventurous.

Analysis

The correct answer is (B). Sid's point is that these modern adventures are with modern inventions. His last statement is trying to say that bungee-jumping is modern. Phil's best counter would be to point out that bungee-jumping is not new.

EXAMPLE

3   *Al:*   **To be a good parent, one must be patient.**

    Bill: **That's not so. It takes much more than patience to be a good parent.**   Pa → GP

Bill has understood Al's statement to mean that

    (A) if a person is a good parent, he or she will be patient

    (B) if a person is patient, he or she will make a good parent

    (C) some patient people make good parents

(D) some good parents are patient
(E) a person cannot be a good parent unless he or she is
     patient

Analysis

The correct answer is (B). This is a problem in grasping an understanding of necessary and sufficient conditions. Al states that if one is a good parent then one is patient. Patience is necessary to be a good parent. However, Bill's response shows that he (Bill) has inferred that Al considers patience to be sufficient to be a good parent, not just a necessary condition. (B) reflects Bill's mistaken inference. (A) is incorrect because it accurately describes Al's statement. (C) and (D) are incorrect because Al's statement concerns "any" or "all" persons and not "some." (E) is incorrect because it is equivalent to (A) and thus accurately describes Al's statement.

Syllogistic Reasoning

Syllogistic reasoning is a slightly more formal type of reasoning. It deals with an argument that has two premises and a conclusion. This type of question gives you short propositions (premises) and asks you to draw conclusions, valid or invalid. You may be expected to evaluate assumptions—information that is or is not assumed.

First, if possible, simplify the propositions to assist your understanding.
Second, draw diagrams (Venn diagrams; see p. 87 in Chapter 2), if possible.
Third, replace phrases or words with letters to help yourself follow the logic.

EXAMPLE

1   **All couples who have children are happy.**
        All couples either have children or are happy.

        Assuming the above to be true, which one of the following
        CANNOT be true?

        (A) All couples are happy.
        (B) Some couples who are happy have children.
        (C) Some couples who have children are not happy.
        (D) Some couples have happy children.
        (E) Children of happy couples are happy.

Analysis

The correct answer is (C). If all couples who have children are happy, and if all couples who don't have children are happy, then all couples are happy. Simplifying the two statements to "all couples are happy" makes this question much more direct and easier to handle. Thus (C) is false, since it contradicts the first statement; we have no information about children.

EXAMPLE

2   All As are Bs.
Some Cs are As.

Which one of the following is warranted based upon the above?

    (A) All Bs are As.
    ✓(B) Some Cs are Bs.
    (C) All Bs are Cs.
    (D) No Bs are As.
    (E) All Cs are Bs.

Analysis

The correct choice is (B). Here is a diagram of the original information:

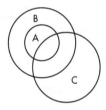

With this diagram, the following is evident:

    (A) "All Bs are As" is false.
    (B) "Some Cs are Bs" is true.
    (C) "All Bs are Cs" is false.
    (D) "No Bs are As" is false. If all As are Bs, then some Bs must be As.
    (E) "All Cs are Bs" is false.

EXAMPLE

3   In this question, the second premise shows up in the actual question.

If the Dodgers do not finally win a championship for their fans this season, the team's manager will definitely not return to guide the club next year.

It follows logically from the statement above that, if the Dodgers win a championship this season, then next year the team's manager

    (A) will definitely not return
    (B) will probably not return

(C) will probably return
(D) will definitely return
(E) may or may not return

Analysis

The correct answer is (E). The passage states, "if the Dodgers do not win the championship [condition A], then the manager will not return [condition B]. Thus we have if A then B. The question then asks, what follows if they *do* win the championship [a negation of condition A]? If A implies B, the negation of A [if the Dodgers do win the championship] does *not* imply the negation of B [the manager will return]. Hence, condition A or not A (win or lose) may be the case; the manager may or may not return. (C) is possible, but he may also not return. All we know for sure is that if he loses, he positively won't return.

Conclusions

Here you will be given a list of conditionals, statements, or a short paragraph, and asked to follow the logic to reach a valid conclusion.

In this type, you will first want to underline key terms to eliminate looking at excess wording.

Second, mark the direction of each statement. Where does it start and end? What connection is it making?

Third, look for the "kicker" statement. That's the one that starts the chain reaction; it gives you the information to work with other statements.

If there is no "kicker" statement, carefully check how the information given in one statement is relative to the information given in the next statement. This relationship may be enough to help you understand the reasoning.

In checking the validity of a conclusion, you should be looking for a key statement that leads you as directly as possible to that conclusion. Sometimes, if the choices don't start with the word "therefore," you may wish to insert the word "therefore" before the answer choices to help you see which one follows logically.

EXAMPLE

1

Senator Jones will vote for the Pork bill if he is reelected. If the Pork bill passes, then Senator Jones was not reelected. Senator Jones was reelected.

Which one of the following can be concluded from these statements?

(A) Senator Jones assisted in the passage of the Pork bill.
(B) The passage of the Pork bill carried Senator Jones to victory.
(C) Senator Jones voted against the Pork bill, but it passed anyway.

(D) The Pork bill didn't pass, even though Senator Jones voted for it.

(E) The Pork bill was defeated by a large majority.

Analysis

The correct answer is (D). Notice that the "kicker" statement that started the chain reaction is "Senator Jones was reelected." From this, we know that he voted for the Pork bill. But the Pork bill could not have passed; otherwise, he could not have been reelected.

EXAMPLE

2   Meteorology may qualify as a science, but there is a great deal of guesswork involved as well. Even with increased knowledge about wind currents and weather patterns, and the most sophisticated equipment, forecasters' predictions are often wrong. Even the movement of a phenomenon as prominent as a hurricane cannot be determined very far in advance.

Which one of the following is the best conclusion to the passage?

(A) Therefore, we should be especially skeptical of weather predictions for the distant future.

(B) Therefore, we cannot control the weather, but we can predict it.

(C) Therefore, even though we cannot accurately predict the weather now, it will be possible in the near future.

(D) Therefore, since we cannot predict the weather, our aim should be to control it.

(E) Therefore, meteorology is a worthless science.

Analysis

The correct answer is (A). The passage points out that, although we can to some extent predict the weather, we are often wrong. This leads us to the conclusion that we cannot predict far in advance. (A) is the best answer. (B) and (D) do not follow since the passage does not mention controlling the weather. (C) does not follow since the passage does not address our gaining additional knowledge or more sophisticated equipment to help us in the future. The passage does not condemn meteorology, so (E) can be eliminated.

Logical Flaws

This common question type gives you a passage, statement, or argument, and asks you to find, understand, analyze, or name the type of flaw in the reasoning.

As you watch for logical flaws, notice that some are very evident especially if the passage or argument seems nonsensical. Others are very subtle, and need a second look. If you don't spot the flaw immediately upon reading the passage, let the choices help. Remember, the choices are showing you some possibilities.

Also, reading the question first will stop you from trying to make complete sense from a nonsensical passage, or trying to follow the logic or reasoning when, by design of the question, it does not follow. You see that the question itself warned you that there was a flaw in the reasoning.

EXAMPLE

1   The new American revolution is an electronic one. Advances in sophisticated circuitry have yielded more gadgets than anyone could have imagined only a few years ago: calculators as small as a wristwatch and automobile dashboards full of digital readouts are two of the many products that have enhanced the quality of life. But we may become so dependent on solid-state circuits to do our thinking that we may forget how to do it ourselves. Certain birds living on islands where there were no predators have, in time, lost their ability to fly. We may just as easily lose the ability to perform even the simplest mathematical calculation without the aid of an electronic gadget.

Which one of the following best describes the flaw in the reasoning in this passage?

(A) It assumes that a temporal sequence implies a causal relation.

(B) It generalizes from one instance to every other instance of the same type.

(C) It draws an analogy between two very different situations.

(D) It wrongly assumes that no new and better electronic devices will be invented.

(E) It assumes that what happens in America also happens in the rest of the world.

Analysis

The correct answer is (C). The flaw in the reasoning here is the comparison of two wholly unlike situations. The analogy compares men and birds and compares an event in the evolutionary history of certain birds that happened under unique circumstances over vast periods of time to what is supposed to be similar situations in the modern world, but which has in fact no real similarity.

EXAMPLE

2   With the continued water shortage in our area, the Water Department has had to restrict the use of water during daylight hours and to increase the cost of water to consumers. An average water bill has risen twenty-four dollars a year for three years in a row. **Three years from now, our water costs will be astronomical.**

A major flaw in the reasoning is that it

    (A) relies upon figures that are imprecise to support a conclusion

    (B) fails to indicate exactly how high expenses will be in three years

    (C) assumes the conditions of the past three years will continue

    (D) overlooks the possibility that conservation methods may improve in the next five years

    (E) ignores the likelihood of the high cost driving down the water usage

Analysis

The correct answer is (C). To follow the author's line of reasoning, the author must assume that "the conditions of the past three years will continue." This assumption is flawed since the conditions could change. The conclusion is therefore based on a faulty assumption.

EXAMPLE

3   In 1982 and 1983, when the limit on class size in grades 7, 8, and 9 was 25, our junior high school students had an average reading score of 79 and an average math score of 75 in the state tests administered at the end of grade 9. But, in 1984 and 1985, when the limit on class size was raised to 28, our junior high school students had average scores of 75 in the state reading tests and 75 in the state math tests. The increase in class size limitations has brought about the decline in state test scores.

Which one of the following is a major flaw in the reasoning in this passage?

    (A) The author believes that test scores are accurate.

    (B) The author fails to realize that some students' math test scores have not declined, though the average has.

    (C) The author regards scores in math tests more important than scores in reading.

    (D) The author assumes class size has caused the variation in test scores.

    (E) The author does not know whether or not class size actually increased.

Analysis

The correct answer is (D). Since the class size limitations were increased and only the reading scores decreased, the author came to the conclusion that class size limitations caused the decline. But the math scores did not decrease, which would lead one to believe other factors are involved in the scores' decline. Also, because there were different class size limitations does not mean the sizes of the classes were different. The author's reasoning is flawed by his assumption that class size caused the variation. (E) is a fact, but is not the flaw in the author's reasoning.

Passage Completion

This question type requires you to choose a phrase or sentence that best completes the passage.

It is initially important that you preserve the meaning of the passage, completing or maintaining the same thought. Unity (same subject) and coherence (order of thoughts) should be carefully noted. Second, it is important that the words you choose fit stylistically, use the same vocabulary, and are from the same context. Many times you will be able to eliminate some choices that "just don't sound good."

EXAMPLE

1   English, with its insatiable and omnivorous appetite for imported food, has eaten until it has become linguistically unbuttoned. And the glutton has cloaked his paunch with the pride of the gourmet. We would not imply that a large vocabulary is bad, but rather that it is self-destructive if uncontrolled by _____.

Which one of the following is the best completion according to the context of this passage?

(A) a smattering of slang
(B) a fine sense of distinction
(C) the removal of all but Anglo-Saxon derivatives
(D) a professor who knows the limits of good usage
(E) an unbuttoned tongue

Analysis

The correct answer is (B). The passage describes the English language itself; therefore, references to individuals, (D) and (E), are inappropriate. They do not maintain the same general level of thought. Since the author does not condemn a large and distinguished vocabulary, (A) and (C), which do, are both poor choices. (B) preserves the meaning of the passage and fits stylistically.

EXAMPLE

2   In a reversal of past trends, last year more lawyers left courtroom practice to go into the teaching of law than vice versa.

Since courtroom practice on average yields a much higher annual income, this shift discredits the theory that _____.

Which one of the following best completes the last sentence in
the passage above?

    (A) incomes in the teaching of law will at some future time
        match those of cour

    (B) the change in profes
        to increase their in

    (C) more lawyers have
        past few years than

    (D) lawyers under 40 y
        professions for fina

    (E) lawyers are likely
        which the income i

Analysis

The correct answer is (E). The passage argues a connection between lawyers, profession changes, and income. Any answer choice that does not address those items cannot be a logical conclusion. (E) addresses the three key items and offers a conclusion
that is logically consistent with the apparent change from higher to lower paying profes-
sions. (A) is irrelevant because the passage does not address the "future." (B) is irrelevant because the passage does not address "prediction." (C) is irrelevant because the
passage does not address "remained" in a profession, only changing. (D) is irrelevant
because the passage does not address the "age" of lawyers.

Word Reference

Here a word, or group of words, is taken out of context, and you are asked either
what the word or words mean or what they refer to. In this type of question, first consider the passage as a whole, then carefully examine the key word or words surrounding the selected ones.

EXAMPLE

English, with its insatiable and omnivorous appetite for imported food, has eaten until it has become linguistically unbuttoned. And the glutton has cloaked his paunch with the
pride of the gourmet. We would not imply that a large vocabulary is bad, but rather that it is self-destructive if uncontrolled
by a fine sense of distinction.

As used here, the word "glutton" refers to

    (A) an English language with a lack of Anglo-Saxon derivation
    (B) one who never stops talking about foreign food
    (C) an English language bursting with pride

(D) one who is bilingual
(E) an English language bursting with derivatives from foreign languages

Analysis
The correct answer is (E). The passage, as a whole, is commenting on the English language, and (E) is the only choice that equates "glutton" with the subject of the passage.

IN CONCLUSION

As you have seen, Logical Reasoning includes a potpourri of problem types all requiring common sense and reasonableness in the answers. You should take care in underlining what is being asked so that you do not (for example) accidentally look for the valid conclusion when the invalid one is asked for. Because of the nature of the Logical Reasoning problems, it is very easy to get tangled in a problem and lose your original thought, spending too much time on the question. If you feel that you have become trapped or stuck, take a guess and come back later if you have time. Remember that you must work within the context of the question, so do not bring in outside experiences or otherwise complicate a problem. The Logical Reasoning question is looking not for training in formal logic, but just for common sense and reasonableness.

Remember: Logical Reasoning accounts for 50% of your LSAT score.

REVIEW OF SOME GENERAL STRATEGIES FOR LOGICAL REASONING

THE PASSAGE
Read *actively,* circling key words.
Note major issue and supporting points.

THE QUESTION
Preread (before reading the passage) *actively.*
Note its reference.
Watch out for *unstated* ideas:
assumptions, implications/inferences, and sometimes conclusions.

ANSWER CHOICES
Sometimes there may not be a *perfect* answer; thus choose the *best* of the five choices.
Use the elimination strategy.
Note that "wrong" words in a choice make that choice incorrect.
Watch for those off-topic key words.

EXTRA PRACTICE: LOGICAL REASONING

Directions: In this section you will be given brief statements or passages and be required to evaluate the reasoning involved. In some instances, more than one choice will appear to be a possible answer. You are to choose the *best* answer. Use common sense and reasonableness in making your selection; then mark the correct answer.

Use the answer sheet found on page 163.

Questions 1–3

Robots have the ability to exhibit programmed behavior. Their performance can range from the simplest activity to the most complex group of activities. They not only can build other robots, but also can rebuild themselves. Physically they can resemble humans, yet mentally they cannot. Even the most highly advanced robot does not have the capacity to be creative, have emotions, or think independently.

1. From the passage above, which one of the following must be true?

   (A) Robots could eventually take over the world.
   (B) The most complex group of activities involves being creative.
   (C) A robot should last forever.
   (D) Emotions, creativity, and independent thought can be written as programs.
   (E) Building other robots involves independent thinking.

2. The author of this passage would agree that

   (A) robots would eventually be impossible to control
   (B) in the near future, robots will be able to think independently
   (C) robots have reached their peak of development

   (D) there are dangers in robots that think for themselves
   (E) there are some tasks that are better done by robots than by humans

3. The author's assertions would be weakened by pointing out that

   (A) humans exhibit programmed behavior for the first few years of life
   (B) robots' behavior is not always predictable
   (C) building other robots requires independent training
   (D) internal feeling is not always exhibited
   (E) the most complex group of activities necessitates independent thinking

4. Life is like a parachute jump—you had better get it right the first time.

   The author of this statement assumes that

   (A) if nothing is ventured, nothing is gained
   (B) risk-taking is foolish
   (C) you only live once
   (D) starting over is possible but difficult
   (E) a second try is usually no better than the first

[handwritten notes at top: "NO Blos Zb is one month", "B, t → All Jan → B, t", "Jan ≠ rest of Year", "All Jan → B, t"]

5. No plant in the botanical gardens blossoms twice in the same month. All of the plants in the botanical gardens that blossom in January are grown from either bulbs or tubers. None of the plants that blossom in January will flower again later in the year.

If the statements above are true, which one of the following must also be true?

(A) No plant in the botanical garden grown from a bulb will blossom in October.

(B) No plants in the botanical garden blossom twice in the year if they blossom first in January.

(C) None of the plants in the botanical gardens that blossom in June are grown from tubers.

(D) All of the plants in the botanical gardens grown from bulbs or tubers that did not blossom in January will flower later in the year.

(E) All plants in the botanical gardens grown from bulbs or tubers flower in January.

6. The simplest conceivable situation in which one human being may communicate with another is one in which structurally complementary communicants have been conditioned to associate the same words with the same things.

The sentence that would best complete this thought is:

(A) Therefore, dictionaries are of little value to foreigners.

(B) Therefore, man cannot communicate effectively with animals.

(C) Therefore, communication is a matter of relation.

(D) Therefore, communication is simplest following a common experience.

(E) Therefore, communication is dependent on complementary structures.

7. In a nationwide survey, four out of five dentists questioned recommended sugarless gum for their patients who chew gum.

Which one of the following would most weaken the above endorsement for sugarless gum?

(A) Only five dentists were questioned.

(B) The dentists were not paid for their endorsements.

(C) Only one of the dentists questioned chewed sugarless gum.

(D) Patients do not do what their dentists tell them to do.

(E) Sugarless gum costs much more than regular gum.

8. In Tom and Angie's class, everyone likes drawing or painting or both, but Angie does not like painting.

Which one of the following statements cannot be true?

(A) Angie likes drawing.

(B) Tom likes drawing and painting.

(C) Everyone in the class who does not like drawing likes painting.

(D) No one in the class likes painting.

(E) Tom dislikes drawing and painting.

9. *Mark:* The big test is tomorrow and I didn't study. I suppose I'll just have to cheat. I know it is wrong, but I have to get a good grade on the test.
Amy: I don't think that's a good idea. Just go to the teacher, tell the truth, and maybe you can get a postponement.

Amy attacks Mark's argument by

(A) attacking his reasoning
(B) applying personal pressure
(C) implying that good triumphs over evil
(D) presenting another alternative
(E) suggesting a positive approach

Questions 10–11

The microwave oven has become a standard appliance in many kitchens, mainly because it offers a fast way of cooking food. Yet, some homeowners believe that the ovens are still not completely safe. Microwaves, therefore, should not be standard appliances until they are more carefully researched and tested.

10. Which one of the following, if true, would most weaken the conclusion of the passage above?

(A) Homeowners often purchase items despite knowing they may be unsafe.
(B) Those homeowners in doubt about microwave safety ought not to purchase microwaves.
(C) Research and testing of home appliances seldom reveal safety hazards.

(D) Microwaves are not as dangerous as steam irons, which are used in almost every home.
(E) Homeowners often purchase items that they do not need.

11. Which one of the following, if true, would most strengthen the conclusion of the passage above?

(A) Homeowners often doubt the advertised safety of all new appliances.
(B) Speed of food preparation is not the only concern of today's homeowner.
(C) Modern homeowners have more free time than ever before.
(D) Food preparation has become almost a science, with more complicated and involved recipes.
(E) Many microwave ovens have been found to leak radioactive elements.

12. A few mimes are sad.
All mimes are always funny.
Children cannot be sad and funny at the same time.

Given that the foregoing are true, which one of the following must be true?

(A) There are no sad children.
(B) No child is funny.
(C) No sad mimes are children.
(D) Mimes cannot be sad and funny simultaneously.
(E) All funny mimes are sad.

13. According to a count of the men and women listed in the Glenarm Telephone Directory, there are 10,000 more men than women in this city of only 100,000. But according to the last census report, the population of Glenarm is 55 percent female. All of the following can be used to explain this discrepancy EXCEPT

(A) not all phone users list their names in the directory
(B) married couples are more likely to use the husband's than the wife's name in the directory
(C) the census report has been faulted for undercounting the minority population of large cities
(D) the phone book count may be misled by initials or names that are not gender specific
(E) there are many more females under 14 than males

14. Given that this rock is white in color, it must be quartz.

The foregoing conclusion can be properly drawn if it is true that

(A) only quartz rocks are white in color
(B) quartz rocks are generally white in color
(C) other white rocks have proved to be quartz
(D) few other types of rocks are white in color
(E) all quartz rocks are white in color

Questions 15–16

"Even the smallest restaurant in Paris serves better breads than the best restaurants in New York," the visiting chef said. He was complaining about the quality of the bread available in America. "I was trained in France," he added, "so I understand bread-making. But in America, there are hardly any good bakers. You can tell just by looking at the roll baskets. In every restaurant I have visited in New York, the roll baskets are still full on every table at the end of the meal."

15. The chef's conclusions depends on all of the following assumptions EXCEPT

(A) if the bread is good, all of it will be consumed
(B) the quality of a restaurant can be determined by the quality of its breads
(C) all good bakers are professionals
(D) the norm for good bread-making is France
(E) restaurants do not replenish roll baskets

16. All of the following are errors in the reasoning of the speaker in the passage above EXCEPT

(A) the argument takes as fact what is unproven personal opinion
(B) the argument assumes that New York restaurants represent American baking
(C) the speaker claims complete knowledge of a large number of small restaurants in Paris
(D) the speaker claims that he knows how to bake bread
(E) the examples the speaker cites of good and bad bread makers are vague and unspecific

Questions 17–18

Some American auto factories are beginning to resemble their Japanese counterparts. In many Japanese factories, the workers enjoy the same status and privileges as their bosses. Everyone works in harmony, and there is much less of the tension and anger that results when one group dominates another.

17. With which one of the following would the author of the above passage most likely agree?

   (A) American work environments ought to emulate Japanese auto factories.
   (B) Japanese automobiles are better built than American automobiles.
   (C) Tension in the workplace enhances worker productivity.
   (D) Japanese culture differs so much from American culture that it precludes any overlap of styles.
   (E) Striving for managerial status induces worker productivity.

18. The argument gives logically relevant support for which one of the following conclusions?

   (A) Some American auto factories are experiencing changes in their work environments.
   (B) American auto workers envy their Japanese counterparts.
   (C) There is no tension or anger in Japanese factories.
   (D) Decrease in tension leads to higher productivity.
   (E) There is no tension or anger in American factories that follow Japanese models.

19. When we approach land, we usually sight birds. The lookout has just sighted birds.

   Which one of the following represents the most logical conclusion based upon the foregoing statements?

   √ (A) The conjecture that we are approaching land is strengthened.
   (B) Land is closer than it was before the sighting of the birds.
   (C) We are approaching land.
   (D) We may or may not be approaching land.
   (E) We may not be approaching land.

20. The presence of the gas Nexon is a necessary condition, but not a sufficient condition, for the existence of life on the planet Plex.

   On the basis of the foregoing, which of the following would also be true?

   (A) If life exists on Plex, then only the gas Nexon is present.
   (B) If life exists on Plex, then the gas Nexon may or may not be present.
   √ (C) If life exists on Plex, then the gas Nexon is present.
   (D) If no life exists on Plex, Nexon cannot be present.
   (E) If no life exists on Plex, Nexon is the only gas present.

21. The absence of the liquid Flennel is a sufficient condition for the cessation of life on the planet Fluke, but it is not a necessary condition.

   On the basis of the foregoing, which of the following would also be true?

   √ (A) If life on Fluke ceased to exist, there would have to have been an absence of the liquid Flennel.

(B) If all liquid Flennel were removed from Fluke, life there would surely perish.

(C) If all liquid Flennel were removed from Fluke, life there might or might not cease.

(D) If all liquid Flennel were removed from Fluke, the cessation of life would depend upon other conditions.

(E) Life on Fluke cannot cease so long as Flennel is present.

22. The gas rates in Edina are low only for the first 30 therms used each month; the next 30 cost twice as much, and all gas over 60 therms costs four times as much as the first 30. The city has very cold winters and warm summers. To heat an average-size two-bedroom home in the winter by gas is prohibitively expensive, but not as costly as electric heating. Consequently

All of the following are logical conclusions to this passage EXCEPT

(A) most homeowners use oil heating

(B) many homes are kept at temperatures below 70 degrees in the winter

(C) the consumption of gas is lower in the winter than in the summer

(D) electric cooling is more common than electric heating

(E) many homes have wood burning stoves and fireplaces

23. If the poodle was reared at Prince Charming Kennels, then it is a purebred.

The foregoing statement can be deduced logically from which one of the following statements?

(A) Every purebred poodle is reared at Prince Charming Kennels or at another AKC approved kennel.

(B) The poodle in question was bred at either Prince Charming Kennels or at another AKC approved kennel.

(C) The poodle in question either is a purebred or looks remarkably like a purebred.

(D) The majority of poodles reared at Prince Charming Kennels are purebred.

(E) There are no dogs reared at Prince Charming Kennels that are not purebred.

24. There is no reason to eliminate the possibility of an oil field existing beneath the Great Salt Lake. Therefore, we must undertake the exploration of the Salt Lake's bottom.

The foregoing argument assumes which one of the following?

(A) Exploration of the Salt Lake's bottom has not been previously proposed.

(B) An oil field located beneath the lake would be easy to identify.

(C) The Great Salt Lake is the only large inland body of water beneath which an oil field may lie.

(D) The quest for oil is a sufficient motive to undertake exploration of the Salt Lake's bottom.

(E) An oil field exists beneath the Great Salt Lake.

Questions 25–26

My course of study had led me to believe that all mental and moral feelings and qualities, whether of a good or of a bad kind, were the results of association; that we love one thing, and hate another, take pleasure in one sort of action or contemplation, and pain in another sort, through the clinging of pleasurable or painful ideas to those things, from the effect of education or of experience. As a corollary from this, I was convinced, that the object of education should be to form the strongest possible associations of the salutary class; associations of pleasure with all things beneficial to the great whole. It now seemed to me, on retrospect, that my teachers had occupied themselves but superficially with the means of forming and keeping up these salutary associations. They seemed to have trusted altogether to the old familiar instruments, praise and blame, reward and punishment. I did not doubt that by these means, begun early, and applied unremittingly, intense associations of pain and pleasure, especially of pain, might be created, and might produce desires and aversions capable of lasting undiminished to the end of life. But there must always be something artificial and casual in associations thus produced.

25. By "salutary" the author means

   (A) "the strongest possible associations"
   (B) ideas that "salute" one's mind
   (C) capable of giving pain
   (D) promoting some good purpose
   (E) those earning a middle-class income or better

26. All of the following questions are answered in the passage EXCEPT

   (A) Is there any sort of thinking that is not associational?
   (B) Is schooling the only cause of our lifelong "desires and aversions"?
   (C) What else besides education causes these associations?
   (D) What do teachers praise and what do they blame?
   (E) How long would the desires and aversions last?

27. The San Diego Chargers practice expertly for long hours every day and keep a written log of their errors.

   The above statement is an example of which one of the following assumptions?

   (A) Practice makes perfect.
   (B) To err is human.
   (C) People make mistakes; that's why they put erasers on pencils.
   (D) Practice is what you know, and it will help to make clear what now you do not know.
   (E) Writing is a mode of learning.

28. Pine trees may be taller than any other tree. Pines are never shorter than the shortest palms, and some palms may exceed the height of some pines. Peppertrees are always taller than palm trees. Peach trees are shorter than peppertrees but not shorter than all palms.

   Given the foregoing, which one of the following would be true?

   (A) Peach trees may be shorter than pine trees.
   (B) Peppertrees may be shorter than some peach trees.

(C) Every pine is taller than every palm.

(D) A particular palm could not be taller than a particular pine.

(E) Now and then a peach tree may be taller than a pepper.

29. Most popular paperback novels are of low intellectual quality; therefore *Splendor Behind the Billboard,* an unpopular paperback novel, is probably of high intellectual quality.

The foregoing argument is most like which one of the following?

(A) Most locusts inhabit arid places; therefore, locusts are probably found in all deserts.

(B) Most acts of criminal violence have declined in number during the past few years; therefore, law enforcement during this period has improved.

(C) Most people who stop drinking gain weight; therefore, if Carl does not cease drinking, he will probably not gain weight.

(D) Most nations run by autocratic governments do not permit a free press; therefore the country of Endorff, which is run by an autocratic government, probably does not have a free press.

(E) Most new motor homes are equipped with air conditioning; therefore, Jim's new motor home may not be equipped with air conditioning.

Questions 30–31

Jane states, "All mammals have hair. This creature possesses no hair. Therefore, it is not a mammal."

30. Which one of the following most closely parallels the logic of Jane's statement?

(A) All reptiles have scales. This creature possesses scales. Therefore, it is a reptile.

(B) All physics tests are difficult. This is not a physics test. Therefore, it is not difficult.

(C) All American cars are poorly constructed. Every car sold by Fred was poorly constructed. Therefore, Fred sells only American cars.

(D) All mammals do not have hair. This creature possesses hair. Therefore, it may be a mammal.

(E) All lubricants smell. This liquid does not have an odor. Therefore, it is not a lubricant.

31. Which one of the following, if true, would most weaken Jane's argument?

(A) Animals other than mammals have hair.

(B) Some mammals do not have hair.

(C) Mammals have more hair than nonmammals.

(D) One could remove the hair from a mammal.

(E) Reptiles may have hair.

Questions 32–33

A recent study of Hodgkin's disease in young adults has examined a large number of sets of twins, half of them identical and half nonidentical. Identical twins have the same genetic makeup, but like any other siblings nonidentical twins share only about 50 percent of their genetic material. In the study of twins with Hodgkin's disease, the researchers found that the chances of the second of a set of identical twins also developing the disease was 100 times higher than in the case of the sibling of a nonidentical twin, or of any other average individual. The number of cases where both identical twins were affected was, however, not a very large proportion of the identical twin pairs.

32. Based on the information in this passage, we can infer all of the following EXCEPT

  (A) genetic inheritance is one factor in determining the susceptibility to Hodgkin's disease

  (B) if one twin of a set of nonidentical twins develops Hodgkin's disease, the chances of the second twin developing Hodgkin's disease are no greater than that of a person who is not a twin

  (C) Hodgkin's disease is more likely to appear first in a twin who is one of a pair of identical twins than one of a pair of nonidentical twins

  (D) genetics alone is not sufficient to cause Hodgkin's disease

  (E) the chances of the second of a pair of identical twins whose twin has developed Hodgkin's disease also developing the disease are not very high

33. For which reason of the following are studies of identical twins likely to be valuable to medical research?

  (A) Identical twins are usually raised in the same environments.

  (B) Researchers using identical twins can discern differences more easily.

  (C) Identical twins may differ psychologically, but not physically.

  (D) Identical twins may reveal information related to genetics.

  (E) It is easier to arrange medical examinations at the same hospital for identical twins than for unrelated persons.

34. The frog population in the lake each year is determined by the number of two avian predators: egrets and blue herons. The weather has little effect on the egret population, but the number of herons varies according to the rainfall in the area. Therefore, a greatly changing frog population in the lake three years in a row will probably occur when the annual rainfall fluctuates widely for three years.

Of the following arguments, which one most closely resembles this paragraph in the pattern of its reasoning?

  (A) The annual profit or loss of Acme Desk Company depends chiefly on the number of new office buildings in the city and on the stability of the mortgage rates. In a year when mortgage rates fluctuate, the building rate is also likely to fluctuate.

  (B) The parking lot at the university is filled to capacity on nights when the business school holds classes at the same hours as the extension college. If there are classes at the business school and no classes at the extension college, or classes at the extension college and no classes at the business school, the parking lots are three-quarters full.

(C) The restaurant can sell a beef and cheese pizza for a one dollar profit if the price of cheese remains at less than two dollars per pound and the price of beef at less than one dollar per pound. For the last six months, cheese has sold at $1.95 per pound. Since the pizzas have failed to earn a profit of one dollar in this period, the price of beef must have risen to above one dollar per pound.

(D) Farmers in the valley can legally purchase federal water at a reduced rate only if they raise cotton or if their farms are no larger than 960 acres. Several of the farmers who continue to purchase federal water at the reduced rate are raising only alfalfa. Therefore, their farms must be larger than 960 acres.

(E) A cake will not collapse in the oven if the eggs have been brought to room temperature before mixing or if the sugar syrup is at a temperature above 140 degrees. The cake must have collapsed because the eggs were too cold or the sugar was not hot enough.

35. Scientific studies have shown that second-hand tobacco smoke in the workplace greatly increases the number of workers who take more than fifteen days of sick-leave and the number of workers who suffer serious respiratory ailments. It has also been shown that the number of workers who die of lung cancer is twice as high in workplaces that permit smoking than in workplaces that do not. Therefore, the state must pass laws that require all companies to forbid smoking in the workplace.

Which one of the following is the underlying principle in this argument?

(A) Every individual has a responsibility for the well-being of every other individual with whom he or she comes into daily contact.

(B) Employers who do not take care of the health of their workers risk increasing losses from absenteeism each year.

(C) States must be permitted to outlaw any dangerous substances or implements.

(D) States must be responsible for the safety of the workplace of all businesses in their jurisdiction.

(E) Workers must be permitted to make their own decisions about their workplace.

36. For the post-election festivities, no
    athlete was invited to the White House
    unless he or she was more than 35
    years old. No one older than 35 was
    both an athlete and invited to the White
    House.

    Which one of the following conclusions
    can be logically drawn from the
    statements above?

    (A) No one but athletes were invited to
        the White House.
    (B) No athlete was invited to the White
        House.
    (C) Only persons older than 35 were
        invited to the White House.
    (D) No one over 35 was invited to the
        White House.
    (E) Some athletes over 35 were invited
        to the White House.

37. At the Brightman Diet Center, 20 men
    and women who wished to lose ten
    pounds undertook a program that
    included an hour of exercise and a limit
    of 200 calories for breakfast and lunch
    each day. A second group of 20 men
    and women, similar in age and weight
    to the first group, exercised for only
    half an hour and ate up to 500 calories
    for breakfast and lunch each day.
    Surprisingly, at the end of three weeks,
    all 20 who had exercised less and
    consumed more calories at breakfast
    and lunch had lost more weight than
    members of the other group.

    Which one of the following best
    explains these unexpected results?

    (A) Some of those who lost more
        weight exercised longer than the
        half hour.
    (B) Forty people is too small a sample
        to produce any meaningful
        statistics.

    (C) The exercise of some of the
        members of those who lost more
        weight was more vigorous than
        that of members of the other
        group.
    (D) Those in the group that ate 500
        calories for breakfast and lunch
        chose foods lower in fat and
        cholesterol than those in the other
        group.
    (E) The group that had eaten more and
        exercised less during the day ate
        fewer calories at dinner than those
        in the other group.

38. Of the 8,000 American victims of
    isochemic optic neuropathy, most are
    over 60. The condition occurs suddenly
    and normally in only one eye. Its cause
    is unknown, though doctors agree that
    an interruption of the blood flow to the
    optic nerve is a major factor. Untreated,
    most people recover full vision in six
    months. The most common treatment,
    an operation called optic nerve
    decompression surgery, has proven to
    be less effective than no treatment at
    all. Fewer regain their sight after the
    operation, and those who do require
    nine months to do so.

    The conclusions of this paragraph
    would be most useful in support of an
    argument for

    (A) increasing federal supervision of
        surgical procedures
    (B) reducing the cost of surgical
        procedures
    (C) reducing the number of surgical
        procedures
    (D) expanding federal oversight of
        cosmetic surgery
    (E) funding a study of isochemic optic
        neuropathy in men and women
        under 40

39. No one who is a member of the tennis team will smoke cigarettes. No first-rate athlete smokes cigarettes. Therefore, only first-rate athletes will become members of the tennis team.

The reasoning here is in error since the conclusion does not allow for the possibility of

(A) a nonsmoker on the tennis team who is a second-rate athlete
(B) a first-rate athlete who doesn't play tennis
(C) an ex-smoker who is a first-rate athlete
(D) a nonsmoker who is not a first-rate athlete
(E) a smoker who is a first-rate tennis player

40. The sale of clothing featuring characters from children's television programs such as Barney or the Power Rangers has increased enormously in the last five years. The number of children who watch television must also have increased greatly in the same period.

Which one of the following would fail to support this conclusion and at the same time explain the rise in clothing sales?

(A) The relaxation of trade barriers has substantially reduced the cost of Asian-made clothes in the last five years.
(B) Five years ago, the most popular children's television program, Sesame Street, was seen on educational television stations.
(C) In many areas, the three most popular children's television programs are carried on both cable and network television stations.

(D) There are now several stations, such as the Disney Channel or Nickelodeon, which intend most or all of their programs for a young or very young audience.
(E) Television programs directed at children have been increasingly attacked in the last five years for excessive violence.

41. Alfred Thomason, one of the ten brokers in the mortgage department of Kean and Landers, will certainly write more than $5 million in mortgages this year. Last year the department's sales totaled more than $50 million and this year's totals will be just as high.

Which one of the following contains the same kind of reasoning error as this passage?

(A) Jacobson expects the dahlias he exhibits in this year's flower show will win a prize. His dahlias failed to win in last year's exhibition, but he believes that the cause was a jealous judge who is not on this year's panel.
(B) The debate squad is expected to win the state tournament in May. They have won all nine of their debates this year, including a large tournament in Memphis competing against most of the teams highly regarded in the state competition.
(C) The Vasquez family plans to drive from Boston to Scottsdale in four days. Last winter the drive took six days, but they were delayed by bad weather in New England, Pennsylvania, and New Mexico.
(D) South Texas State's Edward Meany will represent his college in a two-day tournament for top golfers from 30 different colleges in the

state. Since the team from South Texas State easily won the state intercollegiate golf championship, Meany should have no trouble winning this tournament.

(E) Seeded first in the NCAA championships in Atlanta, Laura Lomax should breeze through the tournament. She already has won the two tournaments she has entered, and has a 38-match winning streak.

42. Although it is subject to the variations of currencies and interest rates, the Asian influx is now a major factor in the Australian real estate market. Although many Australians are nervous about the waves of Asian immigration, their economy welcomes the purchase of Australian properties by investors from Asia who have no residential rights. Foreigners are permitted to purchase up to half of the units of a condominium, provided they do so before the condo is first occupied. They can also purchase real estate in areas designated as "integrated tourism resorts," though few exist at present. The average purchase price paid by foreign investors is 80 percent more than the average paid by Australian residents. The United States is still the largest foreign investor, and Singapore recently has replaced Britain in second place.

From which one of the following can we infer that Australian regulations of foreign investments in real estate are not determined by a policy designed to exclude Asians?

(A) Asians make purchases chiefly of the more expensive dwelling units.

(B) Asians pay higher average purchase prices than Australians.

(C) The largest foreign investor is the United States.

(D) Traditional ties to Great Britain are no longer important to many Australians.

(E) Asians can purchase property in "integrated tourism resorts."

43. Thirty-eight percent of people in America drink unfluoridated water and, as a result, have 25 percent more cavities. Early opponents of fluoridation, like the John Birch Society, claimed it was a demonic communist scheme to poison America. More recent opponents invoke the fear of cancer, though years of scientific studies have continued to declare fluoridation safe. Almost every dental and medical organization has endorsed the process, but cities as large as Los Angeles are still without it, though its yearly cost is about 50 cents per person.

The claim that fluoridation is a communist plot is cited here because

(A) it gives historic breadth to the argument

(B) it exemplifies the eccentricity of the opposition

(C) it is what the argument is attempting to refute

(D) it supports the assumption that fluoridation is dangerous

(E) it supports the conclusion of the argument

44. The sickle-cell trait is usually regarded as a characteristic of black Africans. As a single gene, it confers a resistance to malaria, but if the gene is inherited from two parents, it may lead to a dangerous form of anemia. That trait, however, is not a unique characteristic of black Africans but appears wherever malaria has been common. The gene occurs as often in areas of Greece and of southern Asia as it does in central Africa. A genetic grouping by how well they digest milk would separate Arabs and northern Europeans from southern Europeans, native Americans, and some Africans. Most Europeans, black Africans, and east Asians have a gene that determines how they inherit fingerprint patterns, but Mongolians and the Australian aborigines do not. We have the notion that race is important because the surface is what we see. We now have the means to look beneath the skin.

This paragraph is probably part of a longer article that seeks to show

(A) the importance of genetic inheritance in the incidence of disease
(B) the difficulty of finding a scientific definition of race
(C) the decline of parasitic diseases like malaria in the wake of the discovery of their causes
(D) that most of the genes in a member of one race are likely to be unique to that race
(E) the genetic determination of the higher incidence of certain diseases in different racial groups

Questions 45–46

Auto accident victims in this state can sue for both their medical costs and for "pain and suffering" awards. Because the "pain and suffering" awards can be very large, often when the medical expenses are high, victims have an incentive to inflate their medical needs and medical costs in order to receive a higher total payment. For the victims of automobile accidents of equivalent seriousness, medical costs in this state are 30 percent higher than in all four of the neighboring states that have no-fault insurance programs and do make "pain and suffering" awards. Motorists in this state pay more than $300 more for the same insurance coverage of motorists in the four adjoining states. A no-fault insurance system eliminating the lawsuits for "pain and suffering" and fairly compensating victims for medical costs would save the insured drivers of the state medical costs of nearly $1 billion.

45. This argument depends on all of the following assumptions EXCEPT

(A) juries assume a higher medical cost signifies greater pain and suffering
(B) accident victims may falsify the extent of their injuries
(C) doctors and lawyers have no incentives to keep costs low
(D) accident victims should not be rewarded for "pain and suffering"
(E) the medical costs of automobile accidents exceed their legal costs

46. Which one of the following, if true, would weaken the persuasiveness of this argument?

(A) The per-vehicle accident rate in this state is 4 percent higher than in the four neighboring states.

(B) The average motorist in this state drives fewer miles than the average motorist in two of the four neighboring states.

(C) There are more state patrolmen per driver in this state than in any other in the region.

(D) Medical costs in the four neighboring states are 20 percent lower than in this state.

(E) Though the sales tax rate is lower, the income tax is higher in this state than in any other in the region.

ANSWERS AND EXPLANATIONS

1. **C** The passage states that robots not only can build other robots but also can rebuild themselves; therefore, they should last forever. (B) is probably true, but (C) must be true. According to the passage, (A) and (E) are not implied, and (D) is probably not true.

2. **E** There are tasks that robots can do better than humans. Any task in which not being able to think independently or not having emotions would be advantageous might be better done by robots. Tasks that require exposure to dangerous chemicals or radioactivity are also suitable for robots.

3. **E** The author states that the robot can do the most complex group of activities, but "does not have the capacity to . . . think independently." If the most complex group of activities necessitates independent thinking, then the author's assertions are in *direct* contradiction. (C) would be a good choice if it mentioned independent thinking, not training, as training is not mentioned in the passage.

4. **C** Only position (C) is a clear assumption; if you only live once, you had better get it right the first time. (D)

contradicts the statement. (A), (B), and (E) may be true but they are not assumptions behind this statement.

5. **B** Since none of the January blossoming plants will flower again later in the year, no plants that first blossom in January will flower twice in the year. (A), (C), and (E) may be untrue, because we are not told that all the bulbs and tubers in the garden blossom in January; we are told only that all the plants that blossom in January are from bulbs or tubers. (D) need not be true since some bulbs may not flower every year.

6. **D** (A) and (B) are irrelevant, and (C) and (E) are not as effective as (D) because they are just restatements of the thought, rather than a clarification.

7. **A** The phrase "four out of five" implies 80% of a large sample (nationwide). If only five dentists were in the sample, the reliability would certainly be in question. (B) would strengthen the endorsement, while (D) and (E) are irrelevant. (C) could weaken it, but not nearly as much.

8. **E** (A) must be true by the first statement because everybody in the class likes drawing or painting or both, so if Angie does not like paint-

ing, she must like drawing. This same logic holds for (C). "Everyone in the class who does not like drawing," must like painting. And (D), it is possible that no one in the class likes painting. But (E) cannot be true if everyone likes drawing or painting or both.

9. **D** (A) is incorrect since there is no attack on Mark's reasoning. (B) is incorrect because personal pressure is not implied. (C) is incorrect since it is hearsay. (E) is incorrect, since who is to say what a "positive" approach is? (E) could have been the correct choice if (D) were not a possibility.

10. **C** The conclusion of the passage is that, because of safety concerns, more research and testing ought to be done before microwaves become standard household appliances. If, however, research and testing are ineffective means of discerning safety problems, then research and testing would be irrelevant. This criticism seriously weakens the conclusion.

11. **E** If many microwave ovens have been found to leak radioactive elements, then the conclusion—that microwaves should not be standard appliances until they are more carefully researched and tested—is further strengthened because more safety concerns needed to be addressed.

12. **C** On the basis of the first and second statements, all sad mimes are also funny. From the third statement, we conclude that no child can be both sad and funny; therefore (D) is false. (C) must be true; that is, no sad mimes are children. (A), (B), and (E) need not be true.

13. **C** Choices (A), (B), (D), and (E) are all reasonable ways of explaining the discrepancies. If the census report did undercount, we would still need to know if it undercounted one gender more than the other.

14. **A** The conclusion can be properly drawn only if the condition, *"being white,"* is sufficient to rule out all but quartz. (A) allows the conclusion, *"must* be quartz," to be reached.

15. **B** Though this chef probably believes that the restaurants of Paris are superior, the passage passes judgment only on the breads, not on the restaurants of New York. It does assume that good bread will be eaten, that lacking French training there are hardly any good bakers in America, and that if the bread is good the roll basket will be empty. But it may have been refilled three times.

16. **D** The chef's claim to know how to bake bread is, no doubt, just, but the four other answers point to weaknesses to be seen in the passage. The speaker asserts American incompetence on the basis of flimsy evidence, and the assumption that American food can be judged on the basis of some New York restaurants generalizes about the small restaurants in Paris and is not specific about restaurants in New York or Paris.

17. **A** The tone of the passage is positive: workers "enjoy" the same status; "harmony"; less "tension and anger." One can therefore conclude that the author approves of the work environment of the Japanese auto factory for the workers' well-being, and any resemblance of American factories to those of the Japanese ought to be encouraged. Note that there is no indication at all regarding

the quality of the goods produced (B).

18. **A** Only (A) is logically supported by the passage. There is no direct support regarding worker envy for (B). There may be less tension and anger in Japanese auto factories; however, to conclude that there is no tension or anger is not logically sound. Nothing in the passage describes the relation of tension to productivity (D).

19. **A** The key word in the statements given is "usually." "Usually" suggests a frequent or regular phenomenon. It implies that an event may be normally expected and allows one to draw a conclusion *stronger than* those contained in (D) and (E). "Usually" does not mean "with certainty." Therefore, the categorical conclusions of (B) and (C) are not appropriate.

20. **C** (A) is not true, since Nexon is not a sufficient condition for life; that is, Nexon alone is not enough. (B) is not true because Nexon must be present if there is life (necessary condition). (C) is true; Nexon must be present (it is a necessary condition). (C) does not suggest the absence of things other than Nexon and, therefore, does not contradict the original statement. (D) is untrue since Nexon alone is not a sufficient condition.

21. **B** (A) need not be true, because the absence of Flennel is not a necessary condition; that is, there can be other conditions that result in the end of life. (C) is not true, because the absence of Flennel is sufficient to end life (one cannot say life may "not cease"). (B) is true, given the absence of Flennel is sufficient to end life. Both (D) and (E) are untrue.

Absence of Flennel is sufficient cause (D) but there might be other causes as well (E).

22. **C** Choices (A), (B), (D), and (E) are all logical conclusions. Since electric heat is very expensive and the winters are very cold but the summers are merely warm, choice (D) makes sense. But even with high costs, we expect gas consumption to be higher in the very cold winters.

23. **E** The statement presented can be logically made only if being reared at Prince Charming Kennels assures that a poodle is purebred. (E) provides such assurance. (A) does not state that only purebreds are reared and, therefore, does not assure that any given poodle from the kennels is pure.

24. **D** (A) may be eliminated because the argument does not rule out a possible previous proposal. (B) may be eliminated as no suggestion of easy identification or the necessity of easy identification is presupposed. (C) may be eliminated because the argument is independent of any comparison between the Great Salt Lake and any other body of water. (E) can be eliminated because the argument presents the weaker claim of the *possibility* of oil. (D) allows, if true, the *possibility* of oil to be sufficient cause for exploration.

25. **D** The context suggests that salutary associations are positive ones, and the phrase *associations of pleasure* immediately following the first mention of *salutary* certifies (D) as the best choice.

26. **D** (A) is answered in the first sentence, as are (B) and (C). In the first sentence we are told that all thinking is associational, and in the second, that both education and experience

promote accusations. Nowhere, however, does the author mention just what teachers blame and praise.

27. **D**   Only this choice addresses both parts of the statement, which implies that expert practice helps identify errors. (B) and (C) stress error only; (A) stresses practice only; and (E) stresses writing only.

28. **A**   Refer to the following diagram:

	SHORT	TALL
Pines	•———	———•
Palms	•———•	
Pepper		•——•
Peach	•———•	

On the basis of the foregoing diagram, (B), (C), (D), and (E) are false.

29. **C**   The structure of the given argument may be simplified:
Most are popular and low.
Splendor is not popular and high (not low).
(C) parallels this structure:
Most who stop do gain.
Carl does not stop and will not gain.

30. **E**   The statement given can be simplified:
All have hair (mammal).
This does not have hair.
It is not (mammal).

Only (E) can be reduced to this same form:
All have smell (lubricants).
This does not have smell.
It is not (lubricant).

31. **B**   (A) has no bearing because the argument is concerned only with mammals. (C) is not relevant; the argument does not address the amount of hair. (E) is likewise outside the argument's subject. (D) is a possible answer because the claim

is that the absence of hair indicates a nonmammal. However, (B) is a better choice. (D) is a possibility—"One could remove." (B) points out that, without any other intervention, there are creatures with no hair that are also mammals.

32. **C**   If the chances of a person with the same genetic makeup as someone who has developed the disease are 100 times higher than someone with different genes, genetic material must play some role. But if the proportion of people who do develop the disease is very small, genetics cannot be the only cause. The study supports (B) and (E), but gives no information on whether the disease is more likely to affect one identical twin than one nonidentical twin.

33. **D**   Because they share the same genetic makeup, identical twins are especially useful in medical studies of the role of genes.

34. **C**   The pattern of reasoning here is that X is caused by changes in either Y or Z. If Y is unchanged, and X happens, it must have been caused by Z. In (C), X is the rise in pizza costs, the steady Y is the cost of cheese, and the causative Z is the price of beef.

35. **D**   Since the argument concerns state laws to be passed, the best choices must be those that refer to the responsibility of the state, (C) and (D). Of the two, (D) is clearly the more specific and directly relevant to the situation described in the paragraph.

36. **B**   The first proposition states that if an athlete and invited, then over 35. The second proposition states that if over 35, then not both an athlete and invited. The propositions con-

tradict each other. Therefore, no person can be both an athlete and invited.

37. **E** The most plausible answer here is that the group that lost more weight ate less at dinner. Presumably, members of the other group were much hungrier because they had exercised so much more and had less to eat at lunch, and so they ate more at dinner. (A) and (C) will not work if applied only to "some" of the group.

38. **C** If this surgical procedure does more harm than good, it would be wise not to perform it at all. This would reduce by one the number of needless surgical procedures.

39. **A** The passage insists that the tennis team will be composed only of first-rate athletes and nonsmokers. But there is no reason given to prevent a nonsmoker who is not a first-rate athlete from being on the team. Presumably he or she made up for lack of great natural ability with more practice.

40. **A** If the prices have gone down, the clothing sales might well increase, and television watching would be irrelevant. Options (B), (C), (D), and (E) have no information to explain the rise in sales apart from television.

41. **D** The error in the reasoning is the assumption that what was true of a group (the mortgage sales department) can predict something specific about a single member of that group (Thomason's presumed sales). The correct parallel is in (D), where the individual's performance (Meany's winning the golf championship) is based on the accomplishment of a group (the South Texas State golf team).

42. **C** If the largest foreign investor is the United States and the third largest is Britain, it appears that the rules are not intended to exclude Asians, since the same rules apply even more extensively to Europeans and Americans.

43. **B** The author, whose position is clearly in favor of fluoridation, refers to the "demonic scheme" to suggest the irrationality of the opposition. Choice (C) is careless. The argument is not trying to refute the notion of a communist plot.

44. **B** Only the first example (sickle-cell) is related to disease. The second concerns the response to lactose, and the third to fingerprints. What all three have in common is that they cannot be predicted by race, and the passage is part of a consideration of the difficulty of providing a scientific definition of race.

45. **E** Options (A), (B), (C), and (D) assumptions in the passage, but there is nothing here to support the idea that either medical or legal costs are greater.

46. **D** If all medical costs in the other states are much lower, the fact that the medical costs of automobile accident victims are also lower would be explained, and the argument that "pain and suffering" awards lead to higher medical costs would be weakened.

ANSWER SHEET
EXTRA PRACTICE: LOGICAL REASONING

1. Ⓐ Ⓑ Ⓒ Ⓓ Ⓔ
2. Ⓐ Ⓑ Ⓒ Ⓓ Ⓔ
3. Ⓐ Ⓑ Ⓒ Ⓓ Ⓔ
4. Ⓐ Ⓑ Ⓒ Ⓓ Ⓔ
5. Ⓐ Ⓑ Ⓒ Ⓓ Ⓔ
6. Ⓐ Ⓑ Ⓒ Ⓓ Ⓔ
7. Ⓐ Ⓑ Ⓒ Ⓓ Ⓔ
8. Ⓐ Ⓑ Ⓒ Ⓓ Ⓔ
9. Ⓐ Ⓑ Ⓒ Ⓓ Ⓔ
10. Ⓐ Ⓑ Ⓒ Ⓓ Ⓔ
11. Ⓐ Ⓑ Ⓒ Ⓓ Ⓔ
12. Ⓐ Ⓑ Ⓒ Ⓓ Ⓔ
13. Ⓐ Ⓑ Ⓒ Ⓓ Ⓔ
14. Ⓐ Ⓑ Ⓒ Ⓓ Ⓔ
15. Ⓐ Ⓑ Ⓒ Ⓓ Ⓔ
16. Ⓐ Ⓑ Ⓒ Ⓓ Ⓔ

17. Ⓐ Ⓑ Ⓒ Ⓓ Ⓔ
18. Ⓐ Ⓑ Ⓒ Ⓓ Ⓔ
19. Ⓐ Ⓑ Ⓒ Ⓓ Ⓔ
20. Ⓐ Ⓑ Ⓒ Ⓓ Ⓔ
21. Ⓐ Ⓑ Ⓒ Ⓓ Ⓔ
22. Ⓐ Ⓑ Ⓒ Ⓓ Ⓔ
23. Ⓐ Ⓑ Ⓒ Ⓓ Ⓔ
24. Ⓐ Ⓑ Ⓒ Ⓓ Ⓔ
25. Ⓐ Ⓑ Ⓒ Ⓓ Ⓔ
26. Ⓐ Ⓑ Ⓒ Ⓓ Ⓔ
27. Ⓐ Ⓑ Ⓒ Ⓓ Ⓔ
28. Ⓐ Ⓑ Ⓒ Ⓓ Ⓔ
29. Ⓐ Ⓑ Ⓒ Ⓓ Ⓔ
30. Ⓐ Ⓑ Ⓒ Ⓓ Ⓔ
31. Ⓐ Ⓑ Ⓒ Ⓓ Ⓔ

32. Ⓐ Ⓑ Ⓒ Ⓓ Ⓔ
33. Ⓐ Ⓑ Ⓒ Ⓓ Ⓔ
34. Ⓐ Ⓑ Ⓒ Ⓓ Ⓔ
35. Ⓐ Ⓑ Ⓒ Ⓓ Ⓔ
36. Ⓐ Ⓑ Ⓒ Ⓓ Ⓔ
37. Ⓐ Ⓑ Ⓒ Ⓓ Ⓔ
38. Ⓐ Ⓑ Ⓒ Ⓓ Ⓔ
39. Ⓐ Ⓑ Ⓒ Ⓓ Ⓔ
40. Ⓐ Ⓑ Ⓒ Ⓓ Ⓔ
41. Ⓐ Ⓑ Ⓒ Ⓓ Ⓔ
42. Ⓐ Ⓑ Ⓒ Ⓓ Ⓔ
43. Ⓐ Ⓑ Ⓒ Ⓓ Ⓔ
44. Ⓐ Ⓑ Ⓒ Ⓓ Ⓔ
45. Ⓐ Ⓑ Ⓒ Ⓓ Ⓔ
46. Ⓐ Ⓑ Ⓒ Ⓓ Ⓔ

✂ To remove, cut along dotted rule.

4

WRITING SAMPLE

INTRODUCTION

The LSAT will include a 30-minute writing sample. You will be asked to respond to a general essay topic that requires no specialized knowledge, but does require you to write an argument for selecting one of two candidates or items based on given criteria. You should express yourself clearly and effectively.

The essay will *not* be scored, but will be forwarded to the law schools to which you apply. Different law schools have adopted different approaches to evaluating and weighing the quality of the essay.

You will write the essay in a "Writing Sample booklet," a paper folder with general directions on the outside, and the essay topic plus space for your response on the inside. A sheet of scratch paper is provided for organizing and/or outlining your ideas. A pen is also provided for the essay. The essay booklet restricts the length of your response to about *30 lines, each line about seven inches long*. Anything you write outside this restricted space will not be evaluated. Therefore, for practice purposes, restrict yourself to the same space that you will be given on the LSAT to become more comfortable with writing under these restricted conditions.

Following are general directions for the writing sample, a careful analysis of this essay requirement, and a series of steps you may want to follow as you compose your essay. Next, you will examine two completed essays, each written from a different perspective. The chapter concludes with a review of general tips for the writing sample and nine suggested topics for writing your own essays.

GENERAL DIRECTIONS

You have 30 minutes to write an essay in response to a given topic. Take a few minutes to plan your work before you begin writing. DO NOT WRITE ON A TOPIC OF YOUR OWN CHOICE. ESSAYS THAT DO NOT ADDRESS THE GIVEN TOPIC ARE UNACCEPTABLE.

The quality of your writing is more important than the length of your response and content. There is no "right" or "wrong" answer to the question. Pay attention to organization, appropriate diction, and correct usage. You will not be expected to display any specialized knowledge in your response, nor will you be expected to write a "perfect" essay; law schools understand that you are writing under a time constraint and pressured circumstances.

Only the lined area in your booklet will be reproduced for the law schools, so do not write outside this space. *Do not* skip lines or use wide margins. These precautions, along with careful planning and legible handwriting that is not unduly large, will keep you within the allowed space.

THE APPROACH

ANALYZING THE WRITING SAMPLE TOPIC

You will be asked to write an argument for hiring, promoting, selecting, etc., one of two candidates or items based on two or more criteria and two brief sketches of the candidates or items.

Some recent topics have included writing arguments in support of:

- Purchasing one of two films for a public television station
- Selecting one of two designs submitted for a commemorative sculpture
- Selecting one of two retirement communities for a retiree
- Selecting one of two ways of investing money inherited from an uncle
- Deciding which one of two schools to enter for an undergraduate business degree
- Selecting one of two proposals for an introductory course in computer training
- Selecting one of two athletes for a team

In each case the initial introductory statement was followed by two criteria, and then the background of each candidate, or a description of each film, or a description of each school, or a description of each option.

Let's take a closer look. A recent topic gave us its two criteria for hiring a mathematics teacher: (1) the high school's increased concern with computers and (2) its wish to develop the mathematics program at the school to incorporate work-study projects in the business community. The first candidate had a solid educational background, high school teaching and minor administrative experience, good references, and recent training in computers. The second candidate had a slightly different but equally good educational background and no high school teaching experience, but had worked as a teaching assistant in college and a tutor in community programs, as well as having solid credentials in computers and experience as an employee in financial work for a retail store and a bank.

What should be apparent is that it does *NOT* matter which candidate you choose. The principles and qualifications will be written in such a way that you can write in favor of *EITHER* candidate. Make your choice, and stick to it. Don't worry about the other candidate. What your readers will be looking for are clarity, consistency, relevance, and correctness of grammar and usage. Since you have only one-half hour to read the topic and to plan and write your essay, you will not be expected to produce a long or a subtle essay. But you must write on the topic clearly and correctly.

The questions will make clear the sort of audience you are writing for, and you can be sure that this audience is literate and informed about the issues in your paper. In the math teacher topic, for example, the assumed audience is whoever is to hire the math teacher. You do not need to tell this audience what she already knows, but you do want to make her focus upon the issues that support your case. Let us assume you are making the case for the experienced teacher with some computer training. Your essay should stress the obvious qualifications—his teaching experience and computer training. Where you have no direct evidence of expertise, you can invent, so long as you do so plausibly and work from details that are given in the question. You could, for example, argue that, although there are two criteria, the computer issue is really the more important since the students will not be able to find good work-study projects in the community until they have a greater knowledge of computers.

Assume you have chosen the second candidate. Your essay should focus upon her strengths (for example, her experience in business will help her in setting up a business-related program for the students). Where her qualifications are weaker (her lack of high school teaching experience), your essay can emphasize the other kind of teaching experience she has had. Do not be afraid to introduce details to support your argument that are your own ideas. Just be sure that, when you do present additional information, it is consistent with and arises plausibly from the information on the test.

So far, the writing topics have used two slightly different forms. The first (the math teachers) used two sentences, one for each of two equally weighted criteria, and then described the two equally qualified candidates. Another sample topic type also uses two sentences to describe the principles, but the first contains the two criteria, and the second sentence elaborates on one of them. For example, the two principles might be (1) lifeguards are promoted on the basis of years of service and community activities; and (2) community activities include lifesaving clinics, talks to school children, waterfront safety seminars, and high school swimming-team coaching. The biographies would then describe two candidates whose years of service differ slightly, and each of whom has some strength in the areas listed under (2). Since you are not told which of the two criteria is the more important, or which of the various sorts of community service is most important, you can decide for yourself how to weigh these factors, as long as you do so plausibly. You cannot contradict the question—for example, by saying length of service is not important—but you can argue that, although your candidate's length of service is slightly less than that of her competition, her overwhelming superiority in community service is more important.

Here is a suggested plan for approaching any writing sample of this sort.

THE PHASES OF WRITING

Phase 1—Prewriting

1. Read the two statements of policy or criteria at least twice, *actively.* (Circle or mark the essential points of the topic.) Are they equally weighted? If not, clarify the difference.
2. Read the biographies or descriptions at least twice, *actively.* Test them carefully against the policy or criteria statements.

3. Choose your candidate or item. Again set the qualifications or qualities beside those of the statements. Decide exactly what your choice's greatest strengths are. What are the limitations? Think about how these limitations can be invalidated or turned into strengths.

4. Outline your essay. It should be two or three paragraphs long. If you are selecting a candidate, paragraph 1 might focus on his or her obvious strengths that meet the given criteria. Paragraph 2, or paragraphs 2 and 3, might deal with how the candidate also shows promise of fulfilling the other requirements.

Phase 2—Writing

1. Do *not* waste time with a fancy opening paragraph on an irrelevant topic like the importance of math teachers or lifeguards in this complex modern world.

2. Start with a direction. Your first sentence should serve a purpose.

3. Support your argument with examples or other specifics.

4. Do *not* write a closing paragraph that simply repeats what you have already said.

5. Write legibly. Write clearly. Write naturally. Do *not* use big words for their own sake. Do not try to be cute or ironic or funny.

6. Remember that the assumed purpose of this paper is to convince a reader to prefer one candidate or item to another. Your real purpose, of course, is to show a law school that you can follow instructions and write an essay that is well organized, adheres to the point, and is grammatically correct.

Phase 3—Reading

1. Allow sufficient time to proofread your essay. At this point, add any information that is vital, and delete any information that seems confusing or out of place.

2. Don't make extensive changes that will make your writing less readable.

3. Check each sentence for mechanical errors (spelling, punctuation, grammar). Some common types of errors are these:

   - using pronouns with no clear antecedents;
   - lack of agreement between subject and verb;
   - using the wrong verb tense;
   - faulty parallelism in a series of items;
   - misplaced or dangling modifiers;
   - adjective-adverb confusion;
   - misuse of comparative terms or comparisons.

TWO COMPLETED WRITING SAMPLES

Following are two "model" essays. Notice that each of the two sample essays is written from a different perspective.

Sample Topic

Read the following descriptions of Bergquist and Kretchmer, applicants for the job of Assistant Director on a major motion picture. Then, in the space provided, write an argument for hiring either Bergquist or Kretchmer. The following criteria are relevant to your decision:

- In addition to working closely with and advising the Director on creative decisions, the Assistant Director must work with all types of individuals—from stars to Teamster truck drivers—and elicit the best from every cast and crew member for the good of the motion picture.
- The Assistant Director is responsible for all the planning and organization—including paperwork, travel itinerary, meals, etc.—of the entire film project. He/she lays the groundwork for a successful "shoot."

BERGQUIST began her career in films as an Administrative Assistant to the president of a major film studio. As such, she often accompanied her employer in his wining and dining of stars, or to the set when problems arose. She double-checked contracts, shooting schedules, cast and crew checks, and kept a close eye on the budget of several multimillion-dollar films. When her boss was subsequently fired due to a poor season of films, Bergquist was able to secure a position as Assistant Editor at the studio, helping several highly respected film editors "cut" feature films. It was here that she learned about the creative end of the business, and soon after became the chief editor of an hour-long studio documentary, which won several awards. After two years, Bergquist was accepted into the Assistant Directors Training Program, and is presently a candidate for Assistant Director of this new $15,000,000 motion picture.

KRETCHMER was a principal/teacher for 12 years before embarking on a film career. She taught math at the New York School for the Creative Arts, and also worked with parents in the community, the board of education, and local government representatives in securing financing for the $20,000,000 school building. As Chairperson of the New Building Committee, she worked closely with architects, townspeople, contractors, and even children to understand their needs for the building. Today the building stands as a model for such schools everywhere. Eight years ago Kretchmer came to Hollywood and, through persistence and charm, secured a studio position and worked her way up to Chief Auditor, where she oversaw budgets on several multimillion-dollar films. She enrolled in the Assistant Directors Training Program, which she recently completed, and is now a candidate for the position of Assistant Director of this new film.

Sample Essay

What sets Bergquist apart from Kretchmer is her understanding of, and experience in, the creative element of filmmaking.

An Assistant Director (AD) advises the Director in key creative decisions: how to best structure and order the shooting schedule, how to begin and end scenes, and how best to shoot a scene or sequence. While the ultimate decision rests with the Director, the AD's input is vital. Like a caddy advising a golfer of the distance and terrain of the course, the AD's knowledge of the creative elements of filmmaking enhances her abilities in these tasks. Since a film's success often hinges on these creative decisions, the AD's contributions can be critical.

As an editor, Bergquist learned how a film is cut together and how the pieces must fit coherently. She cut her own films and won numerous awards, thus reflecting her understanding of good creative choices. This special knowledge of film (which Kretchmer lacks)—how shots must match, how moods and sequences build upon each other—is essential to the final success of any film.

Another Approach

Read the following descriptions of Bergquist and Kretchmer, applicants for the job of Assistant Director on a major motion picture. *Then, in the space provided, write an argument for hiring either Bergquist or Kretchmer.* The following criteria are relevant to your decision:

- In addition to working closely with and advising the Director on creative decisions, the Assistant Director must work with all types of individuals—from stars to Teamster truck drivers—and elicit the best from every cast and crew member for the good of the motion picture.
- The Assistant Director is responsible for all the planning and organization—including paperwork, travel itinerary, meals, etc.—of the entire film project. He/she lays the groundwork for a successful "shoot."

BERGQUIST began her career in films as an Administrative Assistant to the president of a major film studio. As such, she often accompanied her employer in his wining and dining of stars, or to the set when problems arose. She double-checked contracts, shooting schedules, cast and crew checks, and kept a close eye on the budget of several multimillion-dollar films. When her boss was subsequently fired due to a poor season of films, Bergquist was able to secure a position as Assistant Editor at the studio, helping several highly respected film editors "cut" feature films. It was here that she learned about the creative end of the business, and soon after became the chief editor of an hour-long studio documentary, which won several awards. After two years, Bergquist was accepted into the Assistant Directors Training Program, and is presently a candidate for Assistant Director of this new $15,000,000 motion picture.

KRETCHMER was a principal/teacher for 12 years before embarking on a film career. She taught math at the New York School for the Creative Arts, and also worked with parents in the community, the board of education, and local government representatives in securing financing for the $20,000,000 school building. As Chairperson of the New Building Committee, she worked closely with architects, townspeople, contractors, and even children to understand their needs for the building. Today the building stands as a model for such schools everywhere. Eight years ago Kretchmer came to Hollywood and, through persistence and charm, secured a studio position and worked her way up to Chief Auditor, where she oversaw budgets on several multimillion-dollar films. She enrolled in the Assistant Directors Training Program, which she recently completed, and is now a candidate for the position of Assistant Director of this new film.

Sample Essay

Kretchmer has what Bergquist seriously lacks: the experience and ability to work well with all kinds of people—a crucial skill in the collaborative art/business of filmmaking.

Any film's lengthy end-credits attest to the huge number of people contributing talent—technicians, laborers, performing artists and others. As the director's right-hand person, the Assistance Director (AD) must help orchestrate that effort. She must "read" the personalities of different individuals and know how to appeal to each ego to garner the best from each.

As chairperson of a building committee, Kretchmer worked successfully with dozens of different personalities in pursuit of a common goal, not unlike a film project. In working with diverse personalities (parents, administrators, children, teachers, architects and builders, each with different goals) Kretchmer had to have a keen understanding of people and be able to know their strengths and limitations. This is precisely her most important task as a motion picture AD.

Working on the set with hundreds of different personalities requires a specially skilled individual: Kretchmer is that person.

REVIEW OF GENERAL TIPS

1. Read the topic question at least twice, *actively:* circle or mark the essential points of the question. Note the main question or parts to be discussed, the audience you are addressing, and the persona or position from which you are writing.

2. Remember to *prewrite,* or plan before you write. Spend at least five minutes organizing your thoughts by jotting notes, outlining, brainstorming, clustering, etc.

3. As you write, keep the flow of your writing going. Don't stop your train of thought to worry about the spelling of a word. You can fix little things later.

4. Leave a few minutes to reread and edit your paper after you finish writing. A careful rereading will often catch careless mistakes and errors in punctuation, spelling, etc., that you didn't have time to worry about as you wrote.

5. Remember that a good essay will be

   - on topic,
   - well organized,
   - well developed with examples,
   - grammatically sound with few errors,
   - interesting to read, with a variety of sentence types,
   - clear, neat, and easy to read.

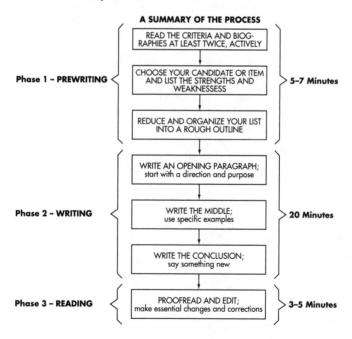

A SUMMARY OF THE PROCESS

Phase 1 – PREWRITING
- READ THE CRITERIA AND BIOGRAPHIES AT LEAST TWICE, ACTIVELY
- CHOOSE YOUR CANDIDATE OR ITEM AND LIST THE STRENGTHS AND WEAKNESSESS
- REDUCE AND ORGANIZE YOUR LIST INTO A ROUGH OUTLINE

5–7 Minutes

Phase 2 – WRITING
- WRITE AN OPENING PARAGRAPH; start with a direction and purpose
- WRITE THE MIDDLE; use specific examples
- WRITE THE CONCLUSION; say something new

20 Minutes

Phase 3 – READING
- PROOFREAD AND EDIT; make essential changes and corrections

3–5 Minutes

PRACTICE: WRITING SAMPLE

After reviewing the completed essays, try some practice on your own. We have provided sample questions.

Try following the steps we have suggested, varying them slightly, if necessary, to suit your personal style. Have an honest critic read and respond to each practice essay you complete.

You will be given a special sheet of paper to write your essay. It will have the essay topic on the top followed by approximately 25 lines of writing. For practice, write your essay on one side of an 8½" by 11" college-ruled lined sheet of paper. *Use only 25 lines.*

Writing Sample Topic 1

Read the following description of Arbit and Blatas, candidates for your party's nomination to the city council. *Then, in the space provided, write an argument for nominating either Arbit or Blatas.* Use the information in this description and assume that two general policies guide your party's decision on nomination:

- Nominations are based upon a combination of the probable success in the election and party service.
- Party service includes seniority, committee work, and fund-raising.

Arbit, a Rumanian-American, has lived in the district and worked for the party for fifteen years. He is chairman of two key party committees and a member of two others. His fund-raising picnic, begun ten years ago, now raises at least $10,000 every year. Arbit is 47, a trial lawyer, with no prior experience in elective office. Twenty percent of the district is Rumanian-American, almost all of whom support the party in every election.

Blatas, of Hungarian background, moved to the district seven years ago. She has worked for the party for seven years as a member of several party committees, and as Arbit's assistant in arranging the fund-raising picnic. A graduate of law school, she is 35, and was recently promoted to director of the city's real estate research office. She narrowly lost an election for city assessor two years ago. Thirty-five percent of the voters in the district are Hungarian-American.

Writing Sample Topic 2

Read the following descriptions of Arnot and Brecht, applicants for the position of head chef at *Chez Moi,* a highly successful New York restaurant. *Then, in the space provided, write an argument for hiring either Arnot or Brecht.* The following criteria are relevant to your decision:

- The chef at *Chez Moi* must be able to socialize freely and to discuss each day's menu with the patrons.
- *Chez Moi's* reputation depends upon the remarkable range and originality of its seafood and its desserts.

Chef Arnot was born in Normandy and trained in Paris. For fifteen years he has been the head chef at major international restaurants in Paris and Marseilles. While in Paris, he won competition among the city's pastry chefs four times. In Marseilles, his specialty was Mediterranean seafood. He is among the most respected chefs in the world, known equally for his inventive recipes for fish and his short temper. His English is competent, but slow and heavily accented. He has, for the first time, agreed to accept a position outside of France.

Chef Brecht was born in Berlin and trained in Paris, London, and Rome. For the last five years, she has been the head chef in one of Chicago's most successful restaurants. Through her books and her television cooking programs, she has become the most widely known and most popular chef in America. She is especially renowned for her recipes for ice creams and sherbets. She has agreed to apply for the position at *Chez Moi* because of the restaurant's reputation and because it is located in New York, a center of the publishing and television industries.

Writing Sample Topic 3

Read the following descriptions of Selig and Druck, two applicants for the position of receptionist for the medical offices of four physicians (general practitioners). *Then, in the space provided, write an argument for hiring either Selig or Druck.* The following criteria are relevant to your decision:

- The receptionist must answer the phone, schedule appointments for each of the physicians, and relay messages from the physicians to their patients when necessary.
- The receptionist must screen patients over the phone, in order to decide whether to schedule an immediate appointment.

Selig has worked as a registered nurse for ten years and in the emergency room at City Hospital for the last eighteen months. Before this, she was the head nurse in a small suburban hospital staffed by twelve physicians and twenty nurses and aides. She recently decided to leave her position as an emergency room nurse and seek a job with more regular hours and duties. Since high school, Selig has spent two evenings each week counseling the distraught people who phone the free, state-supported "crisis hot line" for help. She has prevented a number of suicides by encouraging the caller to reveal his location and wait for help.

Druck recently moved into the area, leaving his position as office manager for a busy medical corporation in another state. He has long been involved in medical work, having completed two years of medical school before deciding that he was most interested in the business and personnel decisions associated with enhanced patient care. After a series of jobs manning the front office for various private practices, Druck accepted the managerial position only to discover that it kept him more out of touch with the patients themselves than he would like. Druck is a regular subscriber to the major medical journals.

Writing Sample Topic 4

The *Times-Herald,* a large metropolitan newspaper, is about to add a new strip to its comic page. The editorial board must decide between two features that do not now appear in any of the city's other newspapers. *In the space provided, write an argument to be presented to the editorial board in support of one of the two following comic strips.* Two considerations should guide your decision:

- The newspaper wishes to improve its reputation for serious journalism.
- The newspaper wishes to increase its circulation.

Described by *Time* magazine as "America's most beloved comic strip," *Tom Jordan, M.D.* is a serial that depicts the life of a handsome young doctor at a large New York hospital. It appears in more newspapers in the United States than any other comic. Its stories combine medical information, romance, and moral uplift. Each story takes thirty-two weeks to complete. An especially popular recent episode dealt with Tom Jordan's saving the life of an orphaned leukemia victim; others in the recent past have dealt with drug addiction among the very rich, kidney transplants, and anorexia. *Tom Jordan, M.D.* is the work of a group of four cartoonists.

Bart Pollard's comic, *D.C.,* was the first strip cartoon to win a Pulitzer Prize. Its satiric treatment of Democrats and Republicans, of clergymen, doctors, lawyers, and athletes, has at one time or another given such offense that a number of newspapers that had contracted to run the feature have refused to print it. In Washington, Pollard's *D.C.* is called the "comic strip that everyone hates, but everyone reads." A cabinet officer who closely resembled a character pilloried in the comic has recently filed a libel suit against Pollard. Readership of the strip is especially high on college campuses.

Writing Sample Topic 5

The Animal Protection Society must decide on a speaker to address its annual fund-raising dinner. *In the space provided, write an argument in support of one of the two following choices.* Two considerations guide your decision:

- The society must immediately raise as much money as possible to support an emergency airlift to save an endangered species of crane.
- The society wishes to increase the number of life members, subscribers who can be counted on to give money every year.

Jan Gilbert is a comedienne and the star of a popular television talk show. On her program, she frequently invites keepers from the San Diego Zoo, who bring with them lion cubs, talking mynah birds, lemurs, and other small animals that appeal to large audiences. A dog lover, she often appears in public and on television with her miniature poodle, which travels with her wherever she goes. She is an active fund-raiser for conservative political causes. Because of her love of animals, she has agreed to waive half of her usual personal appearance fee of $12,000.

Katrina Nelson is a distinguished zoologist. She is an adjunct research professor at Cambridge University and has spent fourteen years in Africa observing the behavior of packs of Cape hunting dogs, jackals, and hyenas. A film she made on the scavengers and predators of Africa has been shown on educational television stations. She is the author of five books, including one on the animals of Africa that have become extinct in this century. She is an experienced and skillful public speaker. Her lecture fee is $500.

Writing Sample Topic 6

Read the following descriptions of two 1-hour television series, *Love 'Em and Leave 'Em* and *Down and Out,* that are competing for a spot in the network lineup. *Then, in the space provided, write an argument for deciding which of the two the network should choose.* The following criteria are relevant to your decision:

- The only available time slot for the chosen series is 10 P.M. on a weeknight.
- Network executives prefer a series that can deal with controversial issues while providing action and adventure.

Love 'Em and Leave 'Em deals with a metropolitan newspaper columnist who writes a daily "advice to the lovelorn" column and often gets involved in the private lives and problems of those who write her letters. Her father is a criminal attorney, and her sister is a police lieutenant. The columnist holds a degree in psychology and provides free counseling a few hours a week at a halfway house for rehabilitated drug addicts. She is always arguing with the managing editor of the newspaper, who wants a column that is entertaining but not controversial.

Down and Out portrays the week-to-week lives of a minor league baseball team. Two members of the team work as private detectives during the off season and are always alert to "shady" situations. The owner of the team is a former U.S. senator who always preferred baseball to politics but still acts as a presidential advisor at times. The team players are an ethnic and racial mix; some are as young as eighteen and some in their early thirties; the private life and personal background of each individual player remain to be developed. The team manager, a former All-Star, has two sons on the team.

PART THREE

PRACTICE

Mastering Problem Types and Time Pressures

5

MODEL TEST ONE

This chapter contains full-length Model Test One. It is geared to the format of the LSAT, and it is complete with answers and explanations. It is equivalent to the LSAT in question structure, number of questions, level of difficulty, and time allotments. (The questions used are not taken directly from the LSAT, as those questions are copyrighted and may not be reproduced.)

Model Test One should be taken under strict test conditions. The test ends with a 30-minute Writing Sample, which is not scored.

Section	Description	Number of Questions	Time Allowed
I.	Reading Comprehension	28	35 minutes
II.	Analytical Reasoning	24	35 minutes
III.	Logical Reasoning	26	35 minutes
IV.	Analytical Reasoning	24	35 minutes
V.	Logical Reasoning	25	35 minutes
	Writing Sample		30 minutes
TOTALS:		127	3 hours 25 minutes

Now please turn to the next page, remove your answer sheet, and begin Model Test One.

ANSWER SHEET—MODEL TEST ONE

Section 1	Section 2	Section 3	Section 4	Section 5
1. Ⓐ Ⓑ Ⓒ Ⓓ Ⓔ	1. Ⓐ Ⓑ Ⓒ Ⓓ Ⓔ	1. Ⓐ Ⓑ Ⓒ Ⓓ Ⓔ	1. Ⓐ Ⓑ Ⓒ Ⓓ Ⓔ	1. Ⓐ Ⓑ Ⓒ Ⓓ Ⓔ
2. Ⓐ Ⓑ Ⓒ Ⓓ Ⓔ	2. Ⓐ Ⓑ Ⓒ Ⓓ Ⓔ	2. Ⓐ Ⓑ Ⓒ Ⓓ Ⓔ	2. Ⓐ Ⓑ Ⓒ Ⓓ Ⓔ	2. Ⓐ Ⓑ Ⓒ Ⓓ Ⓔ
3. Ⓐ Ⓑ Ⓒ Ⓓ Ⓔ	3. Ⓐ Ⓑ Ⓒ Ⓓ Ⓔ	3. Ⓐ Ⓑ Ⓒ Ⓓ Ⓔ	3. Ⓐ Ⓑ Ⓒ Ⓓ Ⓔ	3. Ⓐ Ⓑ Ⓒ Ⓓ Ⓔ
4. Ⓐ Ⓑ Ⓒ Ⓓ Ⓔ	4. Ⓐ Ⓑ Ⓒ Ⓓ Ⓔ	4. Ⓐ Ⓑ Ⓒ Ⓓ Ⓔ	4. Ⓐ Ⓑ Ⓒ Ⓓ Ⓔ	4. Ⓐ Ⓑ Ⓒ Ⓓ Ⓔ
5. Ⓐ Ⓑ Ⓒ Ⓓ Ⓔ	5. Ⓐ Ⓑ Ⓒ Ⓓ Ⓔ	5. Ⓐ Ⓑ Ⓒ Ⓓ Ⓔ	5. Ⓐ Ⓑ Ⓒ Ⓓ Ⓔ	5. Ⓐ Ⓑ Ⓒ Ⓓ Ⓔ
6. Ⓐ Ⓑ Ⓒ Ⓓ Ⓔ	6. Ⓐ Ⓑ Ⓒ Ⓓ Ⓔ	6. Ⓐ Ⓑ Ⓒ Ⓓ Ⓔ	6. Ⓐ Ⓑ Ⓒ Ⓓ Ⓔ	6. Ⓐ Ⓑ Ⓒ Ⓓ Ⓔ
7. Ⓐ Ⓑ Ⓒ Ⓓ Ⓔ	7. Ⓐ Ⓑ Ⓒ Ⓓ Ⓔ	7. Ⓐ Ⓑ Ⓒ Ⓓ Ⓔ	7. Ⓐ Ⓑ Ⓒ Ⓓ Ⓔ	7. Ⓐ Ⓑ Ⓒ Ⓓ Ⓔ
8. Ⓐ Ⓑ Ⓒ Ⓓ Ⓔ	8. Ⓐ Ⓑ Ⓒ Ⓓ Ⓔ	8. Ⓐ Ⓑ Ⓒ Ⓓ Ⓔ	8. Ⓐ Ⓑ Ⓒ Ⓓ Ⓔ	8. Ⓐ Ⓑ Ⓒ Ⓓ Ⓔ
9. Ⓐ Ⓑ Ⓒ Ⓓ Ⓔ	9. Ⓐ Ⓑ Ⓒ Ⓓ Ⓔ	9. Ⓐ Ⓑ Ⓒ Ⓓ Ⓔ	9. Ⓐ Ⓑ Ⓒ Ⓓ Ⓔ	9. Ⓐ Ⓑ Ⓒ Ⓓ Ⓔ
10. Ⓐ Ⓑ Ⓒ Ⓓ Ⓔ	10. Ⓐ Ⓑ Ⓒ Ⓓ Ⓔ	10. Ⓐ Ⓑ Ⓒ Ⓓ Ⓔ	10. Ⓐ Ⓑ Ⓒ Ⓓ Ⓔ	10. Ⓐ Ⓑ Ⓒ Ⓓ Ⓔ
11. Ⓐ Ⓑ Ⓒ Ⓓ Ⓔ	11. Ⓐ Ⓑ Ⓒ Ⓓ Ⓔ	11. Ⓐ Ⓑ Ⓒ Ⓓ Ⓔ	11. Ⓐ Ⓑ Ⓒ Ⓓ Ⓔ	11. Ⓐ Ⓑ Ⓒ Ⓓ Ⓔ
12. Ⓐ Ⓑ Ⓒ Ⓓ Ⓔ	12. Ⓐ Ⓑ Ⓒ Ⓓ Ⓔ	12. Ⓐ Ⓑ Ⓒ Ⓓ Ⓔ	12. Ⓐ Ⓑ Ⓒ Ⓓ Ⓔ	12. Ⓐ Ⓑ Ⓒ Ⓓ Ⓔ
13. Ⓐ Ⓑ Ⓒ Ⓓ Ⓔ	13. Ⓐ Ⓑ Ⓒ Ⓓ Ⓔ	13. Ⓐ Ⓑ Ⓒ Ⓓ Ⓔ	13. Ⓐ Ⓑ Ⓒ Ⓓ Ⓔ	13. Ⓐ Ⓑ Ⓒ Ⓓ Ⓔ
14. Ⓐ Ⓑ Ⓒ Ⓓ Ⓔ	14. Ⓐ Ⓑ Ⓒ Ⓓ Ⓔ	14. Ⓐ Ⓑ Ⓒ Ⓓ Ⓔ	14. Ⓐ Ⓑ Ⓒ Ⓓ Ⓔ	14. Ⓐ Ⓑ Ⓒ Ⓓ Ⓔ
15. Ⓐ Ⓑ Ⓒ Ⓓ Ⓔ	15. Ⓐ Ⓑ Ⓒ Ⓓ Ⓔ	15. Ⓐ Ⓑ Ⓒ Ⓓ Ⓔ	15. Ⓐ Ⓑ Ⓒ Ⓓ Ⓔ	15. Ⓐ Ⓑ Ⓒ Ⓓ Ⓔ
16. Ⓐ Ⓑ Ⓒ Ⓓ Ⓔ	16. Ⓐ Ⓑ Ⓒ Ⓓ Ⓔ	16. Ⓐ Ⓑ Ⓒ Ⓓ Ⓔ	16. Ⓐ Ⓑ Ⓒ Ⓓ Ⓔ	16. Ⓐ Ⓑ Ⓒ Ⓓ Ⓔ
17. Ⓐ Ⓑ Ⓒ Ⓓ Ⓔ	17. Ⓐ Ⓑ Ⓒ Ⓓ Ⓔ	17. Ⓐ Ⓑ Ⓒ Ⓓ Ⓔ	17. Ⓐ Ⓑ Ⓒ Ⓓ Ⓔ	17. Ⓐ Ⓑ Ⓒ Ⓓ Ⓔ
18. Ⓐ Ⓑ Ⓒ Ⓓ Ⓔ	18. Ⓐ Ⓑ Ⓒ Ⓓ Ⓔ	18. Ⓐ Ⓑ Ⓒ Ⓓ Ⓔ	18. Ⓐ Ⓑ Ⓒ Ⓓ Ⓔ	18. Ⓐ Ⓑ Ⓒ Ⓓ Ⓔ
19. Ⓐ Ⓑ Ⓒ Ⓓ Ⓔ	19. Ⓐ Ⓑ Ⓒ Ⓓ Ⓔ	19. Ⓐ Ⓑ Ⓒ Ⓓ Ⓔ	19. Ⓐ Ⓑ Ⓒ Ⓓ Ⓔ	19. Ⓐ Ⓑ Ⓒ Ⓓ Ⓔ
20. Ⓐ Ⓑ Ⓒ Ⓓ Ⓔ	20. Ⓐ Ⓑ Ⓒ Ⓓ Ⓔ	20. Ⓐ Ⓑ Ⓒ Ⓓ Ⓔ	20. Ⓐ Ⓑ Ⓒ Ⓓ Ⓔ	20. Ⓐ Ⓑ Ⓒ Ⓓ Ⓔ
21. Ⓐ Ⓑ Ⓒ Ⓓ Ⓔ	21. Ⓐ Ⓑ Ⓒ Ⓓ Ⓔ	21. Ⓐ Ⓑ Ⓒ Ⓓ Ⓔ	21. Ⓐ Ⓑ Ⓒ Ⓓ Ⓔ	21. Ⓐ Ⓑ Ⓒ Ⓓ Ⓔ
22. Ⓐ Ⓑ Ⓒ Ⓓ Ⓔ	22. Ⓐ Ⓑ Ⓒ Ⓓ Ⓔ	22. Ⓐ Ⓑ Ⓒ Ⓓ Ⓔ	22. Ⓐ Ⓑ Ⓒ Ⓓ Ⓔ	22. Ⓐ Ⓑ Ⓒ Ⓓ Ⓔ
23. Ⓐ Ⓑ Ⓒ Ⓓ Ⓔ	23. Ⓐ Ⓑ Ⓒ Ⓓ Ⓔ	23. Ⓐ Ⓑ Ⓒ Ⓓ Ⓔ	23. Ⓐ Ⓑ Ⓒ Ⓓ Ⓔ	23. Ⓐ Ⓑ Ⓒ Ⓓ Ⓔ
24. Ⓐ Ⓑ Ⓒ Ⓓ Ⓔ	24. Ⓐ Ⓑ Ⓒ Ⓓ Ⓔ	24. Ⓐ Ⓑ Ⓒ Ⓓ Ⓔ	24. Ⓐ Ⓑ Ⓒ Ⓓ Ⓔ	24. Ⓐ Ⓑ Ⓒ Ⓓ Ⓔ
25. Ⓐ Ⓑ Ⓒ Ⓓ Ⓔ	25. Ⓐ Ⓑ Ⓒ Ⓓ Ⓔ	25. Ⓐ Ⓑ Ⓒ Ⓓ Ⓔ	25. Ⓐ Ⓑ Ⓒ Ⓓ Ⓔ	25. Ⓐ Ⓑ Ⓒ Ⓓ Ⓔ
26. Ⓐ Ⓑ Ⓒ Ⓓ Ⓔ	26. Ⓐ Ⓑ Ⓒ Ⓓ Ⓔ	26. Ⓐ Ⓑ Ⓒ Ⓓ Ⓔ	26. Ⓐ Ⓑ Ⓒ Ⓓ Ⓔ	26. Ⓐ Ⓑ Ⓒ Ⓓ Ⓔ
27. Ⓐ Ⓑ Ⓒ Ⓓ Ⓔ	27. Ⓐ Ⓑ Ⓒ Ⓓ Ⓔ	27. Ⓐ Ⓑ Ⓒ Ⓓ Ⓔ	27. Ⓐ Ⓑ Ⓒ Ⓓ Ⓔ	27. Ⓐ Ⓑ Ⓒ Ⓓ Ⓔ
28. Ⓐ Ⓑ Ⓒ Ⓓ Ⓔ	28. Ⓐ Ⓑ Ⓒ Ⓓ Ⓔ	28. Ⓐ Ⓑ Ⓒ Ⓓ Ⓔ	28. Ⓐ Ⓑ Ⓒ Ⓓ Ⓔ	28. Ⓐ Ⓑ Ⓒ Ⓓ Ⓔ
29. Ⓐ Ⓑ Ⓒ Ⓓ Ⓔ	29. Ⓐ Ⓑ Ⓒ Ⓓ Ⓔ	29. Ⓐ Ⓑ Ⓒ Ⓓ Ⓔ	29. Ⓐ Ⓑ Ⓒ Ⓓ Ⓔ	29. Ⓐ Ⓑ Ⓒ Ⓓ Ⓔ
30. Ⓐ Ⓑ Ⓒ Ⓓ Ⓔ	30. Ⓐ Ⓑ Ⓒ Ⓓ Ⓔ	30. Ⓐ Ⓑ Ⓒ Ⓓ Ⓔ	30. Ⓐ Ⓑ Ⓒ Ⓓ Ⓔ	30. Ⓐ Ⓑ Ⓒ Ⓓ Ⓔ

To remove, cut along dotted rule.

SECTION I

Directions: **Read the passages and answer the questions following each passage by blackening the appropriate space on the answer sheet. You may refer back to the passages when answering the questions. Answer all questions on the basis of what is stated or implied.**

Although statutory law (a law enacted by the legislature) expressly forbids strikes by government workers, the constitutional validity of these laws as
(5) well as their interpretative applications have been under attack in various cases, the most publicized case being that of the federal government air traffic controllers.
(10) The First Amendment to the United States Constitution guarantees the right of free speech. The constitutional issue to be resolved therefore is whether strikes are a form of "symbolic
(15) speech" or "symbolic conduct" that should be accorded the same degree of First Amendment protection as verbal communications. In a case that involved private rather than public
(20) employees, a Texas Court held that picketing as an incident to a labor dispute is a proper exercise of freedom of speech. The court went on to say that only a "clear and present danger of
(25) substantive evil will justify an abridgement of the right to picket." Later, the New Jersey state court concluded that even though picketing is protected by freedom of speech, this
(30) does not mean that statutes prohibiting strikes are constitutionally invalid. This case involved a constitutional interpretation of the New Jersey statute. The court stated that the
(35) justification of this statute is based on the ground of "clear and present

danger" that would result to the state if the performance of functions of a public utility was ceased or impaired by
(40) a strike. Those in favor of no-strike clauses seem to concede that strikes are a form of symbolic speech that should be accorded the same degree of First Amendment protection as verbal
(45) speech. Their justification for upholding these clauses is the "clear and present danger" doctrine. They tend to believe that strikes by government employees automatically
(50) present a "clear and present danger of substantive evil." However, according to the U.S. Supreme Court, legislatures cannot be relied upon to make a determination of what constitutes a
(55) "clear and present danger." In effect this is what happened when President Reagan ordered the firing of the air traffic controllers, based on the antistrike clause pronounced by
(60) Congress. The Supreme Court held that courts themselves must determine what constitutes a clear and present danger. The Supreme Court went on to say that mere public inconvenience or
(65) annoyance is not enough to constitute a clear and present danger. Thus, the public inconvenience and annoyance created by the curtailment of air traffic as a result of the controllers' strike may
(70) not be sufficient to constitute such a danger. The argument that a clear and present danger resulted from the

emergency staffing of control towers by military and supervisory personnel (75) is invalidated by the fact that the airlines have run safely since the strike.

This is not to suggest that every employee should automatically have the right to strike. However, (80) constitutional consideration of due process and freedom of speech should bar denying government workers, as a class, the right to strike. A close look should be taken at what actually (85) constitutes a "clear and present danger of substantive evil." It is an evasion for courts to allow legislatures to prejudge all government services to be different for "strike" purposes than those (90) provided by the private sector. The court itself should look at such factors as the nature of the service in determining whether particular no-strike clauses are constitutionally valid. (95) The nature of the provider of the service (i.e., government v. private) is not a compelling justification for upholding no-strike clauses.

1. According to the passage, strikes by government workers are

(A) constitutionally invalid
(B) forbidden by statutory law
(C) permissible when there is no danger of substantial evil
(D) permissible when there is no public inconvenience or annoyance
(E) permissible when there is no danger to national security and safety

2. If government workers as a class are denied the right to strike, it can be argued that they have been denied all of the following EXCEPT

(A) due process
(B) freedom of speech

(C) the clear and present danger doctrine
(D) redress from abnormally dangerous working conditions
(E) an abridgment of the right to picket

3. According to the passage, the "clear and present danger" justification of forbidding a strike has been misapplied for all of the following reasons EXCEPT

(A) the dangers were determined by the executive branch
(B) the dangers are often merely inconveniences
(C) the dangers were determined by the courts
(D) strikes by government workers do not automatically present dangers
(E) the inconvenience caused by the air traffic controllers may not have been a danger

4. The fact that there was no rise in the number of airline accidents in the first six months after the firing and replacement of the striking air traffic controllers undermines the

(A) government's argument that a strike would present a danger to the public
(B) argument that the no-strike clause violates first amendment rights
(C) argument that a strike is a form of symbolic speech
(D) air traffic controllers' argument that they left their jobs because of dangerous working conditions
(E) argument that no-strike clauses discourage more highly qualified individuals from applying for positions

5. The author of the passage objects to the current situation in which

(A) all employees equally have the right to strike
(B) the government regards national security more important than an individual's freedom
(C) the Supreme Court avoids taking a position in its dealing with regret-to-strike cases
(D) an unfair burden of proof is placed upon workers who leave jobs they believe to have unsafe working conditions
(E) a false distinction is made between workers doing similar jobs for the government and private employees

6. Which one of the following might the author cite to exemplify another of the harmful effects of the no-strike rule?

(A) It deters the highly skilled from taking government jobs.
(B) It can be used as a precedent in the private sector.
(C) It places too much power in the hands of the judicial branch of the government.
(D) It encourages the courts to determine whether or not particular no-strike clauses are valid.
(E) It protects some workers from abnormally dangerous working conditions.

F — Art
Art ≠ F

Virginia Woolf's development as a novelist was deeply influenced by her struggle to reconcile feminism and art. Long before the aesthetic creed of
(5) Bloomsbury came into being she had learned from her father that a work of literature is no better than the morality which it is intended to express—a lesson she never forgot. Virginia Woolf
(10) was a passionate moralist, though she directed all her fervor into one narrow channel. The impulse to write *Three Guineas* possessed her for years, "violently . . . persistently, pressingly,
(15) compulsorily," until she carried it into action. This moral fervor was not contained within the limits of her tracts, nor could it have been. Feminism is implicit in her novels. The
(20) novels are not, of course, didactic in the narrow sense of pleading for specific reforms, but they illustrate the dangers of one-sidedness and celebrate the androgynous mind.
(25)   Virginia Woolf's main emphasis in her feminist writings, as in the novels, was on self-reform, and on art as a means to that end. Novels and tracts alike grew out of a preoccupation with
(30) her own spiritual dilemma. Fiction was the medium within which Virginia Woolf controlled and directed this intense self-absorption. When she deserted art for propaganda, as in
(35) *Three Guineas*, her self-absorption got the upper hand. Thus, paradoxically, she was truer to her feminist ideas as a novelist than as a pamphleteer. Her social conscience and her aesthetic
(40) vision were mutually dependent. She could express her feminism only by means of her art; but her art owed its character to her feminism.
    The contrast between Virginia
(45) Woolf's failure in *Three Guineas* and her triumph in *The Years* confirms this impression. In the first, confining herself to political and social controversy, she lost her grasp of
(50) reality and ended up talking to herself. In the second, striving, as she said, "to give the whole of the present society . . . facts as well as the vision," she transcended purely personal
(55) preoccupations and created a lasting work of art. Virginia Woolf's direct

attack on social evil is too shrill and self-indulgent to succeed, even as propaganda. On the other hand, her

(60) symbolic representation of the Wasteland—pollution, faithlessness, remorse—has a lucid objectivity that forces the reader to see through her eyes. The tract, with all its talk of

(65) reform, is one-sided. The novel is whole.

In Virginia Woolf's case, the myth of the artist as more or less helpless agent of his own creative drive seems

(70) to have a foundation in fact. She needed the discipline of art, because it permitted her to express her intense moral indignation, while at the same time controlling the disintegrating

(75) effects of that indignation upon her personality. Art produced feelings of release and harmony, such as she associated with the androgynous mind. When she avoided that discipline, as in

(80) Three Guineas, her writing tended to become morbid. In relation to the radiance of Virginia Woolf's artistic successes, therefore, Three Guineas represents a kind of negative definition.

(85) Through it we can glance into the heart of her darkness.

7. According to the passage, Woolf's father influenced her

(A) choice of writing as a career
(B) belief in the importance of self-reform
(C) belief that literature should have a moral base
(D) desire to write tracts and pamphlets
(E) views on the equality of men and women

8. We can infer from the passage that the "spiritual dilemma" mentioned in line 30 refers to a

(A) need to transcend one-sidedness and encompass both the masculine and feminine
(B) desire to retire from the world rather than participate actively in society
(C) need to choose between artistic endeavors and social work
(D) desire to pursue a writing career and a desire to raise a family
(E) need to transcend lucid objectivity and express passion in her work

9. According to the passage, which one of the following best characterizes Woolf's feminism?

(A) a faith in feminine creativity and intuition
(B) an integration of the masculine and the feminine
(C) an indignation toward social institutions
(D) an emphasis on social equality
(E) a morbid preoccupation with self

10. The function of the third paragraph of the passage is to provide a

(A) concrete example of the points made in paragraph 2
(B) view contrasting with the one presented in paragraph 1
(C) transition between paragraphs 2 and 4
(D) subtopic to the main topic of paragraph 1
(E) exegesis of the works introduced in paragraph 1

11. Which one of the following oppositions does the author principally address in the passage?

(A) Woolf's aesthetic creed and the aesthetic creed of the Bloomsbury group
(B) Woolf's novels of social reform and Woolf's novels of individual soul-searching
(C) masculinity and femininity
(D) social injustice and self-reform
(E) Woolf's propaganda and Woolf's art

12. From the passage we can infer that the author

(A) questions the validity of the Bloomsbury aesthetic creed
(B) approves of symbolism only when used for social reform
(C) finds Woolf's fiction more successful than her nonfiction
(D) believes Woolf's social concerns are trivial
(E) dislikes literature written in the cause of social reform

13. Which one of the following would be the best title for this passage?

(A) *Three Guineas* and *The Years:* A Study
(B) Virginia Woolf's Success
(C) Virginia Woolf: Problems with Nonfiction
(D) Virginia Woolf: Reconciling Feminism and Art
(E) Masculine vs. Feminine: A Study of Virginia Woolf

Much as they may deplore the fact, historians have no monopoly on the past and no franchise as its privileged interpreters to the public. It may have (5) been different once, but there can no longer be any doubt about the relegation of the historian to a back seat. Far surpassing works of history, as measured by the size of their public (10) and the influence they exert, are the novel, works for the stage, the screen, and television. It is mainly from these sources that millions who never open a history book derive such conceptions, (15) interpretations, convictions, or fantasies as they have about the past. Whatever gives shape to popular conceptions of the past is of concern to historians, and this surely includes (20) fiction.

Broadly speaking, two types of fiction deal with the past—historical fiction and fictional history. The more common of the two is historical fiction, (25) which places fictional characters and events in a more or less authentic historical background. Examples range from *War and Peace* to *Gone With the Wind.* Since all but a few novelists (30) must place their fictional characters in some period, nearly all fiction can be thought of as in some degree historical. But the term is applied as a rule only to novels in which historical (35) events figure prominently. Fictional history, on the other hand, portrays and focuses attention upon real historical figures and events, but with the license of the novelist to imagine (40) and invent. It has yet to produce anything approaching Tolstoy's masterpiece. Some fictional history makes use of invented characters and events, and historical fiction at times (45) mixes up fictional and nonfictional characters. As a result the two genres overlap sometimes, but not often enough to make the distinction unimportant.

(50) Of the two, it is fictional history that is the greater source of mischief, for it is here that fabrication and fact, fiction and nonfiction, are most likely to be mixed and confused. Of course,

(55) historians themselves sometimes mix fact with fancy, but it is a rare one who does it consciously or deliberately, and he knows very well that if discovered he stands convicted of betraying his

(60) calling. The writer of fictional history, on the other hand, does this as a matter of course and with no compunction whatever. The production and consumption of fictional history

(65) appear to be growing of late. Part of the explanation of this is probably the fragmentation of history by professionals, their retreat into specializations, their abandonment of

(70) the narrative style, and with it the traditional patronage of lay readers. Fictional history has expanded to fill the gap thus created but has at the same time gone further to create a

(75) much larger readership than history books ever had.

14. We can infer from the passage that the author is probably

(A) a historian
(B) a historical novelist
(C) a literary critic
(D) a social commentator
(E) a literary historian

15. According to the passage, which one of the following is likely to have contributed to the increasing popularity of fictional history?

(A) a change in the demographics of lay readers of history

(B) an increase in the audience for movies and television
(C) a decline in historians' use of a storytelling style
(D) an increase in historians' mixing fact and fancy
(E) a decline in the writing ability of professional historians

16. The author's attitude toward fictional history can best be summarized in which one of the following statements?

(A) Masterpieces such as *War and Peace* and *Gone With the Wind* could not be created in the fictional history genre.
(B) Fictional history is responsible for leading the reading public away from traditional historical works.
(C) Fictional history provides a useful service by filling the gap for readers not interested in traditional history.
(D) Writers of fictional history should not mix historical figures with fictional characters.
(E) Fictional history can mislead readers about actual historical events.

17. Of the following, which one would the author consider most likely to cause a reader to confuse fact and fiction?

(A) a book about the Watergate scandal with fictionalized dialogue between President Nixon and his attorney general, John Mitchell
(B) a book about a fictional platoon in Vietnam during the last days of the war
(C) a fictional account of the adventures of a group of servants in the White House under Eisenhower, Kennedy, Johnson, and Nixon

(D) an account of the assassination of President Kennedy as viewed by a Texas adolescent on the parade route

(E) a book based on newspaper accounts about the reaction to the Cuban missile crisis in the United States, the U.S.S.R., and Western Europe

18. The function of the second paragraph of the passage is to

(A) reinforce the argument about fictionalized history presented in the first paragraph

(B) define and contrast fictional history and historical fiction

(C) emphasize the superiority of historical fiction to fictional history

(D) provide context for the analysis in the third paragraph

(E) clarify the difference between history and fiction

19. According to the passage, the author would agree with all of the following statements EXCEPT

(A) historical fiction and fictional history are of concern to the professional historian

(B) the works of today's professional historians tend to be more specialized than historical works of the past

(C) professional historians understand that they should not mix fact and fiction in their works

(D) a historical event presented as a TV miniseries is likely to be accepted as true by many people

(E) fictional history has succeeded because of a failure of the academic history curriculum

20. The author's attitude about the issue of fiction and history is presented most clearly in

(A) paragraph 1, lines 1–8
(B) paragraph 1, lines 17–20
(C) paragraph 2, lines 35–42
(D) paragraph 3, lines 50–54
(E) paragraph 3, lines 63–65

21. The tone of this passage could best be described as

(A) hostile and didactic
(B) moderate and concerned
(C) pedantic and detached
(D) ironic and condescending
(E) philosophical and enlightened

Most of our knowledge about how the brain links memory and emotion has been gleaned through the study of so-called classical fear conditioning. In
(5) this process the subject, usually a rat, hears a noise or sees a flashing light that is paired with a brief, mild electric shock to its feet. After a few such experiences, the rat responds
(10) automatically to the sound or light even in the absence of the shock. Its reactions are typical to any threatening situation: the animal freezes, its blood pressure and heart rate increase, and it
(15) startles easily. In the language of such experiments, the noise or flash is a conditioned stimulus, the foot shock is an unconditioned stimulus, and the rat's reaction is a conditioned
(20) response, which consists of readily measured behavioral and physiological changes.

Conditioning of this kind happens quickly in rats—indeed, it takes place
(25) as rapidly as it does in humans. A single pairing of the shock to the sound or sight can bring on the conditioned effect. Once established, the fearful

reaction is relatively permanent. If the (30) noise or light is administered many times without an accompanying electric shock, the rat's response diminishes. This change is called extinction. But considerable evidence (35) suggests that this behavioral alteration is the result of the brain's controlling the fear response rather than the elimination of the emotional memory. For example, an apparently (40) extinguished fear response can recover spontaneously or can be reinstated by an irrelevant stressful experience. Similarly, stress can cause the reappearance of phobias in people who (45) have been successfully treated. This resurrection demonstrates that the emotional memory underlying the phobia was rendered dormant rather than erased by treatment.

(50) Fear conditioning has proved an ideal starting point for studies of emotional memory for several reasons. First, it occurs in nearly every animal group in which it has been examined: fruit flies, (55) snails, birds, lizards, fish, rabbits, rats, monkeys, and people. Although no one claims that the mechanisms are precisely the same in all these creatures, it seems clear from studies (60) to date that the pathways are very similar in mammals and possibly in all vertebrates. We therefore are confident in believing that many of the findings in animals apply to humans. In addition, (65) the kinds of stimuli most commonly used in this type of conditioning are not signals that rats—or humans, for that matter—encounter in their daily lives. The novelty and irrelevance of (70) these lights and sounds help to ensure that the animals have not already developed strong emotional reactions to them. So researchers are clearly observing learning and memory at

(75) work. At the same time, such cues do not require complicated cognitive processing from the brain. Consequently, the stimuli permit us to study emotional mechanisms relatively (80) directly. Finally, our extensive knowledge of the neural pathways involved in processing acoustic and visual information serves as an excellent starting point for examining (85) the neurological foundations of fear elicited by such stimuli.

22. Which one of the following best states the main idea of the passage?

(A) Fear conditioning in animals and humans proves the direct link between emotion and memory.

(B) The mechanisms for linking memory and emotion are the same in mammals and possibly all vertebrates.

(C) Fear conditioning is a helpful starting point to use in studying emotional memory.

(D) Fearful reactions created by a conditioned stimulus are relatively permanent in both animals and humans.

(E) Fear conditioning in rats and other mammals is similar to the creation of phobias in humans.

23. Which one of the following statements is best supported by information presented in the passage?

(A) Fear conditioning requires that the conditioned and unconditioned stimuli are paired on many occasions.

(B) Emotional mechanisms in the brain are linked to complicated cognitive processing.

(C) The recurrence of human phobias under stress may be compared to the spontaneous recovery of the fear response in rats.

(D) A conditioned response is weakened in times of stress provided emotion and memory have been successfully linked.

(E) A rat's conditioned response to the pairing of conditioned and unconditioned stimuli diminishes over time.

24. A rat is exposed to a buzzer and an electric shock. After pairing the two stimuli 50 times, the rat exhibits a fear response when the buzzer alone is administered. The buzzer is then sounded *without* the shock an additional 200 times. According to the passage, the rat will probably

(A) continue to exhibit the fear response to the buzzer alone

(B) initially exhibit the fear response to the buzzer alone but then entirely lose the response

(C) initially exhibit the fear response to the buzzer alone, then appear to lose the response, then after the buzzer and shock are paired one additional time, exhibit it again to the buzzer alone

(D) initially exhibit the fear response to the buzzer alone, then appear to lose the response, then exhibit it again after a cat is introduced into the area

(E) initially exhibit the fear response to the buzzer alone, then begin to exhibit the response erratically, then lose the response entirely

25. The author contends that an apparently extinguished fear response that is recovered under stress indicates

(A) learning and memory

(B) complex cognitive processing

(C) previous strong emotional response to stimuli

(D) inadequate pairing of conditioned/unconditioned stimuli

(E) lack of control by the brain

26. The passage lists the nine specific animal groups for which fear conditioning studies have been performed in order to

(A) suggest the neural basis of the fear response

(B) show in how wide a range of animals fear conditioning is exhibited

(C) show the developmental link from fruit flies to people

(D) raise the question of the role of complex cognitive processes in fear conditioning

(E) show that emotions are present in simple as well as complex creatures

27. We can infer that the immediate goal of research described in the passage is to understand

(A) the neural basis of fear

(B) the relationship between cognition and emotion

(C) the mechanism of conditioning

(D) the effects of acoustic and visual stimuli

(E) the similarities among mammalian cognitive processes

28. Which one of the following best describes the relationship of the third paragraph to the passage as a whole?

(A) It completes the definition of the method begun by the author in the first paragraph and elaborated upon in the second paragraph.

(B) It presents qualifications to the points made in the first and second paragraphs and suggests other possible approaches.

(C) It summarizes the evidence and conclusions described in detail in the second paragraph.

(D) It presents further applications of the method explained in the first and second paragraphs.

(E) It justifies the use of the method explained in the first and second paragraphs.

STOP

IF YOU FINISH BEFORE TIME IS UP, CHECK YOUR WORK ON THIS SECTION OF THE TEST ONLY.
DO NOT GO ON TO THE NEXT SECTION OF THE TEST UNTIL TIME IS UP FOR THIS SECTION.

SECTION II

Time — 35 minutes
24 Questions

Directions: **In this section you will be given groups of questions based on different sets of conditions. Drawing a simple diagram may be helpful in answering some of the questions. You are to choose the best answer and mark the corresponding space on your answer sheet.**

Questions 1–6

The Bell Canyon Condominium is a four-story building with a single penthouse apartment on the fourth floor. There are two apartments on each of the three other floors. The apartments are owned by A, B, C, D, E, F, and G.

    A's apartment is on one of the floors higher than B's.

    C's apartment is on one of the floors lower than D's.

    C's apartment is on one of the floors lower than E's.

    F and G's apartments are on the same floor.

1. Which one of the following could be the owner of the penthouse?

    (A) B
    (B) C
    (C) E
    (D) F
    (E) G

2. If F's apartment is on the second floor, which one of the following must be true?

    (A) C's apartment is on the first floor.
    (B) D's apartment is on the third floor.
    (C) A's apartment is on the fourth floor.
    (D) G's apartment is on the first floor.
    (E) B's apartment is on the third floor.

3. If D owns the penthouse apartment, on which floor or floors could G's apartment be located?

    (A) the first floor only
    (B) the second floor only
    (C) the third floor only
    (D) the second or the third floor
    (E) the first, second, or third floor

4. If D's and E's apartments are on the same floor, which one of the following must be true?

    (A) D and E are on the third floor.
    (B) D and E are on the second floor.
    (C) A is on the fourth floor.
    (D) B and C are on the first floor.
    (E) F and G are on the second floor.

5. If C's apartment is on the first floor, and A is the owner of the penthouse, which one of the following must be true?

    (A) G's apartment is on the third floor.
    (B) D's apartment is on the second floor.
    (C) E's apartment is on the second floor.
    (D) B's apartment is on the first floor.
    (E) F's apartment is on the second floor.

6. Which one of the following is possible?

(A) A and C are on the same floor.
(B) A and E are on the same floor.
(C) A is on the first floor.
(D) D is on the first floor.
(E) C is on the fourth floor.

Questions 7–12

A new bank has decided to stay open only on weekends—all day Saturday and Sunday—and no other days. The bank has hired two managers (U and V), four tellers (W, X, Y, and Z), and two operations officers (S and T), for a total of exactly eight full-time employees. No part-time employees are hired. Each employee works a complete day when working.

  A manager must be on duty each day. The managers cannot work on the same day.

  At least two tellers must be working on the same day.

  W and X will not work on the same day.

  S and Z will only work on Saturday.

  No employee can work on consecutive days, but each employee must work on Saturday or Sunday.

7. Which one of the following could be false?

(A) If U works on Saturday, then V works on Sunday.
(B) If X works on Saturday, then W works on Sunday.
(C) T can work either day.
(D) If W works on Saturday and Y works on Sunday, then X works on Sunday.
(E) If U works on Sunday, then X works on Saturday.

8. Which one of the following is an acceptable group of employees that could work on Saturday?

(A) ZWYST
(B) UVWYZS
(C) VWXZT
(D) UZST
(E) VWZS

9. What is the greatest number of employees that can work on Saturday?

(A) 2
(B) 3
(C) 4
(D) 5
(E) 6

10. If W works on Sunday, then which one of the following must be true?

(A) X works on Saturday.
(B) Y works on Saturday.
(C) T works on Sunday.
(D) Z works on Sunday.
(E) U works on Saturday.

11. Which one of the following must be true?

(A) T always works the same day as Y.
(B) S never works the same day as U.
(C) Z never works the same day as X.
(D) If W works on Sunday, then Y always works on Saturday.
(E) Only two tellers work on Saturday.

12. Which one of the following is a complete and accurate list of the employees who have the possibility of working on Sunday?

(A) UWYZ
(B) UWYS
(C) UVWXT
(D) UVWXYT
(E) UVWXYTS

Questions 13–19

Three division office managers, Fred, Al, and Cynthia, draw office assistants each day from the clerical and typing pools available to them. The clerical pool consists of Lyndia, Jim, Dennis, and Sylvia. The typing pool consists of Edra, Gene, and Helen. The office assistants are selected according to the following conditions:

Fred always needs at least one typist, but never more than two assistants.

Al always needs at least two assistants, but never more than three.

Sylvia or Gene and one other assistant always work for Cynthia.

Gene and Lyndia always work together.

Dennis and Edra will not work together.

No more than two typists work for the same manager, but all three typists must work each day.

13. If Gene works for Fred and all of the assistants work, then which one of the following must be FALSE?

(A) Jim works for Cynthia.
(B) Sylvia works for Cynthia.
(C) Lyndia works for Fred.
(D) Dennis works for Al.
(E) Edra works for Al.

14. If Sylvia doesn't work for Cynthia, then which one of the following must be true?

(A) Edra works for Fred.
(B) Gene works for Al.
(C) Lyndia works for Cynthia.
(D) Dennis works for Al.
(E) Helen works for Cynthia.

15. Assume that Lyndia and Jim work for Al. Which one of the following must be true?

(A) Gene works for Al.
(B) Edra works for Cynthia.
(C) Helen works for Fred.
(D) Edra works for Fred.
(E) Helen works for Cynthia.

16. Assume that Sylvia and Jim work for Al. If all of the assistants work, then which one of the following must be true?

(A) Edra works for Al.
(B) Gene works for Fred.
(C) Lyndia works for Al.
(D) Helen works for Fred.
(E) Dennis works for Fred.

17. Which one of the following must be FALSE?

(A) Helen and Edra never work for Cynthia on the same day.
(B) Edra can work for Cynthia.
(C) Dennis and Gene never work for Fred on the same day.
(D) Jim and Sylvia never work for Fred on the same day.
(E) Lyndia and Sylvia can work for Al on the same day.

18. If Jim works for Cynthia and all of the assistants work, then

(A) Dennis works for Al.
(B) Edra works for Al.
(C) Helen works for Al.
(D) Lyndia works for Al.
(E) Sylvia works for Fred.

19. Assume that Al needs only two assistants and Fred needs only one assistant. If Helen works for Fred, then which one of the following must be true?

(A) Jim works for Al.
(B) Sylvia doesn't work.
(C) Dennis doesn't work.
(D) Edra works for Al.
(E) Edra works for Cynthia.

Questions 20–24

Four teams (Red, Blue, Green, and Yellow) participate in the Junior Olympics, in which there are five events. In each event participants place either 1st, 2nd, 3rd, or 4th. First place is awarded a gold medal, 2nd place is awarded a silver medal, and 3rd place is awarded a bronze medal. There are no ties and each team enters one contestant in each event. All contestants finish each event.

The results of the Junior Olympics are:
    No team wins gold medals in two consecutive events.
    No team fails to win a medal within two consecutive events.
    The Blue team wins only two medals, neither of them gold.
    The Red team only wins three gold medals, and no other medals.

20. If the green team wins only one gold medal, then which one of the following must be true?

(A) The yellow team wins two gold medals.
(B) The red team wins only two bronze medals.
(C) The yellow team wins only one gold medal.

(D) The yellow team wins only silver medals.
(E) The green team wins only bronze medals.

21. Which one of the following must be true?

(A) The yellow team wins only bronze and gold medals.
(B) The yellow team wins five medals.
(C) The green team cannot win a silver medal.
(D) The yellow team cannot win a bronze medal.
(E) The green team wins exactly three medals.

22. If the yellow team wins five silver medals, then the green team must win

(A) more silver than gold
(B) more gold than bronze
(C) two gold, two bronze, one silver
(D) two gold, three bronze
(E) six medals

23. All of the following must be true EXCEPT

(A) the green team wins five medals
(B) the yellow team wins five medals
(C) if the green team wins one gold medal, the yellow team wins one gold medal
(D) if the green team wins only one silver medal, the yellow team wins only one silver medal
(E) if the yellow team wins only silver medals, the green team cannot win a silver medal

24. If a fifth team, Orange, enters all events and wins only three consecutive silver medals, which one of the following must be true?

    (A) If green wins a gold in the 2nd event, it also wins a bronze in the 3rd event.

    (B) If green wins a gold in the 2nd event, it also wins a silver in the 4th event.

    (C) If yellow wins a gold in the 2nd event, green wins a bronze in the 3rd event.

    (D) If yellow wins a gold in the 2nd event, blue wins a silver in the 3rd event.

    (E) If red wins a gold in the 1st event, orange wins a silver in the last event.

STOP

IF YOU FINISH BEFORE TIME IS UP, CHECK YOUR WORK ON THIS SECTION OF THE TEST ONLY.
DO NOT GO ON TO THE NEXT SECTION OF THE TEST UNTIL TIME IS UP FOR THIS SECTION.

SECTION III

Time — 35 minutes
26 Questions

**Directions:** **In this section you will be given brief statements or passages and will be required to evaluate the reasoning involved. In some instances, more than one choice will appear to be a possible answer. You are to choose the _best_ answer. Use common sense and reasonableness in making your selection; then mark the proper space on the answer sheet.**

1. Though the benefits of the hot tub and the Jacuzzis have been well publicized by their manufacturers, there are also some less widely known dangers. Young children, of course, cannot be left unattended near a hot tub, and even adults have fallen asleep and drowned. Warm water can cause the blood vessels to dilate and the resulting drop in blood pressure can make people liable to fainting, especially when they stand up quickly to get out. Improperly maintained water can promote the growth of bacteria that can cause folliculitis.

The main point of this passage is that

(A) the benefits of the hot tub and the Jacuzzi have been overrated
(B) the dangers of the hot tub and Jacuzzi outweigh their potential publicized benefits
(C) users of hot tubs and Jacuzzis should be aware of the dangers connected with their use
(D) the hot tub and Jacuzzi are dangerous only when improperly maintained
(E) the hot tub is potentially beneficial in the treatment of high blood pressure

2. _Chariots of Fire_ may have caught some professional critics off guard in 1982 as the Motion Picture Academy's choice for an Oscar as the year's best

film, but it won wide audience approval as superb entertainment.

Refreshingly, _Chariots of Fire_ features an exciting story, enchanting English and Scottish scenery, a beautiful musical score, and appropriate costumes.

All of these attractions are added to a theme that extols traditional religious values—without a shred of offensive sex, violence, or profanity.

Too good to be true? See _Chariots of Fire_ and judge for yourself.

Those who condemn the motion picture industry for producing so many objectionable films can do their part by patronizing wholesome ones, thereby encouraging future Academy Award judges to recognize and reward decency.

Which one of the following is a basic assumption underlying the final sentence of the passage?

(A) Academy judges are not decent people.
(B) The popularity of a film influences academy judges.
(C) Future academy judges will be better than past ones.
(D) There are those who condemn the motion picture industry.
(E) _Chariots of Fire_ is a patronizing film.

3. *Andy:* All teachers are mean.
   Bob: That is not true. I know some doctors who are mean too.

Bob's answer demonstrates that he thought Andy to mean that

(A) all teachers are mean
(B) some teachers are mean
(C) doctors are meaner than teachers
(D) teachers are meaner than doctors
(E) only teachers are mean

4. Theodore Roosevelt was a great hunter. He was the mighty Nimrod of his generation. He had the physical aptitude and adventurous spirit of the true frontiersman. "There is delight," he said, "in the hardy life of the open; in long rides, rifle in hand; in the thrill of the fight with dangerous game." But he was more than a marksman and tracker of beasts, for he brought to his sport the intellectual curiosity and patient observation of the natural scientist.

Which one of the following would most weaken the author's concluding contention?

(A) Theodore Roosevelt never studied natural science.
(B) Actually, Theodore Roosevelt's sharpshooting prowess was highly exaggerated.
(C) Theodore Roosevelt always used native guides when tracking game.
(D) Theodore Roosevelt was known to leave safaris if their first few days were unproductive.
(E) Theodore Roosevelt's powers of observation were significantly hampered by his nearsightedness.

5. The following is an excerpt from a letter sent to a law school applicant:
   "Thank you for considering our school to further your education. Your application for admission was received well before the deadline and was processed with your admission test score and undergraduate grade report.
   "We regret to inform you that you cannot be admitted for the fall semester. We have had to refuse admission to many outstanding candidates because of the recent cut in state funding of our program.
   "Thank you for your interest in our school and we wish you success in your future endeavors."

Which one of the following can be deduced from the above letter?

(A) The recipient of the letter did not have a sufficiently high grade point average to warrant admission to this graduate program.
(B) The recipient of the letter was being seriously considered for a place in the evening class.
(C) The law school sending the letter could not fill all the places in its entering class due to a funding problem.
(D) Criteria other than test scores and grade reports were used in determining the size of the entering class.
(E) The school sending the letter is suffering severe financial difficulties.

Questions 6–7

At birth we have no self-image. We cannot distinguish anything from the confusion of light and sound around us. From this beginning of no-dimension, we gradually begin to differentiate our body from our environment and develop a sense of identity, with the realization that we are a separate and independent human being. We then begin to develop a conscience, the sense of right and wrong. Further, we develop social consciousness, where we become aware that we live with other people. Finally, we develop a sense of values, which is our overall estimation of our worth in the world.

6. Which one of the following would be the best completion of this passage?

(A) The sum total of all these developments we call the self-image or the self-concept.
(B) This estimation of worth is only relative to our value system.
(C) Therefore, our social consciousness is dependent on our sense of values.
(D) Therefore, our conscience keeps our sense of values in perspective.
(E) The sum total of living with other people and developing a sense of values makes us a total person.

7. The author of this passage would most likely agree with which one of the following?

(A) Children have no self-dimension.
(B) Having a conscience necessitates the ability to differentiate between right and wrong.
(C) Social consciousness is our most important awareness.

(D) Heredity is predominant over environment in development.
(E) The ability to distinguish the difference between moral issues depends on the overall dimension of self-development.

8. Opportunity makes the thief. Without thieves there would be no crime. Without opportunity there would be no crime.

Which one of the following most weakens the statements above?

(A) Thieves wait for opportunities.
(B) Without crime there would be no opportunity.
(C) Thieves are not the only criminals.
(D) Some crimes carry greater penalties.
(E) Many thieves are not caught.

Questions 9–10

In a report released last week, a government-funded institute concluded that there is "overwhelming" evidence that violence on television leads to criminal behavior by children and teenagers.

The report based on an extensive review of several hundred research studies conducted during the 1970s, is an update of a 1972 Surgeon General's report that came to similar conclusions.

9. Which one of the following is the most convincing statement in support of the argument in the first paragraph above?

(A) A 50-state survey of the viewing habits of prison inmates concluded that every inmate watches at least 2 hours of violent programming each day.

(B) A 50-state survey of the viewing habits of convicted adolescents shows that each of them had watched at least 2 hours of violent programming daily since the age of 5.

(C) One juvenile committed a murder that closely resembled a crime portrayed on a network series.

(D) The 1972 Surgeon General's report was not nearly as extensive as this more recent study.

(E) Ghetto residents who are burglarized most often report the theft of a television set.

10. The argument above is most weakened by its vague use of the word

(A) violence
(B) government
(C) extensive
(D) update
(E) overwhelming

Questions 11–12

Violence against racial and religious minority groups increased sharply throughout the county last year, despite a slight decline in statewide figures. Compiling incidents from police departments and private watchdog groups, the County Human Relations Committee reported almost 500 hate crimes in the year, up from only 200 last year. It was the first increase since the committee began to report a yearly figure six years ago. The lower statewide figures are probably in error due to underreporting in other counties; underreporting is the major problem that state surveyors face each year.

11. All of the following, if true, would support the conclusion or the explanation of the discrepancy in the state and county figures EXCEPT

(A) the number of hate crimes and those resulting in fatalities has increased in neighboring states

(B) anti-immigration sentiment was fanned this year by an anti-immigration ballot referendum

(C) funding for police departments throughout the state has decreased

(D) many law-abiding members of minority groups are fearful or distrustful of the police

(E) all of the counties in the state have active private watchdog groups that carefully monitor hate crimes

12. The author of this passage makes his case by

(A) establishing the likelihood of an event by ruling out several other possibilities

(B) combining several pieces of apparently unrelated evidence to build support for a conclusion

(C) contrasting a single certain case with several others with less evidence in their support

(D) assuming that what is only probable is certain

(E) using a general rule to explain a specific case

13. The study of village communities has become one of the fundamental methods of discussing the ancient history of institutions. It would be out of the question here to range over the whole field of human society in search for communal arrangements of rural life. It will be sufficient to confine the present inquiry to the varieties presented by nations of Aryan race, not because greater importance is to be attached to these nations than to other branches of humankind, although this view might also be reasonably urged, but principally because the Aryan race in its history has gone through all sorts of experiences, and the data gathered from its historical life can be tolerably well ascertained. Should the road be sufficiently cleared in this particular direction, it will not be difficult to connect the results with similar researches in other racial surroundings.

Which one of the following, if true, most weakens the author's conclusion?

(A) Information about the Aryan race is no more conclusive than information about any other ethnic group.
(B) The experiences and lifestyle of Aryans are uniquely different from those of other cultures.
(C) The Aryan race is no more important than any other race.
(D) The historical life of the Aryans dates back only 12 centuries.
(E) Aryans lived predominantly in villages, while today 90 percent of the world population live predominantly in or around major cities.

14. Although any reasonable modern citizen of the world must abhor war and condemn senseless killing, we must also agree that honor is more valuable than life. Life, after all, is transient, but honor is _____.

Which one of the following most logically completes the passage above?

(A) sensible
(B) real
(C) eternal
(D) of present value
(E) priceless

Questions 15–16

Bill said, "All dogs bark. This animal does not bark. Therefore it is not a dog."

15. Which one of the following most closely parallels the logic of this statement?

(A) All rocks are hard. This lump is hard. Therefore, it may be a rock.
(B) All foreign language tests are difficult. This is not a foreign language test. Therefore, it is not difficult.
(C) All Blunder automobiles are poorly built. Every auto sold by Joe was poorly built. Therefore, Joe sells Blunder automobiles.
(D) Rocks beat scissors, scissors beat paper, and paper beats rocks. Therefore, it is best to choose paper.
(E) All paint smells. This liquid does not smell. Therefore, it is not paint.

16. Which one of the following would weaken Bill's argument the most?

(A) Animals other than dogs bark.
(B) Some dogs cannot bark.
(C) Dogs bark more than cockatiels.
(D) You can train a dog not to bark.
(E) You can train birds to bark.

17. No one cheats on all the exams he takes. Some people cheat on most of the exams they take. Most cheat on some of the exams they take. Everyone has cheated on at least one exam he has taken. Cheating is wrong.

Which one of the following is inconsistent with the preceding facts?

(A) Joe has never been caught cheating.
(B) Cheating is an acceptable procedure.
(C) Jack is never wrong.
(D) More people cheat on none of the exams they have taken than cheat on all of the exams they have taken.
(E) More people cheat on some of the exams they have taken than cheat on most of the exams they have taken.

Questions 18–19

California and Nevada officials have questioned the impartiality of the board of scientists from the National Academy of Science who assess the safety of proposed nuclear dumping sites. They claim that the panels are heavily weighted in favor of the nuclear power companies that have been lobbying for the creation of nuclear dump sites in the deserts of the Southwest. At least ten members of the panels are or have been employees of the Department of Energy, but none is associated with any environmental organization. Environmentalists fear that long-lived nuclear wastes may leach into the groundwater and ultimately into the waters of the Colorado River. They also point out that 90 percent of the budget of the National Academy's Radioactive Waste Management Board is provided by the Department of Energy. The inventory of radioactive waste has been growing larger and larger in temporary storage places, but so far there has been virtually no agreement about a permanent dump site.

18. The officials who question the impartiality of the Management Board assume that the Department of Energy

(A) supports the activities of the nuclear power industry
(B) supports the activities of environmental groups
(C) wishes to delay the selection of permanent nuclear waste dumping sites for as long as possible
(D) is indifferent to the growing mass of nuclear wastes in temporary storage sites
(E) has declined to take a stand for or against the use of nuclear power

19. The Nuclear Waste Management Board could best allay doubt of its impartiality if it were to

(A) publish the results of its studies of the feasibility of locating nuclear waste dumps in the deserts of the Southwest
(B) add one or two environmentalists to the panels that assess locations for nuclear dump sites
(C) make public the sources of all its funding
(D) recommend desert sites at a greater distance from the Colorado River
(E) base decisions on feasibility studies by scientists with no connection to the National Academy

---

20. The law of parsimony urges a strict economy upon us; it requires that we can never make a guess with two or three assumptions in it if we can make sense with one.

Which one of the following is the main point of the author's statement?

(A) Complications arise from economy.
(B) Simplify terminology whenever possible.
(C) Don't complicate a simple issue.
(D) Assumptions are necessarily simple in nature.
(E) Excess assumptions never clarify the situation.

21. You can use a bottle opener to open the new beer bottles. You do not need to use a bottle opener to open the new beer bottles.

Which one of the following most closely parallels the logic of these statements?

(A) You must turn on the switch to light the lamp. If you turn on the switch, the lamp may not light.
(B) A cornered rattlesnake will strike, so do not corner a rattlesnake.
(C) If you do not study you will fail the test. If you do study, you may fail the test.
(D) Every candidate I voted for in the election lost his race. I must learn to vote better.
(E) I can move the sofa with my brother's help. If my brother is not available, I'll get a neighbor to help me.

22. To be admitted to Bigshot University, you must have a 3.5 grade-point average (GPA) and a score of 800 on the admissions test, a 3.0 GPA and a score of 1000 on the admissions test, or a 2.5 GPA and a score of 1200 on the admissions test. A sliding scale exists for other scores and GPAs.

Which one of the following is inconsistent with the above?

(A) The higher the GPA, the lower the admissions test score needed for admission.
(B) Joe was admitted with a 2.7 GPA and a score of 1100 on the admissions test.
(C) No student with a score of less than 800 on the admissions test and a 3.4 GPA will be admitted.

(D) More applicants had a GPA of 3.5 than had a GPA of 2.5.

(E) Some students with a score of less than 1200 on the admissions test and a GPA of less than 2.5 were admitted.

23. The Census Bureau's family portrait of America may remind us of the problems we face as a nation, but it also gives us reason to take heart in our ability to solve them in an enlightened way. The 1980 census was the first in history to show that the majority of the population in every state has completed high school. And the percentage of our people with at least 4 years of college rose from 11 percent in 1970 to 16.3 percent in 1980. That's progress—where it really counts.

Which one of the following assumptions underlies the author's conclusion in the above passage?

(A) Greater numbers of high school and college degrees coincide with other firsts in the 1980 census.

(B) Greater numbers of high school and college degrees coincide with greater numbers of well-educated people.

(C) Greater numbers of high school and college degrees coincide with a great commitment to social progress.

(D) Greater numbers of high school and college degrees coincide with a better chance to avoid national catastrophe.

(E) Greater numbers of high school and college degrees coincide with the 1980 census.

24. Add No-NOCK to your car and watch its performance soar. No-NOCK will give it more get-up-and-go and keep it running longer. Ask for No-NOCK when you want better mileage!

According to the advertisement above, No-NOCK claims to do everything EXCEPT

(A) improve your car's performance

(B) increase your car's life

(C) improve your car's miles per gallon

(D) cause fewer breakdowns

(E) stop the engine from knocking

25. So many arrogant and ill-tempered young men have dominated the tennis courts of late that we had begun to fear those characteristics were prerequisites for championship tennis.

Tennis used to be a gentleman's game. What is sad is not just that the game has changed. With so much importance placed on success, it may be that something has gone out of the American character—such things as gentleness and graciousness.

Which one of the following statements, if true, would most weaken the above argument?

(A) The American character is a result of American goals.

(B) Tennis has only recently become a professional sport.

(C) Some ill-tempered tennis players are unsuccessful.

(D) The "gentlemen" of early tennis often dueled to the death off the court.

(E) Some even-tempered tennis players are successful.

26. *Dolores:* To preserve the peace, we must be prepared to go to war with any nation at any time, using either conventional or nuclear weapons.
Fran: Which shall it be, conventional weapons or nuclear weapons?

Fran mistakenly concludes that the "either . . . or" phrase in Dolores's statement indicates

(A) fear
(B) indecision
(C) a choice
(D) a question
(E) a refusal

STOP

IF YOU FINISH BEFORE TIME IS UP, CHECK YOUR WORK ON THIS SECTION OF THE TEST ONLY.
DO NOT GO ON TO THE NEXT SECTION OF THE TEST UNTIL TIME IS UP FOR THIS SECTION.

SECTION IV

Time — 35 minutes
24 Questions

Directions: In this section you will be given groups of questions based on different sets of conditions. Drawing a simple diagram may be helpful in answering some of the questions. You are to choose the best answer and mark the corresponding space on your answer sheet.

Questions 1–6

A group of tourists is planning to visit a cluster of islands—U, V, W, X, Y, and Z, connected by bridges. The tourists must stay on each island visited for exactly three days and three nights. Each bridge takes one hour to cross, may be crossed in either direction, and can be crossed only in the morning to give the tourists a full day on the island.

   The islands are connected by bridges
      only as indicated below:
   U is connected to W, X, and Y
   V is connected to Y and Z
   X is connected to Z and W
   Y is connected to X and Z

1. If the group visits island W first, eight days later it could NOT be at which one of the following islands?

   (A) U
   (B) V
   (C) X
   (D) Y
   (E) Z

2. If the group stays on island X for three nights, it CANNOT spend the next three days and nights on island

   (A) U
   (B) V
   (C) W
   (D) Y
   (E) Z

3. Which one of the following is a possible order of islands visited in 12 days and nights?

   (A) UWYZ
   (B) UVYZ
   (C) UYVX
   (D) UXZV
   (E) UWYX

4. If the group visits island W first and can visit an island more than once, but does not use a bridge more than once, what is the greatest number of visits it can make?

   (A) 5
   (B) 6
   (C) 7
   (D) 8
   (E) 9

5. Assume the group visits island X first, and does not use a bridge more than once. Assume also that the group does stay at island Y twice. What is the greatest number of different islands the group can visit?

   (A) 3
   (B) 4
   (C) 5
   (D) 6
   (E) 7

6. Assume another island, T, is added to the tour. Assume also that T is connected only to U. Which one of the following statements must be true?

(A) On the eighth day of a tour, starting its visit at island T, the group could be on island V.
(B) On the fifth day of a tour, starting its visit at island T, the group could be on island X.
(C) On the seventh day of a tour, starting its visit at island T, the group could be on island U.
(D) On the eighth day of a tour, starting its visit at island V, the group could be on island T.
(E) On the tenth day of a tour, starting its visit at island Z, the tour group could be on island T.

Questions 7–13

Teams A and B play a series of 9 games. To win the series, a team must win the most games, but must also win a minimum of 3 games.
There are no ties in the first 3 games.
Team A wins more of the last 3 games than team B.
Team B wins more of the last 5 games than team A.
The last game is a tie.
Games 1 and 3 are won by the same team.

7. Which one of the following must be true?

(A) One team must win 5 games to win the series.
(B) There are no ties.
(C) One team wins at least 2 of the first 3 games.
(D) The same team wins the last 5 games.
(E) The last three games are won by one team.

8. Considering all of the conditions mentioned above, game 6

(A) could be won by team A
(B) could be won by team B
(C) could be a tie
(D) must be won by team A
(E) must be won by team B

9. If game 7 is won by team A, then

(A) game 8 is a tie
(B) game 2 is a tie
(C) game 4 is won by team A
(D) game 5 is a tie
(E) game 6 is won by team A

10. Which one of the following must be true?

(A) There is only 1 tie in the last 5 games.
(B) Team A wins 2 of the first 3 games.
(C) Team B can win 3 of the last 5 games.
(D) Game 4 is a tie.
(E) Team A can win only 1 of the last 5 games.

11. If team A wins game 1 and game 4, then which one of the following must be FALSE?

(A) Team A wins game 3.
(B) Team A wins game 2.
(C) Team B wins game 2.
(D) Team A wins the series.
(E) Team B wins the series.

12. Assume that game 4 is won by the winner of game 5. If game 2 is not won by the winner of game 3, then which one of the following must be true?

(A) Team A wins game 7.
(B) Team B is the winner of the series.
(C) Team A wins game 2.
(D) Team B wins game 1.
(E) Team A wins game 3.

13. Which one of the following must be true?

   (A) For team A to win the series, team A must win exactly two of the first four games.
   (B) For team B to win the series, team B must win exactly one of the first four games.
   (C) For team A to win the series, team A must win only three of the first seven games.
   (D) For team B to win the series, team B must win at least three of the first four games.
   (E) For team A to win the series, team A must win two consecutive games.

Questions 14–18

Eight busts of American Presidents are to be arranged on two shelves, left to right. Each shelf accommodates exactly four busts. One shelf is directly above the other shelf. The busts are of John Adams, George Washington, Abraham Lincoln, Thomas Jefferson, James Monroe, John Kennedy, Theodore Roosevelt and Franklin Delano Roosevelt.

   The Roosevelt busts may not be directly one above the other.
   The bust of Kennedy must be adjacent to the bust of a Roosevelt.
   The bust of Jefferson must be directly above the bust of John Adams.
   The busts of Monroe, Adams, Kennedy and Franklin Delano Roosevelt must be on the bottom shelf.
   The bust of Monroe must be third from the left.

14. If the bust of Theodore Roosevelt is second from the left on one shelf, which one of the following must be true?

   (A) The bust of Adams must be first on a shelf.
   (B) The bust of Adams must be third on a shelf.
   (C) The bust of Kennedy must be first on a shelf.
   (D) The bust of Kennedy must be second on a shelf.
   (E) The bust of Kennedy must be third on a shelf.

15. Which one of the following must be true about the bust of Monroe?

   (A) It is next to the bust of Adams.
   (B) It is next to the bust of Kennedy.
   (C) It is next to the bust of Franklin Delano Roosevelt.
   (D) It is directly under the bust of Lincoln.
   (E) It is directly under the bust of Theodore Roosevelt.

16. If the bust of Washington is first, directly above Kennedy's, all of the following must be true EXCEPT

   (A) the bust of Jefferson is fourth
   (B) the bust of Theodore Roosevelt is third
   (C) the bust of Franklin Delano Roosevelt is second
   (D) the bust of Lincoln is third
   (E) the bust of Adams is fourth

17. Which one of the following is not a possible order for the busts on either shelf?

   (A) Washington, Lincoln, Theodore Roosevelt, Jefferson
   (B) Franklin Delano Roosevelt, Kennedy, Monroe, Adams

(C) Theodore Roosevelt, Lincoln,
Washington, Jefferson
(D) Lincoln, Theodore Roosevelt,
Washington, Jefferson
(E) Kennedy, Adams, Monroe, Franklin
Delano Roosevelt

18. If the bust of Lincoln is next to the bust
of Jefferson, all of the following are
true EXCEPT

(A) if the bust of Kennedy is first, the
bust of Theodore Roosevelt is also
first
(B) if the bust of Washington is first,
the bust of Franklin Delano
Roosevelt is also first
(C) if the bust of Washington is
second, the bust of Kennedy is also
second
(D) if the bust of Kennedy is second,
the bust of Theodore Roosevelt is
also second
(E) if the bust of Washington is
second, the bust of Franklin Delano
Roosevelt is also second

Questions 19–24

For a dinner party, a hostess needs several
different three-bean salads.
    Each salad is to contain three types of
    beans, chosen from garbanzos,
    chili beans, wax beans, lima beans,
    and kidney beans.
Chili beans and lima beans do not taste
    good together and therefore are
    never used in the same salad.
Lima beans and kidney beans do not
    look good together and therefore
    are never used in the same salad.

19. How many different salads (using the
above ingredients) could the hostess
serve that contain lima beans?

(A) 0
(B) 1
(C) 2
(D) 3
(E) 4

20. How many different salads could she
serve that do not contain chili beans?

(A) 0
(B) 1
(C) 2
(D) 3
(E) 4

21. How many different salad
combinations could she serve at the
party?

(A) 4
(B) 5
(C) 6
(D) 7
(E) 8

22. Which beans will occur most often in
the salad combinations that could be
served at the party?

(A) chili and garbanzos
(B) chili and limas
(C) limas and wax beans
(D) kidney and limas
(E) garbanzos and wax beans

23. If there are only enough wax beans to
go into two salads, what is the total
number of salads that can be served?

(A) 1
(B) 2
(C) 3
(D) 4
(E) 5

24. If the hostess discovers the garbanzos
    have gone bad, how many three-bean
    combinations can she serve without
    using the rotten garbanzos?

    (A) 0
    (B) 1
    (C) 2
    (D) 3
    (E) 4

STOP

IF YOU FINISH BEFORE TIME IS UP, CHECK YOUR WORK ON THIS SECTION OF THE TEST ONLY.
DO NOT GO ON TO THE NEXT SECTION OF THE TEST UNTIL TIME IS UP FOR THIS SECTION.

SECTION V

Time — 35 minutes
25 Questions

Directions: **In this section you will be given brief statements or passages and will be required to evaluate the reasoning involved. In some instances, more than one choice will appear to be a possible answer. You are to choose the best answer. Use common sense and reasonableness in making your selection; then mark the proper space on the answer sheet.**

1. Chrysanthemums that have not been fertilized in July will normally not blossom in October. In October, the chrysanthemums did not blossom.

   With the premises given above, which one of the following would logically complete an argument?

   (A) Therefore, the chrysanthemums were not fertilized in July.
   (B) Therefore, the chrysanthemums may not have been fertilized in July.
   (C) Therefore, the chrysanthemums may blossom later in the fall.
   (D) Therefore, the chrysanthemums will blossom in the fall.
   (E) Therefore, the chrysanthemums will not blossom later in the fall.

2. When asked about the danger to public health from the spraying of pesticides by helicopters throughout the county, the County Supervisor replied, "The real danger to the public is the possibility of an infestation of harmful fruit-flies, which this spraying will prevent. Such an infestation would drive up the cost of fruits and vegetables by 15 percent."

   Which one of the following is the most serious weakness in the Supervisor's reply to the question?

   (A) He depends upon the ambiguity in the word "danger."

   (B) His response contains a self-contradiction.
   (C) He fails to support his argument concretely.
   (D) He fails to answer the question that has been asked.
   (E) His chief concern is the economic consequences of spraying.

3. So far this year researchers have reported the following:

   Heavy coffee consumption can increase the risk of heart attacks.
   Drinking a cup of coffee in the morning increases feelings of well-being and alertness.
   Boiled coffee increases blood cholesterol levels.
   Coffee may protect against cancer of the colon.

   If all these statements are true, which one of the following conclusions can be drawn from this information?

   (A) Reducing coffee consumption will make people healthier.
   (B) Reducing coffee consumption will make people feel better.
   (C) People at risk for heart attack should limit their coffee drinking.
   (D) Percolated coffee will not affect cholesterol levels.
   (E) People at risk for cancer should reduce their coffee consumption.

4. Compared with children in other states, infants born in California weigh more, survive the first years in greater numbers, and live longer. The hysteria about the danger of pesticides in California has attracted attention simply because a few Hollywood stars have appeared on television talk shows. Pesticides are the responsibility of the California Department of Food and Agriculture, and we can be sure its members are doing their job.

The argument of this paragraph would be weakened if all of the following were shown to be true EXCEPT

(A) rates of melanoma and some forms of leukemia in California are above national norms

(B) the three highest positions at the California Department of Food and Agriculture are held by farm owners

(C) synthetic pesticide residues in food cause more cancer than do "natural pesticides" that the plants themselves produce

(D) more Californians suffer the consequences of air pollution than do the citizens in any other state

(E) children of farm workers are three times more likely to suffer childhood cancers than children of urban parents

5. Should we allow the Fire Department to continue to underpay its women officers by using policies of promotion that favor men?

The question above most closely resembles which one of the following in terms of its logical features?

(A) Should the excessive tax on cigarettes, liquor, and luxury goods be unfairly increased again this year?

(B) Should corrupt politicians be subject to the same sentencing laws as blue-collar felons?

(C) Should the police chief be chosen by examination score regardless of gender or seniority?

(D) Should the religious right be allowed to determine the censorship laws for all of society?

(E) Are liberal political values an appropriate basis for all of the social values in this state?

6. If airline fares have risen, then either the cost of fuel has risen or there are no fare wars among competing companies. If there are no fare wars among competing companies, the number of airline passengers is larger than it was last year.

According to the passage above, if there has been a rise in airline fares this month, which one of the following CANNOT be true?

(A) There are no fare wars among competing airlines.

(B) The cost of fuel has risen, and the number of passengers is the same as last year.

(C) The cost of fuel has risen, there are no fare wars, and the number of passengers is larger than it was last year.

(D) There are no fare wars, and the number of passengers is larger than it was last year.

(E) The cost of fuel has risen, there are no fare wars, and the number of passengers is smaller than it was last year.

7. Only 75 years ago, the best fishing in the world was the Grand Banks of the North Atlantic. But now overfishing and man's pollution have decimated the area. There will be no fishing industry in the Americas in a very few years. The waters off Newfoundland now yield less than half the catch of five years ago, and less than one quarter of the total of ten years ago. The cod has almost disappeared. The number of fishermen in Newfoundland and New England has declined, and their yearly earnings are now at an all-time low. Yet radar has made fishing methods more efficient than ever.

Which one of the following identifies most clearly a faulty assumption in the reasoning of this passage?

(A) Ten years is too short a time period to use to draw conclusions about the natural world.

(B) The argument assumes that the waters off Newfoundland are representative of all the American oceans.

(C) The pollution of the sea may have been caused by natural as well as by human forces.

(D) The argument does not allow for the possibility that the catch may increase in size in the next five years.

(E) The argument fails to consider that the decline in the catch may be due to factors other than pollution.

8. A cigarette advertisement in a magazine asks, "What do gremlins, the Loch Ness monster, and a filter cigarette claiming 'great taste' have in common?" The answer is "You've heard of all of them, but don't really believe they exist."

The advertisement contains no pictures, and no additional text except the words Gold Star Cigarettes and the Surgeon General's warning in a box in the lower corner.

Which one of the following conclusions can be drawn from the information given above?

(A) Cigarette advertising depends upon visual appeal to create images for specific brands.

(B) All cigarette advertising depends on praising a specific brand.

(C) Gold Star Cigarettes are non-filters.

(D) The writers of this advertisement do not believe in advertising.

(E) The writers of this advertisement do not believe the Surgeon General's warning is true.

9. The traffic on the Imperial Highway has always been slowed by the dangerous curves in the road. It was built when cars were much smaller and less powerful, and very few drivers traveled between Imperial City and Fremont. All this has changed. The cost of widening and straightening the road would now be many times greater than building the proposed new toll road on the borders of the Imperial Wetlands reserve. Environmentalists fear the construction noise and waste will harm the wildlife in the reserve, and have urged that the toll road not be constructed.

Which one of the following, if true, would most strengthen the case of the environmentalists?

(A) None of the animals living in the Imperial Wetlands is on the list of endangered species.
(B) The traffic congestion on the Imperial Highway increases each year.
(C) The cost of building the new road will be amortized in ten years by the tolls collected.
(D) There are several less direct routes the toll road could take between Fremont and Imperial City.
(E) The environmentalists threaten to bring a lawsuit in federal court to halt construction of the road.

10. Despite the very large increase in the federal tax on luxury items, the value of the stock of Harry Evans, Inc., seller of the world's most expensive jewelry, continues to rise. Six months after the introduction of the tax, Evans's stock is at an all-time high. Moreover, sales in the United States continue to increase. In other countries, where Evans does 30 percent of its business, there have been no rises in excise taxes and the company will open new stores in Tokyo, Monte Carlo, and Singapore. According to a company spokesperson, _____.

Which one of the following most logically completes this paragraph?

(A) American customers who can afford to shop at Evans are not likely to be deterred by a rise in luxury taxes
(B) American customers are expected to spend far less at Evans because of the tax rise
(C) American sales are not significant enough to affect the overall profits of the firm
(D) the company will probably be forced to close most of its stores in America
(E) state taxes are more likely to influence jewelry sales than federal taxes

11. A recent study of cigarette smokers has shown that, of cancer patients who are heavy smokers of unfiltered cigarettes, 40 percent will die of the disease. For cancer patients who are light smokers of filter cigarettes, the percentage is 25 percent.

Which one of the following conclusions can be drawn from the information above?

(A) There are more heavy smokers of unfiltered cigarettes than light smokers of filter cigarettes.

(B) More heavy smokers of unfiltered cigarettes die of cancer than light smokers of filter cigarettes.

(C) A heavy smoker of unfiltered cigarettes who has cancer is more likely to die than a light smoker of unfiltered cigarettes.

(D) A heavy smoker of unfiltered cigarettes who has cancer may be more likely to die than a light smoker of unfiltered cigarettes.

(E) A heavy smoker of unfiltered cigarettes who has cancer is more likely to die than a light smoker of filtered cigarettes who has cancer.

Questions 12–13

Archeologists have come to the support of Arctic anthropologists. A small minority of anthropologists assert that Stone-Age tribes of the Arctic domesticated wolves and trained them to haul sleds. Excavations have recently found evidence to support this claim. Archeologists have found wolf bones near the site of a Stone-Age village. They have also found walrus bones that might have been used on primitive sleds. The small minority of anthropologists believe that their theories have been proved.

12. Which one of the following is true of the evidence cited in the paragraph above?

(A) It is not relevant to the anthropologists' conclusions.

(B) It conclusively contradicts the anthropologists' conclusions.

(C) It neither supports nor refutes the anthropologists' conclusions positively.

(D) It supports the anthropologists' conclusions authoritatively.

(E) It conclusively supports only a part of the anthropologists' conclusions.

13. Which one of the following, if true, would best support the theory of the anthropologists?

(A) Wolves are known to have fed upon the garbage of villages in northern Europe.

(B) Wolves as a species are easily domesticated and trained.

(C) Almost all Stone-Age Arctic tools were made of walrus bone.

(D) Stone-Age villages were located on the migration routes of the caribou herds upon which wolves preyed.

(E) The earliest sled part found in the Arctic was made one thousand years after the Stone Age.

Questions 14–15

The following criticism of a self-portrait by Vincent van Gogh appeared in a magazine in 1917:

"Here we have a work of art which is so self-evidently a degenerate work by a degenerate artist that we need not say anything about the inept creation. It is safe to say that if we were to meet in our dreams such a villainous looking jailbird with such a deformed Neanderthal skull, degenerate ears, hobo beard and insane glare, it would certainly give us a nightmare."

14. The author of this passage makes his point by using

(A) invective
(B) analogy
(C) citation of authority
(D) paradox
(E) example

15. In relation to the first sentence of the quotation, the second sentence is

(A) an example of an effect following a cause
(B) a specific derived from a general principle
(C) a logical conclusion
(D) a contradiction
(E) a personal experience in support of a generalization

---

16. A company called Popcorn Packaging is promoting the use of popcorn as a cushioning material in packing. Unlike the commonly used Styrofoam beads or chips, popcorn can be recycled as a food for birds or squirrels and can serve as a garden mulch. Used out of doors, popcorn disappears almost overnight, while the Styrofoam beads may be in the environment for centuries. Even before we became ecology conscious, popcorn was used in packing in the 1940s. Since it now costs less to produce than Styrofoam, there is every reason to return to wide-scale use of packaging by popcorn.

Which one of the following, if true, would most seriously weaken the author's argument?

(A) A package using popcorn as a cushioning material will weigh less than a package using Styrofoam beads.
(B) Popcorn may attract rodents and insects.
(C) A large number of squirrels can damage a garden by consuming flowering bulbs.
(D) Less than 1 percent of the material now used for package cushioning is recycled.
(E) Styrofoam replaced popcorn in the early 1950s because it was cheaper to produce.

17. This produce stand sells fruits and vegetables. All fruits are delicious, and all vegetables are rich in vitamins. Every food that is vitamin-rich is delicious, so everything sold at this stand is delicious.

Which one of the following assumptions is necessary to make the conclusion in the argument above logically correct?

(A) The stand sells many fruits and vegetables.
(B) This produce stand sells only fruits and vegetables.
(C) Something cannot be both vitamin-rich and delicious.
(D) Some stands sell fruits that are not delicious.
(E) Some vegetables are delicious.

18. Voter turnout in primary elections has declined steadily from 1982 to 1990. In 1990, more than 80 percent of the Americans eligible to vote failed to do so. Only 11.9 percent of the Democrats and 7.7 percent of the Republicans went to the polls. The largest number of voters turned out for elections in the District of Columbia (28 percent) and in Massachusetts, where the 32 percent total was the highest since 1962. In each of the twenty-four other states holding elections, the number of voters was smaller than it had been in 1986 and 1982.

Based on the information in this passage, which one of the following must be true?

(A) The turnout in the District of Columbia was affected by favorable weather conditions.

(B) Fewer than 20 percent of the eligible major-party voters voted in the 24 states other than Massachusetts.

(C) The voter turnout in Massachusetts is always higher than the turnouts in other states.

(D) The voter turnout decline is a signal of a nationwide voter rebellion.

(E) More voters cast their votes in general elections than in primary elections.

19. Each year the number of schools that no longer allow smoking on school property grows larger. Four states, New Jersey, Kansas, Utah, and New Hampshire, now require tobacco-free schools. The Tobacco Institute has fought against regulations restricting smoking everywhere from airlines to restaurants on the grounds that they trample on the rights of smokers, but is conspicuously absent from school board lobbyists. Tobacco industry spokesmen have denounced the rules treating teachers like children, but have said they will not go on record to defend policies that affect children.

Which one of the following, if true, best accounts for the Tobacco Institute's behavior?

(A) The tobacco industry is presently fighting the charge that it attempts to recruit new smokers among minors.

(B) The tobacco industry can depend on continued high profits from overseas operations, where restrictions do not exist.

(C) Most tobacco companies are highly diversified corporations whose profits no longer depend wholly on tobacco products.

(D) The tobacco industry believes the rights of children to be equal to the rights of adults.

(E) The tobacco industry agrees with the schools that have rules against tobacco.

Questions 20–21

A number of lawsuits have been brought against popular singing groups charging that suicidal themes in their songs have led to teenage suicides. So far, the courts have found that the lyrics are protected by the First Amendment. But what if this should change, and a court decides that suicidal themes in popular songs are dangerous? In fact, the songs that have been charged so far are antisuicide; they present sardonically the self-destructive behavior of drinking, drugs, and escape by death. They describe a pitiful state of mind, but they do not endorse it.

Blaming suicide on the arts is nothing new. In the late eighteenth century, Goethe's popular novel *Werther* was said to be the cause of a rash of suicides in imitation of the novel's hero. If we begin to hold suicide in books or music responsible for suicides in real life, the operas of Verdi and Puccini will have to go, and *Romeo and Juliet* and *Julius Caesar* will disappear from high school reading lists.

20. The author of this passage argues by

    (A) providing examples to support two opposing positions
    (B) using an observation to undermine a theoretical principle
    (C) disputing an interpretation of evidence cited by those with an opposing view
    (D) predicting personal experience from a general principle
    (E) accusing the opposing side of using inaccurate statistical information

21. Which one of the following is an assumption necessary to the author's argument?

    (A) A lyric presenting suicide in a favorable light should not have First Amendment protection.
    (B) Literature or music cannot directly influence human behavior.
    (C) Many record albums already carry labels warning purchasers of their dangerous contents.
    (D) The audience, not the performer, is responsible for the audience's actions.
    (E) Freedom of speech is the most threatened of our personal freedoms.

---

22. Haven't you at some time had a favorite song or book or film that was not well known but later became popular? And didn't you feel somehow betrayed and resentful when what you had thought was unique became commonplace? On a larger scale, the same thing happens to novelists or film makers who have enjoyed critical esteem without popular success. Let them become public sensations, and the critics who praised their work will attack them virulently.

This paragraph most likely introduces an article on a film maker who has made a

    (A) series of commercially successful films
    (B) series of commercially unsuccessful films
    (C) single film, a commercial success
    (D) single film, a commercial failure
    (E) critical success and a commercial success

23. Studies of the effects of drinking four or more cups of coffee per day have shown that coffee consumption increases work efficiency by improving the ability to process information. People who drink two cups of coffee in the morning are more alert and feel better than those who do not. But there are other factors to be considered.

Which one of the following sentences would provide the most logical continuation of this paragraph?

(A) Contrary to popular belief, drinking coffee cannot erase the effect of alcohol.
(B) Some studies suggest that coffee drinking will protect against cancer of the colon.
(C) Combined with the stress of heavy exercise, coffee drinking may be the cause of higher blood pressure.
(D) Drinking two or more cups of coffee per day increases the risk of heart attacks in men.
(E) Many people cannot distinguish between the taste of decaffeinated and that of regular coffee.

24. All of the members of the chorus will sing in the performance of the oratorio *Messiah*. Some of these are highly trained professionals, some are gifted amateurs, and some are singers of mediocre ability.

If the statements above are true, which one of the following must also be true?

(A) *Messiah* will be performed by highly trained professionals, gifted amateurs, and some singers of mediocre ability.

(B) Some of the members of the chorus are not highly trained professionals, gifted amateurs, or singers of mediocre ability.
(C) *Messiah* will be performed by some highly trained professionals, but not all of them are in the chorus.
(D) Not all of those in the chorus who are gifted amateurs will perform in the oratorio.
(E) All of those who will perform *Messiah* are members of the chorus.

25. The passage of laws that limit elected officials to one or two terms in office is an admission that voters are civic fools, unable to tell good lawmakers from bad ones. To ban all the politicians when the real intention is to get rid of the corrupt ones is to burn the house down to get rid of the vermin.

The author of this passage makes his point chiefly by

(A) defining a key term
(B) exposing a self-contradiction
(C) drawing an analogy
(D) questioning the evidence of his opponents
(E) citing an example

STOP

IF YOU FINISH BEFORE TIME IS UP, CHECK YOUR WORK ON THIS SECTION OF THE TEST ONLY.
DO NOT GO ON TO THE NEXT SECTION OF THE TEST UNTIL TIME IS UP FOR THIS SECTION.

WRITING SAMPLE

Directions: You have 30 minutes to write an essay in response to a given topic. Take a few minutes to plan your work before you begin writing. DO NOT WRITE ON A TOPIC OF YOUR OWN CHOICE. ESSAYS THAT DO NOT ADDRESS THE GIVEN TOPIC ARE UNACCEPTABLE.

The quality of your writing is more important than the length of your response or the content. Pay attention to organization, appropriate diction, and correct usage. You will not be expected to display any specialized knowledge in your response, nor will you be expected to write a "perfect" essay; law schools understand that you are writing under a time constraint, and will allow for the minor lapses in writing ability that might occur under this circumstance.

Only the lined area in your booklet will be reproduced for the law schools, so do not write outside this space. _Do not_ skip lines or use wide margins. These precautions, along with careful planning and legible handwriting that is not unduly large, will keep you within the allowed space.

Sample Topic

Read the following descriptions of Jackson and Brown. *Then, in the space provided, write an argument for deciding which of the two should be assigned the responsibility of hiring teachers for the Hapsville School System.* The following criteria are relevant to your decision:

- The taxpayers want educators who can instill in students the desire to learn and an excitement for knowledge, something that has been lacking in their schools.
- A majority of students' parents believe that their children should be equipped, upon graduation, to earn a living, and thus favor a more trade-oriented (rather than academic) approach to schooling.

JACKSON was appointed as Superintendent of Schools by the Hapsville School Board, which was elected by the community's taxpayers. As a 30-year resident of Hapsville (population 45,000), Jackson is unique in that he holds not only a doctorate in administration, but also a master's degree in education. He taught in the Hapsville schools for 16 years until he served on the state Commission on Education. He has always favored a progressive approach to education, although it may not always have been popular with the town's population. Through the years he has brought many fine teachers to the faculty, because of his willingness to encourage new classroom techniques.

BROWN is a 52-year resident of Hapsville, having been born in the same house in which he now lives. He was elected to the School Board 13 years ago, and continues to win nearly unanimous reelection every two years. As the foremost developer in the Four Counties area, Mr. Brown has had the opportunity to build hundreds of new homes in the six housing developments he's planned and actualized, and, in the interim, has employed hundreds of Hapsville residents as carpenters, electricians, plumbers, architects, landscapers, groundskeepers, etc. As such, he is held in high esteem by most of the town, not only for his providing livelihoods for many, but also for his fair and realistic outlook on life. Mr. Brown feels strongly that the key to life is having a marketable skill.

You will be given a special sheet of paper to write your essay. It will have the essay topic on the top followed by approximately 25 lines of writing. For practice, write your essay on one side of an 8½" x 11" college-ruled lined sheet of paper. *Use only 25 lines.*

ANSWER KEY

Section I: Reading Comprehension

1. B	6. A	11. E	16. E	21. B	26. B
2. C	7. C	12. C	17. A	22. C	27. A
3. A	8. A	13. D	18. B	23. C	28. E
4. A	9. B	14. A	19. E	24. D	
5. E	10. A	15. C	20. D	25. A	

Section II: Analytical Reasoning

1. C	5. D	9. D	13. A	17. E	21. B
2. A	6. B	10. A	14. C	18. D	22. D
3. E	7. E	11. E	15. A	19. C	23. D
4. C	8. E	12. D	16. D	20. C	24. C

Section III: Logical Reasoning

1. C	6. A	11. E	16. B	21. E	26. B
2. B	7. B	12. C	17. D	22. E	
3. E	8. C	13. B	18. A	23. B	
4. D	9. B	14. C	19. E	24. E	
5. D	10. E	15. E	20. C	25. D	

Section IV: Analytical Reasoning

1. B	5. D	9. A	13. E	17. E	21. B
2. B	6. E	10. E	14. D	18. C	22. E
3. D	7. C	11. E	15. A	19. B	23. C
4. E	8. E	12. B	16. D	20. C	24. B

Section V: Logical Reasoning

1. B	6. E	11. E	16. B	21. D
2. D	7. B	12. C	17. B	22. E
3. C	8. C	13. B	18. B	23. D
4. D	9. D	14. A	19. A	24. A
5. A	10. A	15. D	20. C	25. C

MODEL TEST ANALYSIS

Doing model exams and understanding the explanations afterwards are of course important in acquainting you with typical LSAT question types and successful approaches to the questions. However, another benefit of carefully analyzing these model tests is to understand the kinds of errors you are making and thus work to minimize them. For instance, if a very high percentage of your incorrect answers is due to "careless error" or "misread problem" then perhaps you are working much too fast and should slow your pace accordingly. If your incorrect answers are due primarily to "lack of knowledge," then a careful rereading and reworking of the appropriate question-type chapter may be in order. Or if you find that you aren't completing a large number of questions because of lack of time, you may need to either increase your speed or learn to use the "one-check, two-check" technique more effectively.

This kind of analysis of the model tests will enable you to identify your particular weaknesses and thus remedy them.

MODEL TEST ONE ANALYSIS

Section	Total Number of Questions	Number Correct	Number Incorrect	Number Unanswered*
I. Reading Comprehension	28			
II. Analytical Reasoning	24			
III. Logical Reasoning	26			
IV. Analytical Reasoning	24			
V. Logical Reasoning	25			
TOTALS:	127			

*At this stage in your preparation, you should not be leaving any blank answer spaces. At least fill in a guess, as there is no penalty for a wrong answer.

REASONS FOR INCORRECT ANSWERS
You may wish to evaluate the explanations before completing this chart.

Section	Total Number Incorrect	Lack of Knowledge	Misread Problem	Careless Error	Unanswered or Wrong Guess
I. Reading Comprehension					
II. Analytical Reasoning					
III. Logical Reasoning					
IV. Analytical Reasoning					
V. Logical Reasoning					
TOTALS:					

EXPLANATION OF ANSWERS

Section I

Passage 1

1. **B** The first sentence of the passage makes it clear that government workers are forbidden to strike by statutory law.

2. **C** If strikes are a form of symbolic speech, the denial of the right to strike is arguably a denial of free speech. It also can be argued that it denies due process, the right to picket, and the right to avoid abnormally dangerous working conditions.

3. **A** The courts, not the legislative or the executive branches, must determine the "clear and present danger," according to the Supreme Court decision described in the second paragraph.

4. **A** Because the firing of the controllers had the same effect as a strike, it appears that there was no danger to the public.

5. **E** The author points out that workers in government who do that same job as workers in private industry cannot strike. The passage argues that the nature of the service should determine the right to strike, not the employer.

6. **A** It is possible that the "highly qualified" may seek employment outside of government, because of the no-strike clause. Choices (B), (C), (D), (E) are not plausible weaknesses of the no-strike rule.

Passage 2

7. **C** See lines 4–9. Her father also may have influenced her in the ways suggested in (A), (B), (D), and (E), but these answers are not suggested by the passage itself.

8. **A** We can infer from lines 19–24 that this was Woolf's dilemma, particularly because in lines 25–28 we learn that the emphasis in her feminism was self-reform. E is incorrect; "lucid objectivity" is cited as a strength of her novel *The Years*, not something that needed to be overcome. C is not supported by the passage because there is nothing to suggest that Virginia Woolf wished to pursue "social work." Similarly, (B) and (D) are not supported by any information in the passage.

9. **B** In the passage, the integration of masculine and feminine (the androgynous mind) and the danger of one-sidedness (lines 19–24) describe Woolf's feminism. Although C and D might also characterize her feminism, the passage emphasizes a need for wholeness. A is not supported by the passage. E might be suggested in lines 30–36 and lines 79–81 but it is *not* presented as a characterization of her feminism.

10. **A** Paragraph two is concerned with the superiority of Woolf's novels to her tracts in dealing with her feminist concerns. Paragraph three contrasts a tract and a novel to illustrate this point. Paragraph three doesn't present a contrast to or a subtopic of paragraph one (B, D), nor does it act as a transition (C). (In fact, the passage could move smoothly from paragraph two to paragraph four even if paragraph three were missing. What would be missing would be a concrete example—i.e., answer A.) Paragraph two does not present an exegesis (E).

11. **E** This opposition is at the heart of the passage—see paragraphs two,

three, and four. Different types of novels are *not* contrasted (B), nor is Woolf's aesthetic creed contrasted to the aesthetic creed of the Bloomsbury group (A). (A contrast is suggested in lines 4–9, but it is minor, and not explained or developed.) C is incorrect; the passage explicitly addresses Woolf's *avoidance* of such a contrast and her belief in the androgynous mind. D is unclear and inaccurate.

12. **C** See paragraph four. Although the author does say that Woolf's primary emphasis was on self-reform, he does not suggest that her social concerns were trivial (D). Nothing in the passage suggests that the author is criticizing the Bloomsbury aesthetic creed (A). Similarly, although the author finds Woolf's novels more successful than her tracts, it is a giant leap to infer that he dislikes social reform literature in general (E). (B) is clearly incorrect.

13. **D** The passage states this idea in the first line and then continues throughout to develop the subject of the importance of both feminism and art in Woolf's writing. See lines 38–43. (A) is too limited; these two works are used to illustrate the main point of the passage. (B) is broad and imprecise. (C) is also imprecise. (E) is incorrect; opposition of masculine and feminine is not part of the passage.

Passage 3

14. **A** The author is obviously most concerned with the work of historians and the current state of written history, which is what prompts his discussion of fiction in relation to history. See lines 4–8, 17–20, 54–60, 65–71. Literature and liter-

ary concerns (answer C) are secondary.

15. **C** See lines 69–70: "...their abandonment of the narrative style. ..." A decline in the writing *ability* of historians (E) is not implied. And although the author does mention the movies and television, he does not attribute the growth of fictional history to an increase in their audiences (B).

16. **E** This attitude is clearly stated in lines 50–54. B may seem correct, but the author does not say that fictional history on its own has won the audience away from traditional history. On the contrary, he suggests that professional historians themselves may be partly responsible for the growth of fictional history (lines 65–69).

17. **A** This book would most clearly fit the definition of fictional history given in lines 35–40. According to the author, it is fictional history that causes the greatest confusion (lines 50–54). (B) and (C) would be classified as historical fiction according to the author's definitions, and (D) and (E) as nonfiction.

18. **B** The second paragraph is devoted to defining and contrasting the two terms. (D) might be considered a possible answer but is less clear and specific. The other answers are simply inaccurate.

19. **E** Nothing in the passage suggests a judgment of history taught in the schools. The other statements are all supported in the passage: (A)—lines 17–20; (B)—lines 65–69; (C)—lines 54–60; (D)—lines 12–16.

20. **D** Throughout the passage the author is most concerned with the growth of fictional history and its effects. None of the other answers present

his *attitude* as clearly, though (C) does define fictional history.

21. **B** The author is obviously concerned with the "mischief" that the mixture of history with fiction can cause. However, he presents his concern in a moderate fashion. He is not hostile, he does not preach, he is not pedantic, nor does he display irony. (E) suggests an elevated tone not present in the passage

Passage 4

22. **C** (C) is the best answer because the author explains fear conditioning in order to show how it is a good method for studying emotional memory. (A) is incorrect; the passage "proves" nothing. (B) is also incorrect. The fact that the mechanisms in mammals and vertebrates may be similar is not the main point of the passage; also, the passage does not state that the mechanisms are "the same." (D) is only a supporting point—not the main point—of the passage. (E) is incorrect; the way that phobias are initially created in humans is not addressed in the passage.

23. **C** The passage makes this connection in lines 39–45. (A) is incorrect—see lines 28–29. (B) is also incorrect; lines 75–77 specifically state that cues to which subjects respond fearfully are not linked to complicated cognitive processing. (D) is incorrect because the passage states that stress, rather than *weakening* a response, may cause its recurrence. (E) is not the right choice. See lines 28–29. The rat's conditioned response diminishes only when the conditioned stimulus is administered many times without the unconditioned stimulus. As long

as the shock and conditioned stimulus are paired, the rat's response to the conditioned stimulus will remain.

24. **D** The passage states than an extinguished fear response can recover spontaneously or can be reinstated by an irrelevant stressful experience (lines 39–42). We can assume that for a rat, introduction of a cat could be an "irrelevant stressful experience." (A) and (B) are incorrect; both are contradicted by information in the passage (lines 29–34 and lines 34–38). (C) and (E) are not supported by information in the passage.

25. **A** This answer is directly supported in lines 73–75. According to lines 28–29, the response is not related to complex cognitive processing. Therefore, (B) is incorrect. (C) and (D) are not supported by any information presented in the passage. (E) is incorrect; in lines 34–38, the brain's control, rather than lack of control, is cited.

26. **B** The author cites the nine animals to show the wide range of animal groups in which fear conditioning occurs. This supports his point that fear conditioning is an ideal starting point for studies of emotional memory. Although fear conditioning occurring in so many animal groups may support (A) (that the fear response is neural), this is not the primary reason for citing them. See lines 50–54. There is no suggestion of a developmental link between the animal groups listed, making (C) an incorrect choice. (D) and (E) are also incorrect; the author's listing of the nine animals is not connected in the passage to the role of the brain, nor is any point made about the

emotions of fruit flies, snails, and so on.

27. **A**   The last line of the passage states that the object of the research is to examine the "neurological foundations of fear." (B) and (E) are incorrect; the primary object of the research is not "cognition" nor how mammals are similar. (C) is also incorrect; conditioning is the *method* to be used to study the neurological basis of fear, not the object of the research itself. (D) should be ruled out because the effects of acoustic and visual stimuli are a small part of the research, not its main object.

28. **E**   The third paragraph is devoted to reasons that fear conditioning is an "ideal starting point" for research of emotional memory, i.e., it occurs in many animal groups, the signals are not the type to which subjects have preexisting strong emotional reactions, and so on. (A) is incorrect because the definition is completed in paragraphs 1 and 2. (B) is incorrect because the author presents no qualifications or reservations about fear conditioning. (C) is not a good choice because the passage adds new information (i.e., reasons or justifications) and does not summarize. Finally, (D) is not correct because the passage does not present any applications other than the study of emotion and memory for the fear conditioning method.

Section II

Answers 1–6

From the information given, you could have made the following diagram:

						Pent.	4	___	
Higher	A	D	E				3	___	___
	?	?	?	FG			2	___	___
Lower	B	C	C				1	___	___

1. **C**   Since F and G are on the same floor, they can't be on 4. Since B and C are below A or D/E, they can't be on 4; therefore only A, D, or E can be on 4.

2. **A**   If F's apartment is on 2, so is G's. For B and C to be below A, D, and E, B and C must be on 1 and A, D, and E on 3 and 4, but we don't know exactly where on 3/4.

3. **E**   If D is on 4, G (and F) *can* be on 3, 2, or 1.

D	D	D
FG	AE	AE
AE	FG	BC
BC	BC	FG

4. **C**   If D and E are on the same floor, A must be on 4. All the other answers are possible but *not* certain.

5. **D**   If A is on 4 or C on 1, the arrangement must be either

A		A
FG	or	DE
DE		FG
BC		BC

6. **B**   A and E can be on the same floor if D is on 4.

D		D
AE	or	AE
FG		BC
BC		FG

Answers 7–12

From the information given, you may have constructed a simple grouping display of information similar to this:

Managers	Tellers	Officers
⟨ U V	⟨ W X	Ⓢ Sat.
	Y	T
	Ⓩ Sat.	

Another possible display might look like this:

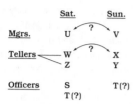

7. **E**   From the original information, a manager must be on duty each day and the managers cannot work on the same day. Therefore (A) must be true. (E) does not have to be true, since U's schedule has no bearing on X's schedule. Since W and X will not work on the same day, (B) must also be true. There is no restriction placed on T.

8. **E**   V, W, Z, S can work on Saturday without breaking any of the conditions given. Choice (A) is missing a manager. Choice (B) has two managers working on the same day. Choices (C) and (D) have W and X working on the same day.

9. **D**   Five employees, U or V, X or W, Z, S, and T are the greatest number to work on Saturday.

10. **A**   Since W and X will not work on the same day, (A) must be true. (B) is false since Y must work on Sunday. (C) could be true. Since W's schedule has no effect on Z and U, (D) and (E) may be true or false.

11. **E**   Since no employee can work on consecutive days, and there are four tellers, then two must work on Saturday.

12. **D**   U, V, W, X, Y, Z, and T have the possibility of working on Sunday; S and Z do not.

Answers 13–19
From the information given, you could have constructed the following simple diagram and display of information:

13. **A**   From the diagram and information above, if Gene works for Fred, then Lyndia also works for Fred, and Sylvia must work for Cynthia. Since Dennis and Edra will not work together, one of them must work for Cynthia; therefore choice (A) must be false. Jim cannot work for Cynthia.

14. **C**   Using the diagram, if Sylvia doesn't work for Cynthia, then Gene must work for Cynthia. If Gene works for Cynthia, then Lyndia must also work for Cynthia, since Gene and Lyndia always work together.

15. **A**   If Lyndia and Jim work for Al, then Gene must also work for Al, and Sylvia must work for Cynthia. The diagram would look like this:

First, (A) is true since Gene and Lyndia always work together. Stop there. Go no further. Edra could work for Cynthia or Fred, and also Helen could work for Cynthia or Fred.

16. **D**   If Sylvia and Jim work for Al, then Gene and Lyndia must work for Cynthia. Since Dennis and Edra cannot work together, one of them must work for Fred and the other for Al. The diagram would now look like this:

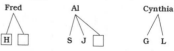

Therefore, only (D) is true.

17. E   From the diagram, if Lyndia and Sylvia work for Al, then Gene also must work for Al. But either Sylvia or Gene must work for Cynthia. Therefore (E) must be false.

18. D   From the diagram, if Jim works for Cynthia, then Sylvia must also work for Cynthia, since Gene and Lyndia must work together. Gene and Lyndia cannot work for Fred, because then Dennis and Edra (who cannot work together) would work for Al. Therefore, Lyndia must work for Al. The diagram would look like this:

19. C   If Al needs only two assistants and Fred needs only one, and if Helen works for Fred, then the diagram would look like this:

Since Gene and Lyndia must work together, they can work for either Al or Cynthia. Since Edra (typist) must work and Dennis and Edra cannot work together, then Dennis doesn't work. Otherwise, Dennis and Edra would work together. Statements A, B, D, and E *could* be true.

Answers 20–24

Drawing a diagram, below, will help answer the questions.

EVENTS

	1	2	3	4	5
RED	G	—	G	—	G
BLUE	—	B/S	—	B/S	—
GREEN					
YELLOW					

Since the red team wins only 3 gold medals, it must win gold medals in events 1, 3, and 5, since no team wins gold medals in consecutive events. Also, note that since blue wins only two medals (neither of them gold), it must have won medals in events 2 and 4, so that it didn't fail to win a medal within two consecutive events. Be aware then that green and yellow, therefore, must each have won medals in all five events.

20. C   If the green team wins only one gold medal, there remains only one gold medal, which the yellow team must win.

21. B   Since three medals are given for each event, and, according to our diagram from the facts, red and blue already account for their total awards with one medal in each event, the other two medals in each event must go to yellow and green. Thus, yellow and green will each be awarded five medals.

22. D   By completing the chart such that the yellow team wins five silver medals, we can see that green must win two gold and three bronze medals.

	1	2	3	4	5
RED	G	—	G	—	G
BLUE	—	B/S	—	B/S	—
GREEN					
YELLOW	S	S	S	S	S

23. D   We know choices (A) and (B) are both true: both the green and yellow teams each must win five medals. Therefore (E) is also true. Choice (C) is true because three of the gold medals are already won by the red team; since blue doesn't win gold, if green wins one gold, yellow wins the remaining gold medal. Choice (D) is not true: if the green team wins only one silver medal, the yellow team must win at least two silver medals.

24. **C** If a fifth team enters all events and wins only three consecutive silver medals, it must win the silver in events 2, 3, and 4, so that it does not fail to win a medal within two consecutive events. Therefore our diagram would look like this:

	1	2	3	4	5
RED	G	—	G	—	G
BLUE	—	B	—	B	—
GREEN					
YELLOW					
ORANGE	—	S	S	S	—

Therefore, if yellow wins a gold in the 2nd event, green must win a medal in the 3rd event (since no team fails to win a medal within two consecutive events). Thus, green must win a bronze in the 3rd event.

Section III

1. **C** The passage is more restrained in its criticism than (A) or (B), while (D) and (E) are only elements of the paragraph, not its main point.

2. **B** By urging moviegoers to patronize films *in order to* influence academy judges, the author reveals his assumption that the academy will be influenced by the number of people paying to see a movie.

3. **E** Bob's answer shows that he thinks that people other than teachers are mean. His thought was that Andy meant otherwise.

4. **D** The author's concluding contention is that Roosevelt was not only a good marksman, but also an intellectually curious and patient man. If Roosevelt was known to leave safaris which were not immediately productive, this fact would substantially weaken the author's contention about Roosevelt's "patient observation."

5. **D** The words "because of a recent cut in state funding of our program" indicate that another criterion was used in determining entering class size besides candidates' scores and grades, namely, the financial situation of the college. The words *seriously* in choice (B) and *severe* in choice (E) are not necessarily supported by the passage, and thus make those choices incorrect. Since grade point average is only one of several criteria for admission, we cannot deduce (A) with certainty.

6. **A** This sentence not only fits well stylistically but completes the thought of the passage by tying it into the opening statement.

7. **B** The author of this passage actually defines conscience as the ability to sense right and wrong.

8. **C** "Without opportunity there would be no crime" fails to consider that thievery is not the only type of crime.

9. **B** This choice offers the most thorough and comprehensive evidence that the viewing of violent television precedes criminal behavior. (A) is not the best choice because it describes viewing habits that follow rather than precede criminal behavior.

10. **E** The use of "overwhelming" leaves the evidence unspecified, thus opening to challenge the extent and nature of the report's data.

11. **E** All of the first four statements can be used to explain the underreporting. In D, for example, if the size of police departments has declined,

they would have less manpower available to gather and report information. E is a reason against underreporting rather than an explanation for it.

12. **C** The argument uses the case of the county to call the state figures into question. The underreported figures are "less evidence."

13. **B** If the experiences and lifestyle of the Aryan race are uniquely different from those of other cultures, it would seriously weaken the author's conclusion that studying the Aryan race will be helpful in understanding the experiences and life styles of other races. That its communal arrangements are *unique* would make comparison between the Aryan race and other cultures impossible.

14. **C** The author presents a *contrast* between life and honor: in particular, the final sentence suggests that life and honor have opposite qualities. Of the choices, the only opposite of *transient* is *eternal.*

15. **E** The logic of this statement goes from the general absolute ("all") to the specific ("this animal"), concluding with specific to specific. Symbolically, if *P* implies *Q,* then *not Q* implies *not P.* (E) goes from general absolute ("all") to specific ("this liquid"), concluding with specific to specific. Notice how and where the inverse ("not") is inserted. Using symbols, we have that, if *P* implies *Q,* then *not Q* implies *not P.*

16. **B** This is a close one. (B) and (D) both weaken the argument by pointing out that all dogs do not always bark, but (B) is absolute. (D) is tentative, since a dog trained not to bark might do so by accident.

17. **D** (D) is the correct answer, since it states "cheat on *none* of the exams," while the passage states, "Everyone has cheated on *at least* one exam." (A) is incorrect, since it says nothing about what Joe actually did. (B) is incorrect, since, although we are told that cheating is "wrong," we do not know what is "acceptable" and what is not. Do not make subjective answers. (C) is not a good choice, since Jack may never have taken an exam. (E) is incorrect, since it just restates two of the given conditions.

18. **A** The complaint about ex-employees of the Department of Energy on the board, and the financial tie of the National Academy Board to the Energy Department indicate the officials' belief that the Department of Energy supports the nuclear power industry against the views of environmentalists.

19. **E** Though adding one or two environmentalists might help, they would still be outnumbered by the ten panel members with ties to the Department of Energy. Of the five choices, E offers the best hope of impartiality.

20. **C** (A) contradicts the statement's urging of economy. (B) introduces an irrelevant word, "terminology." (D) and (E) are *absolute* statements about assumptions, but the statement itself is *relative,* urging us only to simplify our assumptions *if one such simplification is possible; in other words, "If an issue is simple, don't complicate it."*

21. **E** The question demonstrates a solution and the fact that an alternative exists.

22. **E** (A) is obviously true. (B) also satisfies the conditions. (C) is correct,

since 3.5 was required with a score of 800. (D) is correct, since we do not know anything about numbers of applicants. (E) is inconsistent, since a score of 1200 is required with a GPA of 2.5. (E) specifies a score *less than* 1200. Therefore, a GPA greater than (*not less than*) 2.5 would be required for admittance.

23. **B** To speak in positive terms about the increase in school degrees, the author must assume that the degrees indicate what they are supposed to indicate, that is, well-educated individuals. (A) and (E) are empty statements; (C) and (D) are altogether unsubstantiated by either expressed or implied information.

24. **E** Although the brand name is No-NOCK, the advertisement makes no claim to stop the engine from knocking. All the other claims are contained in the advertisement.

25. **D** The choice repudiates the suggestion that gentleness and graciousness were once part of the American character. (B), another choice worth considering, is not best because it does not address the temperament of tennis players as directly as does (D).

26. **B** By asking Dolores to choose between conventional and nuclear weapons, Fran has concluded that Dolores's statement calls for a decision. (C), worth considering, is not best because Fran supposes that Dolores has *not* made a choice—hence her question.

Section IV

Answers 1–6

From the information given, you should have constructed a diagram similar to this:

1. **B** From the diagram, if the group begins on island W, it could not reach island V in the eight days. Remember three days would have to be spent on W and three on X.

2. **B** From the diagram, if the group stays on island X for three nights, then the group cannot get to island V on the next visit.

3. **D** To answer this question, you must try each answer choice and eliminate the ones that do not connect. From the diagram, the only possible order listed would be U X Z V.

4. **E** From the diagram, if the group visits island W first, it could go to X to Y to Z, back to X, to U back to Y, to V and back to Z. A total of 9 visits. You could work from the choices, but remember to start from the highest number.

5. **D** From the diagram, the group could go from X to W to U to Y to V to Z to Y. This would be 6 different islands.

6. **E** Adding island T to the diagram connected only to U could look like this:

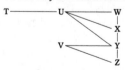

From this revised diagram, only (E) must be true. On the tenth day of a tour starting on Z, the tour group could be on island T. It would go from Z to Y to U to T or Z to X to U to T.

Answers 7–13

From the information given, you could have constructed the following diagram:

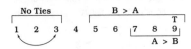

Notice the simple markings to show:
There are no ties in the first 3 games.
Team A wins more of the last 3 games than team B.
Team B wins more of the last 5 games than team A.
The last game is a tie.
Games 1 and 3 are won by the same team.

From this information you could deduce that team A wins either game 7 or 8, but not both, and team B cannot win any of the last 3 games. (If team A won both, team B could not win more of the last 5 games.) If team A wins game 7, then 8 is a tie, and if team A wins game 8, then 7 is a tie.

You could also deduce that team B must win games 5 and 6. Your diagram now looks like this:

```
 No Ties              B > A
┌────────┐         ┌─B──B──A──T──T┐
 1   2   3    4     5  6  7  8  9
     ‿                   └─T──A─┘
```

7. **C** From the information given, since games 1 and 3 are won by the same team, then one team wins at least 2 of the first 3 games.

8. **E** From the diagram, game 6 must be won by team B.

9. **A** From the diagram, if game 7 is won by team A, then game 8 must be a tie.

10. **E** From the diagram, you can see that (E) must be true.

11. **E** If team A wins games 1 and 4, then it must also win game 3. This would give team A four wins total, and team B could only win three, therefore team B could not win the series.

For this question, the diagram would now look like this:

```
 A      A   A   B   B    A      T
 1   2  3   4   5   6   7   8   9
```

12. **B** If game 4 is won by the winner of game 5, then team B wins game 4. If game 2 is not won by the winner of game 3, then team B wins either game 2 or 3. This gives team B at least four wins and team A only a possible three wins, therefore B is the winner of the series.

13. **E** From the original diagram, team A must win either games 1, 2, and 3, or games 1, 3, and 4 to win the series. [This also eliminates choice (A).] If team B wins exactly one of the first four games [choice (B)], then team B cannot win the series as team A will win at least three games. If team A wins only three of the first seven games [choice (C)], then team A could still lose the series as team B could win games 2, 4, 5, and 6, with team A winning only games 1, 3, and 7. Team B could win the series by winning two of the first four games, eliminating choice (D).

Answers 14–18

Drawing a simple diagram, below, will help answer the questions.

```
                              TR
                               *
                ___ ___ ___ J      FDR
M, A, K, FDR →  ___ ___   M  A     K – FDR or
                                   FDR – K
```

Note that, once Madison is placed in position 3 on the bottom, Adams must go in position 4 in order to leave spots for Kennedy to be adjacent to Franklin Delano Roosevelt.

14. **D** If Theodore Roosevelt is second from the left (on top), then Franklin Delano Roosevelt must be first on the bottom since one Roosevelt may not be above the other. Therefore, Kennedy must be second on the bottom.

15. **A** Adams must go to the far right on the bottom to allow Kennedy to be adjacent to Franklin Delano Roosevelt.

16. **D** If Washington and Kennedy are both first on their shelves, then Franklin Delano Roosevelt must be second on the lower shelf. Therefore, Theodore Roosevelt cannot be second on the top shelf and therefore must be third. Thus, statement D cannot be true.

17. **E** Since Adams must be on the right in the second row, only (E) is not possible.

18. **C** If Lincoln is next to Jefferson, that leaves Theodore Roosevelt and Washington for the first two positions on the top shelf. All of the choices are therefore true except (C) because that choice would place one Roosevelt above the other, which is not permitted.

Answers 19–24

19. **B** Since lima beans will not go with kidney beans or chili beans, they can go only with wax beans and garbanzos. Therefore, there is only one salad (limas + wax + garbanzos) that contains limas and that may be served at the party.

20. **C** The combinations of salads without chili beans are as follows:

1. garbanzos + wax + limas
2. garbanzos + limas + kidneys
3. garbanzos + wax + kidneys
4. wax + limas + kidneys

But remember that the *servable* salads may not include limas with kidneys or chili beans, thus reducing the number to two: garbanzos + wax + kidneys, and garbanzos + wax + limas.

21. **B** Without any restrictions there are 10 possible ways to choose three ingredients from a total of five:

CGW	GWL	WLK
CGL	GLK	
CGK	GWK	
CWL		
CWK		
CLK		

However, the imposed restrictions (lima beans do not go with kidney beans or chili beans) narrow the servable salads down to five:

CGW	GWL	~~WLK~~
~~CGL~~	~~GLK~~	
CGK	GWK	
~~CWL~~		
CWK		
~~CLK~~		

22. **E** From the chart above, we can see that garbanzos and wax beans appear more times in the servable salads. The other ingredients do not appear as often.

23. **C** From our chart we can see that having only enough wax beans for two salads will eliminate two of the four wax bean salads. Therefore, instead of five servable salads, there will now be only three.

24. **B** Again from our chart, if we eliminate the servable salads with garbanzos, we are left with only one servable salad: chili + wax + kidneys.

Section V

1. **B** The correct answer must use both premises. The first qualifies the assertion with "normally," so (A) will not follow, but (B) (with the qualifier "may") will. (C) may or may not be true, but it is not a logical conclusion based on the two premises. (D) and (E), like (A), do not use both premises.

2. **D** The question asked concerns the danger to public health, but the reply does not deal with this issue at all. It changes the subject.

3. **C** Reducing coffee consumption in general will not guarantee a healthier population (A) if "heavy" consumers do not reduce their coffee intake. Reducing coffee consumption would make those who drink a morning cup of coffee feel less well (B). (C) is a logical conclusion since heavy consumption increases heart attack risk. There is no information in the passage to justify the assertion about percolated coffee (D). If coffee may protect against colon cancer, (E) is not true.

4. **D** The issue of the danger of pesticides is addressed by (A), (C), and (E), while (B) calls into question the objectivity of the Food and Agriculture Department. But (D) deals with a different issue: air pollution. And if air pollution is a cause of illness, pesticides may be less to blame.

5. **A** The question contains its own prior judgment (underpay, unfair promotion policies) on what it asks, regardless of a "yes" or "no" answer. Similarly, the adjective "excessive" and the adverb "unfairly" prejudge any answer in choice (A).

6. **E** Since fares have risen, the cost of fuel has risen or there are no fare wars. And if there are no fare wars, the number of passengers is larger. Only (E) cannot be true. (B) is possible if fuel costs have risen, and there are fare wars.

7. **B** Though the argument for a decline in fishing off Newfoundland is convincing, the generalization that the "fishing industry in the Americas" will disappear is here based only on information about the Atlantic waters off Canada. It is possible that other areas have not been so affected.

8. **C** The advertisement asserts filter cigarettes cannot have great taste. A reasonable inference is that Gold Star is not a filter cigarette. (A) is contradicted by this ad without visual appeal. (B) is contradicted by this ad, which does not specifically praise a brand. (D) is illogical given the existence of this ad. Nothing in the ad supports (E).

9. **D** Choices (A), (B), and (C) strengthen the case for building the toll road. The environmentalists may be able to make their case for one of the other possible routes that, if less direct, would not disturb the reserve. With the information we have, the value of (E) is indeterminable.

10. **A** There is nothing in the paragraph to support (E), and there are details that contradict (B), (C), and (D). That "sales in the United States continue to increase" supports (A).

11. **E** The passage does not give the information that would lead to the conclusion in (A), (B), or (C). (E) is a better answer than (D), the odds against the heavy smoker being 40 in 100 as opposed to 25 in 100 for the light smoker.

12. **C** The presence of wolf bones and walrus bones near a village is not evidence that wolves were trained to

haul sleds; it does not disprove the theory, however.

13. **B** Choices (A), (C), (D), and (E) would undermine the theory. But if wolves were easily domesticated and trained, it would make the theory of their domestication by Stone-Age tribes more plausible.

14. **A** The author makes his point by invective, an abrasive verbal attack.

15. **D** The first sentence asserts the needlessness of commenting on the picture; the second nonetheless makes a detailed criticism.

16. **B** If popcorn attracts rodents and insects, warehouses where packages using popcorn are stored would have vermin problems.

17. **B** Only (B) is a necessary assumption. It must be assumed that no other items (for example dressings, recipes, spices, etc.) are sold at the stand in order to conclude definitively that everything sold there is delicious.

18. **B** Though (E) is probably true, it is not a conclusion based on the information in the passage. But the passage does assert that only 19.6 percent (11.9 plus 7.7) of the eligible voters in the Democratic and Republican parties went to the polls.

19. **A** Choices (B) and (C), although true, are not relevant, while (D) and (E) are probably untrue. That it is only in the schools that the tobacco spokesmen are silent supports the inference of (A).

20. **C** In both paragraphs, the author disputes the interpretations of his opponents.

21. **D** The author assumes that an audience is able to evaluate a work and determine its own course of action.

22. **E** The opening lines describe esteem without popularity, later followed by popular success.

23. **D** The "But" introducing the last sentence suggests that a contrast, a disadvantage of coffee, is to follow. Either (C) or (D) is possible, but since exercise has not been an issue, (D) is the better choice.

24. **A** Only choice (A) must be true. There may be other performers as well as the chorus members (the orchestra, for example) in the performance, so (E) is incorrect.

25. **C** The passage draws an analogy comparing corrupt politicians to vermin.

6

MODEL TEST TWO

This chapter contains full-length Model Test Two. It is geared to the format of the LSAT, and it is complete with answers and explanations. It is equivalent to the LSAT in question structure, number of questions, level of difficulty, and time allotments. (The questions used are not taken directly from the LSAT, as those questions are copyrighted and may not be reproduced.)

Model Test Two should be taken under strict test conditions. The test ends with a 30-minute Writing Sample, which is not scored.

Section	Description	Number of Questions	Time Allowed
I.	Logical Reasoning	26	35 minutes
II.	Reading Comprehension	28	35 minutes
III.	Analytical Reasoning	24	35 minutes
IV.	Logical Reasoning	26	35 minutes
V.	Reading Comprehension	28	35 minutes
	Writing Sample		30 minutes
TOTALS:		132	3 hours 25 minutes

Now please turn to the next page, remove your answer sheet, and begin Model Test Two.

ANSWER SHEET—MODEL TEST TWO

Section 1	Section 2	Section 3	Section 4	Section 5
1. Ⓐ Ⓑ Ⓒ Ⓓ Ⓔ	1. Ⓐ Ⓑ Ⓒ Ⓓ Ⓔ	1. Ⓐ Ⓑ Ⓒ Ⓓ Ⓔ	1. Ⓐ Ⓑ Ⓒ Ⓓ Ⓔ	1. Ⓐ Ⓑ Ⓒ Ⓓ Ⓔ
2. Ⓐ Ⓑ Ⓒ Ⓓ Ⓔ	2. Ⓐ Ⓑ Ⓒ Ⓓ Ⓔ	2. Ⓐ Ⓑ Ⓒ Ⓓ Ⓔ	2. Ⓐ Ⓑ Ⓒ Ⓓ Ⓔ	2. Ⓐ Ⓑ Ⓒ Ⓓ Ⓔ
3. Ⓐ Ⓑ Ⓒ Ⓓ Ⓔ	3. Ⓐ Ⓑ Ⓒ Ⓓ Ⓔ	3. Ⓐ Ⓑ Ⓒ Ⓓ Ⓔ	3. Ⓐ Ⓑ Ⓒ Ⓓ Ⓔ	3. Ⓐ Ⓑ Ⓒ Ⓓ Ⓔ
4. Ⓐ Ⓑ Ⓒ Ⓓ Ⓔ	4. Ⓐ Ⓑ Ⓒ Ⓓ Ⓔ	4. Ⓐ Ⓑ Ⓒ Ⓓ Ⓔ	4. Ⓐ Ⓑ Ⓒ Ⓓ Ⓔ	4. Ⓐ Ⓑ Ⓒ Ⓓ Ⓔ
5. Ⓐ Ⓑ Ⓒ Ⓓ Ⓔ	5. Ⓐ Ⓑ Ⓒ Ⓓ Ⓔ	5. Ⓐ Ⓑ Ⓒ Ⓓ Ⓔ	5. Ⓐ Ⓑ Ⓒ Ⓓ Ⓔ	5. Ⓐ Ⓑ Ⓒ Ⓓ Ⓔ
6. Ⓐ Ⓑ Ⓒ Ⓓ Ⓔ	6. Ⓐ Ⓑ Ⓒ Ⓓ Ⓔ	6. Ⓐ Ⓑ Ⓒ Ⓓ Ⓔ	6. Ⓐ Ⓑ Ⓒ Ⓓ Ⓔ	6. Ⓐ Ⓑ Ⓒ Ⓓ Ⓔ
7. Ⓐ Ⓑ Ⓒ Ⓓ Ⓔ	7. Ⓐ Ⓑ Ⓒ Ⓓ Ⓔ	7. Ⓐ Ⓑ Ⓒ Ⓓ Ⓔ	7. Ⓐ Ⓑ Ⓒ Ⓓ Ⓔ	7. Ⓐ Ⓑ Ⓒ Ⓓ Ⓔ
8. Ⓐ Ⓑ Ⓒ Ⓓ Ⓔ	8. Ⓐ Ⓑ Ⓒ Ⓓ Ⓔ	8. Ⓐ Ⓑ Ⓒ Ⓓ Ⓔ	8. Ⓐ Ⓑ Ⓒ Ⓓ Ⓔ	8. Ⓐ Ⓑ Ⓒ Ⓓ Ⓔ
9. Ⓐ Ⓑ Ⓒ Ⓓ Ⓔ	9. Ⓐ Ⓑ Ⓒ Ⓓ Ⓔ	9. Ⓐ Ⓑ Ⓒ Ⓓ Ⓔ	9. Ⓐ Ⓑ Ⓒ Ⓓ Ⓔ	9. Ⓐ Ⓑ Ⓒ Ⓓ Ⓔ
10. Ⓐ Ⓑ Ⓒ Ⓓ Ⓔ	10. Ⓐ Ⓑ Ⓒ Ⓓ Ⓔ	10. Ⓐ Ⓑ Ⓒ Ⓓ Ⓔ	10. Ⓐ Ⓑ Ⓒ Ⓓ Ⓔ	10. Ⓐ Ⓑ Ⓒ Ⓓ Ⓔ
11. Ⓐ Ⓑ Ⓒ Ⓓ Ⓔ	11. Ⓐ Ⓑ Ⓒ Ⓓ Ⓔ	11. Ⓐ Ⓑ Ⓒ Ⓓ Ⓔ	11. Ⓐ Ⓑ Ⓒ Ⓓ Ⓔ	11. Ⓐ Ⓑ Ⓒ Ⓓ Ⓔ
12. Ⓐ Ⓑ Ⓒ Ⓓ Ⓔ	12. Ⓐ Ⓑ Ⓒ Ⓓ Ⓔ	12. Ⓐ Ⓑ Ⓒ Ⓓ Ⓔ	12. Ⓐ Ⓑ Ⓒ Ⓓ Ⓔ	12. Ⓐ Ⓑ Ⓒ Ⓓ Ⓔ
13. Ⓐ Ⓑ Ⓒ Ⓓ Ⓔ	13. Ⓐ Ⓑ Ⓒ Ⓓ Ⓔ	13. Ⓐ Ⓑ Ⓒ Ⓓ Ⓔ	13. Ⓐ Ⓑ Ⓒ Ⓓ Ⓔ	13. Ⓐ Ⓑ Ⓒ Ⓓ Ⓔ
14. Ⓐ Ⓑ Ⓒ Ⓓ Ⓔ	14. Ⓐ Ⓑ Ⓒ Ⓓ Ⓔ	14. Ⓐ Ⓑ Ⓒ Ⓓ Ⓔ	14. Ⓐ Ⓑ Ⓒ Ⓓ Ⓔ	14. Ⓐ Ⓑ Ⓒ Ⓓ Ⓔ
15. Ⓐ Ⓑ Ⓒ Ⓓ Ⓔ	15. Ⓐ Ⓑ Ⓒ Ⓓ Ⓔ	15. Ⓐ Ⓑ Ⓒ Ⓓ Ⓔ	15. Ⓐ Ⓑ Ⓒ Ⓓ Ⓔ	15. Ⓐ Ⓑ Ⓒ Ⓓ Ⓔ
16. Ⓐ Ⓑ Ⓒ Ⓓ Ⓔ	16. Ⓐ Ⓑ Ⓒ Ⓓ Ⓔ	16. Ⓐ Ⓑ Ⓒ Ⓓ Ⓔ	16. Ⓐ Ⓑ Ⓒ Ⓓ Ⓔ	16. Ⓐ Ⓑ Ⓒ Ⓓ Ⓔ
17. Ⓐ Ⓑ Ⓒ Ⓓ Ⓔ	17. Ⓐ Ⓑ Ⓒ Ⓓ Ⓔ	17. Ⓐ Ⓑ Ⓒ Ⓓ Ⓔ	17. Ⓐ Ⓑ Ⓒ Ⓓ Ⓔ	17. Ⓐ Ⓑ Ⓒ Ⓓ Ⓔ
18. Ⓐ Ⓑ Ⓒ Ⓓ Ⓔ	18. Ⓐ Ⓑ Ⓒ Ⓓ Ⓔ	18. Ⓐ Ⓑ Ⓒ Ⓓ Ⓔ	18. Ⓐ Ⓑ Ⓒ Ⓓ Ⓔ	18. Ⓐ Ⓑ Ⓒ Ⓓ Ⓔ
19. Ⓐ Ⓑ Ⓒ Ⓓ Ⓔ	19. Ⓐ Ⓑ Ⓒ Ⓓ Ⓔ	19. Ⓐ Ⓑ Ⓒ Ⓓ Ⓔ	19. Ⓐ Ⓑ Ⓒ Ⓓ Ⓔ	19. Ⓐ Ⓑ Ⓒ Ⓓ Ⓔ
20. Ⓐ Ⓑ Ⓒ Ⓓ Ⓔ	20. Ⓐ Ⓑ Ⓒ Ⓓ Ⓔ	20. Ⓐ Ⓑ Ⓒ Ⓓ Ⓔ	20. Ⓐ Ⓑ Ⓒ Ⓓ Ⓔ	20. Ⓐ Ⓑ Ⓒ Ⓓ Ⓔ
21. Ⓐ Ⓑ Ⓒ Ⓓ Ⓔ	21. Ⓐ Ⓑ Ⓒ Ⓓ Ⓔ	21. Ⓐ Ⓑ Ⓒ Ⓓ Ⓔ	21. Ⓐ Ⓑ Ⓒ Ⓓ Ⓔ	21. Ⓐ Ⓑ Ⓒ Ⓓ Ⓔ
22. Ⓐ Ⓑ Ⓒ Ⓓ Ⓔ	22. Ⓐ Ⓑ Ⓒ Ⓓ Ⓔ	22. Ⓐ Ⓑ Ⓒ Ⓓ Ⓔ	22. Ⓐ Ⓑ Ⓒ Ⓓ Ⓔ	22. Ⓐ Ⓑ Ⓒ Ⓓ Ⓔ
23. Ⓐ Ⓑ Ⓒ Ⓓ Ⓔ	23. Ⓐ Ⓑ Ⓒ Ⓓ Ⓔ	23. Ⓐ Ⓑ Ⓒ Ⓓ Ⓔ	23. Ⓐ Ⓑ Ⓒ Ⓓ Ⓔ	23. Ⓐ Ⓑ Ⓒ Ⓓ Ⓔ
24. Ⓐ Ⓑ Ⓒ Ⓓ Ⓔ	24. Ⓐ Ⓑ Ⓒ Ⓓ Ⓔ	24. Ⓐ Ⓑ Ⓒ Ⓓ Ⓔ	24. Ⓐ Ⓑ Ⓒ Ⓓ Ⓔ	24. Ⓐ Ⓑ Ⓒ Ⓓ Ⓔ
25. Ⓐ Ⓑ Ⓒ Ⓓ Ⓔ	25. Ⓐ Ⓑ Ⓒ Ⓓ Ⓔ	25. Ⓐ Ⓑ Ⓒ Ⓓ Ⓔ	25. Ⓐ Ⓑ Ⓒ Ⓓ Ⓔ	25. Ⓐ Ⓑ Ⓒ Ⓓ Ⓔ
26. Ⓐ Ⓑ Ⓒ Ⓓ Ⓔ	26. Ⓐ Ⓑ Ⓒ Ⓓ Ⓔ	26. Ⓐ Ⓑ Ⓒ Ⓓ Ⓔ	26. Ⓐ Ⓑ Ⓒ Ⓓ Ⓔ	26. Ⓐ Ⓑ Ⓒ Ⓓ Ⓔ
27. Ⓐ Ⓑ Ⓒ Ⓓ Ⓔ	27. Ⓐ Ⓑ Ⓒ Ⓓ Ⓔ	27. Ⓐ Ⓑ Ⓒ Ⓓ Ⓔ	27. Ⓐ Ⓑ Ⓒ Ⓓ Ⓔ	27. Ⓐ Ⓑ Ⓒ Ⓓ Ⓔ
28. Ⓐ Ⓑ Ⓒ Ⓓ Ⓔ	28. Ⓐ Ⓑ Ⓒ Ⓓ Ⓔ	28. Ⓐ Ⓑ Ⓒ Ⓓ Ⓔ	28. Ⓐ Ⓑ Ⓒ Ⓓ Ⓔ	28. Ⓐ Ⓑ Ⓒ Ⓓ Ⓔ
29. Ⓐ Ⓑ Ⓒ Ⓓ Ⓔ	29. Ⓐ Ⓑ Ⓒ Ⓓ Ⓔ	29. Ⓐ Ⓑ Ⓒ Ⓓ Ⓔ	29. Ⓐ Ⓑ Ⓒ Ⓓ Ⓔ	29. Ⓐ Ⓑ Ⓒ Ⓓ Ⓔ
30. Ⓐ Ⓑ Ⓒ Ⓓ Ⓔ	30. Ⓐ Ⓑ Ⓒ Ⓓ Ⓔ	30. Ⓐ Ⓑ Ⓒ Ⓓ Ⓔ	30. Ⓐ Ⓑ Ⓒ Ⓓ Ⓔ	30. Ⓐ Ⓑ Ⓒ Ⓓ Ⓔ

SECTION I

Time — 35 minutes
26 Questions

Directions: **In this section you will be given brief statements or passages and will be required to evaluate the reasoning involved. In some instances, more than one choice will appear to be a possible answer. You are to choose the *best* answer. Use common sense and reasonableness in making your selection; then mark the proper space on the answer sheet.**

Questions 1–2

Probability is a curiously unstable concept. Semantically speaking, it is an assumption, a pure artifice, a concept that may or may not be true, but nevertheless facilitates a logical process. It is not a hypothesis because, by its very nature, it cannot be proved. Suppose we flip a coin that has a distinguishable head and tail. In our ignorance of the coming result we say that the coin has one chance in two of falling heads up, or that the probability of a head turning up is one-to-two. Here it must be understood that the one-to-two is not "true" but is merely a species of the genus probability.

1. The author of this passage assumes that

   (A) nothing about our coin influences its fall in favor of either side or that all influences are counterbalanced by equal and opposite influences
   (B) probability can be dealt with without the use of logic
   (C) an assumption must be plausible
   (D) the probability of the coin's landing on an edge is counterbalanced by the probability of its not landing on an edge
   (E) probability can be precisely calculated

2. The last sentence implies that

   (A) probability is not absolute
   (B) one-to-two is merely a guess
   (C) one-to-two is a worthless ratio
   (D) truth is not important
   (E) genus is a category of species

3. Self-confidence is a big factor in success. The person who thinks he can, will master most of the things he attempts. The person who thinks he can't, may not try.

   The author of these statements would agree that

   (A) nothing is impossible
   (B) no task is too large
   (C) success relies on effort
   (D) self-confidence is of most importance
   (E) trying is half the battle

4. Booker T. Washington was criticized by members of his own race for rationalizing the fate of African-American people with the following assertion: "No race shall prosper 'til it learns there is as much dignity in tilling a field as in writing a poem."

Which one of the following, if true, would strengthen the criticism of Washington's assertion?

(A) Most African-American people during Washington's time were denied access to a liberal arts education.

(B) African-American landowners who worked hard running a farm were often able to pay for the artistic or professional education of their children.

(C) White people had respect for both African-American poets and African-American farmers.

(D) The economically dominant countries of the world are mainly agricultural.

(E) Most of Washington's critics had never tilled a field.

5. If no test has no easy questions, then all of the following must be true EXCEPT

(A) every test has some easy questions

(B) some tests have some easy questions

(C) no test has all hard questions

(D) easy tests have easy questions

(E) every test has some hard questions

Questions 6–7

Because college-educated men and women as a group earn more than those without college educations, and because in Eastern Europe and Latin America, 105 women are enrolled in colleges for every 100 men, the total earnings of college women in these areas should be equal to, if not greater than, the earnings of college men. But college women in Eastern Europe and in Latin America earn only 65 percent of what college men in these countries earn.

6. Which one of the following, if true, is most useful in explaining this discrepancy?

(A) The earning power of both men and women rises sharply in accord with their level of education.

(B) In some countries of Western Europe, the earning power of college-educated women is higher than that of men in Eastern Europe and Latin America.

(C) In Eastern Europe, more men than women who enter college fail to complete their educations.

(D) The largest percentage of women in Eastern European and Latin American universities study to become teachers; the largest percentage of men study engineering.

(E) In Eastern Europe and Latin America, about 60 percent of the total workforce is college educated.

7. Which of the following is a faulty assumption based on the statistics of the passage?

(A) The passage assumes all of the college women enter the workforce.

(B) The passage assumes conditions in Eastern Europe and in Latin America are the same.

(C) The passage assumes that men and women should be paid equally.

(D) The passage assumes that college-educated women outnumber women who have not attended college in Eastern Europe and Latin America.

(E) The passage assumes that all college-educated workers will be paid more than workers who do not have college educations.

8. When consumers are in a buying mood, and the cost of money is low, a shrewd retailer with a popular product will reduce prices of items that are selling slowly and make up for any loss by raising prices on the product or products that are popular.

In which one of the following situations are these recommendations observed?

(A) At Easter, John's Markets offered one dozen eggs at half their usual price, hams and turkeys at a 40 percent discount, but because of heavy rains, raised the price of many green vegetables.

(B) This Christmas Arrow Clothiers is offering six-month interest free charge accounts to any customers who purchase $50 or more of merchandise from their stock of discontinued summer wear and the fashionable new op-art neck wear.

(C) Since interest rates have reached a yearly low, the price of tax-free bonds is near an all-time high. Discount Brokerage has launched a campaign to sell off all of its holding in precious metals mutual funds that are now at a their lowest price in years.

(D) Angus Jewelry is offering special savings for customers who make purchases in May. With graduations coming soon, they are offering engraved gold Swiss watches, as well as lower prices on heart-shaped jewelry items that were featured on Valentine's Day.

(E) Travel agents in Orlando are capitalizing on the lowered air-fares to lure tourists by offering special rates on hotel accommodations and discounted admission tickets to two of the large theme parks in the area.

9. While some cities impose tough, clear restrictions on demolitions of older buildings, our city has no protection for cultural landmarks. Designation as a landmark by the Cultural Heritage Commission can delay a demolition for only one year. This delay can be avoided easily by an owner's demonstrating an economic hardship. Developers who simply ignore designations and tear down buildings receive only small fines. There-fore, _____.

Which one of the following best completes the passage above?

(A) the number of buildings protected by Cultural Heritage Commission designation must be increased

(B) developers must be encouraged to help preserve our older buildings

(C) the designation as landmark must be changed to delay demolition for more than one year

(D) developers who ignore designations to protect buildings must be subject to higher fines

(E) if our older buildings are to be saved, we need clearer and more rigorously enforced laws

10. In ballet schools throughout the country, 95 percent of the students and teachers are female, and 5 percent are male, but professional dance companies need at least 45 percent male dancers.

Which one of the following, if true, would help to explain these statistics?

(A) The social acceptance of dancing as a profession is much higher for females than for males.
(B) Modern choreographers can create dances that can be performed by companies with more female than male dancers.
(C) There are fewer dances than songs in most films and stage musicals.
(D) Men who have classical ballet training develop the same muscles as are used in track events such as the hurdles and the high jump.
(E) Women's bodies are more likely to mature at an earlier age than men's.

Questions 11–12

Sixty percent of the American people, according to the latest polls, now believe that inflation is the nation's most important problem. This problem of inflation is closely related to rising prices. The inflation rate has been 10 percent or more most of this year. Undoubtedly, our gluttonous appetite for high-priced foreign oil has been a major factor. We have been shipping billions of dollars overseas, more than foreigners can spend or invest here. Dollars are selling cheaply and this has forced the value of the dollar down. Government programs now being inaugurated to slow this trend are at best weak, but deserve our support, as they appear to be the best our government can produce. Hopefully, they won't fail as they have in the past.

11. The author of this passage implies that

(A) inflation cannot be stopped or slowed, because of a weak government
(B) the fear of inflation is not only unwarranted, but also detrimental
(C) 40 percent of non-Americans believe inflation is not the most important problem
(D) foreign oil is the sole reason for the sudden increase in inflation
(E) the present programs will probably not slow inflation

12. Which one of the following contradicts something in the preceding passage?

(A) Foreign oil is actually underpriced.
(B) The inflation rate has not risen for most of this year.
(C) Overseas investors are few and far between.
(D) Our government is trying a new approach to end inflation.
(E) The weakness of the programs stems from lack of support.

13. Sales of new homes in Arizona fell almost 20 percent in the month of February, compared to last year. Analysts attribute the decline to several factors. Record rainfalls kept both builders and buyers indoors for most of the month. The rise in the interest rates have brought mortgage rates to a ten-month high. Both the sales of new homes and housing starts have reached new lows. With every indication that mortgage rates will remain high for the rest of the year, Arizona home-builders foresee a very grim year ahead.

Which one of the following would add support to the conclusion of this passage?

(A) Last year's sales increased in the second half of the year, despite some increase in interest rates.

(B) Last year's sales were accelerated by good weather in January and February.

(C) Widespread advertising and incentives to attract buyers this February were ineffective.

(D) Rain in Arizona usually ends late in February.

(E) Home sales and building starts throughout the country are about the same this year as last year.

14. No one reads *Weight-Off* magazine unless he is fat. Everyone reads *Weight-Off* magazine unless he eats chocolate.

Which one of the following is inconsistent with the above?

(A) No one is fat and only some people eat chocolate.

(B) Some people are fat and no one eats chocolate.

(C) Everyone is fat.

(D) No one is fat and no one reads *Weight-Off*.

(E) No one who is fat eats chocolate.

15. *Jerry:* Every meal my wife cooks is fantastic.
    Dave: I disagree. Most of my wife's meals are fantastic, too.

Dave's response shows that he understood Jerry to mean that

(A) Dave's wife does not cook fantastic meals

(B) only Jerry's wife cooks fantastic meals

(C) every one of Jerry's wife's meals is fantastic

(D) not every one of Jerry's wife's meals is fantastic

(E) no one cooks fantastic meals all the time

Questions 16–17

Commentators and politicians are given to enlisting the rest of America as allies, sprinkling such phrases as "Americans believe" or "Americans will simply not put up with" into their pronouncements on whatever issue currently claims their attentions. They cite polls showing 60 or 80 or 90 percent support for their views. There may (or may not) have been such polls, but even if the polls are real, their finer points will not be reported because they usually contradict the speaker's point. The alleged 80 percent support for a balanced budget amendment, for example, plummets to less than 30 percent if the pollster so much as mentions an entitlement program like social security. People do have opinions, but they are rarely so specific or so unequivocal as your news broadcaster or your senator would lead you to believe.

16. The argument of this passage would be less convincing if it could be shown that

(A) In a recent poll, 80 percent of the Americans responding supported a balanced budget amendment.
(B) Most polls used by television commentators are conducted by telephone calls lasting less than 35 seconds.
(C) Far more Americans are indifferent to or badly informed about current affairs than are well informed.
(D) The polls' predictions of who will be elected president have been correct about every presidential election since Truman defeated Dewey.
(E) Many polls are based on samples that do not accurately represent the demographics of an area.

17. The argument of this passage proceeds by using all of the following EXCEPT

(A) supporting a general point with a specific example
(B) questioning the honesty of politicians and commentators
(C) reinterpreting evidence presented as supporting a position being rejected
(D) pointing out inherent inconsistencies in the claims of the politicians and commentators
(E) exposing the limitations of arguments based on statistics

18. The most often heard complaint about flights on Scorpio Airlines is that there is insufficient room in the cabin of the plane to accommodate all of the passengers' carry-on baggage. The number of passengers who carry on all of their luggage rather than checking it at the ticket counter has increased so much that on more than half of the flights on Scorpio Airlines passengers have difficulty finding space for their bags in the cabin of the plane. The company is considering ways to alleviate this problem.

All of the following are plausible ways of dealing with the problem EXCEPT

(A) Reducing the allowable size of carry-on luggage.
(B) Charging passengers who carry on more than one bag a fee.
(C) Increasing the fares of flights on lightly traveled routes.
(D) Reducing the seating capacity of the cabins to provide more space for luggage.
(E) Offering a price reduction to ticket buyers who check their bags.

19. X: "We discover new knowledge by the syllogistic process when we say, for example, 'All men are mortal; Socrates is a man; therefore Socrates is mortal.'"

 Y: "Yes, but the fact is that if all men are mortal we cannot tell whether Socrates is a man until we have determined his mortality—in other words, until we find him dead. Of course, it's a great convenience to assume that Socrates is a man because he looks like one, but that's just a deduction. If we examine its formulation—'Objects that resemble men in most respects are men; Socrates resembles men in most respects; therefore Socrates is a man'—it's obvious that if he is a man, he resembles men in *all* necessary respects. So it's obvious we're right back where we started."

 X: "Yes, we must know all the characteristics of men, and that Socrates has all of them, before we can be sure."

Which one of the following best expresses X's concluding observation?

(A) In deductive thinking we are simply reminding ourselves of the implications of our generalizations.
(B) It is often too convenient to arrive at conclusions simply by deduction instead of induction.
(C) Socrates' mortality is not the issue; the issue is critical thinking.
(D) Socrates' characteristics do not necessarily define his mortality.
(E) The key to the syllogistic process is using theoretical, rather than practical, issues of logic.

20. It takes a good telescope to see the moons of Neptune. I can't see the moons of Neptune with my telescope. Therefore, I do not have a good telescope.

Which one of the following most closely parallels the logic of this statement?

(A) It takes two to tango. You are doing the tango. Therefore, you have a partner.
(B) If you have a surfboard, you can surf. You do not have a surfboard. Therefore, you cannot surf.
(C) You need gin and vermouth to make a martini. You do not have any gin. Therefore, you cannot make a martini.
(D) If you know the area of a circle, you can find its circumference. You cannot figure out the circumference. Therefore, you do not know the area.
(E) You can write a letter to your friend with a pencil. You do not have a pencil. Therefore, you cannot write the letter.

Questions 21–22

Over 90 percent of our waking life depends on habits which for the most part we are unconscious of, from brushing our teeth in the morning, to the time and manner in which we go to sleep at night. Habits are tools which serve the important function of relieving the conscious mind for more important activities. Habits are stored patterns of behavior which are found to serve the needs of the individual that has them and are formed from what once was conscious behavior which over years of repetition can become an automatic behavior pattern of the unconscious mind.

21. It can be inferred that the author bases his beliefs on

   (A) the testimony of a controlled group of students
   (B) biblical passages referring to the unconscious state
   (C) an intense psychological research
   (D) extensive psychological research
   (E) recent findings of clinical psychologists

22. The last sentence implies that

   (A) all repetitious patterns become unconscious behavior
   (B) conscious behavior eventually becomes habit
   (C) the unconscious mind causes repetitive behavior
   (D) automatic behavior patterns of the conscious mind are not possible
   (E) habits can be good or bad

Questions 23–24

It should be emphasized that only one person in a thousand who is bitten by a disease-carrying mosquito develops symptoms that require hospitalization, according to Dr. Reeves. But it is a potentially serious disease that requires close collaboration by citizens and local government to prevent it from reaching epidemic proportions.

Citizens should fill or drain puddles where mosquitoes breed. They should repair leaking swamp coolers and be sure swimming pools have a good circulating system. Make sure drain gutters aren't clogged and holding rainwater. Keep barrels and other water-storage containers tightly covered. Use good window screens.

23. Which one of the following statements, if true, would most strengthen the advice given in the second paragraph above?

   (A) Leaking swamp coolers are the primary cause of mosquito infestation.
   (B) It is possible to completely eliminate mosquitoes from a neighborhood.
   (C) No one can completely protect herself from being bitten by a mosquito.
   (D) Tightly covered water containers do not ensure the purity of the water in all cases.
   (E) Window screens seldom need to be replaced.

24. What additional information would strengthen the clarity of the second sentence above?

   (A) The names of some local governments that have fought against disease.

(B) The name of the disease under discussion.

(C) The names of those bitten by disease-carrying mosquitoes.

(D) The full name of Dr. Reeves.

(E) A description of the symptoms that a bitten person might develop.

---

25. That which is rare is always more valuable than that which is abundant. And so we are continually frustrated in our attempts to teach young people how to use time wisely; they have too much of it to appreciate its value.

Which one of the following statements, if true, would most weaken the argument above?

(A) Appreciation is not the same as obedience.

(B) "Abundant" is a term whose definition varies widely.

(C) Currency that is based on rare metals is more valuable than currency that is not.

(D) Many young people possess an intuitive knowledge of what time is, a knowledge they lose around middle age.

(E) The leisure time of people aged 18–24 has decreased by 80 percent over the last 10 years.

26. Many theorists now believe that people cannot learn to write if they are constantly worrying about whether their prose is correct or not. When a would-be writer worries about correctness, his ability for fluency is frozen.

With which one of the following statements would the author of the above passage probably agree?

(A) Writing theorists are probably wrong.

(B) Writing prose is different from writing poetry.

(C) Literacy is a function of relaxation.

(D) Fear blocks action.

(E) Most good writers are careless.

STOP

IF YOU FINISH BEFORE TIME IS UP, CHECK YOUR WORK ON THIS SECTION OF THE TEST ONLY.
DO NOT GO ON TO THE NEXT SECTION OF THE TEST UNTIL TIME IS UP FOR THIS SECTION.

SECTION II

Directions: **Read the passages and answer the questions following each passage by blackening the appropriate space on the answer sheet. You may refer back to the passages when answering the questions. Answer all questions on the basis of what is stated or implied.**

The Sixth Amendment's right to the "assistance of counsel" has been the subject of considerable litigation in twentieth-century American courts.
(5) The emphasis has traditionally centered on the degree to which a criminal defendant can demand the assistance of counsel in various courts and at different hierarchical stages of
(10) the criminal proceeding. Although past courts have alluded to the idea that a defendant has a converse right to proceed without counsel, the issue had not been squarely addressed by the
(15) United States Supreme Court until late in its 1974–75 term. At that time, the Court held that within the Sixth Amendment rests an implied right of self-representation.
(20)   As early as 1964, Justice Hugo Black wrote that "the Sixth Amendment withholds from federal courts, in all criminal proceedings, the power and authority to deprive an accused of his
(25) life or liberty unless he has or waives the assistance of counsel." However, recognizing that the Sixth Amendment does not require representation by counsel, it is quite another thing to say
(30) that the defendant has a constitutional right to reject professional assistance and proceed on his own. Notwithstanding such a logical and legal fallacy, the Court has, by way of
(35) opinion, spoken of a Sixth Amendment "correlative right" to dispense with a

lawyer's help. Many lower federal courts have seized upon this and supported their holdings on it, in whole
(40) or in part.
    The basic motivation behind this proffered right of self-representation is that "respect for individual autonomy requires that (the defendant) be
(45) allowed to go to jail under his own banner if he so desires" and that he should not be forced to accept counsel in whom he has no confidence. Courts have ruled that neither due process nor
(50) progressive standards of criminal justice require that the defendant be represented at trial by counsel. The Supreme Court, in its 1975 decision, held that a defendant in a state criminal
(55) trial has a constitutional right to waive counsel and carry on his own case *in propria persona.* In raising this obscure privilege to a constitutional level, the Court stated that, so long as the
(60) defendant is made aware of the dangers and disadvantages of self-representation, his lack of technical legal knowledge will not deprive him of the right to defend himself personally.
(65)   The Court conceded that the long line of right to counsel cases have alluded to the idea that the assistance of counsel is a prerequisite to the realization of a fair trial. However, the
(70) Court noted that the presence of counsel is of minor significance when a stubborn, self-reliant defendant

prohibits the lawyer from employing his knowledge and skills. This line of
(75) reasoning is concluded with the observation that "the defendant and not his lawyer or the state, will bear the personal consequences of a conviction." The logical extension of
(80) this premise brings the Court to its decision that, recognizing the traditional American respect for the individual, the defendant "must be free personally to decide whether in his
(85) particular case counsel is to his advantage."

1. According to the passage, the chief purpose of the Sixth Amendment is to

   (A) assure a defendant the assistance of counsel in capital cases
   (B) assure a defendant the assistance of counsel in civil cases
   (C) assure a defendant the assistance of counsel in criminal cases
   (D) allow a defendant to represent himself in a criminal trial
   (E) allow a defendant to represent himself in a civil trial

2. The "logical and legal fallacy" referred to in lines 33–34 is probably

   (A) the ability to waive a right does not automatically give rise to a replacement of that right
   (B) the right to reject implies a correlative right to refuse to reject
   (C) the right to dispense with a lawyer's help
   (D) the right to legal assistance
   (E) the defendant who chooses to go to jail is free to do so

3. From the passage, the phrase *"in propria persona"* in lines 56–57 means

   (A) in his own person
   (B) by an appropriate person
   (C) in place of another person
   (D) improperly
   (E) by using a stand-in

4. In allowing a defendant to refuse counsel, the Supreme Court may have reasoned all of the following EXCEPT

   (A) a defendant who objected to a court-appointed attorney would prevent the lawyer from defending him effectively
   (B) the assistance of counsel is necessary to the realization of a fair trial
   (C) in the event of an unfavorable verdict, the defendant will suffer the consequences
   (D) American tradition recognizes the individual's freedom to make decisions that will affect him
   (E) it is possible that a defendant might defend himself more effectively than a court-appointed lawyer

5. A defendant who is acting as counsel in his own defense must be

   (A) given additional legal assistance
   (B) allowed to give up his own defense if he chooses to do so before the trial has concluded
   (C) warned of the disadvantages of self-representation
   (D) assisted by the judge in areas where the defendant's lack of knowledge of technical legal terms is deficient
   (E) tried before a jury

254 Model Test Two

6. All of the following are objections that might be raised to self-representation EXCEPT

(A) by accepting the right to self-representation, a defendant must waive his right to assistance of counsel
(B) a defendant determined to convict himself can do so more easily
(C) if the right to self-representation is not asserted before the trial begins, it is lost
(D) self-representation has a tradition in American law that dates back to the colonial period
(E) a self-representation defendant may be unruly or disruptive

African art could have been observed and collected by Europeans no earlier than the second half of the fifteenth century. Before that time Europe knew
(5) of Africa only through the writing of classical authors such as Pliny and Herodotus and the reports of a few Arabic travelers. Unfortunately, until the latter years of the nineteenth century
(10) Europe was little interested in the arts of Africa except as curiosities and souvenirs of exotic peoples. Indeed, with the growth of the slave trade, colonial exploitation, and Christian
(15) missionizing the arts were presented as evidence of the low state of heathen savagery of the African, justifying both exploitation and missionary zeal. Even with the early growth of the discipline
(20) of anthropology the assumption was that Africa was a continent of savages, low on the scale of evolutionary development, and that these savages, because they were "preliterate," could,
(25) by definition, have no history and no government worth notice.

In recent years the development of critical studies of oral traditions, of accounts by Islamic travelers of the
(30) great Sudanese kingdoms, of the descriptions of the coast by early European travelers, and—above all—of the concept of cultural relativism, has led to a far more realistic
(35) assessment of the African, his culture, history, and arts.

Cultural relativism is, in essence, the attitude whereby cultures other than one's own are viewed in *their* terms
(40) and on *their* merits. As an alternative to the prejudgment of missionaries and colonials it allows us to view the cultures and arts of the African without the necessity of judging his beliefs and
(45) actions against a Judeo-Christian moralistic base, or his art against a Greco-Renaissance yardstick.

Curiously, the "discovery" and enthusiasm for African art early in this
(50) century was not based on an objective, scientific assessment but rather resulted from an excess of romantic rebellion at the end of the last century against the Classical and Naturalist
(55) roots of western art. Unfortunately this uncritical adulation swept aside many rational concerns to focus upon African sculpture as if it were the product of a romantic, rebellious, *fin de siècle,*
(60) European movement. Obviously, African art is neither anti-classical nor anti-naturalistic: to be either it would have had to have had its roots in Classicism or in Naturalism, both
(65) European in origin. Nor was the concept of rebellion a part of the heritage of art in sub-Saharan Africa; rather, as we shall see, it was an art conservative in impulse and stable in
(70) concept.

We may admire these sculptures from a purely twentieth century esthetic, but if we so limit our

admiration we will most certainly fail to
(75) understand them in the context of their
appearance as documents of African
thought and action.

In sharp contrast to the arts of the
recent past in the Western world, by far
(80) the greatest part, in fact nearly all of the
art of the history of the world,
including traditional Africa, was
positive in its orientation; that is, it
conformed in style and meaning to the
(85) expectations—the norms—of its
patrons and audience. Those norms
were shared by nearly all members of
the society; thus, the arts were
conservative and conformist. However,
(90) it must be stressed that they were not
merely passive reflections, for they
contributed actively to the sense of
well-being of the parent culture.
Indeed, the perishable nature of
(95) wood—the dominant medium for
sculpture—ensured that each
generation reaffirmed its faith by re-
creating its arts.

7. According to the passage, before the
latter part of the nineteenth century,
Europeans viewed African art as

(A) simple and direct
(B) odd but beautifully crafted
(C) savage and of little value
(D) ugly and of grotesque proportions
(E) warlike and lacking in beauty

8. According to the passage, which one of
the following contributed to the initial
dismissal of African art by Europeans?

(A) Europeans valued color and
sophisticated techniques, both of
which were absent in African arts.
(B) It was easier to justify exploitation
of Africans if their art was
dismissed as heathen.

(C) Europeans were made
uncomfortable by the Africans'
tendency to depict coarse acts and
vulgar positions.
(D) It was important to reject African
art because it was dangerous to a
stable European society.
(E) It was believed that an influx of
African art could seriously disrupt
the market for European art.

9. According to the passage, all of the
following contributed to a change in
the European view of African art
EXCEPT

(A) the writings of Pliny
(B) cultural relativism
(C) Islamic travel accounts
(D) descriptions by early European
travelers
(E) studies of oral traditions

10. Which one of the following most
accurately represents the concept of
cultural relativism as defined in the
passage?

(A) The words "good" and "bad" are
irrelevant when judging between
works of art.
(B) One cannot enjoy a work of art
without a complete understanding
of the culture from which it came.
(C) The best art will always be art that
is positive in its orientation.
(D) If an artist goes outside his own
tradition in creating a work of art,
that work of art will be inferior.
(E) To determine the success of a work
of art, it should be judged against
the values of its own culture.

11. According to the passage, the early twentieth-century European view of African art was inadequate because it

(A) was based on a limited number of objects available to the Western world
(B) was a result of a romantic rebellion against traditions in Western art
(C) did not take into account the importance of oral traditions
(D) was dependent on classical rather than naturalistic standards
(E) was dictated by the judgments of Christian missionaries

12. Which one of the following best describes the author's point about the relationship between twentieth-century Western art and African art?

(A) African art and twentieth-century Western art both have their roots in a desire to escape tradition and rediscover man's primitive state.
(B) The techniques used in African sculpture are remarkably similar to the techniques used in twentieth-century Western sculpture.
(C) It isn't possible to enjoy African art if we judge it by twentieth-century European aesthetic standards.
(D) Compared to twentieth-century Western art, African art is conservative and conformist, in that it is in keeping with the expectations of its society.
(E) Because it was produced by artists unschooled in technique, African art does not display the sophistication and ingenuity of twentieth-century Western art.

13. According to the author, the use of wood in African art is especially significant because

(A) it is a simpler, more available medium than marble
(B) unlike the hardness of stone, its relative softness allows intricate carvings representing African beliefs
(C) it represents a rebellion from the media used in Western sculpture and a return to African roots
(D) it is unique to primitive cultures uncorrupted by the Western world.
(E) its impermanence ensures that each generation creates new art reaffirming the beliefs of the culture

14. In this passage, one of the principal methods the author uses to develop his subject is

(A) discussion and explanation of reactions to African art in the Western world
(B) examination and analysis of several specific African works of art
(C) criticism and refutation of Western traditions such as Classicism and Naturalism
(D) description and explanation of African religious and social beliefs
(E) discussion and analysis of the aesthetic principles at the foundation of African art

In the competitive model—the economy of many sellers each with a small share of the total market—the restraint on the private exercise of
(5) economic power was provided by other firms on the same side of the market. It was the eagerness of competitors to sell, not the complaints of buyers, that saved the latter from spoliation. It was
(10) assumed, no doubt accurately, that the

nineteenth-century textile manufacturer who overcharged for his product would promptly lose his market to another manufacturer who did not. If all
(15) manufacturers found themselves in a position where they could exploit a strong demand, and mark up their prices accordingly, there would soon be an inflow of new competitors. The
(20) resulting increase in supply would bring prices and profits back to normal.

As with the seller who was tempted to use his economic power against the
(25) customer, so with the buyer who was tempted to use it against his labor or suppliers. The man who paid less than the prevailing wage would lose his labor force to those who paid the
(30) worker his full (marginal) contribution to the earnings of the firm. In all cases the incentive to socially desirable behavior was provided by the competitor. It was to the same side of
(35) the market—the restraint of sellers by other sellers and of buyers by other buyers, in other words to competition—that economists came to look for the self-regulatory
(40) mechanisms of the economy.

They also came to look to competition exclusively and in formal theory still do. The notion that there might be another regulatory
(45) mechanism in the economy had been almost completely excluded from economic thought. Thus, with the widespread disappearance of competition in its classical form and its
(50) replacement by the small group of firms if not in overt, at least in conventional or tacit, collusion, it was easy to suppose that since competition had disappeared, all effective restraint
(55) on private power had disappeared. Indeed, this conclusion was all but

inevitable if no search was made for other restraints, and so complete was the preoccupation with competition
(60) that none was made.

In fact, new restraints on private power did appear to replace competition. They were nurtured by the same process of concentration which
(65) impaired or destroyed competition. But they appeared not on the same side of the market but on the opposite side, not with competitors but with
customers or suppliers. It will be
(70) convenient to have a name for this counterpart of competition and I shall call it countervailing power.

To begin with a broad and somewhat too dogmatically stated proposition,
(75) private economic power is held in check by the countervailing power of those who are subject to it. The first begets the second. The long trend toward concentration of industrial
(80) enterprise in the hands of a relatively few firms has brought into existence not only strong sellers, as economists have supposed, but also strong buyers, a fact they have failed to see. The two
(85) develop together, not in precise step, but in such manner that there can be no doubt that the one is in response to the other.

15. Which one of the following would be the best title for this passage?

(A) Capitalism and the Competitive Model
(B) Competition and the Concept of "Countervailing Power"
(C) Problems in American Capitalism
(D) The Importance of Economic Regulatory Mechanisms
(E) The Failure of the Classic Competition Model

16. In the classic competition model, when competitive manufacturers marked up prices because of strong demand, a return to normal was provided by

(A) new manufacturers entering the market
(B) refusal to buy on the part of customers
(C) governmental intervention in the form of regulation
(D) repositioning of the labor force
(E) failure of weaker manufacturers

17. In the classic competition model, the incentive for manufacturers to behave in a socially desirable way toward workers was provided by

(A) competition for the labor supply
(B) competition for the customer
(C) imbalance between supply and demand
(D) self-regulation among competitors
(E) humanistic economic theory

18. According to the author, which one of the following statements is true?

(A) The classic model of competition was inadequate because it ignored the role of labor and rewarded individual greed.
(B) The classic model of competition provided self-regulation prior to, but not after, the Industrial Revolution.
(C) The classic model of competition was undermined by the "restraint of sellers by other sellers and of buyers by other buyers."
(D) The classic model of competition was replaced by concentration of industrial enterprise and collusion among manufacturers.
(E) The classic model of competition was destroyed by the growth of "countervailing power."

19. Examples of "countervailing power" in the regulation of the economic power of manufacturers could include all of the following EXCEPT

(A) organized customer boycotts
(B) cooperative buying organizations
(C) large retail chains
(D) retailers developing their own sources of supply
(E) organizations that network manufacturers

20. According to the author, a weakness of economic thought has been

(A) a preoccupation with competition
(B) a failure to recognize the need for reasonable government regulation
(C) a belief in the "trickle-down" theory
(D) a failure to recognize concentration of industrial enterprise
(E) a bias toward unregulated capitalism

21. Which one of the following best describes the structure of this passage?

(A) The first three paragraphs describe the strengths of economic competition and the fourth and fifth paragraph describe its weaknesses.
(B) The first paragraph presents the historical perspective on competition, the second and third present examples of its effect on the economy, and the fourth and fifth paragraphs set forth the idea of "countervailing power."
(C) The first two paragraphs describe how competition is thought to work, the third paragraph provides a transition, and the fourth and fifth paragraphs describe "countervailing power."

(D) The first three paragraphs describe the classic model of competition, while the fourth and fifth paragraphs describe "countervailing power."

(E) The first three paragraphs present a view of competition in opposition to the author's, while the fourth and fifth paragraphs present the author's view.

Although genetics is all about inheritance, inheritance is certainly not all about genetics. Nearly all inherited characters more complicated than a
(5) single change in the DNA involve gene and environment acting together. It is impossible to sort them into convenient compartments. An attribute such as intelligence is often seen as a
(10) cake which can be sliced into so much "gene" and so much "environment." In fact, the two are so closely blended that trying to separate them is more like trying to unbake the cake. Failure
(15) to understand this simple biological fact leads to confusion and worse.

Not far from Herbert Spencer's (and his neighbor Karl Marx's) tomb, in Hampstead—a notably affluent part of
(20) London—is a large red-brick house. It was occupied by Sigmund Freud after he fled Austria to avoid racial policies which descended from the Galtonian ideal. On his desk is a collection of
(25) stone axes and ancient figurines. Freud's interest in these lay in his belief that behavior is controlled by biological history.

Everyone, he thought, recapitulates
(30) during childhood the phases which humans experienced during evolution. Freud saw unhappiness as a sort of living fossil, the emergence of ancient behavior which was inappropriate
(35) today. Like Galton he viewed the human condition as formed by inheritance. The libido and ego are, he wrote, "at bottom heritages, abbreviated recapitulations of the
(40) development which all mankind has passed through from its primeval days." Freud hoped that once he had uncovered the inherited fault which underlies mental illness, he might be
(45) able to cure it.

Today's Freudians have moved away from their master's Galtonizing of behavior. They feel that nurture is more important. Analysis looks for childhood
(50) events rather than race-memories. In so doing it is in as much danger as was Freud of trying to unbake the cake of human nature. Any attempt to do so is likely to prove futile.

(55) The Siamese cat shows how futile the task may be. Siamese have black fur on the tips of the ears, the tail and the feet, but are white or light brown elsewhere. The cats carry the
(60) "Himalayan" mutation, which is also found in rabbits and guinea pigs (but not, unfortunately, in humans). Breeding experiments show that a single gene inherited according to
(65) Mendel's laws is involved. At first sight, then, the Siamese cat fur is set in its nature: if coat color is controlled by just one gene then surely there is no room for nurture to play a part.

(70) However, the Himalayan mutation is odd. The damaged gene cannot produce pigment at normal body temperature but works perfectly if it is kept cool. This is why the colder parts
(75) of the cat's body, its ears, nose, and tail (and, for a male, its testicles) are darker than the rest. An unusually dark cat can be produced by keeping a typical Siamese in the cold and a light
(80) one by bringing it up in a warm room. Inside every Siamese is a black cat struggling to get out. It is meaningless

to ask whether its pattern is due to gene or environment. It is due to both. (85) What the Siamese cat—and every living creature—inherits is an ability to respond to the environment in which it is placed.

22. The function of paragraph one in the passage is to

(A) define the terms used in the passage
(B) present arguments against a prevailing viewpoint
(C) state the central thesis of the passage
(D) introduce a metaphor used to unite the passage
(E) provide scientific background for the passage

23. The author uses the example of Freud in paragraph two primarily to

(A) provide a prominent example of the belief that behavior is controlled by biology
(B) present historical context for the nature vs. nurture argument
(C) show Freud's limitations as a scientist and indicate the danger of his approach to therapy
(D) explain how Freud's concepts of ego and libido are related to genetic inheritance
(E) emphasize the close connection between psychology and genetic research

24. The sentence "Inside every Siamese is a black cat struggling to get out" (lines 81–82) refers to the fact that

(A) given the recessive nature of the Himalayan mutation, the black color on a Siamese cat will appear only in particular areas

(B) if the dominant coat-color genes of a Siamese cat can fully suppress the Himalayan-mutated recessive genes, the cat's coat will be light brown
(C) although genetically intended to be light brown, a Siamese cat will show black areas because of the Himalayan mutation and warm temperatures
(D) because of the way the Himalayan mutation operates, the coat color of a Siamese will be dark if the cat is kept in the cold
(E) without the Himalayan mutation combining with cold temperatures, the coat of a Siamese cat will be entirely black

25. Which one of the following summarizes the best example of irony in the passage?

(A) People who believe nature and nurture are inseparable are basically trying to unbake the cake of human nature.
(B) Freud fled Austria because of racial policies based on Galtonian theories that Freud himself believed.
(C) After leaving Austria, Freud came to London, where he was able to live in an expensive neighborhood.
(D) Studying how a gene works in a Siamese cat can explain how genes work in human beings.
(E) Modern Freudians have moved far away from Freud's beliefs concerning the causes of people's problems.

26. Which one of the following statements supports the author's thesis in the passage?

(A) Children of criminals, even when removed from the home environment, will in all likelihood exhibit criminal behavior.

(B) Given a genetic history of lung cancer, a person who smokes will be in greater danger of contracting the disease than one who doesn't.

(C) Although it poses some dangers, genetic engineering will lead in the future to a world free from disease and anti-social behavior.

(D) Social programs for improving living conditions in the inner city are ultimately futile because of the genetic heritage of most people who live there.

(E) Although intelligence seems to be determined largely by environment, creative talent in fields such as art, music, and literature is clearly genetic.

27. All of the following statements are supported by information in the passage EXCEPT

(A) Freud saw the development of child to adult as parallel to the development of primitive man to modern man

(B) although Freud viewed inappropriate behavior as a result of biological history, he did believe therapy might cure it

(C) modern Freudians have shifted their views of behavior from Freud's views and by doing so avoided the danger of oversimplification

(D) in Freud's explanation of human behavior, his definitions of both the libido and the ego depend on his acceptance of Galtonian theory

(E) according to Freud, a person's dysfunctional adult behavior would be an inappropriate manifestation of behavior inherited from ancient man

28. Which one of the following best describes the structure of the passage?

(A) Paragraph one states the author's thesis, paragraphs two and three present ideas opposing the thesis, paragraphs four and five provide a concrete example that supports the thesis.

(B) Paragraph one asks a rhetorical question, paragraphs two and three provide commonly held incorrect answers, paragraphs four and five state the correct answer through use of an example.

(C) Paragraph one states the author's thesis, paragraph two presents an opposing argument, paragraph three is a transition, paragraph four provides an example supporting the thesis, paragraph five restates the thesis.

(D) Paragraph one presents historical background for a commonly held belief, paragraphs two and three develop the belief, paragraph four presents a different view, paragraph five states the author's opinion.

(E) Paragraph one presents one side of a well-known controversy, paragraphs two and three present the other side, paragraphs four and five reconcile the opposing viewpoints.

STOP

IF YOU FINISH BEFORE TIME IS UP, CHECK YOUR WORK ON THIS SECTION OF THE TEST ONLY.
DO NOT GO ON TO THE NEXT SECTION OF THE TEST UNTIL TIME IS UP FOR THIS SECTION.

SECTION III

Directions: In this section you will be given groups of questions based on different sets of conditions. Drawing a simple diagram may be helpful in answering some of the questions. You are to choose the best answer and mark the corresponding space on your answer sheet.

Questions 1–6

There are five flagpoles lined up next to each other in a straight row in front of a school. Each flagpole flies one flag (red, white, or blue) and one pennant (green, white, or blue). The following are conditions that affect the placement of flags and pennants on the poles:

On a given flagpole, the pennant, and the flag cannot be the same color.

Two adjacent flagpoles cannot fly the same color flags.

Two adjacent flagpoles cannot fly the same color pennants.

No more than two of any color flag or pennant may fly at one time.

1. If the 2nd and 5th pennants are blue, the 2nd and 5th flags are red, and the 3rd flag is white, then which one of the following must be true?

   (A) Two of the flags are white.
   (B) Two of the pennants are white.
   (C) The 4th pennant is green.
   (D) If the 1st pennant is green, then the 1st flag is blue.
   (E) If the 1st flag is white, then the 1st pennant is green.

2. If the 1st flag is red and the 2nd pennant is blue, then which one of the following is NOT necessarily true?

(A) The 2nd flag is white.
(B) If the 5th flag is red, then the 3rd flag is blue.
(C) If the 4th pennant is green, then the 1st pennant is white.
(D) If the 1st and 5th flags are the same color, then the 3rd flag is blue.
(E) If the 4th pennant is green and the 5th pennant is white, then the 1st and 3rd pennants are different colors.

3. If the 1st and 3rd flags are white and the 2nd and 4th pennants are blue, then which one of the following is FALSE?

   (A) The 4th flag is red.
   (B) The 1st pennant is green.
   (C) The 3rd pennant is not red.
   (D) The 5th pennant is green.
   (E) There is one blue flag.

4. If the 1st and 4th flags are blue and the 3rd pennant is white, then which one of the following must be true?

   (A) If the 1st pennant is green, then the 5th pennant is white.
   (B) If the 5th pennant is white, then the 1st pennant is green.
   (C) The 2nd flag is red.
   (D) The 5th flag is red.
   (E) The 1st pennant is green.

5. If the 2nd flag is red and the 3rd flag is white, and the 4th pennant is blue, then which one of the following must be true?

   (A) If the 5th flag is white, then two of the pennants are blue.
   (B) If the 1st flag is white, then the 2nd flag is white.
   (C) If the 1st pennant is blue, then the 5th pennant is green.
   (D) If the 1st pennant is green, then the 5th flag is not blue.
   (E) If the 1st and 5th flags are the same color, then the 1st and 5th pennants are not the same color.

6. If the 1st flag and the 2nd pennant are the same color, the 2nd flag and the 3rd pennant are the same color, the 3rd flag and the 4th pennant are the same color, and the 4th flag and the 5th pennant are the same color, then which one of the following must be true?

   (A) The 1st pennant is white.
   (B) The 2nd flag is not white.
   (C) The 5th flag is red.
   (D) The 3rd pennant is blue.
   (E) The 4th flag is white.

Questions 7–13

In the Norfolk Library returned book section there are ten books standing next to each other on a shelf. There are two math books, two science books, three English books, and three poetry books. The books are arranged as follows:
   There is a math book on one end and an English book on the other end.
   The two math books are never next to each other.
   The two science books are always next to each other.
   The three English books are always next to each other.

7. If the 8th book is a math book, then which one of the following must be true?

   (A) The 5th book is a science book.
   (B) The 7th book is an English book.
   (C) The 6th book is not a poetry book.
   (D) The 4th book is next to an English book.
   (E) The 9th book is a science book.

8. If the 9th book is an English book and the 5th and 6th books are poetry books, then which one of the following must be true?

   (A) There is a math book next to a poetry book.
   (B) The 2nd book is a science book.
   (C) The 3 poetry books are all next to one another.
   (D) The 7th book is a math book.
   (E) The 4th book is not a poetry book.

9. If the 1st book is a math book and the 7th book is a science book, then which one of the following could be FALSE?

   (A) Both math books are next to poetry books.
   (B) All three poetry books are next to each other.
   (C) The 2nd book is a poetry book.
   (D) The 10th book is an English book.
   (E) The 6th book is a science book.

10. If the 4th book is a math book and the 5th book is a science book, then which one of the following must be true?

   (A) An English book is next to a science book.
   (B) If the 7th book is a poetry book, then the 3rd book is an English book.
   (C) If the 8th book is an English book, then the 2nd book is a poetry book.

(D) If the 10th book is a math book, then a poetry book is next to an English book.

(E) The three poetry books are next to each other.

11. If no two poetry books are next to each other, then which one of the following must be true?

(A) A science book is next to a math book.
(B) The 7th book is a poetry book.
(C) The 8th book is an English book.
(D) An English book is next to a science book.
(E) A poetry book is next to an English book.

12. If a science book is next to an English book, but not next to a poetry book, then which one of the following must be true?

(A) The 7th book is a poetry book.
(B) The 3rd book is an English book or a math book.
(C) The 5th or the 6th book is a math book.
(D) The 3 poetry books are not next to each other.
(E) The 7th or the 10th book is a math book.

13. If the 7th and 8th books are poetry books, how many different arrangements are there for the 10 books?

(A) 1
(B) 2
(C) 3
(D) 4
(E) 5

Questions 14–19

Freshman at State College must enroll in at least 3 classes chosen from Greek, Latin, Sex Lab, Marriage/Family Relations, American History, and Roman History. In addition to enrolling in at least one language (Greek or Latin), freshman class choices are governed by the following rules:

Enrollment in the Sex Lab requires concurrent enrollment in Marriage/Family Relations.

Enrollment in Marriage/Family Relations does not require concurrent enrollment in the Sex Lab.

Freshmen may not enroll in American History and Latin at the same time.

Anyone enrolled in Roman History must also be enrolled in Greek.

14. What is the maximum number of courses that a freshman can take?

(A) 3
(B) 4
(C) 5
(D) 6
(E) 7

15. If a freshman wishes to enroll in American History and the Sex Lab, then which one of the following is true?

(A) She must enroll in at least four classes.
(B) She cannot enroll in Marriage/Family Relations.
(C) She may enroll in Latin.
(D) She cannot enroll in Roman History.
(E) She must enroll in Roman History.

16. If a freshman does not enroll in Greek, what is the maximum number of classes he can take?

    (A) 1
    (B) 2
    (C) 3
    (D) 4
    (E) 5

17. If a freshman enrolls in Latin, which one of the following classes must be taken in addition to Latin?

    (A) Marriage/Family Relations or Sex Lab
    (B) Greek or American History
    (C) Roman History or Greek
    (D) Roman History or Sex Lab
    (E) Greek or Marriage/Family Relations

18. If a freshman does not wish to take American History or Greek, what is the maximum number of classes he can take?

    (A) 1
    (B) 3
    (C) 4
    (D) 5
    (E) 6

19. If a freshman enrolls in Latin, which one of the following must be true?

    (A) He enrolls in only three classes.
    (B) He enrolls in Sex Lab.
    (C) He may choose from four classes.
    (D) He enrolls in Marriage/Family Relations.
    (E) He cannot enroll in Marriage/Family Relations.

Questions 20–24

Seven track and field coaches, A, B, C, D, E, F, and G, are each assigned to coach exactly one of four activities—sprints, distance, jumpers, and throwers. Coaching assignments are made subject to the following conditions:

   Each sport is coached by one or two of the seven coaches.
   B coaches jumpers.
   Neither E nor F is a distance coach.
   If C coaches sprints, F and G coach throwers.
   If D coaches distance or throwers, A and G do not coach either distance or throwers.

20. If C and E coach sprints, which one of the following must be true?

    (A) Distance has two coaches.
    (B) G coaches jumping.
    (C) A coaches jumping or throwing.
    (D) D coaches jumping.
    (E) Jumping has one coach.

21. If G coaches jumping and A coaches distance, which one of the following must be true?

    (A) D coaches sprints.
    (B) F coaches throwing.
    (C) E coaches sprints.
    (D) C coaches distance.
    (E) F coaches sprints.

22. If D coaches throwing, which one of the following CANNOT be true?

    (A) G coaches sprints.
    (B) A coaches jumping.
    (C) E coaches sprints.
    (D) F coaches throwing.
    (E) C coaches jumping.

23. If G is the only throwing coach, which one of the following could be true?

   (A) D coaches distance.
   (B) If F coaches sprints, D coaches sprints.
   (C) A coaches jumping.
   (D) If F coaches jumping, D coaches jumping.
   (E) C and D coach the same sport.

24. If A does not coach sprints and D coaches distance, which one of the following CANNOT be true?

   (A) C coaches distance.
   (B) E coaches throwing.
   (C) G coaches jumping.
   (D) F coaches sprints.
   (E) E coaches sprints.

STOP

IF YOU FINISH BEFORE TIME IS UP, CHECK YOUR WORK ON THIS SECTION OF THE TEST ONLY.
DO NOT GO ON TO THE NEXT SECTION OF THE TEST UNTIL TIME IS UP FOR THIS SECTION.

SECTION IV

Time — 35 minutes
26 Questions

Directions: In this section you will be given brief statements or passages and will be required to evaluate the reasoning involved. In some instances, more than one choice will appear to be a possible answer. You are to choose the *best* answer. Use common sense and reasonableness in making your selection; then mark the proper space on the answer sheet.

Questions 1–2

The spate of bills in the legislature dealing with utility regulation shows that our lawmakers recognize a good political issue when they see one. Among the least worthy is a proposal to establish a new "Consumers Utility Board" to fight proposed increases in gas and electric rates.

It is hardly a novel idea that consumers need representation when rates are set for utilities which operate as monopolies in their communities. That's exactly why we have a state Public Utilities Commission.

Supporters of the proposed consumer board point out that utility companies have the benefit of lawyers and accountants on their payrolls to argue the case for rate increases before the PUC. That's true. Well, the PUC has the benefit of a $40 million annual budget and a staff of 900—all paid at taxpayer expense—to find fault with these rate proposals if there is fault to be found.

1. Which one of the following is the best example to offer in support of this argument against a Consumers Utility Board?

(A) the percentage of taxpayer dollars supporting the PUC
(B) the number of lawyers working for the Consumers Utility Board
(C) the number of concerned consumers

(D) a PUC readjustment of rates downward
(E) the voting record of lawmakers supporting the board

2. Which one of the following would most seriously weaken the above argument?

(A) Private firms are taking an increasing share of the energy business.
(B) Water rates are also increasing.
(C) The PUC budget will be cut slightly, along with other state agencies.
(D) Half of the PUC lawyers and accountants are also retained by utilities.
(E) More tax money goes to education than to the PUC.

3. Most of those who enjoy music play a musical instrument; therefore, if Maria enjoys music, she probably plays a musical instrument.

Which one of the following most closely parallels the reasoning in the statement above?

(A) The majority of those who voted for Smith in the last election oppose abortion; therefore, if the residents of University City all voted for Smith, they probably oppose abortion.

(B) If you appreciate portrait painting you are probably a painter yourself; therefore, your own experience is probably the cause of your appreciation.

(C) Most of those who join the army are male; therefore, if Jones did not join the army, Jones is probably female.

(D) Over 50 percent of the high school students polled admitted hating homework; therefore, a majority of high school students do not like homework.

(E) If most workers drive to work, and Sam drives to work, then Sam must be a worker.

4. "To be a good teacher, one must be patient. Some good teachers are good administrators."

Which one of the following can be concluded from the above statement?

(A) Some good teachers are not patient.
(B) All good administrators are patient.
(C) Some good administrators are patient.
(D) Only good administrators are patient.
(E) Many good administrators are patient.

5. "Good personnel relations of an organization depend upon mutual confidence, trust, and goodwill. The basis of confidence is understanding. Most troubles start with people who do not understand each other. When the organization's intentions or motives are misunderstood, or when reasons for actions, practices, or policies are misconstrued, complete cooperation from individuals is not forthcoming. If management expects full cooperation from employees, it has a responsibility of sharing with them the information which is the foundation of proper understanding, confidence, and trust. Personnel management has long since outgrown the days when it was the vogue to 'treat them rough and tell them nothing.' Up-to-date personnel management provides all possible information about the activities, aims, and purposes of the organization. It seems altogether creditable that a desire should exist among employees for such information which the best-intentioned executive might think would not interest them and which the worst-intentioned would think was none of their business."

The above paragraph implies that one of the causes of the difficulty that an organization might have with its personnel relations is that its employees

(A) have not expressed interest in the activities, aims, and purposes of the organization
(B) do not believe in the good faith of the organization
(C) have not been able to give full cooperation to the organization
(D) do not recommend improvements in the practices and policies of the organization
(E) can afford little time to establish good relations with their organization

6. Of all psychiatric disorders, depression is the most common; yet, research on its causes and cures is still far from complete. As a matter of fact, very few facilities offer assistance to those suffering from this disorder.

The author would probably agree that

(A) depression needs further study
(B) further research will make possible further assistance to those suffering from depression
(C) most facilities are staffed by psychiatrists whose specialty is not depression
(D) those suffering from depression need to know its causes and cures
(E) depression and ignorance go hand in hand

7. No brown-eyed people have red hair. Some short people have red hair.

Based on the foregoing information, all of the following must also be true EXCEPT

(A) there are short people who do not have brown eyes
(B) there are people without brown eyes who are short
(C) there are people with red hair who do not have brown eyes
(D) some brown-eyed people are short
(E) there are people with red hair who are not short

8. *Ivan:* What the Church says is true because the Church is an authority.
   Mike: What grounds do you have for holding that the Church is a genuine authority?
   Ivan: The authority of the Church is implied in the Bible.
   Mike: And why do you hold that the Bible is true?
   Ivan: Because the Church holds that it is true.

Which one of the following is the best description of the reasoning involved in the argument presented in the foregoing dialogue?

(A) deductive
(B) inductive
(C) vague
(D) pointed
(E) circular

9. *Mary:* All Italians are great lovers.
   Kathy: That is not so. I have met some Spaniards who were magnificent lovers.

Kathy's reply to Mary indicates that she has misunderstood Mary's remark to mean that

(A) every great lover is an Italian
(B) Italians are best at the art of love
(C) Spaniards are inferior to Italians
(D) Italians are more likely to be great lovers than are Spaniards
(E) there is a relationship between nationality and love

Questions 10–11

Mr. Dimple: Mrs. Wilson's qualifications are ideal for the position. She is intelligent, forceful, determined, and trustworthy. I suggest we hire her immediately.

10. Which one of the following, if true, would most weaken Mr. Dimple's statement?

    (A) Mrs. Wilson is not interested in being hired.
    (B) There are two other applicants whose qualifications are identical to Mrs. Wilson's.
    (C) Mrs. Wilson is currently working for a rival company.
    (D) Mr. Dimple is not speaking directly to the hiring committee.
    (E) Mrs. Wilson is older than many of the other applicants.

11. Which one of the following, if true, offers the strongest support of Mr. Dimple's statement?

    (A) All the members of the hiring committee have agreed that intelligence, trustworthiness, determination, and forcefulness are important qualifications for the job.
    (B) Mr. Dimple holds exclusive responsibility for hiring new employees.
    (C) Mr. Dimple has known Mrs. Wilson longer than he has known any of the other applicants.
    (D) Mrs. Wilson is a member of Mr. Dimple's family.
    (E) Mrs. Dimple is intelligent, forceful, determined, and trustworthy.

12. All of the candidates for the spring track team must have participated in fall cross-country and winter track. Some runners, however, find cross-country tedious, and refuse to run in the fall. Thus, some winter track runners who would like to be members of the spring track teams are not permitted to try out.

In which one of the following is the reasoning most like that of this passage?

    (A) Mice become aggressive if confined in close quarters for an extended period of time, or if they are deprived of protein-rich foods. Therefore, highly aggressive mice have been closely confined and denied high-protein foods.
    (B) Roses grown in full sun are less susceptible to mildew than roses grown in partial shade. Roses grown in partial shade are also more susceptible to black spot. Thus, roses should be grown in full sun.
    (C) To qualify for the June primary, a candidate for office must reside in the district for six months and gather 500 signatures of district residents who support the candidate. Thus, a longtime district resident would not qualify for the June primary if she gathered only 300 signatures.
    (D) A convenience store sells three chocolate bars for a dollar, and a large soft drink for 50 cents. A competitor sells four chocolate bars for a dollar, and a medium-size soft drink for 50 cents. Therefore, neither of the two stores offers more for the same price.

(E) The City Council has passed an ordinance that allows cyclists to use the city bike paths only if they are over 12 years old and are wearing bicycle helmets. Thus, parents with children under 12 will be unable to cycle with their families on the city bike paths unless they wear helmets.

13. When a dental hygienist cleans your teeth, you may not see much evidence that she is supervised by a dentist. Hygienists often work pretty much on their own, even though they are employed by dentists. Then why can't hygienists practice independently, perhaps saving patients a lot of money in the process? The patients would not have to pay the steep profit that many dentists make on the hygienists' labors.

Which one of the following statements weakens the argument above?

(A) Some patients might get their teeth cleaned more often if it costs less.
(B) Some dentists do not employ dental hygienists.
(C) Hygienists must be certified by state examinations.
(D) A dentist should be on hand to inspect a hygienist's work to make sure the patient has no problems that the hygienist is unable to detect.
(E) In some states, there are more female hygienists than male.

14. There are those of us who, determined to be happy, are discouraged repeatedly by social and economic forces that cause us nothing but trouble. And there are those of us who are blessed with health and wealth and still grumble and complain about almost everything.

To which one of the following points can the author be leading?

(A) Happiness is both a state of mind and a state of affairs.
(B) Both personal and public conditions can make happiness difficult to attain.
(C) Happiness may be influenced by economic forces and by health considerations.
(D) No one can be truly happy.   ·
(E) Exterior forces and personal views determine happiness.

15. "Keep true, never be ashamed of doing right; decide on what you think is right and stick to it."—*George Eliot*

If one were to follow Eliot's advice, one

(A) would never change one's mind
(B) would do what is right
(C) might never know what is right
(D) would never be tempted to do wrong
(E) would not discriminate between right and wrong

16. To paraphrase Oliver Wendell Holmes, taxes keep us civilized. Just look around you, at well-paved superhighways, air-conditioned schools, and modernized prisons, and you cannot help but agree with Holmes.

Which one of the following is the strongest criticism of the statement above?

(A) The author never actually met Holmes.
(B) The author does not acknowledge those of us who do not live near highways, schools, and prisons.
(C) The author does not assure us that he has been in a modernized prison.
(D) The author does not offer a biographical sketch of Holmes.
(E) The author does not define "civilized."

Questions 17–18

Information that is published is part of the public record. But information that a reporter collects, and sources that he contacts, must be protected in order for our free press to function free of fear.

17. The above argument is most severely weakened by which one of the following statements?

(A) Public information is usually reliable.
(B) Undocumented evidence may be used to convict an innocent person.
(C) Members of the press act ethically in most cases.
(D) The sources that a reporter contacts are usually willing to divulge their identity.
(E) Our press has never been altogether free.

18. Which one of the following statements is consistent with the argument above?

(A) Privileged information has long been an important and necessary aspect of investigative reporting.
(B) Not all the information a reporter collects becomes part of the public record.
(C) Tape-recorded information is not always reliable.
(D) The victim of a crime must be protected at all costs.
(E) The perpetrator of a crime must be protected at all costs.

Questions 19–21

A federal court ruling that San Diego County can't sue the government for the cost of medical care of illegal aliens is based upon a legal technicality that ducks the larger moral question. But the U.S. Supreme Court's refusal to review this decision has closed the last avenue of legal appeal.

The medical expenses of indigent citizens or legally resident aliens are covered by state and federal assistance programs. The question of who is to pay when an undocumented alien falls ill remains unresolved, however, leaving California counties to bear this unfair and growing burden.

19. The author implies that

(A) the U.S. Supreme Court has refused to review the federal court ruling
(B) the burden of medical expenses for aliens is growing
(C) the larger moral question involves no legal technicalities
(D) San Diego should find another avenue of appeal
(E) the federal government is dodging the moral issue

20. Which one of the following arguments, if true, would most seriously weaken the argument above?

(A) There are many cases of undocumented aliens being denied medical aid at state hospitals.
(B) A private philanthropic organization has funded medical aid programs that have so far provided adequate assistance to illegal aliens nationwide.
(C) Illegal aliens do not wish federal or state aid, because those accepting aid risk detection of their illegal status and deportation.
(D) Undocumented aliens stay in California only a short time before moving east.
(E) Judges on the Supreme Court have pledged privately to assist illegal aliens with a favorable ruling once immigration laws are strengthened.

21. Which one of the following changes in the above passage could strengthen the author's argument?

(A) adding interviews with illegal aliens
(B) a description of the stages that led to a rejection by the Supreme Court
(C) a clarification with numbers of the rate at which the burden of medical expenses is growing
(D) the naming of those state and federal assistance programs that aid indigent citizens
(E) the naming of those California counties that do not participate in medical aid to illegal aliens

22. History is strewn with the wreckage of experiments in communal living, often organized around farms and inspired by religious or philosophical ideals. To the more noble failures can now be added Mao Tse-tung's notorious Chinese communes. The current rulers of China, still undoing the mistakes of the late Chairman, are quietly allowing their agricultural communes to _____.

Which one of the following is the most logical completion of the passage above?

(A) evolve
(B) increase
(C) recycle
(D) disintegrate
(E) organize

23. *Sal:* Herb is my financial planner.
Keith: I'm sure he's good; he's my cousin.

Which one of the following facts is Keith ignoring in his response?

(A) Financial planning is a professional, not a personal, matter.
(B) Sal is probably flattering Keith.
(C) Professional competence is not necessarily a family trait.
(D) "Good" is a term with many meanings.
(E) Sal's financial planner is no one's cousin.

24. Many very effective prescription drugs are available to patients on a "one time only" basis. Suspicious of drug abuse, physicians will not renew a prescription for a medicine that has worked effectively for a patient. This practice denies a patient her right to health.

Which one of the following is a basic assumption made by the author?

(A) A new type of medicine is likely to be more expensive.
(B) Physicians are not concerned with a patient's health.
(C) Most of the patients who need prescription renewals are female.
(D) Most physicians prescribe inadequate amounts of medicine.
(E) Patients are liable to suffer the same ailment repeatedly.

Questions 25–26

Forty years ago, hardly anybody thought about going to court to sue somebody. A person could bump a pedestrian with his Chrysler Airflow and the victim would say something like, "No harm done," and walk away. Ipso facto. No filing of codicils, taking of depositions or polling the jury. Attorneys need not apply.

25. Which one of the following sentences most logically continues the above passage?

(A) The Chrysler Airflow is no longer the harmless machine it used to be.
(B) Fortunately, this is still the case.
(C) Unfortunately, times have changed.
(D) New legislation affecting the necessity for codicils is a sign of the times.
(E) But now, as we know, law schools are full of eager young people.

26. Which one of the following details, if true, would most strengthen the above statement?

(A) There were fewer courthouses then than now.
(B) The marked increase in pedestrian accidents is a relatively recent occurrence.
(C) Most citizens of 40 years ago were not familiar with their legal rights.
(D) The number of lawsuits filed during World War II was extremely low.
(E) Most young attorneys were in the armed forces 40 years ago.

STOP

IF YOU FINISH BEFORE TIME IS UP, CHECK YOUR WORK ON THIS SECTION OF THE TEST ONLY.
DO NOT GO ON TO THE NEXT SECTION OF THE TEST UNTIL TIME IS UP FOR THIS SECTION.

SECTION V

__Directions:__ **Read the passages and answer the questions following each passage by blackening the appropriate space on the answer sheet. You may refer back to the passages when answering the questions. Answer all questions on the basis of what is stated or implied.**

In the negotiation of tax treaties, developing nations, as a group, share two objectives somewhat at odds with those of developed-nation treaty
(5) partners. One such goal, attracting foreign investment, is in the broader context of foreign policy objectives. In the narrower realm of tax policy a common developing-country objective
(10) is to maximize the public capture of revenues from foreign investment activities.

Unfortunately for potential Third World treaty partners, this latter goal
(15) can conflict directly with the desires of both First World governments and individual investors. The preference of First World authorities for restricted source-based taxation is due to
(20) considerations of administrative feasibility. Such restrictions, though formally reciprocal, only produce equitable revenue effects when investment flows between treaty
(25) partners are relatively equal. However, when investment flows primarily in one direction, as it generally does from industrial to developing countries, the seemingly reciprocal source-based
(30) restrictions produce revenue sacrifices primarily by the state receiving most of the foreign investment and producing most of the income—namely, the developing country partner. The benefit
(35) is captured either by the taxpayer in the form of reduced excess credits, or by

the treasury of the residence (First World) state as the taxpayer's domestically creditable foreign tax
(40) liabilities decrease. The potential public revenue gain to the residence state further bolsters the industrial nations' preference for restrictions on source-based taxation—at the direct expense
(45) of the treaty partner's revenue goals.

The facilitation of foreign investment by tax treaties, whereas potentially serving the tax-policy goal of maximizing public revenue, also (or
(50) even instead) may serve broader economic objectives of developing countries. Foreign investments may be seen as essential sources of technical and managerial knowledge, capital,
(55) jobs, and foreign exchange. As such, the significance of foreign investments as an immediate source of public revenue could pale next to their longer-term "ripple effect" on development. In
(60) the negotiation of tax treaties, then, a developing country might be expected to ignore revenue goals and accept substantial limitations on source-based taxation, at least insofar as such
(65) limitations could be expected to encourage investment.

Frequently, however, Third World nations take a considerably more aggressive approach, seeking treaty
(70) terms that, in effect, provide subsidies to private investors at the expense of First World treaty partners. The United

States traditionally has followed a strict policy of "capital export neutrality," *(75)* providing no tax incentives for investment in the Third World through either the Internal Revenue Code or tax treaty provisions.

1. Normally, a developing country will negotiate a tax treaty for the purpose of

   (A) attracting foreign workers
   (B) decreasing tax revenues
   (C) attracting international investment and reducing tax revenues
   (D) attracting foreign investment and increasing tax revenues
   (E) decreasing dependence on special interest local investors

2. We can infer that a reciprocal source-based taxation treaty between a First World and a developing nation will produce

   (A) greater revenues for the First World nation
   (B) greater revenues for the developing nation
   (C) equal revenues for each country
   (D) no revenues for either country
   (E) losses to the economy of the First World nation

3. In negotiated treaties with developing countries, a First World country is likely to prefer

   (A) unrestricted source-based taxation
   (B) reciprocal restricted source-based taxation
   (C) nonreciprocal source-based taxation
   (D) equal investment flow between the partners
   (E) limited investment flow between the partners

4. In a treaty with a developing country that generates an excess of foreign tax credits, all of the following are likely EXCEPT

   (A) the treaty will require some reduction of at-source taxation
   (B) the treaty will discourage private investors
   (C) the treaty will not produce what is perceived as the optimal revenue-producing balance
   (D) the treaty will require some expansion of at-source taxation
   (E) the excess of tax credits will be larger if the source country reserves more taxing jurisdiction

5. According to the passage, all of the following are potential advantages of foreign investment to developing countries EXCEPT

   (A) increased managerial expertise
   (B) increased capital
   (C) increased availability of new materials
   (D) increased foreign exchange
   (E) increased employment

6. A developing country that did not insist upon immediate higher public revenues might be expected to

   (A) deter foreign investment
   (B) increase foreign investment
   (C) avoid the "ripple effect"
   (D) decrease employment
   (E) decrease the availability of raw materials

How buildings are depicted indicates how they are perceived. To the serious travelers of the eighteenth century, like James Stuart and Nicholas Revett who (5) took it upon themselves to record the legendary remains of Greece for the first time since antiquity, there are two modes of perception: the topical and the archaeological. To introduce each (10) monument, they resorted to the picturesque tableau. They show the Parthenon at the time of their visit in 1751, when Athens was a sleepy provincial town within the Ottoman (15) Empire and the Akropolis served as the headquarters for the Turkish governor. The temple stands in a random cluster of modest houses; in it we can see a Turk on horseback and, through the (20) colonnade, the vaulted forms of the small Byzantine church that rose within the body of the temple during the Middle Ages. This is what the Parthenon looks like today, the authors (25) are saying; and this depiction carries at once the quaint appeal of an exotic land and that sense of the vanity of things which comes over us at the sight of the sad dilapidation of one-time splendors.

(30)   But when they turn from romance to archaeology, the task of showing the Parthenon not as it is now but as it was then, Stuart and Revett restrict themselves to the measured drawing. (35) They re-create, in immaculate engravings of sharp clear lines, the original design of the temple in suitably reduced scale and with a careful tally of dimensions. We are confronted again (40) with the traditional abstractions of the architect's trade. Indeed, those architects who, in subsequent decades, wished to imitate the Parthenon as a venerable form of rich associational (45) value could do so readily from these precise plates of Stuart and Revett,

without once having seen Athens for themselves. In nineteenth century Philadelphia, for example, the (50) disembodied facade of the Parthenon is reconstructed as the Second Bank of the United States in an urban milieu that is completely alien to the setting of the prototype.

(55)   Against the engravings of Stuart and Revett, we might pit two pencil sketches of the Akropolis made by Le Corbusier during his apprenticeship travels in the early years of this (60) century. The close-up view is neither picturesque nor archaeological. It does not show us the ubiquitous tourists scrambling over the site, for example, nor any other transient feature of local (65) relevance. Nor is the sketch a reproducible paradigm of the essential design of the Parthenon. Instead, we see the temple the way Le Corbusier experienced it, climbing toward it up (70) the steep west slope of this natural citadel, and catching sight of it at a dynamic angle through the inner colonnade of the Propylaia, the ceremonial gate of the Akropolis. The (75) long view shows the building in relation to the larger shapes of nature that complement its form: the pedestal of the Akropolis spur that lifts it up like a piece of sculpture and the Attic (80) mountain chain on the horizon which echoes its mass. And when Le Corbusier draws on this experience later in his own work, it is the memory of the building as a foil to nature that (85) guides his vision.

7. From paragraph one, which one of the following best describes Stuart and Revett's pictures of the remains of ancient Greece?

(A) They show the grandeur of the Akropolis and depict the surrounding mountain ranges.
(B) They emphasize the original design and dimensions of the building.
(C) They show the antiquities as they appeared at the time of the pictures, not as they appeared in ancient Greece.
(D) Human figures and modest houses dominate the scenes that are shown in the pictures, whereas the natural surroundings are missing entirely.
(E) They are designed to contrast classical Grecian architecture with Byzantine architecture from the Middle Ages.

8. Which one of the following best summarizes the author's point about Stuart and Revett's first set of pictures (paragraph one)?

(A) Although the pictures are from 1751, they capture the way the Greek monuments looked to the average Greek citizen at the time they were constructed.
(B) By mixing grand monuments such as the Akropolis with modest houses, Stuart and Revett are making an ironic comment about architecture.
(C) Stuart and Revett's intention was to give as exact a picture as possible of the dimensions, scale, and grandeur of the original Greek antiquities.
(D) The pictures have a quaint appeal but they also convey a sense of the vanity of human efforts by showing

the effects of time on the Greek antiquities.
(E) The pictures capture not just the beauty and grandeur of the Greek antiquities but also suggest the positive spirit possessed by the people who created them.

9. In paragraph two, Stuart and Revett's engravings that depict the Parthenon are best described as

(A) exact and measured
(B) romantic and abstract
(C) topical and picturesque
(D) exotic and quaint
(E) uninteresting and pedantic

10. In paragraph two, the author mentions the Second Bank of the United States (lines 51–52) in order to

(A) show how Stuart and Revett's archaeological plates were exact enough to allow the Parthenon to be copied without an architect ever seeing the original building
(B) emphasize that classical architecture was so timeless that a building such as the Parthenon could be copied in an entirely alien environment and still retain its beauty
(C) indict Stuart and Revett for allowing inferior copies of Greek antiquities to be made, thereby detracting from the splendor of the original structures
(D) show the difference in the way that architecture was depicted in nineteenth-century America from the way it was depicted in eighteenth-century England as illustrated in Stuart and Revett's plates
(E) contrast the inferiority of imitative nineteenth-century architecture with the greatness of classical Greek architecture

11. According to the author, Le Corbusier's sketches of the Akropolis primarily show its

   (A) beauty and importance as a monument
   (B) relationship to its natural surroundings
   (C) importance as a citadel in Athens
   (D) connection to the common man in ancient Greece
   (E) role as a model for other monuments

12. Which one of the following can be inferred from information in the passage?

   (A) Classical Greek architecture, although often imitated, has never been surpassed.
   (B) The engraving process is the most effective way to create accurate architectural drawings.
   (C) The same building, depending on how it is depicted, may elicit various responses from a viewer.
   (D) Romantic depictions of structures are generally superior to strictly archaeological drawings.
   (E) Stuart and Revett were superior to Le Corbusier in depicting architecture in various ways.

13. Which one of the following does the author primarily use to make his point about architectural depiction?

   (A) anecdote and allusion
   (B) irony and understatement
   (C) metaphor and personification
   (D) logical argument and persuasion
   (E) description and contrast

War and change—political and economic foremost, but social and cultural not far behind—have been linked in America from the beginning.
(5) War was the necessary factor in the birth of the new American republic, as it has been in the birth of every political state known to us in history. War, chiefly the Civil War, in U.S. history has
(10) been a vital force in the rise of industrial capitalism, in the change of America from a dominantly agrarian and pastoral country to one chiefly manufacturing in nature. War, in
(15) focusing the mind of a country, stimulates inventions, discoveries, and fresh adaptations. Despite its manifest illth*, war, by the simple fact of the intellectual and social changes it
(20) instigates, yields results which are tonics to advancement.

By all odds, the most important war in U.S. history, the war that released the greatest number and diversity of
(25) changes in American life, was the Great War, the war that began in Europe in August 1914 and engulfed the United States in April 1917. Great changes in America were immediate.
(30)   In large measure these changes reflected a release from the sense of isolation, insularity, and exceptionalism that had suffused so much of the American mind during the nineteenth
(35) century. The early Puritans had seen their new land as a "city upon a hill" with the eyes of the world on it. It was not proper for the New World to go to the Old for its edification; what was
(40) proper was for the Old World, grown feeble and hidebound, to come to America for inspiration. A great deal of that state of mind entered into what

*illth = ill effects (word coined by the author earlier in the full selection)

Tocqueville called the "American
(45) Religion," a religion compounded of
Puritanism and ecstatic nationalism.
   What we think of today as
modernity—in manners and morals as
well as ideas and mechanical things—
(50) came into full-blown existence in
Europe in the final part of the
nineteenth century, its centers such
cities as London, Paris, and Vienna. In
contrast America was a "closed"
(55) society, one steeped in conventionality
and also in a struggle for identity. This
was how many Europeans saw
America and it was emphatically how
certain somewhat more sophisticated
(60) Americans saw themselves. The grand
tour was a veritable obligation of
better-off, ambitious, and educated
Americans—the tour being, of course,
of Europe.
(65)   Possibly the passage of American
values, ideas, and styles from "closed"
to "open," from the isolated to the
cosmopolitan society, would have
taken place, albeit more slowly, had
(70) there been no transatlantic war of
1914–1918. We can't be sure. What we
do know is that the war, and America's
entrance into it, gave dynamic impact
to the processes of secularization,
(75) individualization, and other kinds of
social-psychological change which so
drastically changed this country from
the America of the turn of the century
to the America of the 1920s.

14. In the passage the author makes all of
the following points about war EXCEPT

(A) war increases the pace of changes
that might occur anyway
(B) war stimulates new inventions and
discoveries
(C) war causes social and intellectual
changes

(D) war in a capitalistic society is
inevitable
(E) war sometimes stimulates a closed
society toward greater openness

15. If true, which of the following best
illustrates the author's point about the
effects of war on American society?

(A) During World War II, the Germans
developed a variety of lethal nerve
gas to use in the field.
(B) The development of radioactive
isotopes used in treating cancer
grew out of research to build the
atomic bomb used in World War II.
(C) The American influenza epidemic of
1919 in all likelihood was a result of
the return of infected soldiers from
the battlefields of World War I.
(D) After the Civil War and the abolition
of slavery in the South, racial
intolerance across America grew in
bitterness.
(E) A significant drain on America's
material resources was a result of
relaxed immigration policies
occurring after World War II.

16. According to the author, World War I
was the most important war in U.S.
history because it

(A) ended the notion of a war to end all
wars
(B) resulted in a weakened Germany
that in turn led to Hitler's appeal
(C) changed America from a
dominantly agrarian country to a
manufacturing country
(D) led to more changes and a wider
diversity of changes than any other
American war
(E) made Americans more aware of
advances made in European
centers such as London, Paris, and
Vienna

17. The main purpose of paragraph three is to

   (A) characterize the American mind in the nineteenth century
   (B) define Tocqueville's concept of American religion
   (C) indicate the main cause of America's entrance into World War I
   (D) contrast Civil War America with World War I America
   (E) indicate the areas of America's strength at the start of World War I

18. According to the author, which one of the following contributed to America's insularity before World War I?

   (A) The inability of all but the most wealthy, educated Americans to travel abroad
   (B) The nationalistic view that the New World (America) shouldn't turn to the Old World (Europe) for ideas
   (C) The emphasis on agrarian pursuits as opposed to belief in industry and technology
   (D) The puritanical idea that traveling widely in the world exposed one to sin and corruption
   (E) The superiority of the New World (America) to a feeble, decadent Old World (Europe)

19. Which one of the following best describes the main subject of this passage?

   (A) a comparison of wars in America
   (B) the benefits of war to society
   (C) the importance of World War I to changes in America
   (D) the contrast between the New World (America) and the Old World (Europe)
   (E) secularization and individualization in American society

20. The relationship of paragraph one to the rest of the passage is best described by which one of the following?

   (A) It presents a popular view that is proved inadequate by the rest of the passage.
   (B) It introduces a philosophical question that is then answered in the rest of the passage.
   (C) It outlines the contents of each of the other four paragraphs in the passage.
   (D) It sets up the first of four examples developed in the rest of the passage.
   (E) It presents a general idea that introduces the specific topic developed in the rest of the passage.

21. According to information in the passage, all of the following inferences can be made EXCEPT

   (A) well-to-do nineteenth-century American parents would be more likely to send their son to Europe than to California
   (B) European "ecstatic nationalism" would be greater after World War I than before it
   (C) religious influence in the daily workings of American society would be less evident in 1920 than 1900
   (D) a census in America 20 years after the Civil War would indicate more manufacturing operations than before the war
   (E) in the nineteenth century, avant garde movements in art and literature would be more likely to originate in Europe than in the U.S.

At a particular moment roughly 15 billion years ago, all the matter and energy we can observe, concentrated in a region smaller than a dime, began (5) to expand and cool at an incredibly rapid rate. By the time the temperature had dropped to 100 million times that of the sun's core, the forces of nature assumed their present properties, and (10) the elementary particles known as quarks roamed freely in a sea of energy. When the universe had expanded an additional 1,000 times, all the matter we can measure filled a (15) region the size of the solar system.

At that time, the free quarks became confined in neutrons and protons. After the universe had grown by another factor of 1,000, protons and neutrons (20) combined to form atomic nuclei, including most of the helium and deuterium present today. All of this occurred within the first minute of the expansion. Conditions were still too (25) hot, however, for atomic nuclei to capture electrons. Neutral atoms appeared in abundance only after the expansion had continued for 300,000 years and the universe was 1,000 (30) times smaller than it is now. The neutral atoms then began to coalesce into gas clouds, which later evolved into stars. By the time the universe had expanded to one-fifth its present size, (35) the stars had formed groups recognizable as young galaxies.

When the universe was half its present size, nuclear reactions in stars had produced most of the heavy (40) elements from which terrestrial planets were made. Our solar system is relatively young: It formed five billion years ago, when the universe was two-thirds its present size. Over time the (45) formation of stars has consumed the supply of gas in galaxies, and hence the population of stars is waning. Fifteen billion years from now stars like our sun will be relatively rare, making (50) the universe a far less hospitable place for observers like us.

Our understanding of the genesis and evolution of the universe is one of the great achievements of 20th-century (55) science. This knowledge comes from decades of innovative experiments and theories. Modern telescopes on the ground and in space detect the light from galaxies billions of light years (60) away, showing us what the universe looked like when it was young. Particle accelerators probe the basic physics of the high-energy environment of the early universe. Satellites detect the (65) cosmic background radiation left over from the early stages of expansion, providing an image of the universe on the largest scales we can observe.

Our best efforts to explain this wealth (70) of data are embodied in a theory known as the standard cosmological model or the big bang cosmology. The major claim of the theory is that in the large scale average the universe is (75) expanding in a nearly homogeneous way from a dense early state. At present, there are no fundamental challenges to the big bang theory, although there are certainly unresolved (80) issues within the theory itself. Astronomers are not sure, for example, how the galaxies were formed, but there is no reason to think the process did not occur within the framework of (85) the big bang. Indeed, the predictions of the theory have survived all tests to date.

22. Which one of the following best expresses the main idea of the passage?

(A) Twentieth-century technological achievements, such as particle accelerators, have made it possible for us to understand how the universe evolved.

(B) Over the past 15 billion years the universe has evolved through a process of expansion and cooling, as explained by the big bang theory.

(C) Because in the next 15 billion years the population of stars will greatly diminish, life in the universe will be precarious at best.

(D) Although the big bang theory is widely accepted by astronomers, there are a number of questions and issues that remain unresolved.

(E) Our solar system, formed 5 billion years ago, is relatively young viewed against the 15-billion-year evolution of the universe.

23. Which one of the following statements regarding the formation of the universe is best supported by information in the passage?

(A) Stars were formed only after the universe cooled enough for atomic nuclei to capture electrons.

(B) Helium and deuterium coalesced into gas clouds that gave birth to stars.

(C) Quarks became confined in atomic nuclei at about the same time that our solar system was formed.

(D) Planets came into being when neutral atoms formed gas clouds and heavy elements.

(E) Galaxies were formed as a result of a series of nuclear reactions in stars.

24. According to the passage, which one of the following is a correct sequence of events in the evolution of the universe?

(A) quarks; neutral atoms; stars; gas clouds; galaxies; planets

(B) quarks; neutral atoms; gas clouds; stars; heavy elements; planets

(C) atomic nuclei; helium; gas clouds; electrons; stars; planets

(D) atomic nuclei; gas clouds; electrons; stars; galaxies; planets

(E) quarks; atomic nuclei; electrons; gas clouds; planets; heavy elements

25. At what point does the passage markedly shift in direction?

(A) Lines 16–17: "At that time the free quarks became confined in neutrons and protons."

(B) Lines 41–44: "Our solar system is relatively young: It formed 5 billion years ago, when the universe was two-thirds its present size."

(C) Lines 47–51: "Fifteen billion years from now stars like our sun will be relatively rare, making the universe a far less hospitable place for observers like us."

(D) Lines 52–55: "Our understanding of the genesis and evolution of the universe is one of the great achievements of 20th-century science."

(E) Lines 76–80: "At present, there are no fundamental challenges to the big bang theory, although there are certainly unresolved issues within the theory itself."

26. According to the passage, all of the following statements are true EXCEPT

(A) the formation of planets was possible because of nuclear reactions in stars

(B) helium and deuterium atoms do not include electrons

(C) we are able to know what the universe looked like billions of years ago

(D) without the cooling that accompanied expansion, the evolution of the universe as we know it would have been impossible

(E) according to the big bang theory, it is not possible that other solar systems developed during the same period as ours

27. The information in the first three paragraphs of the passage is presented as if it is

(A) theoretical
(B) factual
(C) hypothetical
(D) evidentiary
(E) axiomatic

28. Which one of the following can be inferred about the future from the information in the passage?

(A) Because the predictions of the big bang theory have so far proved accurate, the theory will soon be accepted as fact.

(B) Although the expansion of the universe will continue, it will slow down over the next 15 billion years.

(C) Because the supply of gas in the galaxies will have been consumed, there will be less chance of a sun being formed 15 billion years from now.

(D) Although the process by which the universe was formed will continue to be studied, the "first cause" will never be determined by scientific means.

(E) Although the universe will continue to expand in the same way it has been expanding, cooling will not accompany the expansion.

STOP

IF YOU FINISH BEFORE TIME IS UP, CHECK YOUR WORK ON THIS SECTION OF THE TEST ONLY.
DO NOT GO ON TO THE NEXT SECTION OF THE TEST UNTIL TIME IS UP FOR THIS SECTION.

WRITING SAMPLE

<u>*Directions:*</u> You have 30 minutes to write an essay in response to a given topic. Take a few minutes to plan your work before you begin writing. DO NOT WRITE ON A TOPIC OF YOUR OWN CHOICE. ESSAYS THAT DO NOT ADDRESS THE GIVEN TOPIC ARE UNACCEPTABLE.

The quality of your writing is more important than the length of your response or the content. Pay attention to organization, appropriate diction, and correct usage. You will not be expected to display any specialized knowledge in your response, nor will you be expected to write a "perfect" essay; law schools understand that you are writing under a time constraint, and will allow for the minor lapses in writing ability that might occur under this circumstance.

Only the lined area in your booklet will be reproduced for the law schools, so do not write outside this space. *Do not* skip lines or use wide margins. These precautions, along with careful planning and legible handwriting that is not unduly large, will keep you within the allowed space.

Sample Topic

Read the following descriptions of Thomas and Peters, candidates for the position of head coach of the Ventura Vultures professional football team. *Then, in the space provided, write an argument for appointing either Thomas or Peters.* Use the information in this description and assume that the two general policies below equally guide the Vultures' decision on the appointment:

- The head coach should possess the ability to work with players and coaching staff toward achieving a championship season.
- The head coach should successfully manage the behind-the-scenes activities of recruiting, analyzing scouting reports, and handling the media and fans in order to enhance the public relations and image of the team.

THOMAS has been General Manager of the Vultures for the past ten years. A physical education major with a masters in psychology, he knows the player personnel as well as anyone, including the coaching staff. His on-target assessment of player skills and weaknesses has been instrumental in building a more balanced team over the past decade through his skillful trading and recruitment of college athletes. As the chief managing officer, he has also enhanced the team's image by his careful press relationship and understated approach when negotiations with star players reached an impasse. He rarely alienates players, coaches, press, or fans with his even-handed (though sometimes unemotional) attitude, and the Vultures' owners feel fortunate that they were able to entice him away from his high school coaching position, which he left 10 years ago. He has never played either pro or college ball.

PETERS is presently a wide receiver and defensive end for the Vultures. A one-time star, Peters has played both offense and defense for the Vultures since their inception in the league 14 years ago, a remarkable feat equaled by few in the game. He was elected captain of the team the past five years because of his charisma, although he occasionally angers management and fellow players with his strong comments about his philosophy of the game. His only experience in the front office was leading a player charity benefit for the Vultures, which raised more than $2,000,000 for abused Ventura County children. Although a high school dropout, Peters is a self-made man who firmly believes the key to life is having a strong educational background, even though he sometimes feels uncomfortable around college-educated athletes. The Vulture owners believe Peters may provide the emotional charge the team needs at its helm to win its first championship.

You will be given a special sheet of paper to write your essay. It will have the essay topic on the top followed by approximately 25 lines of writing. For practice, write your essay on one side of an 8½" x 11" college-ruled lined sheet of paper. *Use only 25 lines.*

ANSWER KEY

Section I: Logical Reasoning

1. **A**	6. **D**	11. **E**	16. **D**	21. **D**	26. **D**
2. **A**	7. **A**	12. **D**	17. **D**	22. **B**	
3. **D**	8. **B**	13. **C**	18. **C**	23. **B**	
4. **A**	9. **E**	14. **A**	19. **A**	24. **B**	
5. **E**	10. **A**	15. **B**	20. **D**	25. **E**	

Section II: Reading Comprehension

1. **C**	6. **D**	11. **B**	16. **A**	21. **C**	26. **B**
2. **A**	7. **C**	12. **D**	17. **A**	22. **C**	27. **C**
3. **A**	8. **B**	13. **E**	18. **D**	23. **A**	28. **A**
4. **B**	9. **A**	14. **A**	19. **E**	24. **D**	
5. **C**	10. **E**	15. **B**	20. **A**	25. **B**	

Section III: Analytical Reasoning

1. **E**	5. **A**	9. **B**	13. **B**	17. **E**	21. **A**
2. **C**	6. **C**	10. **C**	14. **C**	18. **B**	22. **E**
3. **D**	7. **D**	11. **E**	15. **A**	19. **C**	23. **B**
4. **B**	8. **A**	12. **C**	16. **C**	20. **D**	24. **C**

Section IV: Logical Reasoning

1. **D**	6. **B**	11. **A**	16. **E**	21. **C**	26. **D**
2. **D**	7. **D**	12. **C**	17. **B**	22. **D**	
3. **A**	8. **E**	13. **D**	18. **A**	23. **C**	
4. **C**	9. **A**	14. **D**	19. **E**	24. **E**	
5. **B**	10. **B**	15. **B**	20. **B**	25. **C**	

Section V: Reading Comprehension

1. **D**	6. **B**	11. **B**	16. **D**	21. **B**	26. **E**
2. **A**	7. **C**	12. **C**	17. **A**	22. **B**	27. **B**
3. **B**	8. **D**	13. **E**	18. **B**	23. **A**	28. **C**
4. **D**	9. **A**	14. **D**	19. **C**	24. **B**	
5. **C**	10. **A**	15. **B**	20. **E**	25. **D**	

MODEL TEST ANALYSIS

Doing model exams and understanding the explanations afterwards are of course important in acquainting you with typical LSAT question types and successful approaches to the questions. However, another benefit of carefully analyzing these model tests is to understand the kinds of errors you are making and thus work to minimize them. For instance, if a very high percentage of your incorrect answers is due to "careless error" or "misread problem," then perhaps you are working much too fast and should slow your pace accordingly. If your incorrect answers are due primarily to "lack of knowledge," then a careful rereading and reworking of the appropriate question-type chapter may be in order. Or if you find that you aren't completing a large number of questions because of lack of time, you may need to either increase your speed or learn to use the "one-check, two-check" technique more effectively.

This kind of analysis of the model tests will enable you to identify your particular weaknesses and thus remedy them.

MODEL TEST TWO ANALYSIS

Section	Total Number of Questions	Number Correct	Number Incorrect	Number Unanswered*
I. Logical Reasoning	26			
II. Reading Comprehension	28			
III. Analytical Reasoning	24			
IV. Logical Reasoning	26			
V. Reading Comprehension	28			
TOTALS:	132			

*At this stage in your preparation, you should not be leaving any blank answer spaces. At least fill in a guess, as there is no penalty for a wrong answer.

REASONS FOR INCORRECT ANSWERS

You may wish to evaluate the explanations before completing this chart.

Section	Total Number Incorrect	Lack of Knowledge	Misread Problem	Careless Error	Unanswered or Wrong Guess
I. Logical Reasoning					
II. Reading Comprehension					
III. Analytical Reasoning					
IV. Logical Reasoning					
V. Reading Comprehension					
TOTALS:					

EXPLANATION OF ANSWERS

Section I

1. **A** The author must assume that "nothing about our coin influences its fall in favor of either side or that all influences are counterbalanced by equal and opposite influences"; otherwise "our ignorance of the coming result" is untrue. Also, he mentions that the chances are one out of two that the coin will fall heads up; this could not be correct if the coin had been weighted or tampered with.

2. **A** (A) is implied by the author's statement that one-to-two is not "true." (B), (C), (D), and (E) are not implied and would not follow from the passage.

3. **D** The author is actually pointing out that self-confidence is of most importance. (C) and (E) focus on behavior, while the author is focusing on mental attitude.

4. **A** (A) stresses that farmwork is a fate rather than a privilege, and therefore strengthens the criticism of Washington's positive attitude toward labor. (B), (C), and (D) weaken the criticism, and (E) is irrelevant.

5. **E** If "no test has no easy questions," then all tests have at least one question. Thus (A), (B), (C), and (D) are all true. But a test could have all easy questions.

6. **D** None of the other four choices offer information that explains the discrepancy. If the women in college are preparing for a profession that pays less (teaching) than the profession the men will enter (engineering), the discrepancy is explained.

7. **A** To conclude that the women should earn as much or more than the men, the passage must assume that all of the men and all of the women, or at least an equal number, enter the workforce. It also assumes that all of them, or at least an equal number, graduate from college, though the passage says only "are enrolled."

8. **B** The six-month interest-free charge is the money at a low cost; the stock of discontinued summer wear is the slow selling product, and the fashionable new neck wear is the popular product. None of the other choices covers all three conditions.

9. **E** Though all of the choices are plausible, (E) deals with all three of the problems mentioned in the paragraph. Each of the other choices deals only with one.

10. **A** The statistics present the very small percentage of male dance students. Of the five statements, (A) does throw light on the figures. If dancing is not a socially accepted career for men, it is not surprising that there are few students. The other four statements have no real relevance to the statistics.

11. **E** The author states that the present programs are at best weak and hopefully won't fail as they have in the past.

12. **D** The statement that "Hopefully, they won't fail as they have in the past" tells us that our government is *not* trying a new approach to end inflation. (A) is close, but the passage states that foreign oil is "high-priced," not "overpriced." "High-priced" tells us the relative cost, not the actual comparative value.

13. **C** The conclusion is the prediction of a grim year for home-builders. Choices (A), (B), (D), and (E) do not

point to continued bad sales, but (C), revealing that sales fell even with advertising and incentives, supports the prediction of a bad year ahead.

14. **A** Three possibilities exist:
(a) You read *Weight-Off* magazine, are fat, and do not eat chocolate.
(b) You are fat, eat chocolate, but do not read *Weight-Off* magazine.
(c) You eat chocolate, are not fat, and do not read *Weight-Off* magazine.
Thus,
(A) is inconsistent by (a) and (b). (B) is not inconsistent if (b) and (c) are void of people. (C) is not inconsistent if (c) is void of people. (D) and (E) are not inconsistent by (c) and (a).

15. **B** Dave felt that Jerry implied that no one except Jerry's wife cooks fantastic meals.

16. **D** Only (D) offers an instance of success in the polls. (A) simply repeats a point of the passage without including the qualification that comes later. Choices (B), (C), and (E) would support rather than undermine the viewpoint of the passage.

17. **D** The passage does not point inherent inconsistencies. It does support a point with a specific example (the two figures on the balanced budget poll), question the honesty of politicians (the phrase "or may not"), reinterprets the 80 percent support figure, and shows how statistics can be used to mislead.

18. **C** Decreasing the fares on lightly traveled routes might attract some passengers away from the overcrowded more popular flights, but increasing the fares would not help to solve the luggage problem. The four other suggestions are plausible ways of dealing with the lack of space.

19. **A** X's new realization is expressed in his final sentence: "We must know all the characteristics of men, and that Socrates has all of them, before we can be sure." The "characteristics of men" are what is implied by the generalization "man," in "Socrates is a man." Therefore, deductive thinking is simply reminding ourselves of the particular specifics implied by generalizations.

20. **D** Symbolically, A is necessary to have B (a good telescope to see moons of Neptune). You do not have B (can't see moons with my telescope). Therefore, you cannot have A (a good telescope). (D) is the only choice that follows this line of reasoning. Symbolically, A is necessary to have B (knowing area of circle to find circumference). You do not have B (can't figure out circumference). Therefore, you cannot have A (area of circle).

21. **D** Extensive psychological research would most likely give the information that the author discusses. (E) limits the research to clinical psychologists and to recent findings.

22. **B** "Conscious behavior eventually becomes habit" is indirectly stated in the last sentence. (A) is a close answer, but that absolute word "all" is inconsistent with the words "can become" in the last sentence. This does not imply that they *must* become unconscious behavior.

23. **B** The given advice would be strengthened by the assurance that such measures are effective. Each of the other choices either weakens the advice, or addresses only a portion of the paragraph.

24. **B** The disease under discussion is termed "it," and thus its identity is unclear. The other choices either are not applicable to the second sentence or refer to terms that require no further definition.

25. **E** (E) weakens the argument that young people have abundant time. The other choices are only tangentially relevant to the argument.

26. **D** The passage says that worrying about writing unfortunately keeps one from writing at all; (D) summarizes this viewpoint. (B) and (C) are irrelevant notions; (A) contradicts the author's implied support for writing theorists; and (E) is an unreasonable, unsupported conclusion.

Section II

Passage 1

1. **C** The chief purpose of the Sixth Amendment was to assure the assistance of counsel in criminal cases. The guarantee to the right to self-representation was not the chief purpose of the amendment though the amendment has been used to support it.

2. **A** The phrase refers to the end of the second paragraph. The author regards the waiving of the right to counsel as a choice, which should not be seen as a guarantee of the right of self-representation.

3. **A** The phrase *"in propria persona"* means "in his own person," "by himself," or "by herself."

4. **B** If the Court had believed a fair trial was impossible without the assistance of counsel, it would not have allowed self-representation.

5. **C** The passage emphasizes the importance of warning a defendant of the risks of self-representation.

6. **D** Though true, the tradition of self-representation is not a valid objection to the practice. In fact, it might be cited as an argument in favor of self-representing defendants.

Passage 2

7. **C** The passage states that African arts were curiosities, and were presented as evidence of the "low state of heathen savagery of the African." The implication of lines 18–26 is that the arts, like the government and history, were not worth notice. (D) and (E) are incorrect; nothing is implied concerning the proportions or the subjects of African art. (A) and (C) both suggest a positive reaction to the art; this reaction is not supported by the passage.

8. **B** See lines 12–18. (C), whether true or not, is not supported by the passage. (D) is incorrect; Africa wasn't a threat to European society. In fact, Africans were exploited or made objects of missionary zeal. (A) and (E) are clearly irrelevant or incorrect.

9. **A** The writings of Pliny are cited as one of the early sources of knowledge about Africa—not one of the factors contributing to a change in the European view. See lines 27–36 for support of (B), (C), (D), and (E).

10. **E** Lines 37–40 make it clear that cultural relativism refers to viewing a culture in its own terms and on its own merits rather than judging it by the standards of one's own culture. (E) most clearly defines this point of view in relation to art. (A) is incorrect; the passage does not suggest that value judgments about works of art cannot be made, as long as the works are judged against the values of their own culture. (B) and (C) are irrelevant to the idea of cul-

tural relativism. (D) is also irrelevant, and its judgment is not supported by any statements in the
passage.

11. **B** See lines 48–55. The author states
that when the attitude towards
African art did change, it changed as
a result of an "excess of romantic
rebellion" against Classicism and
Naturalism, not as a result of an objective assessment. No point is
made in the passage about the availability of African art (A). (C) is unclear, and (D) is clearly inaccurate.
The judgments of missionaries (E)
were irrelevant to the twentieth-
century European assessment of
African art.

12. **D** See lines 78–89. One of the author's
main points is that African art was
very much in tune with its audience,
unlike modern European art, which
represented a rebellion against European traditions. (A) is the opposite of the point the author makes
about African art. (B) and (E) are irrelevant and not supported by information in the passage. (C) is
incorrect because although the author says we cannot have full understanding of African art if we judge it
by twentieth-century Western aesthetic standards, we can still "admire" the works in a limited way.
See lines 71–77.

13. **E** See lines 94–98. The author states
that the works of art, while conservative and conformist, were not "passive reflections" of the culture; the
perishable nature of wood ensured
that every generation reaffirmed its
faith. No comparison between wood
and stone is made (with the exception of the implied comparison of
impermanence and permanence).
Therefore, (A) and (B) are incorrect.

Also, no point is made about Western art or the Western world (C),
(D).

14. **A** Throughout the passage the author
talks about European or Western reactions to African art, from the earliest knowledge of Africa in Europe
until the twentieth-century re-
assessment of African art. No specific works are analyzed (B), nor is
any information included about African religious and social beliefs (D)
or African aesthetic principles (E).

Passage 3

15. **B** (B) is the best choice because the
passage first describes the classic
model of competition and then introduces what the author refers to
as the concept of "countervailing
power." Although the ideas in (D)
and (E) are both present in the passage, these titles are too restrictive.
(A) is incomplete, and (C) is clearly
wrong, in that the passage doesn't
specifically address "American capitalism."

16. **A** (A) is directly from the passage
(lines 18–22). Although (B) and (C)
might occur, these are not part of
the classic competition model described by the author. (E) would certainly not provide a return to normal
prices; although it might offer a
change in *supply*, it would not alter
demand. Answer (D) is simply unclear.

17. **A** (A) is the best choice. See lines
27–34. (D) and (E) are clearly
wrong. (C) is unclear. The second-
best answer is (B), since the behavior of manufacturers is ultimately
related to competition for the customer. However, (A) is the more
specific answer provided by the
passage.

18. **D** (D) is the best choice. See lines 47–55. (A) is incorrect because the classic model of competition does *not* ignore the role of labor (lines 27–31). Also, although the author might agree that greed undermined the classic model, this is not an issue addressed in the passage. (B) is incorrect because the author does not relate change in self-regulation of competition to any particular event, nor does he place it in a specific time frame. (C) is clearly the opposite of the point made in the passage. The restraint of "sellers by other sellers and buyers by other buyers" is part of the classic model of competition. (E) is incorrect because, according to the author, "countervailing power" did not destroy competition but grew as a result of a change in the classic model, i.e., the reduction of the number of competitors and resulting concentration of power among a small group of firms.

19. **E** Organizations that network manufacturers would not provide a customer- or supplier-generated restraint on them, which is the way the author defines "countervailing power." All of the other choices are possible wielders of "countervailing power."

20. **A** In lines 34–47 and lines 55–60, the author makes it clear that economists have almost exclusively focused on the classic model of competition in considering restraints on manufacturers. (B) is incorrect because the author does not discuss government regulation or the lack of it as part of economic theory. Similarly, (C) is incorrect; the "trickle-down" theory (i.e., that what is good for those at the top will

ultimately benefit those at the bottom) is also not mentioned in the passage. (D) is contradicted in the passage; according to the author, economists did recognize the trend toward concentration (lines 47–55, 78–84). Finally, although the author might agree with (E), the passage suggests that economists have been preoccupied with the classic model of competition (including its built-in restraints) rather than biased toward "unregulated" capitalism. The preoccupation with the classic models led them to ignore other types of restraint in the economy.

21. **C** The passage sets up the classic model of competition in paragraphs one and two. Paragraph three is a shift in the discussion to the idea that there might be a restraining mechanism exclusive of the competitive model that economists haven't recognized. Paragraphs four and five describe this restraining mechanism. The second-best answer is (D); however, paragraph three does provide a transition, which makes (C) the better choice.

Passage 4

22. **C** The second and third sentences of paragraph one state the thesis of the passage, which the rest of the paragraph explains further. (D) is incorrect because although the cake metaphor is introduced, it is referenced only once later in the passage. No terms are defined in paragraph one (A) nor are arguments presented (B).

23. **A** See lines 26–31. Although Freud does provide historical context (B), the author's primary purpose in including him is to explain by using a

prominent example the argument that genetic inheritance is responsible for behavior.

24. **D** In the example of the Siamese cat, the author states that the cat's coat-color gene (the Himalayan mutation) dictates dark fur, but pigment is produced only if the temperature is cold. See lines 70–80. The example is used to show the inseparable contributions of "nature" and "nurture." (A) and (B) are both incorrect because nothing in the passage addresses the concept of dominant or recessive genes. (C) and (E) are simply inaccurate statements.

25. **B** See lines 20–24 and 35–37. There is irony (a disparity) in the fact that Freud would subscribe to theories that led to his flight from Austria. The author uses the irony to underline the point he makes in lines 14–16 of paragraph one. (E) is incorrect because although there may be irony in modern Freudians moving so far away from Freud's beliefs, the author does not make this point ironically.

26. **B** This statement most clearly supports the author's point that what is inherited is an ability to respond to the environment. Trying to separate the effects of inheritance and environment is not productive. Like the Himalayan mutation and its connection to temperature in Siamese cats, if there were a lung-cancer-causing gene in humans, its manifestation might depend on environment (smoking or not smoking). (A), (C), (D), and (E) all suppose being able to separate the effects of genes and environment, which the author argues isn't possible in most cases.

27. **C** The passage does not support this statement. See lines 50–53. The author indicates that today's Freudians separate nature and nurture and therefore oversimplify human behavior. The other statements are supported: (A)—lines 29–31; (B)—lines 42–45; (D)—lines 35–42; (E)—lines 32–35.

28. **A** After the statement of the thesis that traits and behaviors cannot be separated into those that are genetically caused and those that are environmentally caused, the author illustrates the "nature" argument using Freud and the "nurture" argument using modern Freudians. In the final two paragraphs he presents the example of the Himalayan mutation in Siamese cats to support his initial thesis. (B) is incorrect because paragraph one does not pose a rhetorical question; (C) is incorrect because paragraph three is not a transition.

Section III

Answers 1–6

UPPER-case letters denote colors given in the problem, and lower-case letters denote deduced colors.

1. E	1	2	3	4	5	
	b/w	R	W	b	R	(flag)
	w/g	B	g	w	B	(pennant)

The 3rd pennant cannot be blue or white, so therefore it is green. The 4th flag cannot be white or red, so it must be blue. The 4th pennant cannot be green or blue, so it must be white. The 1st flag cannot be red, so it is either blue or white. The 1st pennant cannot be blue, so it must be green or white.

2. **C**

1	2	3	4	5	
R	w	r/b			(flag)
g/w	B	g/w			(pennant)

(A) is clearly true. If the 5th flag is red, then the 3rd flag cannot be, since the 1st flag is red and we can have only two of any one color. Thus, (B) is true. If the 4th pennant is green, then the 3rd pennant must be white. But that does not determine the color of the 1st pennant. Thus, (C) is not necessarily true. (D) is the same as (A) and is also true. If the 4th pennant is green, this implies that the 3rd pennant must be white. If the 5th pennant is white, then the 1st pennant cannot be. Therefore (E) is true.

3. **D**

1	2	3	4	5	
W	r	W	r	b	(flag)
g	B	g	B	w	(pennant)

The facts in this problem determine the complete configuration of flags and pennants. (D) is the one statement that is false.

4. **B**

1	2	3	4	5	
B	w	r	B		(flag)
	W	g			(pennant)

Statement (B) is true since the 1st pennant cannot be blue or white. Statement A is false since the 5th pennant could be blue or white. Statement (C) is false since it is white. Statements (D) and (E) are false since they could be white.

5. **A**

1	2	3	4	5	
	R	W	r		(flag)
	g	B			(pennant)

If the 5th flag is white, then the 5th pennant must be green. Thus the 1st and 2nd pennants cannot be green and cannot be the same color,

so one of them is blue. Therefore, (A) is true. All the other statements are false.

6. **C**

1	2	3	4	5	
W	B	W	B	r	(flag)
g	W	B	W	B	(pennant)

1	2	3	4	5	
B	W	B	W	r	(flag)
g	B	W	B	W	(pennant)

Since blue and white are the two common colors between flags and pennants, the above are the only two arrangements possible. In both cases, the 5th flag is red and the 1st pennant is green.

Answers 7–13

7. **D**

1	2	3	4	5	6	7	8	9	10
E	E	E						M	M

If the 8th book is a math book, then the three English books must be in positions 1, 2, and 3, since they cannot be in positions 8, 9, and 10. Thus, the other math book is in position 10. The 4th book must be next to the English book in position 3.

8. **A**

1	2	3	4	5	6	7	8	9	10
M			P	P			E	E	E

If the 9th book is an English book, then so are the 8th and 10th books. Thus there is a math book in position 1. The science books must be in positions 2 and 3 *or* 3 and 4. This leaves only positions 4 and 7 for the other math book. Thus (A) is always true. (C) could be true, but does not have to be true. The 3rd poetry book could be in position 2.

9. **B**

1	2	3	4	5	6	7	8	9	10
M					S	S	E	E	E

If the 1st book is a math book, then the 8th, 9th, and 10th books must be the English books. If the 7th book is a science book, so must be the 6th book. This means that the other math book must be either the 3rd, the 4th, or the 5th book. The remainder of the books are poetry books, including the 2nd book.

10. **C**

1	2	3	4	5	6	7	8	9	10
M	P	P	M	S	S	P	E	E	E

or

E	E	E	M	S	S	P	P	P	M

If the 4th book is a math book and the 5th book is a science book, then the 6th book is also a science book. This leaves two possible arrangements for the remaining books, as shown above. Statement (C) is the only correct one.

11. **E**

1	2	3	4	5	6	7	8	9	10
E	E	E	P					P	M

or

M	P						P	E	E	E

The poetry books must be in positions 4 and 9 *or* 2 and 7, depending on whether the math book is in position 1 or 10. See diagrams above. For example, let us assume that the math book is the 10th book. In order for no two poetry books to be next to each other, the 4th and 9th books must be poetry books, with the 3rd poetry book in either position 6 or 7, depending on the positions of the science books. The same argument holds if the 1st book is a math book.

12. **C**

1	2	3	4	5	6	7	8	9	10
E	E	E	S	S	M	P	P	P	M

and

M	P	P	P	M	S	S	E	E	E

These are the two possible arrangements. We see that (A) is false, (B) could be false, (D) is false, and (E)

could be false. Only (C) is always true.

13. **B**

1	2	3	4	5	6	7	8	9	10
E	E	E	M	S	S	P	P	P	M

and

E	E	E	S	S	M	P	P	P	M

These are the only two possible combinations; thus, (B) is the correct answer.

Answers 14–19

A simple chart, as follows, will help to answer the questions:

14. **C** From the chart we can see that a freshman can take everything except Latin (if he takes American History) or take everything except American History (if he takes Latin).

15. **A** In order to enroll in American History and the Sex Lab, a freshman must take Marriage/Family Relations plus Greek. Therefore, only (A) is true.

16. **C** If a freshman does not enroll in Greek, he can take only Latin, Sex Lab, and Marriage/Family Relations.

17. **E** If a freshman enrolls in Latin, his course load could consist of Latin, Greek, and Roman History; or it

could consist of Latin, Sex Lab, and Marriage/Family Relations; or it could consist of Latin, Greek, and Marriage/Family Relations.

18. **B** If a freshman does not take Greek or American History, he must take Latin, and cannot take Roman History (because Roman History requires taking Greek). Therefore, the other two courses left for him to take are Sex Lab and Marriage/Family Relations.

19. **C** If a freshman enrolls in Latin, he may choose from any of the classes except American History. Thus, he may choose from Greek, Sex Lab, Marriage/Family Relations, and Roman History—a total of four.

Answers 20–24

From the information given, you could have constructed the following display:

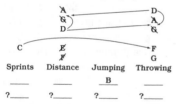

20. **D** If C and E are both sprint coaches, then from the original conditions F and G coach throwers. Since G coaches throwers, D cannot coach distance, so D must coach jumping.

Sprints	Distance	Jumping	Throwing
C		B	F
? E	?	? D	? G

21. **A** If G coaches jumping and A coaches distance we have:

Sprints	Distance	Jumping	Throwing
	A	B	
?	?	? G	?

If D coaches distance or throwing, A must coach sprints or jumping.

Since A coaches distance, D cannot coach distance or throwing. This means D must coach sprints. The other choices are possible, but not necessarily true.

Sprints	Distance	Jumping	Throwing
D	A	B	
?	?	? G	?

22. **E** If D coaches throwing, A and G cannot coach distance or throwing. This leaves only C to be the distance coach. So C CANNOT coach jumping.

Sprints	Distance	Jumping	Throwing
	C	B	D
?	?	?	?
	A̶		A̶
	G̶		G̶

(with E̶ and F̶ struck above Distance)

23. **B** If G is the only throwing coach, we have the following:

Sprints	Distance	Jumping	Throwing
		B	G
?	?	?	? X

(with E̶ and F̶ struck above Distance)

If D coaches distance or throwers, G must coach sprints or jumping. Since G coaches throwing, D does not coach distance or throwers. Thus, A and C must coach distance giving the following arrangement:

Sprints	Distance	Jumping	Throwing
	A	B	G
?	? C	?	? X
	D̶		D̶

(with E̶ and F̶ struck above Distance)

Choice (A) is incorrect since D doesn't coach distance.
Choice (C) is incorrect since A coaches distance.
Choice (D) is incorrect since, if F coaches jumping, D and E must coach sprints.

Choice (E) is incorrect since C and D coach different sports.

24. **C** If D coaches distance, A and G do not coach distance or throwing.

Sprints	Distance	Jumping	Throwing
A̶	D	B	——
?___	?___	?___	?___
	A̶		A̶
	G̶		G̶

E̶
F̶ (above Distance)

Since A does not coach sprints, then A must coach jumping. So A and B coach jumping; therefore, G CANNOT coach jumping.

E̶
F̶ (above Distance)

Sprints	Distance	Jumping	Throwing
A̶	D	B	——
?___	?___	? A	?___
	A̶		A̶
	G̶		G̶

Section IV

1. **D** This choice provides the most direct evidence of the effectiveness of the PUC consumer action. Each of the other choices is only tangentially related to the argument.

2. **D** This choice most seriously weakens the author's contention that the PUC acts in the public interest. (C) is a weaker choice, especially because "slightly" softens the statement.

3. **A** This choice parallels both the reasoning and the structure of the original. The original reasoning may be summarized as follows: most $X \rightarrow Y$; therefore $X \rightarrow Y$ (probably).

4. **C** The reasoning goes as follows: All good teachers are patient (rephrasing of the first statement); some good teachers (patient) are good administrators; therefore, some good administrators are patient. To use a term of degree other than some requires assumptions beyond the information given.

5. **B** Since good personnel relations of an organization, according to the passage, rely upon "mutual confidence, trust and goodwill," one of the causes of personnel difficulties would most certainly be the employees' not believing in the good faith of the organization.

6. **B** In the second sentence, the author implies that the lack of facilities is related to the lack of research mentioned in the first sentence. In any case, the passage reveals the author's concern with both research and assistance, and therefore agrees more fully with (B) than with (A), which mentions research only.

7. **D** Since some short people have red hair, and since anyone with red hair can't have brown eyes, (A) is true: there are short people who do not have brown eyes. Likewise, since there are some short people with red hair, and those red-haired people cannot have brown eyes, (B) is true: there are people without brown eyes who are short.

Or, by using Venn diagrams, three groupings can be drawn that satisfy the given conditions:

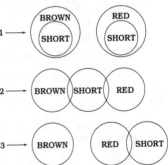

Notice that, based on alternative 3, (D) need not be true. (C) and (E) merely restate the given.

8. **E** The correct answer is "circular." The argument that what the Church says is true is ultimately based upon this same assertion.

9. **A** Kathy believes Mary to have meant that *only Italians* are great lovers. Therefore, Kathy takes issue with this and points out in her reply that there are non-Italians who are great lovers. (A), if replaced for Mary's statement, would make Kathy's reply a reasonable one.

10. **B** Only (B) addresses Dimple's assumption that Mrs. Wilson is the *only* applicant whose qualifications are ideal. Other choices are irrelevant to the *argument,* although some may be relevant to the implied situation.

11. **A** Only (A) addresses the substance of Dimple's argument.

12. **C** The passage offers a pattern in which failure to meet one of two specific requirements results in a failure to qualify for something. In (C), the fall and winter track seasons become the residence requirement and the collecting of signatures. Failure to complete both leads to disqualification (for the spring team, for the June primary).

13. **D** The author of the argument avoids the issue of *quality.* The statement that stresses the incompleteness of the pro-hygienist position weakens it. (B) and (E) are irrelevant.

14. **D** The passage describes two types of obstacles to happiness: exterior forces and personal attitude. Both these factors are mentioned in (A), (B), (C), and (E). (D) requires the assumption that the two categories discussed by the author are the only categories.

15. **B** (A) may be eliminated because changing one's mind need not involve issues of right and wrong (in the moral sense that Eliot implies). (C) and (E) may be eliminated because they refute the underlying assumption of Eliot's words, that one can tell what is right. The passage does not address the issue of temptation (D).

16. **E** Without an implied or explicit definition of "civilized," the relevance of the examples is vague, at best. (A) and (D) are irrelevant considerations, and (B) and (C), although possibly relevant, do not address the most apparent weakness of the passage.

17. **B** (A) and (C) strengthen the argument. Although (D) and (E) partially weaken certain aspects of the argument, only (B) introduces a situation which suggests that freedom of the press may have harmful consequences.

18. **A** (B) and (C) are irrelevant to the argument. (D) and (E) contradict the implied assertion that a free press must be protected at all costs. Only (A) offers a statement both favorable to the concept of a free press and directly relevant to the subject discussed: the use of privileged information.

19. **E** By stating that "a legal technicality . . . ducks the . . . moral question," the author is implying that the federal government which benefits from the technicality is associated with dodging the issue. (A) and (B) restate explicit information; (C) is implausible; and (D) contradicts information in the passage.

20. **B** Private medical aid would render the author's argument unnecessary. (C), a choice worth considering, is not the best one because the author's focus is less on the aliens'

needs than on the monetary burden borne by the counties.

21. **C**   By documenting the rate at which the medical expense burden grows, the author could strengthen the argument that the situation he describes is indeed a burden.

22. **D**   The passage talks about communes as failures. Therefore, the most logical completion must be a negative term consistent with failure. The only negative choice is (D).

23. **C**   By linking Herb's ability with his "cousinhood," Herb is assuming that the latter determines the former; therefore, he is ignoring (C). (B) is irrelevant. (A) is too vague to be the best answer. (D) is inapplicable, because Keith uses "good" in a context that makes its meaning clear. Finally, (E) refers to contradictory information.

24. **E**   In order to argue for the value of renewable prescriptions, the author must first assume that more medicine may be necessary, or, in other words, that the patient may suffer a relapse. Without the possibility of relapse, a call for more medicine that has already effected a cure ("worked effectively") is illogical.

25. **C**   The passage consistently implies a difference between the past and the present, and (C) makes this contrast explicit. (B) contradicts the implication of the passage, while (A) and (D) narrow the focus unnecessarily, and (E) is irrelevant.

26. **D**   This fact would strengthen the merely impressionistic evidence that lawsuits were less prevalent 40 years ago. It is the only choice dealing directly with the implied subject of the passage—lawsuits.

Section V

Passage 1

1. **D**   According to the first paragraph, a developing country hopes to attract foreign investment and increase its revenues from taxation ("maximize the public capture of revenues").

2. **A**   Unless the investment flow is equal in each direction, the First World nation from which the greater revenue is likely to come is more likely to benefit.

3. **B**   According to the second paragraph, reciprocal source-based taxation produces revenue sacrifices by the state receiving most of the foreign investment, that is, the developing country.

4. **D**   Excess foreign tax credits are a disincentive to private investors. If the at-source taxation is reduced, there will be fewer excess foreign credits.

5. **C**   The passage makes no reference to the availability of raw materials. The four other options are cited.

6. **B**   A country that reduced its revenue expectations would be expected to increase foreign investment.

Passage 2

7. **C**   See lines 9–15. The point of the paragraph is to show how Stuart and Revett depicted the way the antiquities looked at the time of their visit in 1751. (A) is incorrect; not only is grandeur not shown but it is also undermined by the modest houses, Turkish influences, and sleepy atmosphere, (B) is also incorrect; these drawings are described in paragraph two. (D) is incorrect because the description does not say that the human figures and houses "dominate" the scenes. (E) is incorrect; although the Byzantine church is briefly mentioned, the

paragraph does not contrast its architecture to the Grecian architecture.

8. **D** See lines 23–29. The author describes Stuart and Revett's topical drawings as being picturesque and conveying a sense of "the vanity of things." (A) is incorrect; the point is clearly made that the drawings do not show the monuments as they originally looked. (B) is also incorrect; although the contrast is shown, there is no implication that Stuart and Revett are making an ironic comment. (C) is true for the depictions described in the second paragraph, not the first. (E) is not supported by any information in the passage.

9. **A** See lines 30–39. The engravings are described by the author as archaeological; they re-create the original design and provide a "careful tally of dimensions." (C) and (D) describe the drawings discussed in paragraph one. The term "romantic," used in answer (B), also describes the drawings discussed in paragraph one. (E) is not supported by the passage; "traditional abstractions of the architect's trade" do not necessarily equal "uninteresting and pedantic" drawings.

10. **A** See lines 41–54. (B) and (E) are incorrect; no judgment is made as to the success of the Philadelphia building. (C) is also incorrect because no criticism of Stuart and Revett is suggested. (D) is inaccurate because the Philadelphia building is not a "depiction," as are the Stuart and Revett plates.

11. **B** The focus of the Le Corbusier sketches, according to the author, is on the way they show the Akropolis in relation to its natural surround-

ings. See lines 74–85. (A), (C), (D), and (E) are not supported by information in the passage.

12. **C** This inference is suggested by the point of the entire passage—that buildings are depicted according to how they are perceived. If they are depicted in various ways, it is implied that a viewer will have different responses, depending on the depiction. None of the other answers is supported by information in the passage. Nothing implies that classical architecture is superior to all other architecture (A) or that engraving is a superior process for depicting architecture (B). Also, there is not sufficient information to rank Stuart and Revett as superior to Le Corbusier (E) or to see romantic depiction as superior to archaeological drawings (D). In fact, the passage indicates that there are different ways to depict architecture, not that one way is superior to another.

13. **E** The author describes the three methods of depiction (topical, archaeological, in relation to nature) and contrasts them. The passage does not employ anecdote or allusion (A), irony or understatement (B), personification (C), or logical argument and persuasion (D).

Passage 3

14. **D** The author says that war and change have been inevitably linked in America, and that war has been a vital force in the rise of capitalism, but he does *not* say that war is inevitable. All of the other answers are supported by the passage: (A)—lines 65–79; (B)—lines 14–16; (C)—lines 16–20; (E)—lines 65–71.

15. **B** See lines 14–21. Radioactive iso-topes used in treating cancer are an example of a positive advance caused by preparations for war. On the other hand, lethal nerve gases (A), in addition to being a German and not an American development, did not lead to positive peacetime uses. (C), (D), and (E), while possibly effects of wars that have changed America, did not "yield results which are tonic to advancement."

16. **D** See lines 22–28. (C) is incorrect; the author states that this is a result of the Civil War. (E) is a statement supported by the passage, but is not the primary reason for World War I's importance. (A) and (B) are not supported by information in the passage.

17. **A** In this paragraph the author paints a picture of, and indicates some of the reasons for, the "isolation, insularity, and exceptionalism" of America before World War I. The paragraph does define "American Religion" (B), but this is too limited an answer to describe the paragraph's main point. (C) and (E) are not covered in this paragraph. There is no contrast drawn between Civil War America and World War I America (D).

18. **B** See lines 35–46. (A) is incorrect; the grand tour is cited as an example that sophisticated Americans saw a trip to Europe as necessary to overcome insularity and complete an education. No social comment is made about its availability only to the rich. (D) is also incorrect; Puritanism is cited in paragraph four, but not in the context indicated in this answer, i.e., the sin and corruption of the world. (E) might seem correct at first, but the passage does not state

that America was in fact superior to Europe; it comments on the *view* that Americans had of their country. (C) is irrelevant; this point is not made in relation to America's insularity.

19. **C** After the first paragraph introduces the idea of war as a force of change, the passage is devoted to the importance of World War I in changing American society. (B) is incorrect; paragraph one concerns some of the benefits of war, but this is not the main topic of the passage; it is an underlying idea. (A) is also incorrect; the passage mentions the Civil War briefly but is mostly concerned with World War I. (D) and (E) are points touched on in the passage, but neither is the main subject.

20. **E** War as a force for change (the topic of paragraph one) is a general idea that introduces the passage's main subject of World War I. It is not a "popular view" that is refuted in the passage (A), nor does the passage ask a question (B). The first paragraph doesn't outline the contents of the passage (C), nor does it set up the first of four examples (D).

21. **B** "Ecstatic nationalism" is part of what Tocqueville called "American Religion." It would not increase in Europe after World War I. (A) can be inferred because Europe was seen as a necessity in a young man's education. (California would have been considered the Wild West.) The inference in (C) is supported by lines 71–79; (D), by lines 8–14, (E), by lines 47–56.

Passage 4

22. **B** (B) is the best answer because most of the passage is devoted to this description of the development of the

universe; the description is then explicitly identified as the big bang theory. (A), (D), and (E) are all accurate statements according to the passage, but they are each a secondary point, not the main idea.

23. **A** See lines 22–33. All the other answers are factually inaccurate according to the passage.

24. **B** This sequence is presented in lines 16–41. (A) and (E) are closest to the correct answer, but each reverses two items in the sequence. (A) reverses stars and gas clouds; (E) reverses planets and heavy metals.

25. **D** Up until lines 52–55 the passage presents a narrative of the evolution of the universe. Lines 52–55 change the direction of the passage because they summarize the methods by which data have been gathered. The second-best answer is (C), because these lines make a future prediction. However, the shift is not as notable as it is in (D), and the future prediction is not developed.

26. **E** There is no indication in the passage that only our solar system could have evolved as the universe expanded. All the other answers are supported by information in the passage. For (A), see lines 37–41; nuclear reactions in stars produced the heavy metals that formed planets. For (B), see lines 16–26. The passage states that helium and deuterium formed early, before the universe had cooled enough for atomic nuclei to capture electrons. For (C), see lines 55–61. Since modern telescopes give us a view of galaxies billions of light years away, we are now seeing the universe in its early stages. For (D), see lines 22–33. Atomic nuclei were unable to capture electrons until the universe had cooled; without electrons, neutral atoms could not have been formed, and the stars as we know them would not have evolved.

27. **B** Although the big bang *theory* is being described, the information in paragraphs one through three is presented as fact. No mention of theory (A) is made until paragraph five.

28. **C** See lines 47–51. Although (A) may appear to be correct, the author indicates only that up until now the big bang theory seems to be borne out by the data. There is no indication that absolute proof will soon be available. (B), (D), and (E) are not supported by any information in the passage.

7

MODEL TEST THREE

This chapter contains full-length Model Test Three. It is geared to the format of the LSAT, and it is complete with answers and explanations. It is equivalent to the LSAT in question structure, number of questions, level of difficulty, and time allotments. (The questions used are not taken directly from the LSAT, as those questions are copyrighted and may not be reproduced.)

Model Test Three should be taken under strict test conditions. The test ends with a 30-minute Writing Sample, which is not scored.

Section	Description	Number of Questions	Time Allowed
I.	Reading Comprehension	28	35 minutes
II.	Analytical Reasoning	24	35 minutes
III.	Logical Reasoning	26	35 minutes
IV.	Reading Comprehension	28	35 minutes
V.	Logical Reasoning	25	35 minutes
	Writing Sample		30 minutes
TOTALS:		131	3 hours 25 minutes

Now please turn to the next page, remove your answer sheet, and begin Model Test Three.

ANSWER SHEET—MODEL TEST THREE

Section 1	Section 2	Section 3	Section 4	Section 5
1. Ⓐ Ⓑ Ⓒ Ⓓ Ⓔ	1. Ⓐ Ⓑ Ⓒ Ⓓ Ⓔ	1. Ⓐ Ⓑ Ⓒ Ⓓ Ⓔ	1. Ⓐ Ⓑ Ⓒ Ⓓ Ⓔ	1. Ⓐ Ⓑ Ⓒ Ⓓ Ⓔ
2. Ⓐ Ⓑ Ⓒ Ⓓ Ⓔ	2. Ⓐ Ⓑ Ⓒ Ⓓ Ⓔ	2. Ⓐ Ⓑ Ⓒ Ⓓ Ⓔ	2. Ⓐ Ⓑ Ⓒ Ⓓ Ⓔ	2. Ⓐ Ⓑ Ⓒ Ⓓ Ⓔ
3. Ⓐ Ⓑ Ⓒ Ⓓ Ⓔ	3. Ⓐ Ⓑ Ⓒ Ⓓ Ⓔ	3. Ⓐ Ⓑ Ⓒ Ⓓ Ⓔ	3. Ⓐ Ⓑ Ⓒ Ⓓ Ⓔ	3. Ⓐ Ⓑ Ⓒ Ⓓ Ⓔ
4. Ⓐ Ⓑ Ⓒ Ⓓ Ⓔ	4. Ⓐ Ⓑ Ⓒ Ⓓ Ⓔ	4. Ⓐ Ⓑ Ⓒ Ⓓ Ⓔ	4. Ⓐ Ⓑ Ⓒ Ⓓ Ⓔ	4. Ⓐ Ⓑ Ⓒ Ⓓ Ⓔ
5. Ⓐ Ⓑ Ⓒ Ⓓ Ⓔ	5. Ⓐ Ⓑ Ⓒ Ⓓ Ⓔ	5. Ⓐ Ⓑ Ⓒ Ⓓ Ⓔ	5. Ⓐ Ⓑ Ⓒ Ⓓ Ⓔ	5. Ⓐ Ⓑ Ⓒ Ⓓ Ⓔ
6. Ⓐ Ⓑ Ⓒ Ⓓ Ⓔ	6. Ⓐ Ⓑ Ⓒ Ⓓ Ⓔ	6. Ⓐ Ⓑ Ⓒ Ⓓ Ⓔ	6. Ⓐ Ⓑ Ⓒ Ⓓ Ⓔ	6. Ⓐ Ⓑ Ⓒ Ⓓ Ⓔ
7. Ⓐ Ⓑ Ⓒ Ⓓ Ⓔ	7. Ⓐ Ⓑ Ⓒ Ⓓ Ⓔ	7. Ⓐ Ⓑ Ⓒ Ⓓ Ⓔ	7. Ⓐ Ⓑ Ⓒ Ⓓ Ⓔ	7. Ⓐ Ⓑ Ⓒ Ⓓ Ⓔ
8. Ⓐ Ⓑ Ⓒ Ⓓ Ⓔ	8. Ⓐ Ⓑ Ⓒ Ⓓ Ⓔ	8. Ⓐ Ⓑ Ⓒ Ⓓ Ⓔ	8. Ⓐ Ⓑ Ⓒ Ⓓ Ⓔ	8. Ⓐ Ⓑ Ⓒ Ⓓ Ⓔ
9. Ⓐ Ⓑ Ⓒ Ⓓ Ⓔ	9. Ⓐ Ⓑ Ⓒ Ⓓ Ⓔ	9. Ⓐ Ⓑ Ⓒ Ⓓ Ⓔ	9. Ⓐ Ⓑ Ⓒ Ⓓ Ⓔ	9. Ⓐ Ⓑ Ⓒ Ⓓ Ⓔ
10. Ⓐ Ⓑ Ⓒ Ⓓ Ⓔ	10. Ⓐ Ⓑ Ⓒ Ⓓ Ⓔ	10. Ⓐ Ⓑ Ⓒ Ⓓ Ⓔ	10. Ⓐ Ⓑ Ⓒ Ⓓ Ⓔ	10. Ⓐ Ⓑ Ⓒ Ⓓ Ⓔ
11. Ⓐ Ⓑ Ⓒ Ⓓ Ⓔ	11. Ⓐ Ⓑ Ⓒ Ⓓ Ⓔ	11. Ⓐ Ⓑ Ⓒ Ⓓ Ⓔ	11. Ⓐ Ⓑ Ⓒ Ⓓ Ⓔ	11. Ⓐ Ⓑ Ⓒ Ⓓ Ⓔ
12. Ⓐ Ⓑ Ⓒ Ⓓ Ⓔ	12. Ⓐ Ⓑ Ⓒ Ⓓ Ⓔ	12. Ⓐ Ⓑ Ⓒ Ⓓ Ⓔ	12. Ⓐ Ⓑ Ⓒ Ⓓ Ⓔ	12. Ⓐ Ⓑ Ⓒ Ⓓ Ⓔ
13. Ⓐ Ⓑ Ⓒ Ⓓ Ⓔ	13. Ⓐ Ⓑ Ⓒ Ⓓ Ⓔ	13. Ⓐ Ⓑ Ⓒ Ⓓ Ⓔ	13. Ⓐ Ⓑ Ⓒ Ⓓ Ⓔ	13. Ⓐ Ⓑ Ⓒ Ⓓ Ⓔ
14. Ⓐ Ⓑ Ⓒ Ⓓ Ⓔ	14. Ⓐ Ⓑ Ⓒ Ⓓ Ⓔ	14. Ⓐ Ⓑ Ⓒ Ⓓ Ⓔ	14. Ⓐ Ⓑ Ⓒ Ⓓ Ⓔ	14. Ⓐ Ⓑ Ⓒ Ⓓ Ⓔ
15. Ⓐ Ⓑ Ⓒ Ⓓ Ⓔ	15. Ⓐ Ⓑ Ⓒ Ⓓ Ⓔ	15. Ⓐ Ⓑ Ⓒ Ⓓ Ⓔ	15. Ⓐ Ⓑ Ⓒ Ⓓ Ⓔ	15. Ⓐ Ⓑ Ⓒ Ⓓ Ⓔ
16. Ⓐ Ⓑ Ⓒ Ⓓ Ⓔ	16. Ⓐ Ⓑ Ⓒ Ⓓ Ⓔ	16. Ⓐ Ⓑ Ⓒ Ⓓ Ⓔ	16. Ⓐ Ⓑ Ⓒ Ⓓ Ⓔ	16. Ⓐ Ⓑ Ⓒ Ⓓ Ⓔ
17. Ⓐ Ⓑ Ⓒ Ⓓ Ⓔ	17. Ⓐ Ⓑ Ⓒ Ⓓ Ⓔ	17. Ⓐ Ⓑ Ⓒ Ⓓ Ⓔ	17. Ⓐ Ⓑ Ⓒ Ⓓ Ⓔ	17. Ⓐ Ⓑ Ⓒ Ⓓ Ⓔ
18. Ⓐ Ⓑ Ⓒ Ⓓ Ⓔ	18. Ⓐ Ⓑ Ⓒ Ⓓ Ⓔ	18. Ⓐ Ⓑ Ⓒ Ⓓ Ⓔ	18. Ⓐ Ⓑ Ⓒ Ⓓ Ⓔ	18. Ⓐ Ⓑ Ⓒ Ⓓ Ⓔ
19. Ⓐ Ⓑ Ⓒ Ⓓ Ⓔ	19. Ⓐ Ⓑ Ⓒ Ⓓ Ⓔ	19. Ⓐ Ⓑ Ⓒ Ⓓ Ⓔ	19. Ⓐ Ⓑ Ⓒ Ⓓ Ⓔ	19. Ⓐ Ⓑ Ⓒ Ⓓ Ⓔ
20. Ⓐ Ⓑ Ⓒ Ⓓ Ⓔ	20. Ⓐ Ⓑ Ⓒ Ⓓ Ⓔ	20. Ⓐ Ⓑ Ⓒ Ⓓ Ⓔ	20. Ⓐ Ⓑ Ⓒ Ⓓ Ⓔ	20. Ⓐ Ⓑ Ⓒ Ⓓ Ⓔ
21. Ⓐ Ⓑ Ⓒ Ⓓ Ⓔ	21. Ⓐ Ⓑ Ⓒ Ⓓ Ⓔ	21. Ⓐ Ⓑ Ⓒ Ⓓ Ⓔ	21. Ⓐ Ⓑ Ⓒ Ⓓ Ⓔ	21. Ⓐ Ⓑ Ⓒ Ⓓ Ⓔ
22. Ⓐ Ⓑ Ⓒ Ⓓ Ⓔ	22. Ⓐ Ⓑ Ⓒ Ⓓ Ⓔ	22. Ⓐ Ⓑ Ⓒ Ⓓ Ⓔ	22. Ⓐ Ⓑ Ⓒ Ⓓ Ⓔ	22. Ⓐ Ⓑ Ⓒ Ⓓ Ⓔ
23. Ⓐ Ⓑ Ⓒ Ⓓ Ⓔ	23. Ⓐ Ⓑ Ⓒ Ⓓ Ⓔ	23. Ⓐ Ⓑ Ⓒ Ⓓ Ⓔ	23. Ⓐ Ⓑ Ⓒ Ⓓ Ⓔ	23. Ⓐ Ⓑ Ⓒ Ⓓ Ⓔ
24. Ⓐ Ⓑ Ⓒ Ⓓ Ⓔ	24. Ⓐ Ⓑ Ⓒ Ⓓ Ⓔ	24. Ⓐ Ⓑ Ⓒ Ⓓ Ⓔ	24. Ⓐ Ⓑ Ⓒ Ⓓ Ⓔ	24. Ⓐ Ⓑ Ⓒ Ⓓ Ⓔ
25. Ⓐ Ⓑ Ⓒ Ⓓ Ⓔ	25. Ⓐ Ⓑ Ⓒ Ⓓ Ⓔ	25. Ⓐ Ⓑ Ⓒ Ⓓ Ⓔ	25. Ⓐ Ⓑ Ⓒ Ⓓ Ⓔ	25. Ⓐ Ⓑ Ⓒ Ⓓ Ⓔ
26. Ⓐ Ⓑ Ⓒ Ⓓ Ⓔ	26. Ⓐ Ⓑ Ⓒ Ⓓ Ⓔ	26. Ⓐ Ⓑ Ⓒ Ⓓ Ⓔ	26. Ⓐ Ⓑ Ⓒ Ⓓ Ⓔ	26. Ⓐ Ⓑ Ⓒ Ⓓ Ⓔ
27. Ⓐ Ⓑ Ⓒ Ⓓ Ⓔ	27. Ⓐ Ⓑ Ⓒ Ⓓ Ⓔ	27. Ⓐ Ⓑ Ⓒ Ⓓ Ⓔ	27. Ⓐ Ⓑ Ⓒ Ⓓ Ⓔ	27. Ⓐ Ⓑ Ⓒ Ⓓ Ⓔ
28. Ⓐ Ⓑ Ⓒ Ⓓ Ⓔ	28. Ⓐ Ⓑ Ⓒ Ⓓ Ⓔ	28. Ⓐ Ⓑ Ⓒ Ⓓ Ⓔ	28. Ⓐ Ⓑ Ⓒ Ⓓ Ⓔ	28. Ⓐ Ⓑ Ⓒ Ⓓ Ⓔ
29. Ⓐ Ⓑ Ⓒ Ⓓ Ⓔ	29. Ⓐ Ⓑ Ⓒ Ⓓ Ⓔ	29. Ⓐ Ⓑ Ⓒ Ⓓ Ⓔ	29. Ⓐ Ⓑ Ⓒ Ⓓ Ⓔ	29. Ⓐ Ⓑ Ⓒ Ⓓ Ⓔ
30. Ⓐ Ⓑ Ⓒ Ⓓ Ⓔ	30. Ⓐ Ⓑ Ⓒ Ⓓ Ⓔ	30. Ⓐ Ⓑ Ⓒ Ⓓ Ⓔ	30. Ⓐ Ⓑ Ⓒ Ⓓ Ⓔ	30. Ⓐ Ⓑ Ⓒ Ⓓ Ⓔ

SECTION I

Directions: **Read the passages and answer the questions following each passage by blackening the appropriate space on the answer sheet. You may refer back to the passages when answering the questions. Answer all questions on the basis of what is stated or implied.**

The Constitution of the United States protects both property rights and freedom of speech. At times these rights conflict. Resolution then requires
(5) a determination as to the type of property involved. If the property is private and not open to the general public, the owner may absolutely deny the exercise of the right of free speech
(10) thereon. On the other hand, if public land is at issue, the First Amendment protections of expression are applicable. However, the exercise of free speech thereon is not absolute.
(15) Rather it is necessary to determine the appropriateness of the forum. This requires that consideration be given to a number of factors including: character and normal use of the
(20) property, the extent to which it is open to the public, and the number and types of persons who frequent it. If the forum is clearly public or clearly private, the resolution of the greater of
(25) rights is relatively straightforward.

In the area of quasi-public property, balancing these rights has produced a dilemma. This is the situation when a private owner permits the general
(30) public to use his property. When persons seek to use the land for passing out handbills or picketing, how is a conflict between property rights and freedom of expression resolved?
(35) The precept that a private property owner surrenders his rights in

proportion to the extent to which he opens up his property to the public is not new. In 1675, Lord Chief Justice
(40) Hale wrote that when private property is "affected with a public interest, it ceases to be private." Throughout the development of Anglo-American law, the individual has never possessed
(45) absolute dominion over property. Land becomes clothed with a public interest when the owner devotes his property to a use in which the public has an interest. In support of this position the
(50) chairman of the board of the Wilde Lake Shopping Center in Columbia, Maryland said:

The only real purpose and justification of any of these centers
(55) is to serve the people in the area— not the merchants, not the architects, not the developers. The success or failure of a regional shopping center will be measured
(60) by what it does for the people it seeks to serve.

These doctrines should be applied when accommodation must be made between a shopping center owner's
(65) private property rights and the public's right to free expression. It is hoped that when the Court is asked to balance these conflicting rights it will keep in mind what Justice Black said in 1945:
(70) "When we balance the Constitutional rights of owners of property against

those of the people to enjoy (First Amendment) freedom(s) . . . we remain mindful of the fact that the (75) latter occupy a preferred position."

1. In which one of the following cases would the owner of the property probably be most free to restrict the freedom of speech?

   (A) an amusement park attended by five million people each year owned by a multinational company
   (B) a small grocery store owned by a husband and wife
   (C) an enclosed shopping mall owned by a single woman
   (D) a fenced public garden and park owned by a small town
   (E) an eight-unit residential apartment building owned by a large real estate company

2. A conflict between property rights and freedom of speech might arise in all of the following situations, EXCEPT

   (A) protesters carrying signs outside a cinema in an enclosed shopping mall
   (B) a disgruntled employee passing out leaflets in front of a hairdresser's salon
   (C) a religious order soliciting funds and converts in the swimming pool area of a condominium
   (D) a candidate for mayor handing out flyers in front of his opponent's headquarters
   (E) environmentalists carrying signs at the entrance to an oil refinery

3. According to the passage, an owner's freedom to deny freedom of speech on his property is determined by all of the following EXCEPT

   (A) whether or not the land is open to the public
   (B) the nature of and the usual use of the property
   (C) the type of person who frequents the land
   (D) the nature of character of the owner
   (E) how many people use the property

4. We can infer from the passage that the author believes that shopping malls in America

   (A) should be in the service of the people who frequent them
   (B) have a right to prohibit distribution of advertising handbills
   (C) have a right to prohibit the distribution of religious printed matter
   (D) have a right to control any distributed materials
   (E) should permit any charitable solicitations

5. According to the passage, the idea that a property owner's rights decline as the property is more used by the general public

   (A) is peculiar to recent Supreme Court decisions
   (B) is attested to by a three-hundred-year-old opinion
   (C) conflicts with the idea that property affected with a public interest ceases to be private
   (D) is in accord with the idea that ownership confers absolute dominion
   (E) is now universally accepted in Great Britain and in Canada

6. All other things being equal, the courts must favor

(A) First Amendment rights over property rights
(B) Fourth Amendment rights over property rights
(C) property rights over First Amendment rights
(D) property rights and First Amendment rights equally
(E) property rights and Fourth Amendment rights equally

When completing *David Copperfield,* Dickens experienced a powerful aftereffect that left him confused about "whether to laugh or to cry . . .
(5) strangely divided . . . between sorrow and joy." He felt that he had been turned inside out, his inner life now visible, in partly disguised forms, in the shadowy world of ordinary daylight.
(10) The story he had written was so deeply personal that "no one can believe [it] in the reading, more than I have believed it in the writing." Having transformed his private memories and his emotional
(15) life into a public myth about himself, particularly his development from an abandoned child into a great popular artist surrounded by love and success, he felt the excitement both of exposure
(20) and catharsis. Exorcising the wounds of childhood and young adulthood, he also dramatized the unresolved problems of his personality and his marriage, anticipating the turmoil that
(25) was to come. Though energized by the process of writing, he was also exhausted by "heaps of Copperfieldian blots," by that "tremendous paroxysm of Copperfield." Towards the end, he
(30) felt "rigid with Copperfield . . . from head to foot." When he finally put down his pen in October 1850, he took

up his "idea of wandering somewhere for a day or two." Almost inevitably, he
(35) went back "to Rochester . . . where I was a small boy."

In *David Copperfield* he re-created in mythic terms his relationship with his mother, his father, his siblings,
(40) particularly Fanny, and with his wife and his wife's sisters. The novel was more precious to him than his own children because the favorite child was himself. Soon after beginning, he
(45) confessed that he had stuck to that fictional name through the exploration of alternative titles because he had, even at the earliest stage, recognized that he was writing a book about
(50) himself.

His passion for names also expressed his need to pattern and control. After the birth of Katie in 1839, he assumed the right to name all his
(55) children (Catherine had "little or nothing to say" about that). The elaborate christening of Alfred D'Orsay Tennyson Dickens provides the representative example of the novelist
(60) imposing his literary constructs on other people's lives as well as his own. When it came to his family, he did not admit of any distinction. When it came to his novels, the distinction between
(65) self and other was subordinated to the dramatization of the many varieties of the single self. Changing Charles Dickens into David Copperfield had the force both of unconscious reversal and
(70) of minimal autobiographical distancing. At the heart of the novel was a partly mediated version of himself that represented his effort to claim that he had come through, that all was well
(75) with him as he approached the age of forty.

7. Which one of the following best expresses the main idea of the passage?

  (A) The creation of *David Copperfield* was, for Dickens, a painful, wrenching experience.
  (B) While writing *David Copperfield*, Dickens put his novel above everything else, including his children.
  (C) In creating *David Copperfield*, Dickens transformed his memories and feelings into a public myth about himself.
  (D) In addition to being auto-biographical, *David Copperfield* is a prophetic novel.
  (E) *David Copperfield*, in addition to being Dickens' most auto-biographical novel, is also his greatest masterpiece.

8. The author's primary intention in this passage is to

  (A) provide a psychological study of Dickens' motivations for writing *David Copperfield* and suggest a basis for evaluating the novel
  (B) create a picture of Dickens as a writer burdened by childhood memories and contrast this with his public image
  (C) show the connection between Dickens as a self-centered husband and father and as a literary genius
  (D) present Dickens' reactions to writing *David Copperfield* and comment on the novel's relationship to his life and personality
  (E) describe Dickens as he finished *David Copperfield* and show how that novel became a turning point in his career

9. The purpose of the last sentence of paragraph one (lines 34–36) is to

  (A) show Dickens' complete exhaustion after finishing *David Copperfield*
  (B) emphasize the connection between Dickens' writing of *David Copperfield* and his own childhood memories
  (C) indicate Dickens' emotional response to writing *David Copperfield* and his inability to separate reality from fiction
  (D) inform the reader of Dickens' actual origins as opposed to the fictional origins created in *David Copperfield*
  (E) show that in finishing *David Copperfield* Dickens had finally exorcised the traumas of his childhood

10. Which one of the following can be inferred about Charles Dickens' life from information presented in the passage?

  (A) His marriage would end badly.
  (B) His most successful works were heavily autobiographical.
  (C) He was a distant, uncaring father.
  (D) His relationship with his sister Fanny had been significant to him.
  (E) Because of the problems in his childhood, he was a man driven by the need for public success.

11. According to the passage, the title of *David Copperfield* is most significant because it

  (A) demonstrates Dickens' view of the protagonist as a version of himself
  (B) with the unconscious reversal of initials, shows Dickens' inability to come to terms with his life
  (C) demonstrates Dickens' need to pattern and control his experience

(D) is a prime example of Dickens'
passion for names

(E) represents both Dickens seeing the
protagonist as himself and playing
a game with the reader

12. The primary effect of lines 53–56—
"After the birth of Katie in 1839, he
assumed the right to name all his
children (Catherine had 'little to say'
about that")—is to

(A) suggest that Catherine Dickens was
an inadequate mother

(B) indicate that Dickens' creativity with
names extended to his family

(C) show that Dickens tended to
confuse art with life

(D) suggest the relationship between
Dickens and Catherine

(E) indicate that Dickens put his work
over his family life

13. Which one of the following best
describes the author's tone in the
passage?

(A) cool and ironic

(B) argumentative and sarcastic

(C) detached and condescending

(D) intimate and persuasive

(E) objective and analytical

14. Which one of the following best
describes the structure of the passage?

(A) Paragraph one focuses on Dickens'
reactions to writing *David
Copperfield,* while paragraph two
includes more of the author's
comments and ties in related
points.

(B) Paragraph one recounts Dickens'
problems in writing *David
Copperfield,* while paragraph two
describes his creative solutions and
his reactions to the work.

(C) Paragraph one presents Dickens'
opinions of *David Copperfield,*
while paragraph two provides the
author's critique and relates the
book to Dickens' other works.

(D) Paragraph one describes Dickens'
relationship to his novels, while
paragraph two describes his
relationship to his family.

(E) Paragraph one shows the effect of
his childhood on Dickens, while
paragraph two describes his later
life and its effect on his novels.

American society in the eighteenth
century operated according to the logic
of a closed system. Whatever the
scope of concern—a family, a
(5) community, a new nation, an empire—
the guiding assumptions in each case
established a framework of rules or
principles, a container of truth that
defined relationships and
(10) consequences inside its bounds.
Sometimes the source of these
principles lay in heavenly writ,
sometimes in natural law, more often
in some blend of the sacred and the
(15) secular. Always, however, they existed
above and prior to human actions, and
therefore they always stood ready as a
measure of virtue in the present and a
basis for prescriptions about the
(20) future. Rarely were these truths
considered incomprehensible.
Although ordinary citizens might
require a learned elite to explain them,
their meaning nevertheless fell within
(25) the ken of human reason. Hence,
everyone was obligated to adapt their
ways to these overarching rules, as
they were commonly understood, and
anyone could reasonably judge others,
(30) wherever they lived, by their degree of
conformity to the same immutable
principles.

Applying these principles was a delicate art that demanded quite

(35) different skills in a familiar, local setting than in a broad, impersonal one. The center of eighteenth-century society was the family in a community. Across an impressive American diversity,

(40) family and community interconnected in a great many forms, ranging from Mennonite settlements where the community almost swallowed its families to kinship systems in South

(45) Carolina and Virginia with a very loose attachment to a county seat or a region. Every variation, however, set family units to manage the particulars of everyday life in a manner that

(50) constrained each unit by the values all of them held in common. These controls, in turn, were reinforced by an assumption of the community's permanence. People expected to spend

(55) a lifetime with the same faces, the same family names, the same pattern of institutions, the same routines of work and pleasure, and as they judged these intimate relations by their

(60) superstructure of truths, they drew upon an accretion of knowledge about individuals and families and customary ways to estimate, day by day, the state of their immediate society.

(65)   The farther their vision extended beyond the community however, the more people relied upon an explicit demonstration that the affairs concerning them in a wider

(70) environment were actually abiding by the correct principles. An obsession with the exact privileges of a colonial legislature and the precise extent of Britain's imperial power, the specifics

(75) of a state constitution and the absolute necessity of a federal one, all expressed this urge for a careful articulation as proof that the right

relationship with external powers did

(80) indeed prevail. Unlike the calculations of a community's health, which gave significance to everybody's accumulated knowledge about their neighbors and their traditions, these

(85) broad applications of principle belonged almost exclusively to an elite. The more a wider world affected the life of a community, the more its members looked to an elite for mediation—to

(90) explain distant events, to negotiate with distant authorities. During times of crisis relationships inside a community that might otherwise have been quite fluid tended to solidify behind a very

(95) few leaders in order to meet an external danger.

15. According to the passage, which one of the following best describes the closed nature of eighteenth-century American society?

(A) People in the society were expected to stay in the positions they were born to rather than to strive to achieve higher rank.

(B) The society was run according to principles laid down in the Bible, and all citizens were expected to adhere to these.

(C) A respect for tradition led citizens to entrust the workings of the community to a knowledgeable elite and to follow a small group of strong leaders.

(D) The society operated on the assumption that set principles existed that could be used both to live by and to measure actions against.

(E) People in the society expected to remain in the same area and among the same people for their entire lives, which ensured they would know each other well.

16. In paragraph two of the passage, the author refers to Mennonite settlements and kinship systems (lines 38–47) in order to

    (A) suggest that America in the eighteenth century was inhabited by a diverse population with different ideas
    (B) provide examples of the variety of religious sects existing in eighteenth-century America
    (C) illustrate that while eighteenth-century American families and communities interacted, they did so in different ways
    (D) emphasize that religious principles were essential in eighteenth-century America to ensure the strength of the society
    (E) show the superiority of eighteenth-century American communities based on religious ties to those based on kinship ties alone

17. According to information in the passage, which one of the following was an effect of a community's permanence?

    (A) It allowed people to develop looser state governments that did not require written laws and principles.
    (B) It allowed people to know their communities well enough to make confident judgments about them.
    (C) It limited the growth of communities and therefore the dissemination of principles necessary to maintain a closed system.
    (D) It prevented an influx of outsiders who would stand in opposition to the community's principles.
    (E) It limited innovations in thought and action that might ultimately lead to changes in the community's principles.

18. The function of the second paragraph of the passage is to

    (A) explain in detail the historical background of the closed system introduced in paragraph one
    (B) describe the roles of family and community in maintaining the closed system defined in paragraph one
    (C) illustrate the contrast between the strong influence of communities and the closed system described in paragraph one
    (D) provide a transition between the closed system shown in paragraph one and the political activities described in paragraph three
    (E) contrast communities built on religious ties with communities built on kinship ties

19. From information in the passage, which one of the following best explains the statement that a federal constitution was "absolute necessity" (lines 75–76)?

    (A) People did not trust a strong centralized government because of their past experiences.
    (B) People wanted explicit details set forth in matters that affected them but were outside their immediate community.
    (C) People wanted to prevent the development of an elite governing body that would operate without any restrictions.
    (D) People demanded strong safeguards in writing to prevent British imperial power from encroaching on them.
    (E) People trusted written documents much more than they trusted unwritten principles, in spite of their respect for the principles.

20. Which one of the following best describes the relationship between the points made in paragraph three and the description of the society in paragraph one?

(A) Because the society operated in adherence to immutable general principles (paragraph one), people needed assurance that events beyond their usual scope of activities were also in accordance with these principles (paragraph three).

(B) Because people lived in a closed system that allowed little variation in belief (paragraph one), they mistrusted anyone outside who seemed to adhere to a different set of principles (paragraph three).

(C) Because the society was based heavily on religious principles and beliefs (paragraph one), people were unsure of themselves in dealing with secular concerns such as legislatures and constitutions (paragraph three).

(D) Because eighteenth-century American society was generally stable and operated on clear principles (paragraph one), people found it difficult to deal with change and tended to follow strong leaders in times of crisis (paragraph three).

(E) Because the society relied on families to pass on general principles and community ideals (paragraph one), people judged outside events and affairs according to the way their own family units operated (paragraph three).

21. From information in the passage, which one of the following can we infer would be the *least likely* advice to come from an average eighteenth-century American?

(A) Trust the voice within you, and always question authority.

(B) Gain wisdom by listening to those older and more experienced than you.

(C) Hold your reputation dear, for you may be judged by your good name.

(D) Be a pillar of strength in both community and family.

(E) Be vigilant in pursuing truth, and turn to God for guidance.

22. Which one of the following best expresses the main idea of the passage?

(A) Eighteenth-century American society was both a culmination of and a reaction to America's colonial status.

(B) Eighteenth-century American society relied primarily on families and communities to ensure that rules and laws were obeyed.

(C) The primary contrast in eighteenth-century American society was between self-enclosed communities and communities as part of a wider environment.

(D) Eighteenth-century American society was based on a set of accepted rules that provided a framework for people's actions and judgments.

(E) The set principles upon which eighteenth-century American society was built were applied both effectively and ineffectively, depending on the context.

Taxonomy, the science of classifying and ordering organisms, has an undeserved reputation as a harmless, and mindless, activity of listing,
(5) cataloguing, and describing—consider the common idea of a birdwatcher, up at 5:30 in the morning with binoculars, short pants, and "life list" of every bird he has seen. Even among scientists,
(10) taxonomy is often treated as "stamp collecting." It was not always so. During the eighteenth and early nineteenth centuries, taxonomy was in the forefront of the sciences. The
(15) greatest biologists of Europe were professional taxonomists—Linnaeus, Cuvier, Lamarck. Darwin's major activity during the twenty years separating his Malthusian insights
(20) from the publication of his evolutionary theory was a three-volume work on the taxonomy of barnacles. Thomas Jefferson took time out from the affairs of state to publish one of the great
(25) taxonomic errors in the history of paleontology—he described a giant sloth claw as a lion's three times the size of Africa's version. These heady days were marked by discovery as
(30) naturalists collected the fauna and flora of previously uncharted regions. They were also marked by the emergence of intellectual structure, as coherent classifications seemed to mirror the
(35) order of God's thought.

America played its part in this great epoch of natural history. We often forget that 150 years ago much of our continent was as unknown and
(40) potentially hazardous as any place on earth. During the eighteenth century, when most naturalists denied the possibility of extinction, explorers expected to find mammoths and other
(45) formidable fossil creatures alive in the American West. There are a number of passionate, single-minded iconoclasts who fought the hostility of the wilderness, and often of urban literary
(50) people, to disclose the rich fauna and flora of America. For the most part, they worked alone, with small support from patrons or government. The Lewis and Clark expedition is an
(55) exception—and its primary purpose was not natural history. We may now look upon tales of frontier toughness and perseverance as the necessary mythology of a nation too young to
(60) have real legends. But there is often a residue of truth in such tales, and naturalists are among the genuine pioneers.

Alexander Wilson walked from New
(65) England to Charleston peddling sub-scriptions to his *American Ornithology*. Thomas Nuttall—oblivious to danger, a Parsifal under a lucky star, vanquishing every Klingsor in the woods, discov-
(70) ered some of the rarest, most beautiful, and most useful of American plants. J. J. Audubon drank his way across Europe selling his beautiful pictures of birds to lords and kings. John Lawson,
(75) captured by Tuscarora Indians, met the following fate according to an eyewitness: "They struck him full of fine small, splinters or torchwoods like hog's bristles and so set them
(80) gradually afire." David Douglas fell into a pit trap for wild cattle and was stomped to death by a bull.

23. According to the passage, taxonomy was considered to be an important science from about

(A) 1700 to 1800
(B) 1700 to 1830
(C) 1700 to 1950
(D) 1800 to 1930
(E) 1818 to 1918

24. As they are used in the first paragraph (line 30), "flora and fauna" refer to

    (A) lands and waters
    (B) botanists and zoologists
    (C) plants and animals
    (D) cataloging and describing
    (E) mythology and folklore

25. We can infer from the passage that

    (A) taxonomy was favorably regarded in the sixteenth and seventeenth centuries
    (B) taxonomy was invented in the eighteenth century
    (C) the number of kinds of barnacles is very large
    (D) Lamarck and Linnaeus were amateur scientists
    (E) most of the world's plants have already been classified

26. The relation of the third paragraph to the rest of the passage may be best described as

    (A) a comic contrast to the seriousness of the first two paragraphs
    (B) specific examples of the pioneers mentioned in the second paragraph
    (C) examples of American taxonomists to set against the exclusively European names of the first paragraph
    (D) real taxonomists of the western United States as opposed to the legendary figures of the second paragraph
    (E) examples of the tall tales of the frontier days

27. In the third paragraph, Parsifal and Klingsor were probably a

    (A) hunter and his prey
    (B) German taxonomist and his subject of study
    (C) knight and his enemy
    (D) a colonizer and the colonized
    (E) a mythical animal and its master

28. This passage is best described as a(n)

    (A) description of the modern bias against taxonomy
    (B) comparison of nineteenth-century and twentieth-century scientists
    (C) account of famous American naturalists
    (D) history and defense of taxonomy
    (E) argument for the renewed study of the classification of organisms

STOP

IF YOU FINISH BEFORE TIME IS UP, CHECK YOUR WORK ON THIS SECTION OF THE TEST ONLY.
DO NOT GO ON TO THE NEXT SECTION OF THE TEST UNTIL TIME IS UP FOR THIS SECTION.

SECTION II

Directions: In this section you will be given groups of questions based on different sets of conditions. Drawing a simple diagram may be helpful in answering some of the questions. You are to choose the best answer and mark the corresponding space on your answer sheet.

Questions 1–6

A radio station will play eight songs during its "Winners" hour. Each song will be played once. The eight songs represent the following types of music: Jazz, Rock, and Country, with at least two songs of each type. The following restrictions are placed on the order and type of songs:

All the jazz songs are played consecutively.

No two rock songs are played consecutively.

No two country songs are played consecutively.

A rock song must be played before a jazz song is played.

There are more jazz songs than country songs.

1. If four jazz songs are played and the first and last songs are of the same type, which one of the following must be true?

   (A) A jazz song is played second.
   (B) A jazz song is played third.
   (C) A rock song is played seventh.
   (D) A rock song is played eighth.
   (E) A country song is played first.

2. If three rock songs are played and a country song is played sixth, which one of the following CANNOT be true?

   (A) A jazz song is played second.
   (B) A rock song is played fifth.

   (C) A rock song is played first.
   (D) A country song is played last.
   (E) A country song is played first.

3. If a jazz song is played third, and the first and last songs are of the same type, which one of the following CANNOT be true?

   (A) A jazz song is sixth.
   (B) A country song is sixth.
   (C) A country song is first.
   (D) A rock song is second.
   (E) A rock song is seventh.

4. If all the jazz songs are played last, how many different arrangements of song types are possible?

   (A) one
   (B) two
   (C) three
   (D) four
   (E) five

5. If a country song is played first and seventh, which one of the following must be true?

   (A) A country song is sixth.
   (B) A jazz song is sixth.
   (C) A country song is third.
   (D) A jazz song is second.
   (E) A jazz song is third.

6. If a single classical song is added to the play list (making nine songs in all) and it is to be played fourth and a country song is to be played fifth, which one of the following must be true?

(A) A jazz song is sixth.
(B) A jazz song is last.
(C) A rock song is second.
(D) A rock song is third.
(E) A country song is last.

Questions 7–13

Seven students—George, Hal, Ken, Jon, Neil, Lynn, and Melanie—are playing a game involving play money. The only bills used are play dollar bills. No coins are used.

   Jon has more bills than Lynn, Melanie, and Neil combined.
   The total of Lynn's and Melanie's bills are equal to Neil's bills.
   Melanie has more bills than Ken and George combined.
   Hal has fewer bills than George.
   Ken and George have the same number of bills.

7. Which one of the following students has the most bills?

(A) Ken
(B) George
(C) Jon
(D) Lynn
(E) Melanie

8. Which one of the following students has the fewest bills?

(A) Melanie
(B) Neil
(C) George
(D) Ken
(E) Hal

9. Which one of the following must be true?

(A) Melanie has fewer bills than Ken.
(B) Neil has more bills than Lynn.
(C) Lynn has fewer bills than Melanie.
(D) Lynn has more bills than George.
(E) George has more bills than Melanie.

10. Assume that Ken is given one bill from Hal. Assume also that Melanie has more bills than Ken, George, and Lynn combined. If none of the students has the same number of bills, which one of the following is a possible order from highest to lowest of students who have the most bills?

(A) Jon, Melanie, Lynn, Neil, Ken, George, Hal
(B) Jon, Neil, Melanie, Lynn, George, Ken, Hal
(C) Neil, Jon, Melanie, George, Ken, Hal, Lynn
(D) Jon, Neil, Ken, Melanie, George, Lynn, Hal
(E) Jon, Neil, Melanie, Ken, George, Hal, Lynn

11. Assume that Lynn does not have the same number of bills as Ken. Which one of the following must be FALSE?

(A) Lynn has the same number of bills as Hal.
(B) Neil has twice as many bills as Melanie.
(C) George has more bills than Hal and Lynn combined.
(D) George does not have the same number of bills as Lynn.
(E) Jon has fewer than twice the number of Lynn's and Melanie's bills combined.

12. If Lynn and Melanie have the same number of bills, then which one of the following must be FALSE?

(A) Neil has more bills than Melanie.
(B) Melanie has more bills than Ken, George, and Hal combined.
(C) George has fewer bills than Hal and Ken combined.
(D) Neil has fewer bills than Lynn, George, and Hal combined.
(E) Jon has more bills than Lynn, Ken, George, and Hal combined.

13. Assume that Tom decides to join the game. Assume also that he is given bills from the bank. If his total number of bills are more than Ken's and fewer than Lynn's, which one of the following must be true?

(A) Melanie has fewer bills than Tom.
(B) Tom has fewer bills than George.
(C) Lynn has fewer bills than Melanie.
(D) Melanie and Lynn have the same number of bills.
(E) Lynn has more bills than Hal.

Questions 14–20

At the snack bar at a party, Alli, Boris, Cisco, and Dan are eating cookies. There are five kinds of cookies to choose from—chocolate chip cookies, oatmeal cookies, sugar cookies, peanut butter cookies, and raisin cookies. Each of these four people eat at least two kinds of cookies. Their choices are governed by the following rules:

> At most two of them eat oatmeal cookies.
> At least two of them eat sugar cookies.
> Alli does not eat any sugar cookies.
> Boris and Cisco do not eat the same type of cookie.
> Boris eats chocolate chip cookies.

Cisco eats sugar cookies.
No one eats both raisin cookies and sugar cookies.
If someone eats raisin cookies, they also eat peanut butter cookies.

14. Which one of the following must be true?

(A) Cisco eats chocolate chip cookies.
(B) Alli eats chocolate chip cookies.
(C) Boris does not eat peanut butter cookies.
(D) Dan does not eat raisin cookies.
(E) Alli does not eat peanut butter cookies.

15. If Boris eats exactly three kinds of cookies, which one of the following must be true?

(A) Cisco eats exactly three kinds of cookies.
(B) Dan eats only sugar cookies.
(C) If Alli eats oatmeal cookies, Dan eats oatmeal cookies.
(D) Boris eats oatmeal cookies.
(E) Cisco eats oatmeal cookies.

16. Which one of the following CANNOT be true?

(A) No one eats raisin cookies.
(B) Alli and Dan both eat oatmeal cookies.
(C) Alli and Dan both eat chocolate chip cookies.
(D) Boris and Cisco eat the same number of kinds of cookies.
(E) Dan does not eat raisin cookies.

17. Which pair of cookie types could each be eaten by at least three different people?

(A) chocolate chip and oatmeal
(B) oatmeal and peanut butter

(C) chocolate chip and peanut butter
(D) oatmeal and sugar
(E) sugar and raisin

18. Which pair of cookie types contains a cookie type eaten by exactly two different people?

(A) chocolate chip and oatmeal
(B) oatmeal and peanut butter
(C) chocolate chip and peanut butter
(D) oatmeal and raisin
(E) sugar and raisin

19. If Alli does not eat chocolate chip or raisin cookies, which one of the following could be true?

(A) Dan eats oatmeal cookies.
(B) More people eat chocolate chip cookies than sugar cookies.
(C) Only one person eats peanut butter cookies.
(D) Cisco does not eat peanut butter cookies.
(E) Boris eats sugar cookies.

20. Which cookie type could be eaten by none of the people?

(A) chocolate chip
(B) oatmeal
(C) sugar
(D) peanut butter
(E) raisin

Questions 21–24

The National Domino League is planning to expand by adding one more team. All of the players for the new team will be chosen from the existing teams. Each team must make three players eligible to be chosen for the new team.

   (1) The players eligible to be chosen from Team 1 are A, B, and C.

   (2) The players eligible to be chosen from Team 2 are D, E, and F.

   (3) The players eligible to be chosen from Team 3 are G, H, and K.

   (4) The new team must choose two players from each of the three teams.

   (5) B refuses to play with D.

   (6) If C is chosen, then K must be chosen.

   (7) G and H refuse to play together.

21. If A is not chosen, then how many members of the new team are determined?

(A) 2
(B) 3
(C) 4
(D) 5
(E) 6

22. If D is chosen, then which one of the following groups of three players could NOT be chosen?

(A) A, G, K
(B) B, C, G
(C) C, E, K
(D) A, E, G
(E) E, H, K

23. Which one of the following is (are) true?

(A) C must be chosen.
(B) If A is chosen, then F must be chosen.
(C) If B is chosen, then E must be chosen.
(D) E must be chosen.
(E) If G is chosen, then K is not chosen.

24. In addition to facts (1), (2), (3), and (4), which of the facts lead(s) to the conclusion that K must be chosen?

    (A) (5)
    (B) (6)
    (C) (7)
    (D) (6) and (7)
    (E) (5), (6), and (7)

STOP

IF YOU FINISH BEFORE TIME IS UP, CHECK YOUR WORK ON THIS SECTION OF THE TEST ONLY.
DO NOT GO ON TO THE NEXT SECTION OF THE TEST UNTIL TIME IS UP FOR THIS SECTION.

SECTION III

Directions: **In this section you will be given brief statements or passages and will be required to evaluate the reasoning involved. In some instances, more than one choice will appear to be a possible answer. You are to choose the *best* answer. Use common sense and reasonableness in making your selection; then mark the proper space on the answer sheet.**

1. Recent studies show that reduction in the maximum speed limit from 65 mph to 55 mph substantially reduces the number of highway fatalities.

   The preceding statement would be most weakened by establishing that

   (A) most fatal car accidents occur at night
   (B) most accidents occurring at speeds between 45 and 55 mph are nonfatal
   (C) few fatal accidents involve only one vehicle
   (D) prior to this reduction, 97 percent of fatal accidents occurred below 45 mph
   (E) prior to the reduction, 97 percent of fatal accidents occurred between 55 and 65 mph

2. Board member Smith will vote for the busing of students if she is reelected to the board. If the busing of students is passed by the board, then Smith was not reelected to the board. Smith was reelected to the board.

   Given the foregoing information, which one of the following can be concluded?

   (A) Smith assisted in the passage of student busing.
   (B) The passage of busing carried Smith to a reelection victory.
   (C) Smith voted against busing; however, it still passed.

   (D) Busing was defeated despite Smith's vote in favor of it.
   (E) Student busing was voted down by a majority of the board.

3. Daniel Webster said, "Falsehoods not only disagree with truths, but usually quarrel among themselves."

   Which one of these would follow from Webster's statement?

   (A) Quarreling is endemic to American political life.
   (B) Truth and falsehood can be distinguished from one another.
   (C) Liars often quarrel with each other.
   (D) Those who know the truth are normally silent.
   (E) Truth and falsehood are emotional, rather than intellectual, phenomena.

4. A recording industry celebrity observed: "I am not a star because all my songs are hits; all my songs are hits because I am a star."

   Which one of the following most nearly parallels this reasoning?

   (A) A college professor noted: "I am the final word in the classroom not because my judgment is always correct, but my judgment in the classroom is always correct because I am the instructor."

(B) A nurse observed: "I am not competent in my duties because I am a nurse, but I am competent in my duties because of my training in nursing."

(C) A dance instructor noted: "I am not the instructor because I know all there is about dance; rather I am an instructor because of my ability to teach dancing."

(D) A recording industry celebrity observed: "I am not wealthy because I am a star; I am wealthy because so many people buy my recordings."

(E) A recording industry celebrity observed: "I am not a star because my every song is enjoyed; I am a star because people pay to watch me perform."

5. The enzyme Doxin cannot be present if the bacterium *Entrox* is absent.

Given the foregoing condition, which one of the following would NOT be true?

(A) *Entrox* may be present without the presence of Doxin.

(B) Doxin and *Entrox* may be present together.

(C) There may be a case in which neither Doxin nor *Entrox* is present.

(D) If Doxin is present, *Entrox* cannot be absent.

(E) Doxin may be present without *Entrox*.

6. If a speaker were highly credible, would an objectively irrelevant personal characteristic of the speaker influence the effectiveness of her communication? For example, if a Nobel prize-winning chemist were speaking on inorganic chemistry, would she induce a lesser change in the opinions of an audience if she were known to be a poor cook? Would the speaker's effectiveness be different if she were obese rather than trim, sloppy rather than neat, ugly rather than attractive?

By failing to consider irrelevant aspects of communicator credibility, studies in communication science have unknowingly implied that audiences are composed of individuals who are responsive only to objectively relevant aspects of a speaker.

Which one of the following represent(s) assumptions upon which the foregoing passage is based?

(A) Audiences are composed of people who are responsive only to objectively relevant aspects of a communicator.

(B) Objectively irrelevant personal characteristics have a bearing on a speaker's effectiveness.

(C) Some characteristics of a communicator are of greater relevance than others.

(D) A trim speaker is likely to be more persuasive than an obese one.

(E) Irrelevant aspects of a communication have more effect on an audience than the content of a speech.

Questions 7–8

I read with interest the statements of eminent archaeologists that the presence of a crude snare in an early Neolithic grave indicates that man of this period subsisted by snaring small mammals. I find this assertion open to question. How do I know the companions of the deceased did not toss the snare into the grave with the corpse because it had proved to be totally useless?

7. The author employs which one of the following as a method of questioning the archaeologists' claims?

   (A) evidence that contradicts the conclusion drawn by the archaeologists
   (B) a doubtful tone about the motives of the archaeologists
   (C) a body of knowledge inconsistent with that employed by the archaeologists
   (D) an alternative to the conclusion drawn by the archaeologists
   (E) the suggestion that archaeological studies are of little use

8. Which one of the following best expresses the author's criticism of the archaeologists whose statements he questions?

   (A) They have not subjected their conclusions to scientific verification.
   (B) They have stressed one explanation and ignored others.
   (C) They have drawn a conclusion that does not fit the evidence upon which it was based.
   (D) They failed to employ proper scientific methods in arriving at their conclusion.

   (E) They have based their conclusion on behaviors exhibited by more modern humans.

9. Semanticists point out that words and phrases often acquire connotations tinged with emotions. Such significances are attached because of the context, the history of the usage of the expression, or the background of the person reading or listening. Thus, "the hills of home" may evoke a feeling of nostalgia or a pleasant sensation; but "Bolshevik" may arouse derision or disgust in the minds of many people.

   The term "progressive education" has gone through several stages in the connotative process. At one time progressive education was hailed as the harbinger of all that was wise and wholesome in classroom practice, such as the recognition of individual differences and the revolution against formalized dictatorial procedures. However, partly because of abuses on the fanatical fringe of the movement, many people began to associate progressive schools with frills, fads, and follies. What had been discovered and developed by Froebel in Germany, by Pestalozzi in Switzerland, by Montessori in Italy, and by men like Parker and Dewey in the United States was muddled in a melange of mockery and misunderstanding and submerged in satirical quips. As a result, many educators have recently avoided the expression and have chosen to call present educational practices "new" or "modern" rather than "progressive."

Which one of the following would most seriously weaken the author's argument?

(A) In a recent poll of American voters, 76 percent responded that they would certainly not vote for the Progressive Labor Party.

(B) Open classrooms have recently fallen out of the educational limelight.

(C) New techniques in teaching cognitive skills, called "progressive learning," have recently met with widespread approval in middle class public schools.

(D) Parker and Dewey were well respected by academicians and educational theorists.

(E) Every new advance in education is first denounced as a "fad."

10. *Bill:* Professor Smith has been late for class almost every morning.
Dave: That can't be true; he was on time yesterday.

Dave apparently believes that Bill has said which one of the following?

(A) Professor Smith is seldom late.

(B) Professor Smith does not enjoy teaching.

(C) Professor Smith has been late every day without exception.

(D) Professor Smith was late yesterday.

(E) Professor Smith informs Bill of his whereabouts.

11. Sunbathers do not usually spend much time in the shade. Shade prevails during most of June in La Jolla. It is June 14.

Which one of the following conclusions would be logically defensible, based upon the foregoing premises?

(A) La Jolla is the site of frequent sunbathing.

(B) The sun is not shining today.

(C) There are sunbathers in La Jolla today.

(D) There may be sunbathers in La Jolla today.

(E) There are more sunbathers in La Jolla in July than in June.

12. Although American politicians disagree about many things, none of them disagrees with Wendell Wilkie's assertion that "the Constitution does not provide for first- and second-class citizens."

Wilkie's statement implies that

(A) the Constitution provides for third- and fourth-class citizens

(B) first-class citizens don't need to be provided for

(C) there is no such thing as a second-class citizen

(D) the Constitution makes no class distinctions

(E) no citizens can be first and second class simultaneously

13. There are 500 students in the school. In the fall semester, 30 were in the glee club, 30 were members of the debating society, and 40 were on the staff of the school newspaper. In the spring semester, all three of these activities had twice as many participants. Thus, in the course of the school year, all but 200 of the 500 students in the school participated in these extracurricular activities.

All of the following can be used to question the conclusion of this passage EXCEPT

(A) some students participated in more than one activity in the fall semester

(B) some students participated in an activity in more than one semester

(C) some students participated in activities in only the fall semester

(D) some students never participated in activities

(E) some students participated in more than one activity in both semesters

14. Nothing can come of nothing; nothing can go back to nothing.

Which one of the following follows most logically from the above statement?

(A) Something can come out of something; something can go back to something.

(B) Something can come out of nothing; something can go back to nothing.

(C) Nothing can come out of something; nothing can go back to something.

(D) Something must come out of something; something must go back to something.

(E) Something must come out of something; nothing can go back to nothing.

15. The president has vowed in speeches across the country that there will be no increase in taxes and no reduction in defense; he has repeatedly challenged Congress to narrow the deficit through deeper spending cuts. Congressional critics have responded with labored comparisons between a bloated Pentagon and the nation's poor being lacerated by merciless budget cutters. In Democratic cloakrooms, laments about the "intolerable deficit" are code words for higher taxes.

Which one of the following additions to the passage would make clear the author's position on the budget issue?

(A) Everyone agrees that the president's budget deficit of around 100 billion is highly undesirable, to say the least.

(B) Everyone agrees that the president's budget deficit is both undesirable and unavoidable.

(C) Everyone agrees that this will be a summer of hot debate in Congress over the president's budget proposal.

(D) Everyone agrees that the partisan disagreement over the president's budget proposal will be won by those who create the most persuasive terminology.

(E) Everyone agrees that the president's budget proposal is a product of careful, honest, but sometimes misguided analysis.

16. *The average wage in this plant comes to exactly $7.87 per working day.* In this statement *average* has the strict mathematical sense. It is the quotient obtained by dividing the sum of all wages for a given period by the product of the number of workers and the number of days in the period.

Which one of the following is the most logical implication of the passage above?

(A) More workers in the plant earn $7.87 per day than those who do not earn $7.87 per day.

(B) Any particular worker in the plant receives $7.87 per day.

(C) There must be workers in the plant who earn far more than $7.87 per day.

(D) If some workers in the plant earn more than $7.87 per day, there must be others in the plant who earn less than $7.87 per day.

(E) There must be workers in the plant who earn exactly $7.87 per day.

17. *Magazine article:* Davy "Sugar" Jinkins is one of the finest boxers to have ever fought. Last week Davy announced his retirement from the ring, but not from the sport. Davy will continue in boxing as the trainer of "Boom Boom" Jones. With Jinkins handling him, we are sure that Boom Boom will become a title contender in no time.

The foregoing article is based upon all of the following assumptions EXCEPT

(A) boxers who have a good trainer can do well

(B) those who were good boxers can be fine trainers

(C) Jones is capable of being trained

(D) title contenders should be well trained

(E) Jinkins did well as a boxer

18. You can solve a problem. You cannot solve a dilemma, for it requires a choice between two disagreeable alternatives.

All of the following exemplify a dilemma EXCEPT:

(A) Amleth must avenge his father's death by killing his assassins. He must also protect his mother who was one of the murderers.

(B) the zoo has one vacant enclosure that is suitable for the exhibition of hyenas or lesser kudus. Hyenas prey upon kudus. The zoo will lose a federal grant if it fails to exhibit both kinds of animals.

(C) Ames must relocate his business in Belmont or Arlington. Office rentals are much more expensive in Belmont; office locations in Arlington are inconvenient for customers.

(D) to have enough meat to feed the four guests I must buy two pounds of beef. But one pound of beef costs two dollars and I have only three dollars.

(E) I must park my car on Ash or Maple Street and go to the market. If I park on Ash Street, I will probably get a parking ticket; if I park on Maple Street, my radio will probably be stolen.

19. The stores are always crowded on holidays. The stores are not crowded; therefore, it must not be a holiday.

Which one of the following most closely parallels the kind of reasoning used in the above sentences?

(A) The stores are always crowded on Christmas. The stores are crowded; therefore, it must be Christmas.

(B) Reptiles are present on a hot day in the desert. Reptiles are absent in this desert area; therefore, this cannot be a hot desert day.

(C) There is a causal relationship between the occurrence of holidays and the number of people in stores.

(D) The voting places are empty; therefore, it is not an election day.

(E) The stores are always empty on Tuesdays. It is Tuesday; therefore, the stores will be empty.

Questions 20–21

For one to be assured of success in politics, one must have a sound experiential background, be a polished orator, and possess great wealth. Should an individual lack any one of these attributes, he most certainly will be considered a dark horse in any campaign for public office. Should an individual be without any two of these attributes, he cannot win an election. If Nelson Nerd is to win the presidency, he must greatly improve his ability as a public speaker. His extraordinary wealth is not enough.

20. The author of the above passage appears to believe that

 (A) Nerd is the wealthiest candidate
 (B) Nerd is a sufficiently experienced politician
 (C) being a good public speaker alone can win one a high public office
 (D) if Nerd's public speaking improves, he will win the presidency
 (E) Nerd is not a dark horse now

21. Which one of the following would most weaken the speaker's claims?

 (A) Nerd is not the wealthiest candidate running for president.
 (B) The incumbent president had little relevant experience before coming into office and has always been a poor public speaker.
 (C) Of the individuals elected to public office, 0.001 percent have lacked either oratory skill, experience, or money.
 (D) Nerd failed in his last bid for the presidency.
 (E) The incumbent president, who is running for reelection, is as wealthy as Nerd.

22. Tom is test driving a blue car. After driving for a short while he comes to the following conclusion: Since this car is blue, it must not accelerate quickly.

 The foregoing conclusion can be properly drawn if it is also known that

 (A) all red cars accelerate quickly
 (B) there are some slow blue cars
 (C) all blue cars may not accelerate slowly
 (D) all cars that accelerate quickly are red
 (E) all slow cars are red

Questions 23–24

As almost everyone is painfully aware, the federal government has butted into almost every sector of human existence in recent years. But this manic intrusiveness isn't always the government's fault. Sometimes there is a compulsion to enlist Uncle Sam as a superbusybody.

23. Which one of the following is one of the author's basic assumptions?

 (A) Most of his readers have suffered government intrusion.
 (B) All government intrusion is unwarranted.
 (C) Government intrusion is always government-initiated.
 (D) All memories of government intrusion are painful memories.
 (E) At no time has the federal government practiced nonintrusiveness.

24. Which one of the following most nearly restates the final sentence?

 (A) Most of the time government is responsible for government intrusion.

(B) Sometimes government does more than intrude; it compels intrusion.

(C) Sometimes Uncle Sam himself enlists in the ranks of the intruders.

(D) Sometimes Uncle Sam is compulsive rather than merely symbolic.

(E) Sometimes the government itself is not responsible for government intrusion.

---

25. Those who dictate what we can and cannot see on television are guilty of falsely equating knowledge with action. They would have us believe that to view violent behavior is to commit it.

On the basis of the content of the above passage, we may infer that the author would believe which one of the following?

(A) Knowing how to manufacture nuclear weapons leads to nuclear war.

(B) Those guilty of committing a crime were not necessarily influenced by an awareness that such crimes occurred.

(C) Media censorship is based upon logical justification.

(D) Know your enemy.

(E) The truth shall set you free.

26. In 1975, the U.S. Supreme Court ruled that the federal government has exclusive rights to any oil and gas resources on the Atlantic Outer Shelf beyond the three-mile limit.

Which one of the following must be true in order for this ruling to be logical?

(A) The U.S. Supreme Court has met recently.

(B) The Atlantic Outer Shelf may possibly contain oil and gas resources.

(C) No oil and gas resources exist within the three-mile limit.

(D) In 1977, the Court reversed this ruling.

(E) Oil and gas on the Atlantic Shelf has not been explored for in the past three years.

STOP

IF YOU FINISH BEFORE TIME IS UP, CHECK YOUR WORK ON THIS SECTION OF THE TEST ONLY. DO NOT GO ON TO THE NEXT SECTION OF THE TEST UNTIL TIME IS UP FOR THIS SECTION.

SECTION IV

Time — 35 minutes
28 Questions

Directions: Read the passages and answer the questions following each passage by blackening the appropriate space on the answer sheet. You may refer back to the passages when answering the questions. Answer all questions on the basis of what is stated or implied.

The Constitution gives the Congress power to make the laws that determine the election of senators and representatives. At first Congress
(5) exercised its power to supervise apportionment by simply specifying in the statutes how many representatives each state was to have. From 1842 until the 1920s, it went further and
(10) required that the districts be relatively compact (not scattered areas) and relatively equal in voting population.

Major shifts in population occurred in the twentieth century: large numbers of
(15) farmers could no longer maintain small farms and moved to the cities to find employment; rapidly growing industries, organized in factory systems, attracted rural workers; and
(20) many blacks who could no longer find work in southern agriculture moved to the North to get better jobs and get away from strict Jim Crow living conditions. The rural areas of the
(25) country became more sparsely populated while the city populations swelled.

As these changes were occurring, Congress took less interest in its
(30) reapportionment power, and after 1929 did not reenact the requirements. In 1946, voters in Illinois asked the Supreme Court to remedy the serious malapportionment of their state
(35) congressional districts. Justice Frankfurter, writing for the Court,

said the federal courts should stay out of "this political thicket." Reapportionment was a "political
(40) question" outside the jurisdiction of these courts. Following this holding, malapportionment grew more severe and widespread in the United States.

In the Warren Court era, voters again
(45) asked the Court to pass on issues concerning the size and shape of electoral districts, partly out of desperation because no other branch of government offered relief, and partly
(50) out of hope that the Court would reexamine old decisions in this area as it had in others, looking at basic constitutional principles in the light of modern living conditions. Once again
(55) the Court had to work through the problem of separation of powers, which had stood in the way of court action concerning representation. In this area, too, the Court's rulings were
(60) greeted by some as shockingly radical departures from "the American way," while others saw them as a reversion to the democratic processes established by the Constitution, applied
(65) to an urbanized setting.

1. The primary purpose of the passage is to

(A) criticize public apathy concerning apportionment

(B) describe in general the history of political apportionment

(C) argue for the power of the Supreme Court

(D) describe the role of the Warren Court in political apportionment

(E) stress that reapportionment is essentially a congressional concern

2. The author implies which one of the following opinions about federal supervision of apportionment?

(A) Federal supervision is unnecessary.

(B) Federal supervision is necessary.

(C) Apportionment should be regulated by the Court.

(D) Apportionment should be regulated by Congress.

(E) Court rulings on apportionment violate "the American way."

3. In the third paragraph, "malapportionment" refers to the

(A) influx of farmers into the city

(B) Jim Crow phenomenon

(C) shift from rural to urban populations

(D) distribution of voters in Illinois

(E) unfair size and shape of congressional districts

4. We may infer that during the Warren Court era

(A) the most dissatisfied voters lived in cities

(B) the constituency was dissatisfied

(C) the separation of powers became important for the first time

(D) the public turned its attention away from issues of apportionment

(E) a ballot issue concerning electoral apportionment passed

5. The passage answers which one of the following questions?

(A) Does the Constitution delegate authority for supervising apportionment?

(B) Do population shifts intensify racism?

(C) Should the Constitution still be consulted, even though times have changed?

(D) Why did the Warren Court agree to undertake the issue of representation?

(E) How did the Warren Court rule on the separation of powers issue?

6. We may conclude that Justice Frankfurter was

(A) a member of the Warren Court

(B) not a member of the Warren Court

(C) opposed to reapportionment

(D) skeptical about the separation of powers

(E) too attached to outmoded interpretations of the Constitution

7. In the passage the author is primarily concerned with

(A) summarizing history

(B) provoking a controversy

(C) suggesting a new attitude

(D) reevaluating old decisions

(E) challenging constitutional principles

Alain Robbe-Grillet is not as cerebral a writer as Nathalie Sarraute or Michel Butor. But he has been more popular, particularly in America. Perhaps that is

(5) one reason. There are others. He relies even more heavily than his fellow novelists on the *roman policier* for basic structure, and detective stories have a built-in popular fascination.

(10) Most of his characters, so far as we can determine, seem to be psycho-pathological. He is therefore a kind of Alfred Hitchcock of the novel. He has also devoted himself to film writing and

(15) film making in association with the *Nouvelle Vague*. His cinema-novels as he called them, rather than film scripts, *L'Année Dernière à Marienbad* (1961) and *L'Immortelle* (1963), have certainly

(20) brought him a wider public exposure than would have been possible with the novels alone. Furthermore his novels have had wide paperback distribution in English translation. But he is an

(25) authentic New Novelist and therefore disturbing but not easy. He is reported to have said that he *wants* his readers to feel disappointed (in their expectation of clarification,

(30) presumably), that if they feel disappointed he knows he has succeeded in what he was trying to do. At least one critic has placed Robbe-Grillet at "the most advanced point of

(35) evolution of the twentieth-century novel and film."

He first turned to the cinema in collaboration with the film director Alain Resnais. In 1961 *L'Année*

(40) *Dernière à Marienbad* hit the movie world with an originality that for a time usurped the attention customarily given to the Italian films of Fellini or the Swedish films of Bergman. *Last Year at*

(45) *Marienbad* played long runs in the art film houses in New York and across the United States. Bruce Morrissette in a critique of the film pointed out to less perceptive critics that it represented a

(50) continuation of techniques established in the earlier novels: "False scenes and objectified hypothesis as in *The Voyeur,* a subjective universe converted into objective perceptions as in *Jealousy*—

(55) with its detemporalization of mental states, its mixture of memories (true and false), of desire images and affective projections—the 'dissolves' found in *The Labyrinth:* all these reach

(60) a high point in *Marienbad.* . . . The spectator's work, like that of the reader, becomes an integral part of the cinematic or novelistic creation." The viewer like the reader was expected to

(65) collaborate in creating meaning. *Marienbad* takes place at an ornate Bavarian palace; the action is circular beginning with "Once more" as the camera moves through Freudian

(70) corridors, empty rooms and a formal garden (with a return at the end); characters emerge as a young woman, A, and older man, M (presumably her jealous husband), and a persistent

(75) lover, X. Fantasies of seduction, resistance, desire, fear, rape, and even murder are projected; but whose they are, A's or M's or X's, is never clear. You take your choice.

8. We may conclude that Nathalie Sarraute and Michel Butor are

(A) interested in Robbe-Grillet
(B) masters of detective fiction
(C) contemporaries of Robbe-Grillet
(D) antagonistic to Robbe-Grillet
(E) comparable to Robbe-Grillet

9. The "that" in line 4 refers to which one of the following?

   (A) the cerebral quality of most French fiction
   (B) the contention that Robbe-Grillet's work does not appeal to the intellect
   (C) the brainlessness of Robbe-Grillet's work
   (D) Robbe-Grillet's reliance on emotional effects
   (E) a fact apparently discussed elsewhere

10. We may assume that the plot of a *roman policier* involves

   (A) French characters
   (B) a crime
   (C) psychopathological characters
   (D) an omniscient narrator
   (E) the collaboration of other novelists

11. According to the passage, one might finish a successful Robbe-Grillet novel feeling

   (A) more intelligent
   (B) in the mood to read the novel
   (C) as if he had seen an Alfred Hitchcock film
   (D) wondering "Who dunnit?"
   (E) disappointed

12. Robbe-Grillet is paradoxical because he

   (A) uses a popular form of the novel yet seeks to alienate his readers
   (B) writes for the cinema and for novel readers
   (C) refers to his works as "cinema-novels" rather than film scripts
   (D) is more well-known for his films than for his novels
   (E) refuses to clarify the meaning of his novels and films

13. According to the passage, the viewer of *Last Year at Marienbad* is a

   (A) participant in the clearly delineated fantasy
   (B) fan of triangular love relationships
   (C) detached spectator
   (D) reader as well
   (E) partner in constructing the plot

14. In a novel or film by a New Novelist like Robbe-Grillet we should expect to find distortion or obscurity in the handling of

   (A) time
   (B) the identity of the characters
   (C) language
   (D) the point of view from which the work is presented
   (E) memory

   The paganism of the Greeks and Romans, though a religion without salvation or afterlife, was not necessarily indifferent to man's moral
(5) behavior. What has misled some historians is that this religion, without theology or church, was, if I may put it this way, more an á la carte religion than a religion with a fixed menu. If an
(10) established church is a "one-party state," then paganism was "free enterprise." Each man was free to found his own temple and preach whatever god he liked, just as he might
(15) open a new inn or peddle a new product. And each man made himself the client of whichever god he chose, not necessarily his city's favorite deity: The choice was free.
(20)   Such freedom was possible because between what the pagans meant by "god" and what Jews, Christians, and Moslems mean, there is little in common but the name. For the three
(25) religions of the Book, God is infinitely

greater than the world which he created. He exists solely as an actor in a cosmic drama in which the salvation of humankind is played out. The pagan (30) gods, by contrast, live their lives and are not confined to a metaphysical role. They are part of this world, one of three races that populate the earth: animals, which are neither immortal nor gifted (35) with reason; humans, who are mortal but reasonable; and gods, who are immortal and reasonable. So true is it that the divine race is an animal genus that every god is either male or female. (40) From this it follows that the gods of all peoples are true gods. Other nations might worship gods unknown to the Greeks and Romans, or they might worship the same gods under different (45) names. Jupiter was Jupiter the world over, just as a lion is a lion, but he happened to be called Zeus in Greek, Taranis in Gallic, and Yao in Hebrew. The names of the gods could be (50) translated from one language to another, just like the names of planets and other material things. Belief in alien gods foundered only where it was the product of an absurd superstition, (55) something that smacked of a fantastic bestiary. The Romans laughed at the gods with animal bodies worshiped by the Egyptians. In the ancient world religious people were as tolerant of one (60) another as are Hindu sects. To take a special interest in one god was not to deny the others.

This fact was not without consequence for man's idea of his own (65) place in the natural order. Imagine a circle, which represents the world according to the religions of the Book. Given man's importance in the cosmic drama, he occupies at least half the (70) circle. What about God? He is so exalted, so awesome, that he remains

far above the circle. To represent Him, draw an arrow, pointing upward from the center of the circle and mark it with (75) the sign of infinity. Now consider the pagan world. Imagine a sort of staircase with three steps. On the lowest step stand the animals; on the next step, humans; and on the third (80) step, the gods. In order to become a god, one did not need to rise very far. The gods stood just above humans, so that it often makes sense to translate the Latin and Greek words for "divine" (85) as "superhuman."

15. Which one of the following best expresses the main idea of the passage?

(A) Under Greek and Roman paganism, people were not bound by a set theology or teachings from a sacred book.

(B) In Greek and Roman paganism, humans differed from animals in that they possessed reason.

(C) Greek and Roman paganism was not, as some historians have claimed, indifferent to man's morality.

(D) Central to Greek and Roman paganism was the belief that the gods were of this world, not above it.

(E) Greek and Roman paganism cannot accurately be called a "religion" because of its concept of the gods.

16. In the first paragraph, the effect of the metaphors "à la carte/fixed menu" and "free enterprise/one-party state" is to

(A) suggest the immorality of the gods

(B) indicate the origins of the gods

(C) suggest the earthbound quality of the gods

(D) suggest the selfishness and pettiness of the gods

(E) indicate the economic role of the gods

17. The central contrast between an "à la carte" religion and a "fixed menu" religion is best expressed as

(A) choice among many gods vs. obedience to one true god

(B) belief in female gods vs. belief in male gods

(C) choice among holy books vs. adherence to one holy book

(D) belief in life on earth vs. belief in life in heaven

(E) choice among varieties of worship vs. acceptance of one liturgy

18. To develop his points, the author uses all of the following methods EXCEPT

(A) contrast

(B) example

(C) figurative language

(D) irony

(E) explanation

19. From information in the passage, we can infer which one of the following would be true under Greek and Roman paganism?

(A) People would be happier and more fulfilled.

(B) Religious wars would be less likely.

(C) Family life would be less significant.

(D) The arts would flourish.

(E) People would behave immorally.

20. According to the author, why have some historians assumed that the Greeks and Romans were indifferent to man's moral behavior?

(A) Their gods had no significant power.

(B) They laughed at the religious practices of others.

(C) Their religion did not include salvation.

(D) Their gods were immoral role models.

(E) They viewed gods and animals as the same.

21. The passage attributes the religious tolerance under paganism to the fact that

(A) human reason was valued over faith

(B) no one god was seen as the "true god"

(C) religion was not at the center of human activity

(D) the same gods were worshiped by different nations

(E) gods were not taken seriously

22. The purpose of the third paragraph of the passage is to

(A) summarize and evaluate the contrasts between paganism and religions of the Book

(B) show the connection between the concepts of the "divine" and the "superhuman"

(C) contrast the place of man in relation to God under paganism and under religions of the Book

(D) explain the conflicts between the concept of monotheism and the concept of polytheism

(E) simplify the points made in paragraphs one and two so that they will be more understandable to the reader

The word *science* is heard so often in modern times that almost everybody has some notion of its meaning. On the other hand, its definition is difficult for (5) many people. The meaning of the term is confused because many endeavors masquerading under the name of science do not have any valid connection with it. Therefore everyone (10) should understand its import and objectives. Just to make the explanation as simple as possible, suppose science is defined as classified knowledge (facts). An (15) example that adequately meets the requirements is astronomy. On the other hand, astrology, regardless of how sincerely it is believed by some, must be excluded since it is not based (20) on fact. Even in the true sciences distinguishing fact from fiction is not always easy. For this reason great care should be taken to distinguish between beliefs and truths. There is no danger (25) as long as a clear difference is made between temporary and proved explanations. For example, hypotheses (tentative theories) and theories are attempts to explain natural (30) phenomena. From these tentative positions the scientist continues to experiment and observe until they are proved or discredited. The exact status of any explanation should be clearly (35) labeled to avoid confusion.

The objectives of science are primarily the discovery and the subsequent understanding of the unknown. Man cannot be satisfied with (40) recognizing that secrets exist in nature or that questions are unanswerable; he must solve them. Toward that end specialists in the field of biology and related fields of interest are directing (45) much of their time and energy. A beginning student should understand the motivation of science and acquire the spirit of inquiry. That kind of spirit, plus practice in the methods of (50) science, should make a course more meaningful.

Actually, two basic approaches lead to the discovery of new information. One, aimed at satisfying curiosity, is (55) referred to as *pure* science. The other is aimed at using knowledge for specific purposes—for instance, improving health, raising standards of living, or creating new consumer (60) products. In this case knowledge is put to economic use. Such an approach is referred to as *applied* science.

Sometimes practical-minded people miss the point of pure science in (65) thinking only of its immediate utilization for economic rewards. One can see that an extraordinary amount of knowledge about chemistry is necessary before one can possibly (70) understand functions of protoplasm like respiration or photosynthesis. Chemists responsible for many of the discoveries could hardly have anticipated that their findings would (75) one day result in applications of such a practical nature as those directly related to life and health. Furthermore, geneticists working on insects could not foresee all the possible applications (80) of their findings to the improvement of plants and animals through selective breeding. The discovery of one bit of information opens the door to the discovery of another. Some discoveries (85) seem so simple that one is amazed they were not made years ago; however, one should remember that the construction of the microscope had to precede the discovery of the cell, (90) and a knowledge of the chemical nature of oxygen and carbon dioxide had to come before a breakthrough in the understanding of photosynthesis. The host of scientists dedicating their (95) lives to pure science are not apologetic about ignoring the practical side of their discoveries; they know from experience that most knowledge is eventually applied. Probably one can (100) safely say that even from a practical point of view all discoveries will eventually be used.

23. To define science, we may simply call it

(A) the complementation of unrelated fields
(B) the convergence of unrelated fields
(C) biology, chemistry, geology, physics, and anthropology
(D) biology, chemistry, geology, and anthropology
(E) classified knowledge

24. According to the passage, which one of the following cannot be classified as a science?

(A) phrenology
(B) astronomy
(C) astrology
(D) chemistry
(E) botany

25. Pure science, leading to the construction of a microscope,

(A) may lead to antiscientific, "impure" results
(B) necessarily precedes applied science, leading to the discovery of a cell
(C) is not always pure

(D) comes largely from the efforts of eccentric scientists
(E) necessarily results from applied science and the discovery of a cell

26. A scientist interested in adding to our general knowledge about oxygen would probably call his approach

(A) applied science
(B) beginning science
(C) agricultural science
(D) pure science
(E) botanical science

27. Of the following, which one is an example of pure as opposed to applied science?

(A) the search for a rust-resistant metal
(B) the search for an antidote to cobra venom
(C) the search for an undiscovered element
(D) the search for archeological evidence of early life in Arizona
(E) the search for a disease resistant rose

28. The best title for this passage is

(A) Manifestations and Relationships of Life
(B) Biology and the Scientific Age
(C) The Nature of Science and Scientists
(D) Organisms and Their Environments
(E) Changing Life

STOP

IF YOU FINISH BEFORE TIME IS UP, CHECK YOUR WORK ON THIS SECTION OF THE TEST ONLY.
DO NOT GO ON TO THE NEXT SECTION OF THE TEST UNTIL TIME IS UP FOR THIS SECTION.

SECTION V

Time — 35 minutes
25 Questions

Directions: In this section you will be given brief statements or passages and will be required to evaluate the reasoning involved. In some instances, more than one choice will appear to be a possible answer. You are to choose the *best* answer. Use common sense and reasonableness in making your selection; then mark the proper space on the answer sheet.

Questions 1–2

By passing more and more regulations allegedly to protect the environment, the state is driving the manufacturing industry away. And when the employers leave, the workers will follow. The number of new no-growth or environmental rules passed each year is increasing by leaps and bounds. Rich environmentalists who think they are sympathetic to workers have no real sympathy for the blue-collar employees who are injured by their activities. One major manufacturer has been fined for failing to establish a car-pool plan. Another is accused of polluting the air with industrial emissions, although everyone knows that two thirds of the pollutants come from cars and trucks. No wonder the large manufacturers are moving to states with fewer restrictive laws. And as the manufacturers go, unemployment and the number of workers leaving the state will rise more rapidly than ever before.

1. The author's argument that strict environmental laws will eventually lead to loss of workers in the state will be most weakened if it can be shown that

   (A) so far, the number of manufacturers who have left the state is small
   (B) the unemployment rate has climbed steadily in the last three years

   (C) most workers who leave the state give as their reason for leaving the poor environmental quality
   (D) several other manufacturing states have strict environmental laws
   (E) rich environmentalists are more powerful in many other states

2. Which one of the following is NOT an argument of this passage?

   (A) Environmentalists are responsible for depriving workers of their jobs.
   (B) When workers leave a state, it is a sign that manufacturers will follow.
   (C) A car-pool law should not be enforced, as cars and trucks are responsible for most air pollution.
   (D) Large manufacturers prefer states with fewer restrictions.
   (E) A rise in unemployment will lead to an increase in workers leaving the state.

3. This supermarket has the highest prices in town. I had to pay $3.00 per pound for hamburger today.

   Which one of the following statements best expresses the main premise that underlies the author's conclusion?

   (A) Hamburger should cost less than $3.00 per pound.
   (B) No other supermarket charges as much as $3.00 per pound for hamburger.

(C) All hamburger is of the same quality.
(D) Prices for other items at this store are equally high.
(E) Other supermarkets may charge less for hamburger, but more for other items.

4. Unlike most graduates of American high schools, all graduates of high schools in Bermuda have completed four years of advanced mathematics.

Which one of the following, if true, would best explain the situation described above?

(A) Math anxiety is higher in the United States than in Bermuda.
(B) There are far more high schools and high school students in the United States than in Bermuda.
(C) More students in America take full-time jobs without completing high school.
(D) Math programs in American high schools are frequently understaffed.
(E) High schools in Bermuda require four years of advanced mathematics for graduation.

5. Psychological novels are superior to novels of adventure. Immature readers prefer novels of adventure to novels with less action and greater psychological depth. The immature reader, who prefers James Bond's exploits to the subtleties of Henry James, can be identified easily by his choice of inferior reading matter.

A criticism of the logic of this argument would be likely to find fault with the author's

(A) presupposing the conclusion he wishes to prove

(B) failure to define "adventure" clearly
(C) failure to cite possible exceptions to this rule
(D) hasty generalization on the basis of a limited specific case
(E) inaccurate definitions of key terms

6. All mathematicians are physicists. Some chemists are mathematicians. Some physicists are biologists. No biologists are chemists.

If all of these statements are true, which one of the following statements must also be true?

(A) Some chemists are biologists.
(B) Some chemists are physicists.
(C) No mathematicians are biologists.
(D) All biologists are physicists.
(E) All physicists are mathematicians or biologists.

7. In professional athletics, the small number of record-setting performers in each thirty-year span is remarkably consistent. In hockey, for example, 5 percent of all the professional players were responsible for more than half of the new records, and 95 percent of the new records were set by only 8 percent of the players. Similar percentages were found in baseball, football, and basketball records, where the numbers of participants are much higher.

If the statements above are true, which one of the following conclusions may be most reasonably inferred?

(A) An increase in the number of athletic teams playing hockey, football, or baseball would significantly increase the number of record-setting performances.

(B) Reducing the number of athletic teams playing hockey, football, or baseball would not necessarily cause a decrease in the number of record-setting performances.

(C) Record-setting performances would increase if the number of amateur teams were increased.

(D) Many record-setting performances are not recorded by statisticians.

(E) As records become higher with the passage of time, fewer and fewer records will be broken.

8. By refusing to ban smoking in restaurants, the city council has put the financial well-being of restaurant owners above the health of the citizens of this city. No doubt the council would support the restaurateurs if they decided to use asbestos tablecloths and to barbecue using radioactivity. These devices would be no more risky.

The author of this paragraph makes her case by arguing

(A) from experience
(B) from example
(C) by authority
(D) from observation
(E) from analogy

9. The GOP's attempt to win the South has, however indirectly, played on the racial anxiety of white voters. It has produced a vocabulary of civility to conceal their opposition to school integration ("forced busing") and affirmative action ("quotas"). And, to the horror of regular Republicans, the party's candidate for senator in Louisiana is a neo-Nazi and Ku Klux Klan alumnus. The ease with which this candidate has merged his bigotry with a respectable conservative social

agenda is frightening. There is, however, a ray of hope. The candidate is sup- ported by about 30 percent of the voters.

The passage above is structured to lead to which one of the following conclusions?

(A) If the candidate disavows his views, he will lose his support; but if he does not disavow them, he cannot gain any new supporters.

(B) And that 30 percent has grown from only 15 percent three weeks ago.

(C) We cannot predict now whether that percentage will increase or decrease before the election.

(D) Two opponents also have about 30 percent of voters with another 10 percent undecided.

(E) There is still a possibility that Louisiana, with its unmatched history of corrupt, demagogic, and ineffectual state politics, will support his candidacy.

Questions 10–11

The gill-net is used to catch halibut and sea bass, but up to 72 percent of what it ensnares is not marketable and is thrown back dead. Gill-nets are often called "walls of death" because they entangle and pain- fully kill mammals such as dolphins, whales, and sea otters. To use the gill-net at sea is like strip mining or clear-cutting on land.

Powerful lobbyists representing the commercial fishing industry have prevented the legislature from passing a ban on the use of gill-nets within the three- mile limit. They claim that the banning of gill-nets will raise the price of fish. They also charge that the law would benefit rich sport fishermen who want the ocean for their yachts.

10. In the first paragraph, the case against gill-nets is made by using

    (A) statistical analysis
    (B) ambiguity and indirection
    (C) biased definitions
    (D) simile and metaphor
    (E) understatement

11. Which one of the following, if true, would support the argument in favor of a ban on gill-nets within the three-mile limit?

    (A) Less than one percent of the fish sold in this country is imported from abroad.
    (B) Gill-net users catch all but two percent of their fish within the three-mile limit.
    (C) The halibut population has fallen to a near extinction level.
    (D) There is a serious overpopulation of the coastal sea otter.
    (E) Coastal sea otters have nearly destroyed the abalone beds along the coast.

12. According to the Supreme Court, the First Amendment does not protect "obscene" speech. To the "obscene," the Court explained, speech must appeal to a "prurient" interest, describe conduct in a way "patently offensive to contemporary community standards," and lack serious literary, artistic or scientific value.

    All of the following arguments can be used to question the validity of the Court's definition of "obscene" EXCEPT

    (A) there is no certain way of knowing just what an "appeal" to "prurient interest" is
    (B) the phrase "patently offensive" is impossible to define precisely

    (C) no two communities are likely to have the same standards of decency
    (D) most juries are incapable of determining what is "serious" artistic or literary value
    (E) there is no writing that is without some "scientific value"

13. There are no edible fish in the streams of this county because there are no pesticide controls.

    Which one of the following assumptions must be made before the conclusion above can be reached?

    (A) Edible fish cannot be found in areas where there are no pesticide controls.
    (B) If there are pesticide controls, there will be many edible fish.
    (C) Without adequate pesticide controls, the fish population will rapidly decline.
    (D) If there are pesticide controls, there will be some edible fish.
    (E) With pesticide controls, the fish population will rapidly increase.

14. For eighteen years, a state has had three conservative congressmen, all representing the agricultural counties in the northern parts of the state. It also has three liberal congressmen from the large capital city in the south. One of the two senators is a liberal from the south, and the other is a conservative from the north.

    Which one of the following can be inferred from this passage?

    (A) Voters in the southern parts of the state will always vote liberal.
    (B) Voters in the northern part of the state are likely to vote liberal in the next election.

(C) Voters in the state are influenced more by a candidate's political leanings than by where the candidate lives.

(D) The population of the three northern counties is about equal to the population of the capital city.

(E) The governor of the state is probably a liberal.

15. African-Americans have periodically raised the issue of reparations for injury and damage to Africans in America from slavery. The granting of reparations to Japanese-Americans has renewed the hope that the government will meet its moral obligation to address the claim of African-Americans. Free black labor helped to develop America, but slavery only injured African-Americans. The "freed" slaves were released into a hostile, racist, capitalistic society without land, capital, or any meaningful form of compensation. The oppression continued through terror, lynching, segregation, discrimination, and disenfranchisement.

Which sentence is the most logical conclusion of this passage?

(A) Historically, leaders from Frederick Douglass to Malcolm X have kept the issue of reparations alive.

(B) After World War II, West Germany paid reparations to the Jewish victims of the Holocaust.

(C) There can be no final reconciliation between African-Americans and the U.S. government until the just claim of reparations is recognized.

(D) Reparations in the form of cash, land, or government securities could be placed in a national development fund and used for the collective benefit of African-Americans.

(E) A small compensation bill was passed by Congress after the Civil War, but vetoed by President Andrew Johnson.

16. Over the last three decades, the President's party has lost an average of 22 House of Representatives seats and two Senate seats in the midterm elections. This year, with a popular Republican President in the White House, GOP strategists had hoped to pick up seats in the House and the Senate. But the polls show these expectations are unrealistic. This should be an election with results much like those of the recent past.

According to information in this passage, the election should

(A) produce large Republican gains in the House and the Senate

(B) produce about 25 new House and Senate seats for the Democrats

(C) result in virtually no change in the balance of Republican and Democratic members of the House

(D) produce small Republican gains in the House and even smaller gains in the Senate

(E) produce two new Republican seats in the Senate

17. Ten percent of the state lottery winners interviewed by researchers of the paranormal have reported that they had visions or other signs instructing them to select the winning numbers. On the basis of these results, the researchers claim to have proved the existence of paranormal gifts.

Which one of the following pieces of additional information would be most relevant in assessing the logical validity of the researcher's claim?

(A) the total sum of money these men and women win on the lottery
(B) the percentage of lottery players who win money
(C) the percentage of contestants interviewed who were not lottery winners
(D) the percentage of lottery players who had visions or signs but did not win money
(E) the amount of money the lottery winners spend each year on lottery tickets

18. By spraying with pesticides like malathion, we can eradicate dangerous pests like the fruit-fly. But malathion spraying also destroys the ladybug, the best natural predator of aphids. Areas that have been sprayed with malathion are now free of the fruit-fly, but infested with aphids. This is the price we must pay to protect our citrus crop.

The argument above assumes all of the following EXCEPT

(A) pesticide spraying is the only way to eradicate the fruit-fly
(B) the aphid infestation is caused by the lack of ladybugs
(C) a pesticide that would kill fruit-flies and spare ladybugs cannot be made

(D) the use of pesticides has disadvantages
(E) the aphid infestation could be prevented by introducing a natural predator other than the ladybug

19. The Superintendent of Education complains that the share of the total state budget for education has decreased in each of the last four years; he blames the fall-off on the steady rise in the cost of law enforcement. Organizations opposing increased spending on education point out that the amount of money the state has spent on education has increased by at least three million dollars in each of the last four years.

Which one of the following, if true, best resolves the apparent contradiction in the passage above?

(A) The total state budget has increased more rapidly than the expenditure for education.
(B) Both the pro- and con-educational-spending spokesmen have failed to take inflation into account.
(C) Law-enforcement costs have not risen as rapidly as the superintendent claims.
(D) Some educational expenses are not included in the state budget, but are paid by local taxes.
(E) School construction is paid for by funds from bonds, not by funds from the state budget.

20. How can I write any of the essays when there are so many essays to be written?

In terms of its logical structure, the remark above most closely resembles which one of the following?

(A) How can he buy a new car when he is already deeply in debt?
(B) How can she increase her collection of books when it is already so large?
(C) How can he iron any of his shirts when he has so many shirts that need ironing?
(D) How can she visit London and Paris when she has not yet visited New York and Washington?
(E) How can they raise horses when they already raise so many cows?

21. Great playwrights do not develop in countries where there is no freedom of opinion. Repressive countries are likely to produce great satiric writers.

If both of these statements are true, which of the following is the most logical continuation?

(A) Therefore, countries with no restrictions on expression will produce great satiric playwrights.
(B) Therefore, great satirists in repressive countries will use forms other than the play.
(C) Therefore, playwrights in repressive countries will not write satire.
(D) Therefore, great satiric writers will not develop in countries where there is freedom of speech.
(E) Therefore, no great satire is likely to be written in dramatic forms.

22. Contrary to the expectations of the Canadian government, a majority of the Mohawk population in Quebec is calling for native sovereignty. The Mohawk separatists cite a written agreement from colonial times in which Great Britain recognized the Mohawks' separateness from Canada. Unfortunately, the various Mohawk factions, each with its own agenda, have made it difficult to reach lasting agreements. What satisfies one group displeases another. The bleak outlook is for _____.

Which one of the following most logically concludes this paragraph?

(A) continued struggle within the tribe and between the tribe and the Canadian government
(B) some kind of compromise which recognizes the rights of both the Indians and the government of Canada
(C) some sort of agreement among the divided groups within the Mohawk tribe
(D) the establishment of a separate Mohawk state with its sovereignty recognized by the Canadian government
(E) a decline in Mohawk militarism and a series of fence-mending conferences

23. A new law will require labels giving consumers more nutritional information on all prepackaged foods manufactured in the United States. Food sold by restaurants or grocers with annual sales of less than $500,000 will be exempt. The required labels will reveal the number of servings, the serving size, the number of calories per serving, and the amount of fat, cholesterol, sodium, and dietary fiber.

The effectiveness of the new labels in improving overall U.S. nutrition could be seriously questioned if which one of the following were shown to be true?

(A) More than 80 percent of the food sold in this country is not prepackaged.

(B) More than 80 percent of the prepackaged food sold in this country is marketed by the eight major food corporations.

(C) The amount of money Americans spend on prepackaged foods for microwaving has more than tripled every year for the last five years, and the trend is expected to continue.

(D) An increasingly large number of consumers now read the nutritional information on food packages.

(E) Small retailers who manufacture packaged foods sell to only a tiny percentage of American food buyers.

24. A year ago the presidential science advisor announced prematurely that the United States would reveal its plan for combating global warming at the World Climate Conference in Geneva, Switzerland. Five European countries have already announced plans to make reductions in carbon dioxide emissions, and five others have committed themselves to goals of stabilizing their emissions. But the United States is still unprepared to announce targets or a schedule for reducing carbon dioxide emissions.

Which one of the following sentences would provide the most logical continuation of this paragraph?

(A) The Geneva Conference will be the last international meeting before negotiations on a global-warming convention begin next year.

(B) The United States accounts for about 22 percent of the carbon dioxide pumped into the atmosphere, while the former Soviet Union accounts for 18 percent.

(C) By adopting renewable energy strategies that would permit stabilization of carbon dioxide emissions, the United States could save millions of dollars.

(D) The British Prime Minister and top environmental officials of many nations will attend the conference in Geneva.

(E) Anticipating a debate in which the Europeans will criticize the United States for failing to act, the administration is downplaying the importance of the conference.

25. There is increasing reason to believe that Americans are talking themselves into a recession. Consumers are becoming more and more pessimistic, and the index of consumer confidence has plunged to its lowest level in years. What bothers analysts is fear that consumer pessimism about the economy will lead to spending cuts and become a self-fulfilling prophecy, speeding the onset of a recession.

Widespread predictions in the media of a coming recession may be one reason for the pessimistic attitudes of consumers. They may be bracing for a recession by cutting back on spending plans for new cars, vacations, and restaurant meals—the very behavior pattern that analysts say will intensify the slump. Real estate values have been in decline for a year and a half, and the stock market has declined for four months in a row. When the economy is on the ropes, waning consumer confidence can deliver the knock-out punch.

The argument in the passage above would be weakened if it were shown that

(A) in the 1955 recession, the widespread concern over the President's health precipitated an economic downturn
(B) although consumer spending in the last fiscal quarter was the same as last year's, most of that strength stemmed from unusual government military spending
(C) the steady rise in car sales has continued, despite the phasing out of discount prices and low-interest car loans
(D) the predicted recession after the steep fall in stock prices two years ago did not lead to recession
(E) some consumers are more eager than ever to maintain the living standards they have enjoyed for the last two years

WRITING SAMPLE

Directions: You have 30 minutes to write an essay in response to a given topic. Take a few minutes to plan your work before you begin writing. DO NOT WRITE ON A TOPIC OF YOUR OWN CHOICE. ESSAYS THAT DO NOT ADDRESS THE GIVEN TOPIC ARE UNACCEPTABLE.

The quality of your writing is more important than the length of your response or the content. Pay attention to organization, appropriate diction, and correct usage. You will not be expected to display any specialized knowledge in your response, nor will you be expected to write a "perfect" essay; law schools understand that you are writing under a time constraint, and will allow for the minor lapses in writing ability that might occur under this circumstance.

Only the lined area in your booklet will be reproduced for the law schools, so do not write outside this space. *Do not* skip lines or use wide margins. These precautions, along with careful planning and legible handwriting that is not unduly large, will keep you within the allowed space.

Sample Topic

The State Legislature has appropriated funds to build a new maximum security prison some-where in Metropolis County. The prison is to house one hundred prisoners convicted of seri-ous crimes and also the two hundred prisoners awaiting trial or being tried in Metropolis City. These prisoners are now held at the overcrowded and antiquated Metropolis City Jail. Two lo-cations have been proposed.

As an aide to the state senator who represents Metropolis County, you have been asked to write an argument to be presented to the Legislature in support of one of the sites. Two considerations guide your decision:

- The state funds for building and maintaining the prison and for transporting the prisoners to the courts are limited.
- The senator is eager to increase his popular support in anticipation of the upcom-ing election.

The Metropolis City site is located ten minutes from the court buildings near the down-town district. This area of the city is densely populated and has a high, slowly declining, crime rate. Residents of the district strongly oppose the building of the prison in their neighbor-hood, especially since a number of prisoners have recently escaped from the old Metropolis City Jail. Art preservation groups also oppose the proposed location since it would require the destruction of two buildings with unique architectural features. The estimated cost for the land and the construction of the prison on the Metropolis City site is eight million dollars.

The Deer Valley site is located in the sparsely populated Metropolis County, seventy-five miles from the court buildings. Deer Valley is a small town in a depressed rural area. Many of the residents of Deer Valley favor the construction of the prison, since they believe it will bring new jobs to the area. The roads between Deer Valley and Metropolis are narrow, and in a win-ter when the rains or snows are heavy, they may be impassable. The cost of utilities in Deer Valley is about twice the cost of utilities in Metropolis City. The estimated building cost in Deer Valley is seven million dollars.

You will be given a special sheet of paper to write your essay. It will have the essay topic on the top followed by approximately 25 lines of writing. For practice, write your es-say on one side of an 8½" x 11" college-ruled lined sheet of paper. *Use only 25 lines.*

ANSWER KEY

Section I: Reading Comprehension
1. E	6. A	11. A	16. C	21. A	26. B
2. C	7. C	12. D	17. B	22. D	27. C
3. D	8. D	13. E	18. B	23. B	28. D
4. A	9. B	14. A	19. B	24. C	
5. B	10. D	15. D	20. A	25. C	

Section II: Analytical Reasoning
1. B	5. E	9. B	13. E	17. C	21. D
2. E	6. D	10. E	14. D	18. E	22. B
3. B	7. C	11. E	15. E	19. D	23. C
4. C	8. E	12. D	16. B	20. E	24. C

Section III: Logical Reasoning
1. D	6. C	11. D	16. D	21. B	26. B
2. D	7. D	12. D	17. E	22. D	
3. C	8. B	13. D	18. D	23. A	
4. A	9. C	14. D	19. B	24. E	
5. E	10. C	15. A	20. B	25. B	

Section IV: Reading Comprehension
1. B	6. B	11. E	16. C	21. B	26. D
2. B	7. A	12. A	17. A	22. C	27. C
3. E	8. E	13. E	18. D	23. E	28. C
4. E	9. B	14. C	19. B	24. C	
5. A	10. B	15. D	20. C	25. B	

Section V: Logical Reasoning
1. C	6. B	11. C	16. B	21. B
2. B	7. B	12. E	17. D	22. A
3. D	8. E	13. A	18. E	23. A
4. E	9. A	14. D	19. A	24. E
5. A	10. D	15. C	20. C	25. C

MODEL TEST ANALYSIS

Doing model exams and understanding the explanations afterwards are of course important in acquainting you with typical LSAT question types and successful approaches to the questions. However, another benefit of carefully analyzing these model tests is to understand the kinds of errors you are making and thus work to minimize them. For instance, if a very high percentage of your incorrect answers is due to "careless error" or "misread problem," then perhaps you are working much too fast and should slow your pace accordingly. If your incorrect answers are due primarily to "lack of knowledge," then a careful rereading and reworking of the appropriate question-type chapter may be in order. Or if you find that you aren't completing a large number of questions because of lack of time, you may need to either increase your speed or learn to use the "one-check, two-check" technique more effectively.

This kind of analysis of the model tests will enable you to identify your particular weaknesses and thus remedy them.

MODEL TEST THREE ANALYSIS

Section	Total Number of Questions	Number Correct	Number Incorrect	Number Unanswered*
I. Reading Comprehension	28			
II. Analytical Reasoning	24			
III. Logical Reasoning	26			
IV. Reading Comprehension	28			
V. Logical Reasoning	25			
TOTALS:	131			

*At this stage in your preparation, you should not be leaving any blank answer spaces. At least fill in a guess, as there is no penalty for a wrong answer.

REASONS FOR INCORRECT ANSWERS

You may wish to evaluate the explanations before completing this chart.

Section	Total Number Incorrect	Lack of Knowledge	Misread Problem	Careless Error	Unanswered or Wrong Guess
I. Reading Comprehension					
II. Analytical Reasoning					
III. Logical Reasoning					
IV. Reading Comprehension					
V. Logical Reasoning					
TOTALS:					

EXPLANATION OF ANSWERS

Section I

Passage 1

1. **E**   Each of the first four cases is public or quasi-public land. The last is private, not likely to be open to the general public and therefore the owner may deny free speech on the property.

2. **C**   In this instance, the property is clearly private; in the other cases, it is not always clear whether the property is public or private.

3. **D**   The nature or character of the owner of the property is not a factor mentioned by the passage. All of the four other options are alluded to in the opening paragraphs of the passage.

4. **A**   The author approvingly quotes the words of a mall chairman in support of this position. Choice (E) may not be true if the charity seekers are offensive.

5. **B**   The passage cites Lord Chief Justice Hale's remarks of 1675. (C) and (D) are false and the passage does not discuss current practice in Canada and Great Britain (E).

6. **A**   The passage concludes with Justice Black's remarks on the "preferred position" of First Amendment freedoms.

Passage 2

7. **C**   This is the best answer because the passage recounts both Dickens' realization that the novel, based on his memories, was deeply personal and also his recognition that he was creating a "mediated version" of himself. See lines 13–20, 67–76. (A) covers only paragraph one of the passage; (B) is a secondary point,

not the main idea. The novel can hardly be called prophetic (C), although one line suggests it "anticipated" turmoil in his marriage. However, this is not a main idea. (E) is an opinion not presented or suggested in the passage.

8. **D**   This answer is supported by the main points in both paragraphs one and two. The author does not present a "psychological study of motivations" (A) nor does he primarily contrast two aspects of Dickens (B), (C). (E) is inaccurate; the passage does not show that the novel became a turning point in his life.

9. **B**   The line indicates that writing the book has called up his childhood memories and therefore "almost inevitably" led him back to the place where he was a small boy. The line does not indicate complete exhaustion (A) nor does it suggest that he was unable to separate reality and fiction (C). (D) is simply inaccurate. It is too far a leap to infer that because he returns to Rochester, he has overcome the trauma of his childhood (E), particularly because of the inclusion of the words "almost inevitably."

10. **D**   This is the best of the answers because Fanny's significance is clearly suggested in lines 37–41. Although (A) might seem correct because future turmoil in his marriage is indicated (lines 22–25), an end to the marriage is not implied. (C) is incorrect because although it is suggested that he sometimes put his work and his own ego above his family, coolness and distance are not implied. (B) and (E) are not supported by information in the passage.

11. **A**   Although (C) and (D) are accurate statements, they are not the *most significant* reasons for Dickens' choice of the name. Lines 67–76 suggest that (A) is the correct answer. (B) and (E) are not supported by information in the passage.

12. **D**   This is the best answer because the parenthetical phrase concerning Catherine indicates her reaction to her husband's assumption of the right to name the children, which in turn suggests something about their relationship. Failing to insist on naming her children does not indicate that she is an inadequate mother (A). (B), (C), and (E) are simply not suggested in this line.

13. **E**   The author is primarily objective and analytical in the passage. (A) is incorrect because although there is perhaps some irony (e.g., lines 41–44), it is minor. (B), (C), and (D) are simply incorrect; the author is neither argumentative, condescending, nor persuasive, for example.

14. **A**   The first paragraph includes an account of Dickens' reactions to writing the novel, using many of his own quotations. The second paragraph relies on more commentary from the author, and also introduces related points, such as Dickens' choice of the novel's title and his interest in names. (E) is incorrect because paragraph one doesn't show the *effect* of Dickens' childhood on him, nor does the second paragraph connect his later life with his novels. Similarly, (B), (C), and (D) all include inadequate (or inaccurate) descriptions of the two paragraphs of the passage.

Passage 3

15. **D**   This summarizes the main point of paragraph one. See lines 3–10, 25–32. (B) is incorrect because the principles were only sometimes laid down in "heavenly writ." (E) is a correct statement but not the best description of the society. (A) is not supported by the passage. (C) is inaccurate.

16. **C**   The author gives two examples—a settlement where community was dominant and settlements where kinship was dominant—to illustrate that although community and family always operated together, they did so in different ways. The examples are not included to show a diverse population (A) nor is any point illustrated or judgment made of religious and nonreligious communities (B), (D), (E).

17. **B**   See lines 51–64. Permanence allowed people to have a much better knowledge of others in their community, the routines, customs, and history. This in turn made it easier to measure the state of the community against a "superstructure of truth." (D) and (E), while possibly true, are not supported by the passage. (A) and (C) are simply inaccurate.

18. **B**   Paragraph two focuses on the roles of both community and family and shows how they operated together to maintain the principles of the closed system of society. See lines 47–54. Paragraph two does not provide historical background (A) nor does it provide a contrast with paragraph one (C). It is not a transition (D) nor does it contrast types of communities (E).

19. **B**   The point of paragraph three is that people required "careful articulation" and "explicit demonstration" in

matters that were beyond their local community. A federal constitution would be an absolute necessity to them so that they could ensure it was in agreement with correct principles. (E) is incorrect because people did trust unwritten general principles on matters within their communities. (A), (C), and (D) are either irrelevant or unsupported by information in the passage.

20. **A** Paragraph one stresses the importance of general governing principles, and paragraph three is concerned with how people ensured adherence to those principles when events were beyond their immediate community. (B) is incorrect; there is no reference to mistrust of outsiders. (D) is also incorrect because there is no reference to people's reaction to change. (C) and (E) are simply inaccurate statements.

21. **A** The passage emphasizes the framework of rules and principles that defined the society. Questioning authority and trusting yourself above all would not be likely advice. (B), (C), (D), and (E) are all suggested by information given in the passage.

22. **D** This states the main idea presented in paragraph one, with its implications developed in paragraphs two and three. (B) is the second-best answer but emphasizes a secondary point rather than the main point. (E) is incorrect because the passage does not draw the contrast between effective and ineffective application of the principles. (C) suggests a minor point, and (A) is inaccurate.

Passage 4

23. **B** The first paragraph says that taxonomy was "in the forefront of the sci-

ences" in "the eighteenth and early nineteenth centuries."

24. **C** The terms refer to plants and animals.

25. **C** The passage gives us no information to support (A), (B), or (E). (D) is untrue (they were among the "greatest biologists of Europe"). That Darwin spent many years and wrote three volumes about the taxonomy of barnacles suggest that there are a large number of kinds to describe.

26. **B** The third paragraph gives examples of the "genuine pioneers" mentioned at the end of the second paragraph. The scientists of the first paragraph are not "exclusively European," (Jefferson).

27. **C** Parsifal was a naive knight of German legend and Klingsor was his enemy, a magician with an enchanted garden. The reference to Parsifal's bravery and the use of the word "vanquished" should suggest this answer.

28. **D** Though the passage does include (A), (B), and (C), the best choice here is (D), which describes all three paragraphs in the passage.

Section II

Answers 1–6

From the information given you should pull out information and list the two possibilities:

```
        1  2  3  4  5  6  7  8
JJJJ or JJJ
  RR
  CC
┌─────────┐
│  R ? J  │
└─────────┘
```

Two Possibilities:

JJJJ		JJJ
R R	or	R R R
C C		C C

1. **B** If four jazz songs are played and the first and last song are of the same type, there are two possible arrangements. Remember, at least two of each type of song are required. Start by placing the first and last song; for example, two rock songs. It is apparent that there is only one place for the four jazz songs, since, other than jazz, no two songs of the same type can be consecutive.

| R | C | J | J | J | J | C | R |
| C | R | J | J | J | J | R | C |

In both arrangements a jazz song is played third. For each of the other answer choices, there are two types of songs played.

2. **E** If three rock songs are played, the remaining five songs must be made up of two country songs and three jazz songs, since there must be more jazz songs than country songs. Since a rock song must precede the first jazz song, there is only one arrangement where a country song is played sixth.

| R | J | J | J | R | C | R | C |

3. **B** There are four possible arrangements where a jazz song is played third and the first and last songs of the same type.

R	J	J	J	C	R	C	R
R	C	J	J	J	R	C	R
R	C	J	J	J	J	C	R
C	R	J	J	J	J	R	C

In none of the arrangements is the sixth song a country song.

4. **C** There is only one arrangement containing three jazz songs where all

three jazz songs are last. There are two arrangements containing four jazz songs. The songs at the beginning of the play list must alternate.

R	C	R	C	R	J	J	J
R	C	R	C	J	J	J	J
C	R	C	R	J	J	J	J

5. **E** If a country song is played first and seventh, there is only one possible arrangement using three jazz songs and one arrangement using four jazz songs. In both cases, a jazz song is being played third.

| C | R | J | J | J | R | C | R |
| C | R | J | J | J | J | C | R |

6. **D** Since a country song was fifth, the first three songs must be rock-country-rock. This leaves only three arrangements for the remaining songs.

R	C	R	K	C	J	J	J	J
R	C	R	K	C	J	J	J	R
R	C	R	K	C	R	J	J	J

In all three arrangements, there is a rock song played third.

Answers 7–13
From the information given, you could have made the following relationships:

$$J > L + M + N$$
$$N = L + M$$
$$M > K + G$$
$$G > H$$
$$K = G$$

7. **C** From the diagram above, since Jon has more bills than Lynn, Melanie, and Neil combined and since Melanie has more bills than Ken and George combined, then Jon has the most bills.

8. **E**   Since Hal has fewer bills than George, and George has fewer bills than Melanie, and Melanie has fewer bills than Neil, and Neil has fewer bills than Jon, then Hal has the fewest number of bills. At this point you may have deduced most of the order of students:

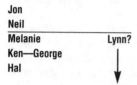

Jon
Neil
Melanie   Lynn?
Ken—George
Hal

If you realized these relationships immediately from the initial conditions, you should have made this part of your first diagram.

9. **B**   From the chart for the previous problem we see that only choice (B) must be true.

10. **E**   Using this new information with the order chart, we have the following chart:

Jon
Neil
Melanie
Ken   Lynn?
George
Hal

You may have approached this problem by eliminating the incorrect choices.

11. **E**   Since Neil has the same number of bills as Lynn and Melanie combined, and Jon has more bills than Lynn, Melanie, and Neil combined, therefore Jon has more bills than twice the number of Lynn's and Melanie's bills. Choice (E) is false.

12. **D**   If Lynn and Melanie have the same number of bills, then Lynn has more bills than Ken and George combined. Since George has more bills

than Hal and since Neil has the same number of bills as Lynn and Melanie combined, then Neil has more bills than Lynn, George, and Hal combined.

13. **E**   If Tom has more bills than Ken and fewer than Lynn, the order of students would now be as follows:

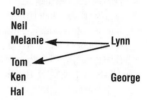

Jon
Neil
Melanie ◄———————— Lynn
Tom ◄
Ken   George
Hal

Therefore, Lynn having more bills than Hal is the only one that must be true.

Answers 14–20
From the information given, you may have set up the following display:

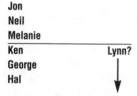

Since Boris eats chocolate chip cookies, Cisco does not. Since Cisco eats sugar cookies, Boris does not. We are given that Alli does not eat sugar cookies and at least two people must eat sugar cookies, so Dan must eat sugar cookies. Anyone who eats sugar cookies does not eat raisin cookies, thus Dan does not eat raisin cookies. Your display should now look like this:

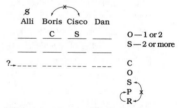

14. D From the display you can see that Dan does not eat raisin cookies.

15. E If Boris eats exactly three kinds of cookies they must be chocolate chip, peanut butter, and raisin. Since Boris eats chocolate chip cookies but does not eat sugar cookies, he must eat two of the remaining three—peanut butter, raisin, oatmeal. But Cisco cannot eat raisin, so if Boris eats raisin, he must eat peanut butter. Since Cisco must eat at least two types, he must eat sugar cookies and oatmeal cookies. The display should look like this:

```
         S̸    ⌒x⌒
     Alli  Boris  Cisco  Dan
     ____    C      S      S
     ____    P      O     ____
             R      R̸      R̸
                    C̸
```

16. B At most, two people eat oatmeal cookies, thus, if Alli and Dan eat oatmeal cookies, Boris and Cisco cannot. Thus, Boris must eat at least one more type of cookie. Either Boris eats peanut butter cookies, or raisin and peanut butter cookies. Either way, Boris eats peanut butter cookies. Thus, Cisco cannot eat peanut butter cookies. This is not a possible arrangement since Cisco must eat at least two types of cookies. The display would look like this:

```
         S̸    ⌒x⌒
     Alli  Boris  Cisco  Dan
     ____    C      S      S
       O     S̸     ____     O
             P      R̸       R̸
                    C̸
                    P̸
```

17. C The general conditions state that oatmeal cookies can only be eaten by a maximum of two people, thus, choices (A), (B), and (D) are incorrect. Choice (E) can be eliminated since Alli cannot eat sugar cookies and Boris does not eat them either. Therefore, by process of elimination, choice (C) must be correct.

18. E This problem follows directly from the given conditions. Sugar cookies is the only cookie type that must be eaten by exactly two different people.

19. D If Alli does not eat chocolate chip or raisin cookies (or sugar cookies), she must eat oatmeal and peanut butter cookies, since those are the only ones left.

```
         S̸    ⌒x⌒
     Alli  Boris  Cisco  Dan
       O     C      S      S
       O     R      R̸      R̸
       C̸     P      C̸
       R̸
```

It is possible for Boris to eat raisin and peanut butter cookies, which would preclude Cisco from eating peanut butter cookies.

Choice (A) is not possible. If Dan eats oatmeal cookies, Boris and Cisco cannot, since at most two people eat oatmeal cookies. In order for Cisco to eat two kinds of cookies, he must eat peanut butter cookies. If Cisco eats peanut butter cookies, Boris cannot. But this is not possible, since Boris needs to eat two types of cookies too, and he cannot eat raisin cookies without peanut butter cookies.

Choice (B) is incorrect, since two people eat sugar cookies and at most two can eat chocolate chip cookies.

Choice (C) is incorrect. If only Alli eats peanut butter cookies, Boris does not eat peanut butter or raisin cookies. Thus Boris would have to eat oatmeal cookies in order to eat two types. But Cisco would also have to eat oatmeal cookies in order to eat two types. Boris and Cisco cannot both eat oatmeal cookies. Choice (E) is incorrect because the initial conditions state that Cisco eats sugar cookies, so Boris could not.

20. **E** Raisin cookies cannot be eaten by Cisco and Dan, and they do not have to be eaten by Alli or Boris. We can also eliminate the other choices. From initial conditions, chocolate chip cookies are eaten by at least one person and sugar cookies are eaten by two people. This eliminates choices (A) and (C). If no one eats peanut butter cookies, no one can eat raisin cookies either. This would force Boris and Cisco to eat oatmeal cookies, but they can't eat the same cookie. This eliminates choice (D). If no one eats oatmeal cookies, Cisco must eat peanut butter cookies, since he must eat two kinds of cookies. Boris must eat raisin cookies in order to eat at least two kinds of cookies, but if he eats raisin cookies, he must eat peanut butter cookies as well. This is not possible, since Cisco is already eating peanut butter cookies. This eliminates choice (B).

Answers 21–24

From the information given, it would be helpful to construct the following chart to answer the questions:

A   B   C*
D   E   F   Two from each row
G   H   K   must be chosen.
*If C, then also K.

21. **D** If A is not chosen, then B and C are chosen. Since C is chosen, K is chosen too. Since B is chosen, D is not chosen. Thus, E and F are chosen. So, if A is not chosen, B, C, E, F, and K must be chosen.

22. **B** If D is chosen, then B is not chosen. Therefore, (B) could NOT be cho-

sen. Also, A and C must be chosen. If C is chosen, then so is K. E or F is chosen. G or H is chosen.

23. **C** If B is chosen, then D is not chosen. Thus, E and F are chosen. Notice that statement 6 is not two-directional.

24. **C** Since G and H do not play together, only one will be chosen. Thus, K must be chosen.

Section III

1. **D** If 97 percent of fatalities occurred *below 45 mph,* then a reduction in the maximum speed from 65 to 55 mph would have little impact, no more than a 3 percent reduction (if we assume that all other fatalities occurred between 55 and 65 mph). (A) and (C) are not relevant, (B) provides no conclusive data, and (E) *strengthens* the argument.

2. **D** The information states:
   1. If busing passes, then Smith was not reelected.
   2. Smith was reelected.
   Therefore, busing failed.
   3. If Smith is reelected she will vote for busing.
   4. Smith was reelected.
   Therefore, Smith voted for busing. (A) and (B) are wrong, because busing failed. (C) is wrong because Smith voted for busing. (E) is wrong because there are insufficient data to support it.

3. **C** Webster is stating that not only do lies disagree with truth, but they usually also disagree with other lies. Thus, it would follow that liars often quarrel with other liars.

4. **A** The given argument can be reduced to:

is not   S (star)   because   H (hit)

is   H   because   S

(A) exhibits the structure closest to that of the given argument:

is not   F   because   C
          (final   (correct)
          word)

is   C   because   F ("Instructor"
      (correct)   is the final
                          word.)

5. **E**   *Setting aside the condition given* in the question, there are four possible states that could exist:

	Doxin	*Entrox*
1.	Present	Present
2.	Present	Absent
3.	Absent	Present
4.	Absent	Absent

The condition contained in the question rules out state 2 only. (A) (state 3), (B) (state 1), and (C) (state 4) are true. (E) (state 2) is false.

6. **C**   The discussion points out that (A) is an implication (rather than an assumption) of the studies. (B) is also not an assumption but is a restatement of the discussion's central issue. In order to consider speaker characteristics as either relevant or irrelevant, the author must assume that such a distinction exists; that assumption is expressed by (C). The passage does not assume a trim speaker will be "more persuasive" (D) or that irrelevant aspects are more influential than content (E), though it does suggest that these are issues worth examining.

7. **D**   The final sentence of the passage offers an alternative explanation of the phenomenon introduced in the first sentence.

8. **B**   The author, by offering an alternative explanation, stresses the scientists' unwillingness to consider such alternatives. (A), a choice worth considering, should be eliminated because the alternative suggested by the author is no more verifiable than the assertion he criticizes.

9. **C**   The author argues that the term "progressive" is avoided by educators because of abuses in the progressive education movement, and that therefore, recently new, educational practices have avoided being tagged with the name "progressive." If choice (C) were true—that "progressive learning" has recently met with approval in middle class public schools—it would contradict the author's statement about the connotation of the word "progressive" and seriously weaken his argument.

10. **C**   The misunderstanding arises from Dave's assumption that Bill has said *every* morning, not *almost* every morning. (D), although worth considering, is not best because it does not address the scope of Bill's remark.

11. **D**   Because the first two statements are not absolute, we may conclude sunbathing is unlikely but still possible. There is no information in the passage to support (A), (B), (C), or (E).

12. **D**   (A) and (B) are, by commonsense standards, implausible. (C) might be a valid statement, but it is not implied by Wilkie's assertion, which makes no distinction between first- and second-class citizens, and so implies (D).

13. **D**   Since the passage does not say that the 200 students in spring activities were all different and all different from the 100 in fall activities, the total number of students could be much lower than 300. A single stu-

dent could participate in all three activities in both semesters. (C) could apply if there were more than one activity, but (D) is a correct assumption in any case.

14. **D** If *nothing* produces only nothing, then the production of something *must* require something. (A) makes the production of something from something a possibility; however, the original statement implies that the something/something relationship is imperative.

15. **A** Only (A) makes an unqualified negative assessment; each of the other choices is either a neutral statement or one that attempts to balance positive and negative terms.

16. **D** The term *average* in the passage implies that if some workers earned more than $7.87 per day, others must have earned less. In choice (C) the words *far more than* make that choice not necessarily true.

17. **E** The magazine is sure that Jones will be a contender soon, and all that is offered to support this is the fact that Jinkins will train him. Therefore, (A) and (B) are the assumptions motivating the passage. (E) is not an assumption, but rather a statement made explicitly in the article.

18. **D** All the other examples are dilemmas. Amleth must choose between failure to avenge or failure to protect his mother; the zoo must choose between the loss of the grant and the loss of a kudu. Ames must choose between higher rent and customer inconvenience. The driver must choose between a parking ticket and losing a radio. In (D), there is no choice between disagreeable alternatives. If you don't

have enough money, you can't buy enough meat.

19. **B** The structure of question 19 may be simplified as follows:

$\underline{C}$ (crowded) <u>whenever</u> H (holiday)
<u>Not C</u>; therefore, <u>not H</u>

(B) is most nearly parallel to the relationships presented in the question:

$\underline{\underline{R}}$ (reptiles) <u>whenever</u> $\underline{D}$ (hot desert day)
<u>Not R</u> (absent); therefore, not $\underline{\underline{D}}$.

20. **B** (A) is not a strong choice; the author indicates only that Nerd is *very* wealthy. The author does not compare Nerd's wealth to that of the other candidates. (C) contradicts the third sentence of the author's statement. Since the author tells us that Nerd has the necessary wealth and should acquire skill as a speaker, the author must believe that the third attribute (experience) is not an issue. In other words, the author believes that Nerd has satisfactory experience. The passage does not assert that an improvement in Nerd's public speaking will guarantee a win (D). Since Nerd has wealth and experience but inadequate speaking skills, he is a dark horse (E).

21. **B** (A) would not weaken the argument, since being wealthy, but not necessarily wealthiest, is all that is called for. (D) and (E) are consistent with the expressed or implied information in the argument. Although (C) is a possible answer choice, (B) is superior; it directly contradicts the author's assertions.

22. **D** The given statement tells us only that the car is blue. For us to be *assured* that it is slow we must know either that every blue car is slow *or*

that no blue car accelerates quickly. (D) restricts quick acceleration to red cars.

23. **A** The argument obviously avoids absolute terms, relying instead on words such as "almost" and "sometimes." Therefore, it would seem consistent that a basic assumption would also avoid absolute terms; only (A) does so. In addition, (A) makes explicit the assumption underlying the first sentence of the passage.

24. **E** The second sentence diminishes the government's "fault" and the final sentence continues this idea; the only restatement that takes into account extragovernmental responsibility for intrusion is (E).

25. **B** The key phrase in the author's remarks is "*falsely* equating knowledge [viewing] with action [crime]." (A) is poor because it links knowledge with action. (C) is poor because the author indicates that those who dictate what we see (in other words, the censors) are guilty of drawing false (illogical) relationships. (D) and (E) are not relevant to the author's argument. (B) is consistent with the author's position that knowledge and action do not necessarily go hand in hand.

26. **B** A ruling on resources must at least presume the possibility that such resources exist; otherwise it is absurd. All other choices are irrelevant to the ruling.

Section IV

Passage 1

1. **B** Each of the other choices is too specific and/or not indicative of the *neutral* rather than argumentative *tone* of the passage.

2. **B** In the fourth paragraph, the author notes that after Congress had stopped enacting its reapportionment power, "serious malapportionment" problems ensued; the author thus implies that federal supervision is necessary. (C), (D), and (E) are issues on which the author does not imply an opinion.

3. **E** A clue to this answer occurs in paragraph 5, in which "malapportionment" is replaced by "the size and shape of electoral districts." Each of the other choices *may contribute* to malapportionment, but each is too specific to be the best choice.

4. **E** In the fifth paragraph we learn that the *voters* asked the Warren Court to rule on apportionment issues; therefore, we must assume that a ballot was taken that expressed the voters' opinions.

5. **A** Question 1 is answered in the first paragraph. The other questions, although they may be implied as *issues* in the passage, are not answered.

6. **B** Justice Frankfurter did not declare his opinion about reapportionment per se, but did declare that the Supreme Court should not address the issue; the Warren Court, on the other hand, did deliberate over the reapportionment issue. Therefore, we may conclude that Frankfurter was not a member of the Warren Court.

7. **A** The passage is a summary of events that occurred through the century, relative to apportionment. Each of the other choices has the author writing a passage calculated to persuade rather than to inform.

Passage 2

8. **E** In the reference to Serrate and Butor at the beginning of the passage, the author declares only that they can be compared to Robbe-Grillet. All the other choices require more information than is given.

9. **B** The first and second sentence imply a connection between popularity and less cerebral (intellectual) work, and the only logical antecedent to "that" is the initial statement that Robbe-Grillet is less cerebral.

10. **B** Directly following the mention of a *roman policier,* we have a coordinate statement about detective stories; the indication is that a *roman policier* is a detective story. Also, note that *policier* suggests the English word "police." Altogether, it appears that a *roman policier* centers on the investigation of a crime.

11. **E** The first paragraph states that he "wants his readers to feel disappointed," and that their disappointment tells him he has been successful.

12. **A** A paradox is an apparent contradiction, such as Robbe-Grillet's choice of form that appeals to a large audience and his deliberately "disappointing" his audience. Choices (B), (C), (D), and (E) are not paradoxical.

13. **E** After enumerating the possible components of the plot of *Marienbad,* the author says, "You take your choice"; earlier he notes that "the spectator's work" becomes part of the "creation." (D) is possibly but not necessarily true.

14. **C** The second paragraph describes the distortions of Robbe-Guillet's works, but his language is not cited.

Passage 3

15. **D** The passage is concerned with the earthly nature of the pagan gods and the implications of that earthly nature. (A), (B), and (C) are correct statements but are subtopics or minor points.

16. **C** Both metaphors, which involve eating out in restaurants and conducting business, suggest the earthbound nature of the gods. (A) and (D) are incorrect because they address qualities not attributed to the gods in this passage.

17. **A** "A la carte" means that each menu item is chosen separately (cf. choice of gods), while "fixed menu" refers to an entire meal ordered as one item (cf. one true god). It is clear in paragraph one that the choice is among deities, not among holy books (C) or varieties of worship (E).

18. **D** There is no irony in the passage. For examples of *contrast,* see lines 24–31; for *example,* see lines 41–52; for *figurative language,* see lines 7–17; for *explanation,* see lines 63–80.

19. **B** See lines 58–65. According to the passage, tolerance was an aspect of paganism, making religious wars unlikely. (A), (C), and (D) are not implied in the passage, and (E) is contradicted.

20. **C** Lines 1–9 imply that "morality" is sometimes erroneously linked to salvation and an afterlife, and that historians have made this error with paganism because of the nature of the religion. (A) and (D) are not suggested by information in the passage, (B) is irrelevant, and (E) is inaccurate.

21. **B** See lines 40–41, 58–62. (D) is a correct statement but does not ex-

plain the basis of religious tolerance. (A), (C), and (E) are not supported anywhere in the passage.

22. **C**   Paragraph three essentially creates a diagram in words to explain man's relationship to God in both paganism and the religions of the Book. (A) and (E) might be considered correct but both are imprecise; paragraph three doesn't actually summarize or evaluate, nor does it simplify all the points in paragraphs one and two.

Passage 4

23. **E**   The first paragraph says, ". . . suppose science is defined as classified knowledge."

24. **C**   Paragraph one specifically excludes astrology as a science (last sentence). Phrenology is also not a science, though the passage does not say so.

25. **B**   Paragraph four compares pure science to applied science, stating, "The discovery of one bit of information opens the door to the discovery of another."

26. **D**   This example of pure science is mentioned in paragraph four.

27. **C**   An undiscovered element may or may not have a practical value. The other four choices are examples of applied science.

28. **C**   Clearly, the passage is a general discussion of the characteristics of science and scientists. The other choices are science-related but deal with other, more specific aspects of science.

Section V

1. **C**   The passage argues that environmental restrictions will lead to losses of jobs and hence workers, but if workers are already leaving because the environmental quality is poor, the argument is seriously weakened.

2. **B**   The passage makes no comment on workers leaving before a manufacturer. It argues that the loss of manufacturers leads to a loss of workers (E).

3. **D**   The conclusion is a comment on the prices, not just on the price of hamburger. The speaker has inferred from the high price of hamburger that the prices of other items are also very high.

4. **E**   Though choices (A), (B), (C), and (D) might contribute to increased study of math in Bermuda, (E) leaves no doubt. High schools in Bermuda require four years of advanced math for graduation; high schools in the United States do not.

5. **A**   Though all of the choices are plausible here, (A) is the best choice. The first sentence asserts the conclusion ("superior"), and the second asserts a consequence ("immature . . . prefer"). The last repeats what has already been insisted upon.

6. **B**   If all mathematicians are physicists and some chemists are mathematicians, those chemists are also physicists. Therefore, some chemists are physicists.

7. **B**   The passage suggests that records are set only by rare, superior performers, and an increase or decrease in the number of participants would not significantly change the number of record-setting performances.

8. **E**   The passage makes its point by analogy, comparing the dangers of smoking to the dangers of asbestos and radioactivity.

9. **A**   The passage is clearly hostile to the racist candidate, and has found a

"ray of hope." The conclusion should logically predict his defeat. Choice (A) also draws a conclusion related to the part of the paragraph that refers to "regular Republicans."

10. **D** The argument uses both simile ("like strip mining or clear-cutting") and metaphor ("walls of death").

11. **C** If the halibut population is endangered, the banning of gill-nets would improve the fish's chance for survival. If (A) and (B) are true, the fisheries' argument about the price rise has more merit. If (D) and (E) are true, the reduction of the sea otter population would be more defensible.

12. **E** Choices (A), (B), (C), and (D) are reasonable objections, but the argument that *no* writing is without some scientific value is an overstatement.

13. **A** The assumption is that where there are no pesticide controls, no edible fish can be found, not the reverse as in (B), (D), and (E).

14. **D** The results of the elections and the fact that there are three congressmen from the north and three from the south suggest that the populations are nearly equal. Choice (A) would be a likely choice if "always" were changed to "usually." Choice (B) is unlikely, and the passage gives us no reason either to believe in or to disbelieve (C) and (E).

15. **C** The passage makes it clear that the author regards the reparations claim as "just," for example, by the reference to the government's "moral obligation." This conclusion keeps the focus on the African-Americans, whose suffering is recounted in the two preceding sentences.

16. **B** If the results are like those of the "recent past," the total should approximate "an average of 22 House" and "2 Senate seats."

17. **D** The conclusion could be more reasonably assessed if we knew how often the paranormal signs had been false. The issue is not how many contestants win money or how much money they win. The issue is the paranormal aid.

18. **E** The words "this is the price we must pay" (that is, we must suffer aphid infestation because the rutabagas have been destroyed) indicated that the author makes all of the assumptions of (A), (B), (C), and (D). The idea of (E) may be true, but it is not an assumption of the passage.

19. **A** The apparent contradiction disappears if the total state budget has increased enough so that the *expenditure* on education has been raised by three million each year while at the same time the *percentage* spent on education is a smaller part of the whole budget.

20. **C** In each case, the verb ("iron" ... "need ironing"; "write" ... "to be written") is repeated, while the adjective ("many") modifies the repeated noun.

21. **B** The first statement asserts that great playwrights will not develop in repressive countries. Therefore, the great satirists which repressive countries will produce (the second statement) will not write plays.

22. **A** The details of the paragraph and the phrase "bleak outlook" suggest that a settlement is not likely.

23. **A** If the new labels will appear on less than 20 percent of the food sold, they will not be very effective.

24. **E** As the United States is still unwilling to act, its downplaying the confer-

ence is a predictable response. Though several of the other choices are plausible, none follows so clearly from what the paragraph has already said.

25. **C**   If there has been a steady rise in car sales, consumers cannot be "cutting back on spending plans for new cars," as the predictions assert.

PART FOUR

FINAL TOUCHES

Reviewing the Important Techniques

8

A SUMMARY OF STRATEGIES

DIRECTIONS AND STRATEGIES

GENERAL TIPS

- Use the "one-check, two-check" system, doing the easier questions first, and saving the time-consuming and difficult questions for later.
- Don't leave any blank answer spaces. At least guess on your unanswered questions.
- Eliminate unreasonable or irrelevant answers immediately, marking them out on your question booklet.
- Highlight key words and phrases by marking right in your question booklet. Use the margins to draw diagrams, set up charts, and so on.
- Mark "T" and "F" (for "True" and "False") alongside the Roman numeral statements in "multiple-multiple-choice" questions. Often these will allow you to immediately eliminate incorrect answer choices. This type of question has not appeared recently.
- Watch out for the common mistake—the MISREAD.
- Spend some extra time reviewing Logical Reasoning problems. Remember, Logical Reasoning will comprise two of the four scored sections of your exam.

REVIEW OF LSAT AREAS

Reading Comprehension

Directions: **Read the passages and answer the questions following each passage by blackening the appropriate space on the answer sheet. You may refer to the passages when answering the questions.**

Strategies:

- Skim the questions first, marking key words and phrases. (Don't read the answer choices.)
- Skim the passage (optional). Read and mark the first sentence of each paragraph.
- Read actively, marking the passage. In particular, look for answer spots, repeat spots, intuition spots.
- Answer the questions. Skip if necessary. Eliminate weak choices. Don't "read into" the passage.

Analytical Reasoning

Directions: In this section you will be given groups of questions based on different sets of conditions. Drawing a simple diagram may be helpful in answering some of the questions. You are to choose the *best* answer and mark the corresponding space on your answer sheet.

Strategies:

- No formal logic is required.
- Make simple charts or diagrams.
- Fill in as much of the diagram as possible, but don't worry if you cannot complete it.
- Look for the framework of the diagram that would be most effective.
- Apply evidence in both directions, that is, also use what you know is *not* true.
- Use question marks for information that is variable.
- Sometimes looking at the questions can tip off the framework of the diagram that would be most helpful.
- If no standard applies, simply pull out information or use simple notes.

Logical Reasoning

Directions: In this section you will be given brief statements or passages and will be required to evaluate the reasoning involved. In some instances, more than one choice will appear to be a possible answer. You are to choose the *best* answer. Use common sense and reasonableness in making your selection; then mark the proper space on the answer sheet.

Strategies:

- Read the question first; then go back and read the argument or statement. This will give insight into what is going to be asked.
- Watch for items in the answer choices that are irrelevant or not addressed in the given information. Eliminate these immediately.
- Notice the overall tone of the question: Positive or negative? Agreeing with and strengthening the author's argument or criticizing and weakening the statement?
- Watch for key words: *some, all, none, only, one, few, no, could, must, each, except.*

Writing Sample

Directions: You have 30 minutes to write an essay in response to a given topic. Take a few minutes to plan your work before you begin writing. DO NOT WRITE ON A TOPIC OF YOUR OWN CHOICE. ESSAYS THAT DO NOT ADDRESS THE GIVEN TOPIC ARE UNACCEPTABLE.

The quality of your writing is more important than the length of your response or the content. Pay attention to organization, appropriate diction, and correct usage. You will not be expected to display any specialized knowledge in your response, nor will you be expected to write a "perfect" essay; law schools understand that you are writing under a time constraint, and will allow for the minor lapses in writing ability that might occur under this circumstance.

Only the lined area in your booklet will be reproduced for the law schools, so do not write outside this space. *Do not* skip lines or use wide margins. These precautions, along with careful planning and legible handwriting that is not unduly large, will keep you within the allowed space.

Strategies:

- Read statements and biographies or descriptions at least twice, actively.
- Choose your candidate or item.
- Outline your essay.
- Start with a direction. Your first sentence should serve a purpose.
- Support your argument with examples or other specifics.
- Do *not* write a closing paragraph that simply repeats what you have already said.
- Write legibly. Write clearly. Write naturally.
- Proofread and edit your essay.

A FINAL CHECKLIST

A Few Days before the Test

- Review the test directions and strategies for each area.
- Become familiar with the test site; visit it if necessary.
- Follow your normal daily routine; don't make drastic changes.

The Night before the Test

- Review briefly, but don't cram.
- Get a normal night's sleep; don't go to bed too early or too late.

On the Day of the Test

- Arrive on time, equipped with three or four sharpened No. 2 pencils, a good eraser, proper identification, your admission ticket, and a watch.
- Dress comfortably. (You may wish to dress in "layers" so that you can add or remove a sweater or jacket if the room temperature changes.)
- Read the test directions carefully.
- Use the "one-check, two-check" system.
- Read *actively.*
- In Reading Comprehension and Logical Reasoning, remember to look at all choices before marking your answer.
- In Analytical Reasoning, be aware that you may not always need to review all of the choices before marking your answer.
- Before you leave a problem, be sure to take a guess. Try to make it an educated guess by eliminating some choices.
- If there are only a few minutes left for a section, fill in the remaining problems with guesses before time is called.
- Remember: look for problems that you CAN DO and SHOULD GET RIGHT, and DON'T GET STUCK on any one problem.

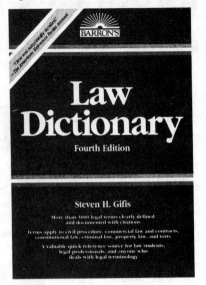